shift the scenery and so forth ..."

Daily Express, 10th February, 1969.

NAB 1

Portrait of a Politician

With very best wishes
from
Gerald Nabarro M.P.
18.x.1969

NAB 1

Portrait of a Politician

SIR GERALD NABARRO, MP

ROBERT MAXWELL · PUBLISHER
A DIVISION OF PERGAMON PRESS LIMITED

ROBERT MAXWELL · PUBLISHER
Headington Hill Hall, Oxford
A DIVISION OF PERGAMON PRESS LIMITED

First edition 1969

Printed in Great Britain by A. Wheaton and Co., Exeter

08 007109 0

TO JO—WHO LISTENED

Who can find a virtuous woman? For her price is far above rubies.
The heart of her husband doth safely trust in her, so that he shall have no need of spoil.
She will do him good and not evil all the days of her life.

Proverbs **31**, v. 10–12

Contents

ERRATA

(Sir Gerald Nabarro M.P. NAB 1—Portrait of a Politician)

In the following places the correct detail is as stated:

Page 25, line 14: Hicks Beach.

Page 79, 4th line from bottom: Nicholls.

Page 82, 3rd line: Whitaker.

Page 206, line 4: £1800 (not £1500).

Page 258, line 18: Wentworth Schofield.

Page 335, col. 2, line 11: Chataway.

Page 341, col. 1, 6th line from bottom: Sir Godfrey Nicholson.

Page 344, col. 1, line 19: Whitaker.

60th Riflemen Photograph: "The Rhodesians" in the principal caption should refer to the quotation and not to the individuals pictured.

"Kidderminster 1946—1965" should read "1950—1964", "Lieut. Col. J. D. H. Butcher, OBE." should read: "Lieut. Col. F. D. H. Burcher, OBE."

ADDITIONAL ACKNOWLEDGEMENTS

Under Photographers, the following should be included:

Kidderminster Times & Stourport News; Associated Newspapers; The Sun; The Press Association.

On the back end paper the acknowledgement should be added: *Punch*, 2nd April 1969.

Under Book Publishers, the following should be included:

William Heinemann Ltd (*The Fight for The Tory Leadership*—Randolph Churchill)

Arthur Barker (*Peaceful Change*)

List of Cartoons

List of Photographs

Preface

An autobiography would be the story of my life, written by myself.

My memoirs might be my autobiography, or a history of matters of which I have special knowledge, or both these things.

This book, *NAB 1—Portrait of a Politician*, is neither autobiography nor memoirs, for in politics the time to write these is when one retires. I have no intention of retiring yet, subject only to the vagaries of the electorate and the good health of my mind and body. I shall write my autobiography just as soon as I retire from the House of Commons, long before dotage and mindful of the late Rt Hon. Alfred Duff Cooper's awful warning: "OLD MEN FORGET."

This book records my impressions of the House of Commons and Westminster; of two Worcestershire constituencies which I have been privileged to serve as Tory Member of Parliament; of more than four hundred Parliamentary constituencies I have spoken in during the quarter of a century since 1945; of television, of sound broadcasting and the press; and of course, the political leaders of my generation. I write of Wilson and of Heath, of Jenkins and of Macleod, of Maudling and of Wedgwood Benn; of John Freeman, Lord Snow and Aubrey Jones, as well as of former Tory Prime Ministers Mr Harold Macmillan and Sir Alec Douglas-Home. Throughout I give my personal impressions and assessments of politics, policies and my Parliamentary colleagues, both friends and opponents.

Max Beerbohm is said to have written to Sir Colin Coote, DSO, formerly Managing Editor of the *Daily Telegraph*, "that it is difficult to write anything in a book of one's own, without seeming self-important". I agree. And what Max Beerbohm called "a hideous pitfall" is undoubtedly what I cannot escape falling into, in this book. I have written my own impressions of two decades in party politics, the fifties and sixties, illustrated by my own experiences and my own speeches, broadcasts, television performances and reproductions of cartoons of myself, mostly hostile, rude or mocking. All this is the portrait of a politician which I have set out, for better or worse, to commit to print.

Of course, the press and the critics will call it bumptious, egocentric, swanky, conceited, pompous and the remainder. I am not Max Beerbohm's "self-important". I have related in this book much about political matters and contemporary controversies which intelligent electors ought to know, if they do not know it already. There is a shortage of Party orthodoxy in the book and a surfeit of personal policies I should like to see adopted for the future good fortune and happiness of the entire British community; and, moreover, a commitment to my Right-wing faith for the seventies.

Thus, the book is written as a personal retrospection of the fifties and sixties and a prospect for the seventies. *Respice, Prospice.*

Many people have helped me in the preparation of the voluminous material at my disposal and I should like particularly to thank the Right Honourable Anthony Wedgwood Benn, MP, Minister of Technology, for allowing me to make use of our correspondence throughout his noble struggle to renounce his peerage, as a basis for Chapter 11; Mr Speaker, the Right Honourable Horace Maybray King, Ph.D, MP, for allowing me to reproduce his address given at William Barkley's Memorial Service; Mr Frank Gillard, Managing Director of Sound Radio at the British Broadcasting Corporation and Mr Michael Bowen, Producer of "Any Questions?"; Mr D. C. L. Holland, Librarian of the House of Commons, and his staff; Mr George Clark, of *The Times*, who read the entire manuscript; Mr Timothy O'Sullivan, who has laboured for nine months and scrutinized thousands of documents; and, of course, the newspapers—the *Daily Express*, the *Daily Telegraph*, *The Times*, the *Daily Mirror*, the *Guardian*, the *News of the World*, the *Sunday Express*, *The Economist*, and many more —for copious quotation from their columns.

Might I also record my gratitude to the cartoonists. That great artist Michael Cummings, of Express Newspapers, who adds vivacity and insight to every political situation he depicts; Nick Garland, of the *Daily Telegraph*, Norman Mansbridge and David Langdon, and several others. I should also like to pay a posthumous tribute to "Vicky", whom I loved for his perspicacity and artistry, and because whenever I sent him my cheque for an addition to my personal collection of cartoons, the recipient—it was later revealed—was always a refugee or some charitable organization. "Vicky" himself never took a penny from me and he always played the game, dead straight, by ensuring that the organization was not one to which I was politically opposed.

Finally, let me thank my Worcestershire constituents who have inspired, encouraged and succoured me, and elected me again and again to serve them in the Commons, House of Parliament. I love sitting in Parliament assembled, which is what this book is really all about.

The Orchard House, GERALD NABARRO
Broadway,
Worcestershire.
1st October, 1969

Acknowledgements

THE author and publisher wish to express their thanks to the newspapers, periodicals, artists, photographers and publishers who have so kindly given permission for their copyright material to be included in this book.

Extracts from Newspapers and Periodicals: *Achievement, Daily Express, Sunday Express, Daily Mail, Daily Mirror, Daily Telegraph, Sunday Telegraph, Weekend Telegraph, The Economist, Everybody's, Guardian, The Listener, Liverpool Daily Post, News of the World, New Statesman, Mayfair* (incorporating *King*), *Observer, Punch, People, Sun, Sunday Graphic, Sunday Times* and *The Times*. The Controller of Her Majesty's Stationery Office (*Hansard*), The British Broadcasting Corporation.

Cartoons

Cummings	*Daily Express, Punch*
Vicky	*Evening Standard, New Statesman*
Garland	*Daily Telegraph*
David Langdon	*Punch, Sunday Mirror*
Lewis Williams	*Birmingham Mail*
Norman Mansbridge	*Sunday Times*
Belsky	*Daily Herald*
Trog	*Daily Mail*
Eccles	*Morning Star*
Jon	*Daily Mail*
Fred May	*Tatler*
Illingworth	*Punch*

Photographers: Lionel Photography, Solihull; The Associated Press Ltd; *Evesham Journal*; Keystone Press Agency Ltd; South West Picture Agency Ltd; *Daily Telegraph*; Berrow's Newspapers; Three Star Press Agency, London; Geo. R. Kendrick, Tenbury Wells.

Book Publishers: Hodder & Stoughton (*The Greasy Pole*); Macmillan (*Wyndham and Children First*); Hollis & Carter (*The Ayes and the Noes*); Weidenfeld & Nicolson (*Political Adventure*).

1. The Great Tory Vintage of 1950

THE architect of Conservative post-war recovery was undoubtedly the Right Honourable Richard Austen Butler, CH, now Lord Butler of Saffron Walden and Master of Trinity College, Cambridge, since 1965.

Among the countless achievements of this remarkable man were the fashioning of post-war policies for his party and the installation in the back room of Conservative Central Office of some of the best brains of our times. These were the nucleus of the ninety-three Conservatives who entered the House of Commons for the first time at the General Election of 23rd February, 1950. RAB Butler handpicked, nurtured and trained them in their political infancy. They became Cabinet Ministers in the Conservative Governments of 1951 to 1964 and the leaders of Conservative thought in the two decades, the fifties and the sixties.

This massive infusion of new post-war Tory blood transformed the political scene. This was the counter attack to 1945. It frightened the life out of the Socialists, who had vaingloriously boasted as they sang the "Red Flag" in the House in 1945, that the Tory Party, utterly decimated, would never rise again. It caused Mr Aneurin Bevan, MP for Ebbw Vale—predecessor of Mr Michael Foot in that Labour stronghold—and husband of Miss Jennie Lee, MP for Cannock, to observe that this was the finest Tory vintage in history. Here is the state of the parties before and after the 1950 General Election:

Before		*After*	
Labour	384	Labour	315
Conservative	193	Conservative	298

Before		*After*	
Ulster Unionist	10	Liberal	9
National Liberal	13	Irish Nationalist	2
Liberal	10	Speaker	1
National	2		
Communist	2		
Irish Nationalist	2		
Independent	16		
Speaker	1		
Vacant (all Labour)	7		

Mr Aneurin Bevan did not exaggerate. I have lived with the members of the 1950 Tory vintage for twenty years. In the House of Commons, on the hustings at six General Elections and scores of by-elections, in industry, trade and commerce, and performing on radio and television. Twenty years after, I concede Bevan's acute powers of perception and prophecy.

The number of the 1950 intake who remain in Parliament dwindles fast. Originally there were ninety-three; there were sixty-seven in February, 1960; now there are thirty-five, and nine of these have announced their intention to retire at the end of the present Parliament. The survivors dine together on the tenth and twentieth anniversaries of their first election, with an avuncular Butler savouring this rare, if not unique vintage.

Heath and Powell, Maudling and Macleod, Soames and Smyth VC, Watkinson and Ryder VC, Smithers and Deedes, Ormsby-Gore and Hill, Aubrey Jones and Alport, Redmayne and Carr, Amery and Maude, Vosper and Bevins, Hylton-Foster and Hornsby-Smith, Leather and Wood, is to name just two dozen of the 1950 entry. And, though politics as a career may be the most speculative, chancy and dangerous that any intelligent Briton may choose of the many different ways of serving his fellow creatures and influencing the course of events, yet the rewards for the successful are glittering and can be accomplished incomparably faster than in any other profession.

The three contestants in the ballot for the Tory leadership when Sir Alec Douglas-Home retired as leader of the Opposition in July 1965—Heath, Maudling and Powell—had all entered the House of Commons in 1950 and been Ministers for years. Thus all three were in the running to become Prime Minister within fifteen years of their first election. Winston Churchill waited forty years, Attlee twenty-seven years, Eden thirty-three years, Macmillan thirty-three years and even Wilson, with the incredibly fortuitous circumstance of three rivals dropping out—Gaitskell and Bevan sadly by their early deaths and Robens by accepting the Chairmanship of the National Coal Board—waited nineteen years, or eighteen years before becoming leader of the Opposition. Progress nowadays for the exceptionally talented, such as these three Tories, Heath, Maudling and Powell, is incomparably more rapid than in any other walk of life.

Iain Macleod, that curious mixture of Celtic visionary (who conducted his 1945 General Election campaign in the Western Isles largely in Gaelic and finished bottom of the poll) and intellectual, was promoted by the then Prime Minister, Sir Winston Churchill, straight on to the Front Bench in 1952 as Minister of Health, because in a series of speeches from the Opposition back-benches he had clobbered and reduced to frothy fulminations that architect of the Health Service, Mr Aneurin Bevan. Any debunker of Bevan was Winston's friend. Never has promotion come so rapidly and dramatically to a backbencher as to Iain Macleod. This tough and talented Fettesian has held with distinction nearly all the great portfolios in Conservative Ministries. He has been Minister of Labour, Colonial Secretary, Minister of Health, Chancellor of the Duchy of Lancaster and Leader of the House of Commons. He has been Chairman of the Conservative Party, Editor of the *Spectator* and Bridge correspondent of *The Sunday Times*. He is a man of tremendous courage and of all Conservative speakers, he is the most feared by Mr Harold Wilson and his colleagues. Yet he will never lead the Conservative Party. Bent with arthritis and widely mistrusted by Tories because of his African policies, which were thought by many to be precipitate and ill-advised; dubbed "too clever by half" by the Marquess of Salisbury and strongly criticised for refusing to serve under Sir Alec Douglas-Home in 1963, Macleod is unlikely now ever to overtake Heath or Maudling or Powell. Nevertheless, he is always a titan of debates and a talented Parliamentarian.

Then two ambassadors emerged from the 1950 Tory vintage. First, Christopher Soames, son-in-law of Sir Winston Churchill and Parliamentary Private Secretary to him as Prime Minister, 1952–55; and successively the occupant of many ministerial jobs, including the Ministry of Agriculture, 1960–64. Understandably the farmers liked him. He looked like a farmer and behaved like one. He did not have himself photographed holding piglets upside down by their back legs. An ardent Common Marketeer, Wilson appointed him the British Ambassador to Paris in 1968, where he flourishes. An Etonian and former officer in the Coldstream Guards, holder of the French Croix de Guerre and married to a Churchill, he had everything on his appointment to Paris to commend him to an intransigent de Gaulle and to ease Britain into Europe. Also, the cross fertilisation in British politics, so different to the United States of America and other foreign democracies, is both curious and satisfying to note. Wilson, as Labour Prime Minister, appoints Soames, an ex-Tory Minister, Ambassador to France; Macmillan, as Tory Prime Minister, appoints Alfred Robens Chairman of the National Coal Board. Presumably because Wilson strives to make his Common Market policy succeed, as Macmillan had striven to cause the nationalised coal induscry to succeed.

As Soames, now an Ambassador, so also Ormsby-Gore, former British Ambassador in Washington. Macmillan sent him there in 1961 after eleven years as MP for Oswestry. A close friend of the Kennedy family and confidant of the President of the United States, Mr John F. Kennedy, until his assassination in 1963, the fifth Lord Harlech, as Ormsby-Gore now is, is the archetypal British aristocrat: gentle, kind, well-mannered and well-loved. He will rank by any standards as one of our greatest ambassadors in Washington. Harlech and Soames, both Etonians, took the oath together on the floor of the House in March, 1950.

So did two holders of the Victoria Cross: Captain Robert Ryder, VC, RN (Merton and Morden), hero of St Nazaire and the midget submarine raids on the German battleship *Tirpitz* in 1943; and Brigadier the Rt Hon. Sir John Smyth, VC, MC (Norwood) who won his Victoria Cross serving with the Indian division in France in 1915 and commanded the forlorn and grossly under-armed brigade of British and Indian troops against the Japanese in South East Asia in 1941–42. Ryder did not much care for Parliamentary politics and left the House in 1955. Jackie Smyth, who founded the splendid Victoria Cross and George Cross Association, remained a Member of Parliament until 1966. Two VCs entering the House together, as Ryder and Smyth did in 1950, is memorable indeed.

Charlie Hill, the Radio Doctor, merits a chapter to himself. He is one of the most versatile and intelligent men one could meet. Nothing gave me greater pleasure than the fact that he referred to me in his splendid autobiography as one of his closest friends. Actually, I was browsing in the House of Commons Library in March, 1950, looking up some facts for a constituency speech, when I heard that deep, fruity voice, so reminiscent of his broadcasts to as many as fourteen million listeners in the dark and cheerless war days. "Ah, you're Nabarro, I believe?" "Yes," I replied, "the Radio Doctor, I believe?" Said Charlie, "I recognise your moustache." I replied, mimicking his best Radio Doctor style, "Have your bowels been open this morning, Mrs Snooks?" We both burst out laughing. He said that he had learned some of his medicine from Dr David Nabarro, the pathologist of Great Ormond Street Children's Hospital and what was he to do with me, the new Member for Kidderminster. I replied that the Doctor was my uncle, godfather, mentor and friend. "Follow his path," said Charlie, "and you could not earn a greater reputation."

We remained mutual confidants until Charlie left the House in 1963, his departure lamented by all. He had been successively Postmaster-General, Chancellor of the Duchy of Lancaster, with special responsibilities for Government Public Relations and Publicity and finally, Minister of Housing and Local Government, 1961–62. How foolish of Macmillan to have sacked this splendid administrator, first rank politician and wit. I wanted him to be made Chairman of the Conservative Party instead of being put out to grass and ignominiously dropped which is what happened as a result of the Macmillan slaughter-house of Friday, 13th July, 1962. A couple of years of Charlie Hill at Conservative Central Office, instead of the ineffective Lord Blakenham (formerly John Hare, MP for Sudbury and Woodbridge, 1945–63) would have won the 1964 General Election for the Tory Party. A master of Party politics, a darling of the constituencies ever since his immortal "Chuck it Priestley" rejoinder in a party political broadcast in the 1950 General Election campaign, Charlie Hill was a Conservative leader the Party could ill afford to lose in the critical months of the run-up to the 1964 General Election. Macmillan blundered badly.

Characteristic of Hill was his light-hearted manner in the *Sunday Telegraph* of July 22nd, 1962, nine days after leaving Ministerial office for the first time in nine years:

> A former Minister who has no ambition to return to the fray is forgotten as quickly as last year's Mayor. In future he is likely to gain public notice only by criticising former colleagues (which I have no intention of doing), or by falling down the stairs (which I hope to escape), or by using a naughty word on television—though nowadays it would have to be very naughty.

Charlie Hill made his maiden speech in the Commons on 14th March, 1950; I made mine shortly after, on 29th March. He left the House in 1963, took a peerage, called himself Lord Hill of Luton, became Chairman of the Independent Television Authority, 1963–67, and then Chairman of the Governors of the British Broadcasting Corporation. I went to open the by-election campaign at Luton which followed Charlie's departure from the Commons. The Tory candidate, an ex-colonial administrator, was hardly the ideal choice for an industrial seat and lacked any previous Parliamentary election experience. He (Sir John Fletcher-Cooke) lost by 3,749 votes, compared with Hill's victory in 1959 by 5,019 votes. In fact Luton demonstrated the decisive influence of a really first class candidate and Member. Charlie Hill won Luton from Labour in 1950 and held it with increased majorities at three subsequent General Elections. I know as a visiting speaker for him from time to time, how the ordinary industrial worker and his wife loved this earthy, companionable and industrious Member. He is a supreme example of the electoral value of personality in politics and the lie direct to those psephological pundits who have never been on the hustings themselves, and who pontificate that a great party candidate is worth only five hundred votes over a poor opponent. Luton would probably have been a Labour seat all the years between 1950 and 1963 but for the splendid electoral assets of Lord Hill.

Slaughtered by Macmillan on the same day in 1962—and no one denies that an essential attribute of a good Prime Minister is to be a butcher —was Harold Watkinson. Unlike Charlie Hill, he sat in the Commons from 1962 to 1964 as a backbencher, then became Lord Watkinson of Woking and later Chairman of Schweppes. Like Charlie Hill he was in Ministerial office throughout the years between 1952 and 1962, culminating with five years in the Cabinet as Minister of Transport and then Minister of Defence. He built Britain's first substantial motorway, the M.1., and made effective the nuclear deterrent of the early 1960s. He has not written his memoirs yet, so neither I nor anyone else really knows what he thought of the Macmillan purge, which abruptly ended his Ministerial and Cabinet career. For me, and many more like me on the Conservative benches, Watkinson and Hill were tragic losses to my party, at a time when we could not afford such a drain on the available talent and experience.

Then a couple of Foreign Office types, very, very much part of the establishment: Cuthbert Alport, who won Colchester from Labour in 1950, and Peter Smithers, who won Winchester. Alport, a prosaic and unimpressive Parliamentarian took a peerage in 1961 and became High Commissioner to preside over the disintegration of the Central African Federation of Southern Rhodesia, Northern Rhodesia and Nyasaland. He was sent back to Salisbury in 1968 by Mr Wilson to talk to Mr Ian Smith but he returned empty-handed. His has been a frustrating career since RAB Butler enrolled him in Conservative Central Office as director of the

Conservative Political Centre, an executive post which he occupied from 1945 to 1950. He would have made a better Foreign Office official than party politician and was never really at home in the Commons.

Likewise Peter Smithers. Charming, erudite, a complete diplomatist, he left the House of Commons after nearly fifteen years to become Secretary of the Council of Europe, which he remained until 1969. Winchester has preferred an Admiral, Morgan-Giles, as Conservative Member, since Smithers retired in 1964.

Julian Amery occupied Preston North for the Tories from 1950, when his majority was less than a thousand, until 1966 when he lost by over two thousand votes, having held it by only fourteen votes in 1964. As he contested the two Member seat in 1945, he had been associated with Preston for over twenty years. Now, after three years in the wilderness he is back again in the House, succeeding Sir William Teeling in the very safe Conservative seat of Brighton, Pavilion, at a by-election in March, 1969. A fine Parliamentarian is Julian Amery. Swept-back black hair, plummy voice, Eton and Balliol and a gallant war record, he occupied many Ministerial posts until the Tories went out in 1964. But Edward Heath dropped him very smartly from the Opposition Front Bench when he took over from Sir Alec Douglas-Home in the summer of 1965. No doubt Heath has painful memories of Suez. The Suez Group, led by the Rt Hon. Charles Waterhouse, Conservative Member for Leicester, South-East, opposed in many divisions the withdrawal of the British Army from Suez. Julian Amery was the secretary of the Group and Edward Heath was the deputy chief Whip. Enoch Powell, Angus Maude, Harry Legge-Bourke, Lord Hinchingbrooke and many other militant Tory back-benchers including myself, were opposed to the Suez party line, Amery as much as, if not more so than any other. It may explain Edward Heath's swift vengeance in 1965. As Cross-Bencher observed in the *Sunday Express* of 5th January, 1969, under the title the "New Brighton Belle":

> Needless to say, he [Julian Amery] will get no heroic welcome from Mr Edward Heath. The two never did get on. Indeed, one of the first things Mr Heath did on becoming party leader in 1965 was to drop Mr Amery from his Front Bench. And of course, the views Mr Amery has since been taking on issues such as Rhodesia have done nothing to soften the Boss's heart towards him. They are altogether too true blue.

Immigration and racial issues, Rhodesia and taxation reform, will ensure that a clamant right wing will characterise Conservative Party affairs for very many years ahead. With two decades of political life yet to run, Amery has an important future role in the party. Significant, too, that he has two decades of tumultuous political experience behind him, 1950–70. He was born into a great Unionist tradition—son of the Rt Hon. L. S. Amery—and young Julian married the daughter of Harold Macmillan. The pedigree is impeccable for a leader of the Right.

And who could excel those great lawyers who came to the Commons in 1950? The Rt Hon. Sir Lionel Heald, QC (Chertsey) and the Rt Hon. Sir Harry Braustyn Hylton Hylton-Foster, QC (York, 1950–59 and the Cities of London and Westminster, 1959–65). Heald was Sir Winston Churchill's Attorney-General, an exacting post indeed, from 1951 to 1954; and Hylton-Foster, a great advocate, was Solicitor-General, 1954–59 and elected Speaker of the House of Commons on October 21st, 1959. When responding to the unanimous call of the House to the Chair, he said:[1]

> In accordance with our ancient custom, I beg to submit myself to the will of the House. At this moment I cannot help thinking about the last occupant of the Chair[2] and how desperately difficult it will be for any hon. Member to follow one who so assuredly commanded the confidence, respect and affection of the whole House.
>
> On a personal note, I wish to acknowledge to the House that I have all those defects in this connection to which the Leader of the Opposition referred. I am greatly obliged to him for referring to them in such courteous terms. I was not going to say this to the House but it occurs to me now. The time was when the Chair was considered a kind of perquisite of the office of Solicitor-General. However, all that came to grief in the year 1601, when one of my predecessors in the office of Solicitor-General—a certain Serjeant Fleming—was said to be too lawyer-like and uncouth for the Chair, and the House was advised to find someone more presentable. I hope that the House will forgive that digression, which was a little prompted by the Rt Hon. Gentleman's observations.
>
> I should like to thank my hon. Friends the Members for South Angus (Sir James Duncan) and Manchester, Withington (Sir Robert Cary) for what they have said. I cannot claim the qualities which, in their kindness, they bestow upon me, but I can and do claim this: that I love and revere this House—its long history and the gay vigour of its modern life; the good humour most of the time; the friendships that it makes; the quick changes of mood; the sure collective judgement of this House about a man—this House,

[1] *Hansard*, 20th October, 1959, cols. 14–15.

[2] Rt Hon. William Shepherd Morrison, MC, QC, MP, Speaker, 1951–59.

> an institution so much greater than the sum of all of us of whom it is at any one time composed.
>
> There have been references to certain discussions—a misery for a candidate in my position to have to listen to. I can only say that there is only one will to which I beg to submit myself and that is the will of this House. Should the House do me the great honour of calling me to its service, I can promise that it will be not only my duty but my whole ambition in life to serve it faithfully and well to the best of my ability and, with the help and with the forbearance of my fellow-Members, to maintain in full vigour those traditions that have made this House at once the origin and example of Parliamentary institutions throughout the world. I beg to submit myself to the will of the House.

And later, after the traditional struggles, and being placed in the Chair by Sir James Duncan and Sir Robert Cary, he said:

> Before I take the Chair as Speaker-elect, I beg most sincerely to thank the House for the great honour it does me in calling me to its service in this place.

Sir Harry's wife—now Baroness Hylton-Foster of the City of Westminster—was the daughter of a previous Speaker of the House of Commons, Colonel Douglas Clifton Brown, later Lord Ruffside, Speaker from 1943 to 1951. Hylton-Foster was firm, courteous, witty, majestic and possessed of a fine voice. He had all these assets and the intellectual equipment too. I admired his abilities and we were long friends, though never too closely. My last memory of this great man was sitting in a deep armchair in the library of my home at Broadway. That afternoon, as Speaker, he had walked in procession around the streets of the ancient Borough of Evesham, greeted the Archbishop of Canterbury and other ecclesiastical and civic dignitaries, at ceremonies to mark the 700th anniversary of the death of Simon de Montfort—creator of the Model Parliament—at the Battle of Evesham in 1265. Hylton-Foster inscribed thus my volume of "The Office of Speaker" by Philip Laundy, Librarian of the Legislative Assembly of Southern Rhodesia (it was still four months before UDI on 11th November, 1965):

> Gratefully, to Gerald,
> My Host, 18th July, 1965.
> Harry Hylton-Foster: Speaker.

Shortly afterwards, on 2nd September, he collapsed and died at the early age of sixty, while taking his morning stroll around the streets of his

Westminster constituency. The very heavy burden of the Speaker's office had brought its toll. He was succeeded by his Deputy, as first Labour Speaker, Dr the Rt Hon. Horace Maybray King.

The most famous of the lady Tory Members to arrive in 1950 was Patricia Hornsby-Smith. Redheaded, vivacious, loquacious, fiery and another of Lord Woolton's former Young Conservative area chairmen from the late 1940s. She won Chislehurst by 167 votes in 1950, when Edward Heath won the nearby Kent constituency of Bexley by an equally small margin. By sheer pertinacity and assiduity, Patricia held on to her marginal seat for sixteen years but just lost it in 1966. Nothing daunted and spurning any thought of a life peerage, Patricia battles on as prospective Tory candidate for Chislehurst, her political home for twenty years.

Dennis Vosper, later Lord Runcorn (he took the name from the constituency which elected him in 1950) was an interesting character and a Member of great promise. Dour and forthright, it is sad that he was dogged by ill-health, and after holding many junior ministerial posts he was forced to resign as Minister of Health in 1957. For the same reason, he had to resign as Minister of Technical Co-operation—that is, overseas aid as run by the Tories—in 1963. He became, as Lord Runcorn, Chairman of the National Assistance Board but could not carry on for long. He died in 1968 at the age of fifty-two.

Martin Redmayne, Brigadier and holder of the Distinguished Service Order, was Tory Chief Whip (after Edward Heath) from 1959 to 1963 and the stalwart who saw Harold Macmillan through all his Profumo troubles in 1963 and weathered the leadership storms later that year. He was briefly shadow Minister of Transport from 1964 to 1966, before being defeated at Rushcliffe, Nottinghamshire in the General Election, by the narrow margin of 380 votes. Here was one of the best Parliamentarians in the Conservative Party, thrown out of a seat he had occupied for sixteen years. A better Chief Whip than Edward Heath, less irascible, a mild and firm persuader, a leader of men and admired by men. Macmillan and his Patronage Secretary Redmayne were an impressive, if not magnificent pair. All the qualities of imperturbability and urbanity that characterised Macmillan were there in abundance in Redmayne. He deserves a better resting place than the cocoonery of their Lordships' House, and as a Director of Customer Relations at Harrods, although his training as Chief Whip during those turbulent years will stand him in good stead there.

The Rt Hon. Richard Wood, Member for Bridlington, the Rt Hon. Robert Carr, Member for Mitcham and Mr Bernard Braine, Member for

South East Essex are long-serving professionals. Unsensational, even pedestrian, they are worthy and utterly faithful party men: ballast for future Tory Ministries. Sir Edwin Leather, a great Canadian, sat for North Somerset from 1950 until he retired through illness in 1964. Today, he is Vice-Chairman of the Conservative Party Organisation, a business man, televiser, broadcaster and eloquent platform performer, one of the most sought after public speakers in the party. Reginald Bevins, council school

"BIG BROTHER" NABARRO, MP, by Cummings, *Punch*, 27th June, 1956.

PEER AND PAUPER by Cummings, *Punch*, March/ April, 1954.

"PIED PIPER NABARRO" by Cummings, *Punch*, 16th May, 1956.

The *Daily Express*, 11th May, 1956.

boy and author of *The Greasy Pole*, was one of the victims of the Macmillan slaughter house of July 1962 and lost his seat at Liverpool, Toxteth in 1964 by 2784 votes after an unprecedented anti-ministerial swing of 11·1%. He has abandoned politics. In *The Greasy Pole*, after fifteen years of friendship in the House of Commons, he knocked me about, thus:

> Gerald Nabarro was undoubtedly the greatest House of Commons character since the War. He was at once a first-rate House of Commons man, an ebullient and belligerent debater, a good constituency Member, extremely industrious, sincere and possessed of an unerring flair for publicity surpassing that of Ernest Marples, which is saying something. He was also immodest, vain, ostentatious, arrogant and in no sense a conformist. Even so, he was

popular both in the House of Commons, and in Kidderminster. But he was an exception to the rule. For the English as a rule dislike vanity in public men.[1]

I liked Reginald Bevins who was a good, down-to-earth Liverpudlian. His judgement of his colleagues was fair, inside the House and out.

The richness of talent and the variety of the fine Tory vintage of 1950 is manifest. Here they are, all ninety-three of them:

Name and age in 1950	*Constituency & career, 1950–70*	*Present status*
William AITKEN. 45	Bury St Edmunds, 1950–64 (died); nephew of Lord Beaverbrook.	Sir William Aitken, KBE (died, 1964).
Cuthbert ALPORT, TD. 37	Colchester, 1950–61 (resigned); High Commissioner, Federation of Rhodesia and Nyasaland, 1961–63.	Rt Hon. Lord Alport of Colchester, TD.
Julian AMERY. 30	Preston, North, 1950–66 (defeated); Brighton, Pavilion, since 1969; son of Rt Hon. L. S. Amery; son-in-law of Harold Macmillan; Minister of Aviation, 1962–64; biographer of Joseph Chamberlain.	Rt Hon. Julian Amery, MP, Backbencher.
John ARBUTHNOT. 38	Dover, 1950–64 (defeated).	Sir John Arbuthnot, Bart, MBE, TD.
Hubert ASHTON, MC. 52	Chelmsford, 1950–64 (retired).	Sir Hubert Ashton, KBE, MC, DL.
P. A. D. BAKER. 29	Norfolk, South, 1950–54; dismissed from the House of Commons, following his imprisonment for fraud.	
John BALDOCK. 34	Harborough, 1950–59 (retired).	

[1] Reginald Bevins, *The Greasy Pole: A personal account of the realities of British politics* (Hodder & Stoughton, 1965), page 19.

Name and age in 1950	*Constituency & career, 1950–70*	*Present status*
Col. Cyril BANKS, MBE. 49	Pudsey, 1950–59 (retired); an Independent, 1956–58.	
Maj. William HICKS BEACH, TD. 42	Cheltenham, 1950–64 (retired).	
Gordon BENNETT. 55	Glasgow, Woodside, 1950–55 (retired).	Sir Gordon Bennett.
Dr Reginald BENNETT. 38	Gosport and Fareham.	Dr Reginald Bennett, MP. Backbencher.
Reginald BEVINS. 41	Liverpool, Toxteth, 1950–64 (defeated); Postmaster-General, 1959–64.	Rt Hon. Reginald Bevins.
Frank BISHOP, MBE. 49	Harrow, Central, 1950–64 (retired).	Sir Frank Bishop, MBE.
Cyril BLACK. 48	Wimbledon; has more directorships than any other MP; concerned with morality; retiring at the end of the present Parliament.	Sir Cyril Black, MP. Backbencher.
Bernard BRAINE. 35	Billericay, 1950–55; Essex, South East, since 1955.	Bernard Braine, MP. Spokesman on Foreign and Commonwealth Affairs.
Jack NIXON BROWNE, CBE. 46	Glasgow, Govan, 1950–55; Glasgow, Craigton, 1955–59 (defeated); Minister of State, Scottish Office, 1959–64.	Rt Hon. Lord Craigton of Renfield, CBE.

Name and age in 1950	*Constituency & career, 1950–70*	*Present status*
Wing-Cdr Eric BULLUS. 43	Wembley, North.	Wing-Cdr Sir Eric Bullus, MP. Backbencher.
Sq-Ldr Frederick BURDEN. 44	Gillingham.	Sq-Ldr Frederick Burden, MP. Backbencher.
Robert CARR. 33	Mitcham.	Rt Hon. Robert Carr, MP. Shadow Minister of Employment and Productivity.
Brig. Terence CLARKE, CBE. 46	Portsmouth, West, 1950–66 (defeated).	
James CLYDE, KC (Scotland). 51	Edinburgh, North, 1950–54 (resigned).	Rt Hon. Lord Clyde, LL.D. Lord Justice General of Scotland and President of the Court of Session, since 1954.
Sq-Ldr A. E. COOPER, MBE. 39	Ilford, South, 1950–66 (defeated).	
Beresford CRADDOCK. 51	Spelthorne (retiring at the end of the present Parliament).	Sir Beresford Craddock, MP. Backbencher.
Viscount CRANBORNE. 33	Bournemouth, West, 1950–54 (retired); heir of 5th Marquess of Salisbury, KG.	
Robert CROUCH. 55	Dorset, North, 1950–57 (died); responsible for bringing Crichel Down case.	Died, 1957.

Name and age in 1950	*Constituency & career, 1950–70*	*Present status*
Petre CROWDER. 30	Ruislip-Northwood.	Petre Crowder, QC, MP. Recorder of Gravesend since 1960; Chairman of Hertfordshire Quarter Sessions, since 1963.
Nigel DAVIES. 29	Epping, 1950–51 (retired).	
William DEEDES, MC. 36	Ashford; Minister without Portfolio, 1962–64.	Rt. Hon. William Deedes, MC, MP.
Lord Malcolm DOUGLAS-HAMILTON, OBE, DFC. 40	Inverness, 1950–54 (retired); 3rd son of 13th Duke of Hamilton; killed in an air crash in Africa, 1964.	Died, 1964.
Nigel FISHER, MC. 36	Hitchin, 1950–55; Surbiton, since 1955.	Nigel Fisher, MC, MP. Backbencher.
Richard FORT. 42	Clitheroe, 1950–59 (died).	Died, 1959.
Richard READER HARRIS. 36	Heston and Isleworth (retiring at the end of the present Parliament).	Richard Reader Harris, MP. Backbencher.
Ian HARVEY, TD. 36	Harrow East, 1950–58 (resigned).	
John HAY. 30	Henley-on-Thames.	John Hay, MP. Backbencher.

Name and age in 1950	*Constituency & career, 1950–70*	*Present status*
Lionel HEALD, KC. 52	Chertsey; Attorney-General, 1951–54 (retiring at the end of the present Parliament).	Rt Hon. Sir Lionel Heald, QC, MP.
Edward HEATH, MBE. 33	Bexley; Chief Whip, 1955–59; Minister of Labour, 1959–60; Lord Privy Seal with Foreign Office responsibilities, especially Europe, 1960–63; President of the Board of Trade, 1963–64; elected leader of the Conservative Party, 27th July, 1965.	Rt Hon. Edward Heath, MBE, MP; Leader of Her Majesty's Opposition since 1965.
Michael HIGGS. 37	Bromsgrove, 1950–55 (retired).	Sir Michael Higgs. Chairman of Worcs. CC since 1959.
Dr Charles HILL. 46	Luton, 1950–63 (resigned); formerly the Radio Doctor; Postmaster-General, 1955–57; Chancellor of the Duchy of Lancaster, 1957–61; Minister of Housing, 1961–62 (victim of the July Purge); Chairman, ITA, 1963–67.	Rt Hon. Lord Hill of Luton. Chairman of the Governors of the BBC since 1967.
Mrs Eveline HILL. 51	Manchester, Wythenshawe, 1950–64 (defeated).	
Geoffrey HIRST, TD. 45	Shipley (retiring at the end of the present Parliament).	Geoffrey Hirst, TD, MP. Backbencher; Independent Conservative.
Henry HOPKINSON, CMG. 48	Taunton, 1950–56 (Peerage); Delegate, General Assembly of the United Nations, 1952–55; served in Foreign Office, up to the rank of Minister, 1924–46.	Rt Hon. Lord Colyton, CMG.

Name and age in 1950	*Constituency & career, 1950–70*	*Present status*
Patricia HORNSBY-SMITH. 25	Chislehurst, 1950–66 (defeated).	Rt Hon. Dame Patricia Hornsby-Smith, DBE. Prospective Conservative candidate for Chislehurst.
Hon. Greville HOWARD. 40	St Ives, 1950–66 (retired); Lord Mayor of Westminster, 1946–47.	
Gerald HOWARD, KC. 53	Cambridgeshire, 1950–61 (resigned).	Hon. Mr Justice Howard. Judge of the High Court, Queen's Bench Division, since 1961.
Walter HUDSON. 55	Hull, 1950–59 (retired).	Walter Hudson, CBE.
H. Montgomery HYDE. 42	Belfast, North (UU). 1950–59 (retired).	H. Montgomery Hyde, Criminologist and Writer.
Harry HYLTON-FOSTER, KC. 44	York, 1950–59; Cities of London and Westminster, 1959–65; Solicitor-General, 1954–59; Speaker, 1959–65.	Rt Hon. Sir Harry Hylton-Foster, QC, LL.D. (died, 1965).
Howard JOHNSON. 38	Brighton, Kemptown, 1950–59 (retired).	
Aubrey JONES. 38	Birmingham, Hall Green, 1950–65 (resigned); Minister of Fuel and Power, 1955–57; Minister of Supply, 1957–59.	Rt Hon. Aubrey Jones. Chairman of the National Board for Prices and Incomes, 1965–70.

Name and age in 1950	*Constituency & career, 1950–70*	*Present status*
Donald KABERRY, TD. 42	Leeds, North-West.	Sir Donald Kaberry, Bt, TD, MP. Backbencher.
Edwin LEATHER. 30	Somerset, North, 1950–59 (retired sick)	Sir Edwin Leather. A Vice-Chairman of the Conservative Party.
David LLEWELLYN. 34	Cardiff, North, 1950–59 (retired sick)	Sir David Llewellyn.
Gilbert LONGDEN, MBE. 47	Hertfordshire, South-West.	Gilbert Longden, MBE, MP. Backbencher.
Percy LUCAS, DSO & Bar. 34	Brentford and Chiswick, 1950–59 (retired); "Laddie Lucas"—Battle of Britain Pilot.	
Stephen MCADDEN. 42	Southend, East	Sir Stephen McAdden, CBE, MP. Backbencher.
Iain MACLEOD. 36	Enfield, West; Minister of Health, 1952–55; Minister of Labour and National Service, 1955–59; Colonial Secretary, 1959–61; Chancellor of the Duchy of Lancaster and Leader of the House of Commons and Chairman of the Conservative Party, 1961–63.	Rt Hon. Iain Macleod, MP. Shadow Chancellor of the Exchequer.
Revd J. G. MACMANAWAY, MBE. 52	Belfast, West (UU), Feb.–Oct. 1950; declared ineligible, as a Minister of the Church of Ireland, to sit in the House of Commons.	

Name and age in 1950	*Constituency & career, 1950–70*	*Present status*
Angus MAUDE, TD. 37	Ealing, South, 1950–58; Independent Conservative, 1957–58 (resigned); Editor, *Sydney Morning Herald*, 1958–61; re-entered Parliament as Member for Stratford-upon-Avon, 1963.	Angus Maude, TD, MP. Backbencher.
Reginald MAUDLING. 32	Barnet; Minister of Supply, 1955–57; Paymaster-General, 1957–59; President of the Board of Trade, 1959–61; Colonial Secretary, 1961–62; Chancellor of the Exchequer, 1962–64.	Rt Hon. Reginald Maudling, MP. Deputy Leader of the Opposition.
Gerald NABARRO. 36	Kidderminster, 1950–64 (retired sick); Worcestershire, South, since 1966.	Sir Gerald Nabarro, MP. Backbencher.
Harmar NICHOLLS. 37	Peterborough (majority of 3 in 1966).	Sir Harmar Nicholls, Bart, MP. Backbencher.
George NUGENT. 42	Guildford, 1950–66 (retired).	Rt Hon. Lord Nugent of Guildford.
Lt-Col. Hendrie OAKSHOTT, MBE. 45	Bebington, 1950–64.	Rt Hon. Lord Oakshott, MBE.
David ORMSBY-GORE. 31	Oswestry, 1950–61 (resigned); Ambassador to USA, 1961–65.	Rt Hon. Lord Harlech, KCMG, DCL. Chairman, British Board of Film Censors; Chairman of Harlech Television.
Capt. L. P. S. ORR. 31	South Down (UU).	Capt. L. P. S. Orr, MP. Backbencher.

Name and age in 1950	*Constituency & career, 1950–70*	*Present status*
Ian ORR-EWING, OBE. 38	Hendon, North; Civil Lord of the Admiralty, 1959–63.	Sir Ian Orr-Ewing, Bart, OBE, MP. Backbencher.
Enoch POWELL, MBE. 37	Wolverhampton, South-West; Financial Secretary to the Treasury, 1957–58 (resigned); Minister of Health, 1960–63; dismissed from the Shadow Cabinet, 1968.	Rt. Hon. Enoch Powell, MBE, MP. Backbencher.
Henry PRICE, 39	Lewisham, West, 1950–64 (retired).	Henry Price, CBE.
Martin REDMAYNE, DSO. 39	Rushcliffe, 1950–66 (defeated); Chief Whip, 1959–64.	Rt Hon. Lord Redmayne, DSO.
Lt-Col. the Hon. Peter REMNANT. 52	Wokingham, 1950–59 (retired).	Died, 1969.
William ROBSON BROWN. 50	Esher (retiring at the end of the present Parliament).	Sir William Robson Brown, MP. Backbencher.
John RODGERS 43	Sevenoaks.	Sir John Rodgers, Bart, MP. Backbencher.
Sir Harold ROPER, CBE, MC. 58	Cornwall, North, 1950–59 (retired).	
Ronald RUSSELL. 55	Wembley, South.	Sir Ronald Russell, MP. Backbencher.

Name and age in 1950	*Constituency & career, 1950–70*	*Present status*
Capt. Robert RYDER, VC, RN. 52	Merton and Morden, 1950–55 (retired).	
Martin SMITH. 42	Grantham, 1950–51 (died) Banker.	Died, 1951.
Peter SMITHERS, D.Phil. 36	Winchester, 1950–64 (resigned), Delegate, United Nations General Assembly, 1960–62; Secretary-General of the Council of Europe, 1964–69.	
Brig. John SMYTH, VC, MC. 56	Norwood, 1950–66 (retired)	Rt Hon. Sir John Smyth, Bart, VC, MC.
Christopher SOAMES. 29	Bedford, 1950–66 (defeated); son-in-law of Sir Winston Churchill; Minister of Agriculture, 1960–64.	Rt Hon. Christopher Soames, CBE. Ambassador to France since 1968.
Capt the Hon. Oliver STANLEY. 30	North Fylde, 1950–66 (retired); heir presumptive to 18th Earl of Derby.	
Geoffrey STEVENS, FCA. 47	Portsmouth, Langstone, 1950–64 (retired).	
William STEWARD. 48	Woolwich, West, 1950–59 (retired).	Sir William Steward.
William TAYLOR, OBE. 47	Bradford, North, 1950–64 (defeated).	Sir William Taylor, Bart, KBE, Hon. Air Commodore.

Name and age in 1950	*Constituency & career, 1950–70*	*Present status*
Kenneth THOMPSON. 41	Liverpool, Walton, 1950–64 (defeated).	Sir Kenneth Thompson, Bart.
Richard THOMPSON. 47	Croydon, West, 1950–55; Croydon South, 1955–66 (defeated)	Sir Richard Thompson, Bart. Prospective Conservative candidate for Croydon, South.
Col. John TILNEY, TD. 42	Liverpool, Wavertree.	Col. John Tilney, TD, MP. Backbencher.
John VAUGHAN-MORGAN. 45	Reigate (retiring at the end of the present Parliament).	Rt Hon. Sir John Vaughan-Morgan, Bart, MP.
Dennis VOSPER, TD. 34	Runcorn, 1950–64 (retired); Minister of Health, 1957 (resigned sick); Secretary for Technical Co-operation, 1961–63 (resigned sick); Chairman of the National Assistance Board, 1964.	Rt Hon. Lord Runcorn of Heswall. Died 1968.
Edward WAKEFIELD, CIE. 46	Derbyshire, West, 1950–62 (resigned); Commissioner, then High Commissioner, for Malta, 1962–65.	Sir Edward Wakefield, Bart, CIE. Died, 1969.
Harold WATKINSON. 40	Woking, 1950–64 (retired); Minister of Transport and Civil Aviation, 1955–59; Minister of Defence, 1959–62 (victim of the July Purge).	Rt Hon. Lord Watkinson of Woking, CH.
Gerald WILLS, MBE. 45	Bridgwater (retiring at the end of the present Parliament).	Sir Gerald Wills, MBE, MP. Backbencher.

Name and age in 1950	*Constituency & career, 1950–70*	*Present status*
Geoffrey WILSON. 46	Truro (retiring at the end of the present Parliament).	Geoffrey Wilson, MP. Backbencher.
Richard WOOD. 29	Bridlington; 2nd son of 1st Earl of Halifax, KG, Viceroy of India, etc; Minister of Pensions and National Insurance, 1963–64.	Rt Hon. Richard Wood, MP.

These were the original ninety-three Members. Now only thirty-five remain:

Rt Hon. Julian Amery.	Brighton, Pavilion.
Dr. Reginald Bennett.	Gosport and Fareham.
*Sir Cyril Black.	Wimbledon.
Mr Bernard Braine.	Essex, South-East.
Wing Commander Sir Eric Bullus.	Wembley, North.
Squadron Leader Frederick Burden.	Gillingham.
Rt Hon. Robert Carr.	Mitcham.
*Sir Beresford Craddock.	Spelthorne.
Mr Petre Crowder, QC.	Ruislip-Norwood.
Rt Hon. William Deedes, MC.	Ashford.
Nigel Fisher, MC.	Surbiton.
*Mr Reader Harris.	Heston & Isleworth.
Mr John Hay.	Henley-on-Thames.
*Rt Hon. Sir Lionel Heald, QC.	Chertsey.
Rt Hon. Edward Heath, MBE.	Bexley.
*Mr Geoffrey Hirst.	Shipley.
Sir Donald Kaberry, Bart.	Leeds, North-West.
Mr Gilbert Longden, MBE.	Hertfordshire, South-West.
Sir Stephen McAdden, CBE.	Southend, East.
Rt Hon. Iain Macleod.	Enfield, West.
Mr Angus Maude.	Stratford-upon-Avon.
Rt Hon. Reginald Maudling.	Barnet.
Sir Gerald Nabarro.	South Worcestershire.
Sir Harmar Nicholls, Bart.	Peterborough.
Captain L. P. S. Orr.	South Down.
Sir Ian Orr-Ewing, Bart, OBE.	Hendon, North.

* Retiring at the end of the present Parliament.

Rt. Hon. J. Enoch Powell, MBE.	Wolverhampton, South-West.
*Sir William Robson Brown.	Esher.
Sir John Rodgers, Bart.	Sevenoaks.
Sir Ronald Russell.	Wembley, South.
Mr John Tilney.	Liverpool, Wavertree.
*Rt Hon. Sir John Vaughan-Morgan, Bart.	Reigate.
*Sir Gerald Wills, MBE.	Bridgwater.
*Mr Geoffrey Wilson.	Truro.
Rt Hon. Richard Wood.	Bridlington.

* Retiring at the end of the present Parliament.

Many of these ninety-three new Tories were from untraditional Tory backgrounds. Of course, there was the usual bevy of Old Etonians—Amery, Arbuthnot, Hicksbeach, Cranborne, Crowder, Davies, Douglas-Hamilton, Fisher, Fort, Hopkinson, Greville Howard, Hylton-Foster, Llewellyn, Ormsby-Gore, Remnant, Smith, Soames, Stanley, Tilney, Vaughan-Morgan and Wood—but the constituencies chose them and for the most part they have proved to be competent Members. Some have even made good Ministers. All the other great schools were well represented but for the first time the 1950 entry contained a high percentage of Members from non-public schools, many of them not even non-Oxbridge graduates. These were the real self-made men. They were a minority and accounted for about a third of the 1950 vintage—about the same in number as those from the most traditional Tory backgrounds. The like of these non-U Members, such as Banks, Gordon Bennett, Bevins, Bishop, Braine, Bullus, Craddock, Hay, Heath, Dr Hill, Mrs Hill, Hudson, Jones, Kaberry, McAdden, Nicholls, Powell, Price, Steward, Taylor, Kenneth Thompson and myself, had never been seen in such numbers in the Tory Parliamentary Party before. Thus wrote *The Times* on 22nd February, 1960, the eve of the tenth anniversary of the 1950 General Election:

> There were men like Mr Bevins, the Postmaster-General, Mr Henry Price and Mr Nabarro, who were self-made; there were shrewd professional men like Sir Donald Kaberry, a Leeds solicitor, who is now vice-chairman of the party; there were technologists like Mr Robert Carr and Mr Harold Watkinson. And above all there was an extraordinarily gifted group of purely professional politicians of a kind the Conservative Party has not known in Parliament before: Mr Macleod, Mr Maudling, Mr Alport and Mr Enoch

Powell (a one-time Professor of Greek). All these had been Members of the Conservative Party's 'Civil Service' working in close partnership with Mr Butler and servicing the Opposition front-bench with briefs of the sort Departments prepare for Ministers in office.

Thus, it is fair to say that the Conservative recruits of 1950, although they certainly did not represent a breakthrough of the social barrier as a whole, did illustrate a deep change that came over Conservative politics after the trauma of 1945. It could be said that the Conservative Party, from Central Office to constituency level, had been forced by the scale of Labour's victory to go in search of merit in unexpected places.

They found a Richmond girl, a secretary, whom we know as Miss Patricia Hornsby-Smith. They found young Conservative leaders like Mr Bernard Braine and Mr John Hay. They found in plenty young and youngish men who had made their mark in local government and who, until now, had had no grand political ambitions—or hopes.

And having found them, the Conservative Party gave them a mission and a purpose. This is why many of them are to this day what Mr Butler and Lord Woolton made them. In fact, it would be misleading to label them as Mr Butler's men, if that were to seem to mean that, say, Mr Nabarro and Brigadier Clarke can hardly contain their ecstasy when Mr Butler develops his views on juvenile crime. But a high proportion are in political life because Mr Butler brought them into it, or gave them good reason to enter it, and perhaps most of them continue to see Conservatism through his eyes.

Tomorrow night, then, Mr Butler will have occasion for pride in some of the careers he largely helped to launch. But he may well wonder, with the 1950 example before him, when there is likely to be such another vintage crop. It is true that the men of 1950 had, as the men of 1959 have not, the advantage of being in opposition at a time when reputations could quickly be made, and the further advantage that there were soon to be vacancies as the old guard were relieved.

But there is some evidence to suggest that in the days of prosperity the party, especially in the constituencies, has forgotten some of the lessons of 1945. There is a danger that the base of the Parliamentary party may be shrinking again. The gallimaufry of talent and proved ability found in the men of 1950 is the best possible warning to the party chairman that the net can hardly be cast too wide.

A short and hesitant step had indeed been taken by the Tory Party towards broadening its social base in Parliament under the guidance of RAB Butler, Lord Woolton and Sir David Maxwell-Fyfe. But the ravages of political fortune, of the electors and personal sickness have been considerable. Even in 1960, only sixty-seven of the original ninety-three Members remained in Parliament. Now there are thirty-five and after the next General Election there may not be more than twenty-five. To restore the Tory Party after the depredations of the sixties it urgently needs in 1970 another vintage comparable in quality to that of twenty years ago.

VICKY'S DREADFUL NIGHTMARE AFTER HIS RETURN FROM COVERING THE AMERICAN PARTY CONVENTIONS

THE AMERICAN PRESIDENTIAL ELECTIONS, *Evening Standard*, 2nd August, 1960. Vicky's impressions after returning from the American Party Conventions.

2. *The Tory Leadership: The Rt Hon. Harold Macmillan*

I HAVE served under five Tory leaders during the last quarter of a century:

(i) Sir Winston Churchill, 1945 to 1955.
(ii) Sir Anthony Eden, 1955 to 1957.
(iii) Mr Harold Macmillan, 1957 to 1963.
(iv) Sir Alec Douglas-Home, 1963 to 1965.
(v) Mr Edward Heath, 1965 to 1970.

And with the exception of Mr Edward Heath, I have sat behind them all in the House of Commons as Prime Ministers.

Traditionally, Conservative leaders were said to "emerge". That is to say, the succession was rigged by a small section of the party, usually with Cabinet inspiration. Of course, soundings of opinion were taken throughout the party and the results weighed rather than counted; and if there was any dispute, these "opinions" could easily be lost in the confusion which such a system inevitably created. At any rate, that is what happened in 1963.

It has not always been so. Sir Winston Churchill, the exception in almost everything, came to power as the head of a Coalition in 1940 to win the war and then carried on as head of the Caretaker Government of May–July, 1945. After six years as leader of the Opposition, he won the election in October, 1951 and returned to Downing Street with a tiny majority of fourteen seats, to reign as Prime Minister until April, 1955.

Sir Anthony Eden, war-time Foreign Secretary and again from 1951 to 1955, was the heir apparent. He had been groomed for the succession for ten years and when the time came for Sir Winston to retire amid the adulation of the entire nation, Sir Anthony was accepted without dissent. Less than two months later, on 26th May, the Conservatives were returned to power at the General Election, with a majority increased to sixty. The Suez affair overtook Sir Anthony and his short period in office ended with his resignation on grounds of grave ill health, in January, 1957.

Since then, the succession to the leadership of the Tory Party has become increasingly deranged. A leader with the necessary stature and unanimous support obstinately refused to emerge, both in the last days of 1956 and the first days of 1957 and, worse still, in the autumn of 1963. This 1963 contest regrettably degenerated into a public brawl, gravely discrediting this gentlemanly party.

It was inevitable that sooner or later some democratic method of electing a leader would develop. It was the survivor of the 1963 farrago, Sir Alec Douglas-Home, who took the initiative in abandoning "emergence" and substituting election. The reform was long overdue. The conception of it is generally attributed to Mr Humphry Berkeley, MP for Lancaster and later Chairman of the United Nations Association, who lost his seat in the 1966 General Election. Anyway, Mr Edward Heath was the first elected leader in the history of the Tory Party, for better or worse. The actual electors were the Tory MPs who consulted their constituency organisations about their preferences. I was temporarily out of the House at the time, and so played no direct part in the proceedings. I think the system is an improvement on "emergence". It ensures "rough justice" of a sort and is pretty much the same as the Labour Party system.

The succession to Sir Anthony Eden in 1956, however, had to be determined by the traditional methods. There was a rough poll of the Cabinet and Mr Harold Macmillan, Chancellor of the Exchequer since 1955, was successful. Mr Macmillan had warned during the Suez crisis of the collapse of sterling if Britain persisted in going it alone with France. He has been widely accused of disloyalty to Eden over Suez but nothing is further from the truth. All Macmillan did, and he did so rightly, as Chancellor of the Exchequer, was to warn of the consequences to sterling, in the absence of American support.

The fascination of the old system, whereby Tory leaders "emerged", was its mystery, but in the case of Mr Macmillan we already have one reliable account from Lord Egremont, who as Mr John Wyndham was

Macmillan's Principal Private Secretary from soon after he took office until 1963:

> I heard afterwards that when Anthony Eden announced his resignation to the Cabinet appropriate tributes of affection and sorrow were paid to him by Rab Butler and Harold Macmillan, after which Eden withdrew. The rest of the Cabinet, on filing out, were stopped by Sir Norman Brook, the Cabinet Secretary, who asked them to go, one by one, into another room where Lord Salisbury and Lord Kilmuir were seated at a table. This pair interrogated their colleagues on the succession. They thought it best, they said, that there should be no discussion. What they wanted was a straight answer to the question: 'Who's best—Rab or Harold?' They got it.[1]

There was no indecision. There was not even any doubt as to who was in the running. Nothing was clear when the Tory succession again became first political news in 1963.

On the evening of 10th January, 1957, I was delivering a speech in the village hall at Wichenford (electorate 262) in rural Worcestershire. My chairman was the delightful and gallant Grenadier Guardsman, Brigadier C. R. Britten, OBE, MC, who lived nearby at Kenswick Manor, the house which was to have been Winston Churchill's war-time headquarters if 10 Downing Street had to be evacuated because of Hitler's bombing of London during the Second World War. Before the meeting, Charles Britten said to me "We will hear tonight whether Harold Macmillan goes to the Palace". We waited agog for news as to whether it was to be Harold Macmillan or RAB Butler for Prime Minister. During the meeting the news arrived that it was Harold Macmillan. The Brigadier asked me to go back to Kenswick Manor with him to celebrate, and accompanied by our respective wives we drank a few glasses of whisky.

What made the evening memorable were the Brigadier's reminiscences of Harold Macmillan from the Kaiser's War. There was the Brigadier's photograph album; there was a faded photograph of the officers of the 4th Battalion The Grenadier Guards before embarking for France in 1915. Through a great magnifying glass, I could recognise the boyish features of my host, the Brigadier, and by his side, looking ridiculously young, my new Conservative leader and Prime Minister, the Rt Hon. Harold Macmillan, MP, "kissing hands" that very evening at Buckingham Palace

[1] Lord Egremont, *Wyndham and Children First* (Macmillan, 1968), pp. 158–59.

as Her Majesty's first Minister. "The bravest man in the Brigade of Guards," said the Brigadier, and he continued:

> Harold and I went to Eton together in the same Half so we were old friends when we met again in July, 1915 on the formation of 4th Battalion Grenadier Guards at Marlow.
>
> In a few weeks we proceeded overseas to join the newly formed Guards Division, and on September 27th the Battalion had its christening at the Battle of Loos. With three other officers I was personally left behind in Vermelles as first reinforcements. That night Ludlow, the Quartermaster, went up to Loos with the rations whilst we remained in a cellar in the village.
>
> In the early hours of next morning, Ludlow came back to Vermelles and, to our horror, told us of the terrible casualties the Battalion had suffered. Well do I remember how he spoke of Harold Macmillan:
>
> The Artillery Commander, when Harold arrived at Loos, was almost demented because there were no Infantry between his guns and the enemy. Regardless of shot and shell, Harold, aged 21, walked up and down the road in full view of the enemy holding the General by the arm and saying his men would be there in a few minutes and all would be well.
>
> 'The whole Battalion is talking of Harold Macmillan's bravery,' he added and, I know that, during the next two years or so, anything brave was described by the Guardsmen as 'nearly as brave as Mr Macmillan'. What higher tribute could there be!
>
> Finally he was wounded and taken to hospital.
>
> Within a few months he was back again in France, this time with another Battalion where he was wounded twice and received a commendation from the Brigade Commander for his report gained on patrol within the enemy lines. The first wound in the knee did not stop him, he carried on.
>
> It is remarkable, with this astounding record as a young officer and three times wounded, that no decoration came his way. This may well have been due to casualties amongst senior officers, but I do feel the public should be reminded of Harold Macmillan's great record as a Guardsman in the First World War.

Several Guards veterans of the First World War, notably the late Harry Crookshank (Rt Hon. Harry Crookshank, Conservative MP for thirty years and sometime Leader of the House of Commons), confirmed to me the Grenadier legend in the trenches, on every brave deed by a serving member of the Brigade of Guards: "Nearly as brave as Mr Macmillan". Yet Mr Macmillan wore no decoration, just the three Great War ribbons. It is all in keeping with his noble concept of service. Forty-five years later, after nearly seven years as Prime Minister, he refused an earldom, the established perquisite and sinecure of any Premier. He chose to remain "Mister", which he is to this day.

"Nearly as brave as Mr Macmillan", in the Brigade; "unflappable" in Parliament. These are true expressions of esteem for a remarkable man by his contemporaries and countrymen.

Had Mr Macmillan handed over to Mr R. A. Butler at the end of five years, that is to say in 1961—and five years is quite enough for, and of, any Prime Minister nowadays—Macmillan would have left behind him the memory and achievement of a very great Tory peace-time premier and party leader. This was destroyed in his last two years of power. Up to then, RAB was the heir apparent insofar as people thought about replacing Macmillan at all and he would have succeeded with as little dispute as when Neville Chamberlain followed Baldwin in 1937. But Macmillan clung to office. Many of his senior Cabinet colleagues have written of everything which I sensed so painfully from the backbenches. Watching him from my corner seat on the second bench below the gangway in the House of Commons, I became aware of the stale and lustreless character of his Ministry. Lord Kilmuir, Lord Chancellor from 1954 until he fell in the purge of July 1962, diagnosed the problem in a way which is representative of the attitude of much of the Cabinet at that time:

> After ten years of power, there was a too dominant preoccupation with administrative matters. Ministers had become obsessed with the work of their own departments and the Government as a whole lost interest in political thinking and the impact of the measures they proposed on ordinary people.[1]

Cummings, the cartoonist of the *Daily Express*, put his finger on it all on 20th February, 1963, when he depicted a patriarchal, Moses-like Macmillan descending from Sinai, carrying a tablet inscribed "To promised land via MacMoses' visions" and a broken tablet, cast aside inscribed "To promised land via Common Market". There is no sign of Mr Edward Heath, the Mr Europe who failed; there is no sign of the Earl of Home, then Foreign Secretary; but a shifty Iain Macleod whispers to a smug Lord Hailsham "If you ask me, it's not a new tablet we need but a new Moses." RAB gazes at MacMoses incredulously, Maudling scowls. I, clearly dubious about the omniscience of MacMoses, raise my eyes heavenwards and beat my chest. Over all hovers a pipe-smoking vulture: he had then only twenty months to wait.

[1] *Political Adventure: The Memoirs of the Earl of Kilmuir* (Weidenfeld & Nicolson, 1964), pp. 320–21.

" If you ask me it's not a new tablet we need but a new Moses "

CONSERVATIVE PARTY POLICY, *Daily Express*, 20th February, 1963.

Cummings, as usual, had it all quite right. The opinion polls showed that the Labour Party, with their new leader, Mr Harold Wilson, were 12½% ahead and this was the month before the Profumo affair.

I had exploded nine months earlier in a speech at Chaddesley Corbett, in my Kidderminster constituency and what I said then, on 18th May, 1962, represented the opinions of the Tory backbenches, restive and apprehensive about the Government's performance:

> Mr Macmillan must shuffle his pack. He must put new men into office and get rid of the dead wood and rotten Ministers. Some of them have been there a long time and they are probably tired of the burdens and responsibilities of office. He must give the Tory Party a new dynamic and get rid of the dunderheads.

The national and provincial press supported me. The *Daily Express* of 19th May, 1962, printed the following banner headline on the front page:

Nabarro hots up Tory row and tells Premier

SHUFFLE THE PACK!

The same newspaper's William Hickey column on 21st May had an item under the heading "Looking beyond the old school tie. Why not pick these for the Cabinet?" and pictured:

Mr Edward du Cann	MP for Taunton
Mr Brian Harrison	MP for Maldon
Mr Ray Mawby	MP for Totnes
Mrs Patricia McLaughlin	MP for Belfast, West
Mr Anthony Fell	MP for Yarmouth

as well as myself, with the question whether the Cabinet would ever recover from my sitting in it.

The *Liverpool Daily Post* said in a leader on the same day:

> Mr Nabarro has a talent for blowing away cobwebs. Can he blow them away from the Cabinet? He is undoubtedly right to say that some Ministers must go. Reshuffling the same dog-eared pack just will not do.

Mr John Freeman, now British Ambassador in Washington, wrote in the *News of the World* on Sunday, 20th May, "It's time for the knife, Mac" and continued:

> Gerald Nabarro's brash outburst against Government 'dead wood and rotten Ministers' is a large straw in a high wind.

THE LIFE AND TIMES OF MR RUBBER-STAMP, MP, *Daily Express*, 28th November, 1960.

On the same day, Cyclops of the *People* asked "Have they one friend?"

> Gerald Nabarro's outburst against the Government was surely the last straw. Is it conceivable that a Government could end its term of office without any friends at all?
>
> In an extraordinary way Mr Macmillan and his cronies seem determined to achieve this remarkable feat.
>
> Those whose lot is to watch the day-by-day processions through the lobbies at Westminster have never seen anything like it.
>
> Normally it is the lunatics and the agitators who make up most of the pressure groups which chivvy MPs. In recent weeks their places have been taken by the most docile members of society.

John Freeman's "large straw in a high wind" was a remarkable piece of prophecy. The slaughter of Friday, 13th July, only eight weeks after my "Shuffle the pack" speech, was a desperate act affecting a large part of the Cabinet and the rest of the Government. As I observed at the time, Westminster "had been made to look like an abattoir". But was the purge really effective? RAB Butler said in 1966, after he had left politics:

> I think the Prime Minister has to be a butcher, and know the joints. That is perhaps where I have not been quite competent in knowing the ways you cut up a carcass.[1]

In so far as the slaughter failed to restore Government popularity, Mr Macmillan was not a very effective butcher either.

From March to June, 1963, the Government was further embarrassed by the Profumo episode. I was completely loyal to Mr Macmillan throughout.

On the night of the Profumo debate when more than two dozen Tory MPs ignored a three-line whip and refused to support Macmillan, I willingly followed him into the Lobby. On the evening of the debate, 17th June, 1963, I was interviewed on "Panorama" by Robin Day in Parliament Square and I said then that I did not think that the affair cast any sort of slur on the Prime Minister personally or on his competence. I had previously said that it was no part of the Prime Minister's function to secrete himself beneath the beds of his Ministers in order to obtain evidence of their moral behaviour.

From this time on, the departure of Mr Macmillan was a matter for daily discussion which built up until the Blackpool Conference in October.

[1] Interview with Kenneth Harris, printed in *The Listener*, 28th June, 1966.

" Why, it's just like the Socialist Party in office — except I doodled and he reads Trollope "

Resignation of Chancellor of the Exchequer, The Rt Hon. Peter Thorneycroft, MP, the Financial Secretary to the Treasury, J. Enoch Powell, Esq., MP, and the Economic Secretary to the Treasury, Nigel Birch, Esq., MP, January, 1958 by Cummings, *Daily Express*, 8th January, 1958.

The hub of the contemporary problem was the lack of an obvious successor. In the same week as the Profumo debate, *The Economist* wrote on 22nd June:

> Unlike Sir Winston Churchill eight years ago, Mr Harold Macmillan had no long-waiting and long-accepted crown prince to put in almost automatically.

And in the same issue, *The Economist* dealt with the other part of the problem which was that while there was no obvious successor, there were far too many possible ones, which it identified as:

Mr R. A. Butler	First Secretary of State
Mr Reginald Maudling	Chancellor of the Exchequer
Lord Hailsham	Lord President of the Council and Minister for Science
Mr Edward Heath	Lord Privy Seal
Mr Iain Macleod	Chancellor of the Duchy of Lancaster

while regarding Lord Home (Foreign Secretary), Mr Selwyn Lloyd (former Chancellor of the Exchequer and Foreign Secretary but on the backbenches since the Purge) and Mr Enoch Powell (Minister of Health), as unlikely contenders, let alone successful ones.

On the eve of the Party Conference, 7th October, Mr Macmillan announced that his illness would necessitate an operation and that he would therefore enter hospital and be unable to attend the conference. But he did not take any immediate action about resigning. On Wednesday, 9th October, I had a long-standing engagement to address a public meeting from the best platform in the north of England, the Bolton Town Hall. It was a Central Office engagement and I always address meetings in nearby constituencies during Party Conferences. The large hall was completely full and, for fire precautionary reasons, the Police closed the doors forty minutes before I was due to speak. The entire national press was represented in view of my provocative advance Press Association handout, designed to test public opinion about the leadership struggle which was now imminent. What I said received the greatest possible newspaper, television and wireless coverage and was eventually quoted in the late Mr Randolph Churchill's extraordinary book *The Fight for the Tory Leadership*.

> How much I deplore the illness of the Prime Minister! May he recover completely and enjoy a long, happy and well-earned retirement. His magnificent service to Britain in war and in peace, should command the admiration

and deep gratitude of us all. He has been a great Prime Minister for seven years.

But, Britain cannot be governed or led by a sick septuagenarian. The Prime Minister should hand over within the next few weeks.

Effectively, there are three probable contestants for the succession:

Butler . . . donnish, dignified and dull.
Hailsham . . . ebullient, erudite and erratic.
Maudling . . . manly, matey and money-wise.
The mantle of the Premiership should fall on Hailsham.

The reaction from the audience at Bolton was extraordinary. At the mention of Butler's name, they groaned; Maudling produced no reaction of any kind; the mention of Hailsham brought them cheering to their feet. Of course, this was before Hailsham's wet histrionics about renouncing his peerage; and before his intemperate and impetuous behaviour on television, when he alienated a large body of public opinion which had formerly supported his candidature.

On the following day, Thursday 10th October, my speech received, as I have said, very extensive coverage. *The Times* had an unambiguous leading article with the same intention as my speech:

> The Prime Minister is a realist, he knows that politics is a harsh master. It is necessary for the nation's future political health that the coming election finds both parties at their best and the battle be closely fought.

Mr Macmillan then capitulated, although when he had taken the decision I do not know. His letter to the Party Conference was written that morning and read out to the assembly of four thousand delegates the same afternoon by Lord Home in his capacity as president of the Conference:

> It will not be possible for me to carry the physical burden of leading the party at the next General Election. . . . In these circumstances I hope that it will soon be possible for the customary processes of consultation to be carried out within the party about its future leadership.

Throughout the week of the Conference and the week after, with the House still in recess and the Party dispersed all over the country, the leadership struggle continued. Much of it, or at any rate, most of the superficial nonsense which surrounded it, was conducted in public, on the television and on radio. The contestants were still supposed to be Butler, Maudling and Hailsham. Maudling, the youngest of these was by no means the least able or satisfactory of them but he suffered from what *The Economist* candidly described on October 19th:

> The party's younger contenders are anxious that none of their number should slip into the leadership while still in his forties, and thus keep the rest of them out for twenty years.

Lord Home remained aloof. Nobody seriously considered him. After careful discussions around the Conference, I was able to give odds for the candidates when I addressed the Lytham St Annes Ladies Tea Club in the Lowther Pavilion at Lytham on the afternoon following my Bolton speech. I made the speech on behalf of my friend Colonel C. G. Lancaster, MP for South Fylde, who was for many years Chairman of the Conservative Parliamentary Fuel and Power Committee of which I was vice-Chairman. Considerable sums of money had already been placed on the various contestants, with national firms of book-makers notably Ladbrokes, so that the odds were of great topical interest:

Lord Hailsham	5–4	against
Mr R. A. Butler	2–1	,,
Mr Reginald Maudling	15–2	,,
Lord Home	33–1	,,
Mr Edward Heath	60–1	,,
Mr Enoch Powell	60–1	,,
Mr Iain Macleod	66–1	,,

Elsewhere I had seen myself listed as a candidate, with the odds of 500 to 1. A rank outsider, said my detractors.

The Tory Party "stuffed-shirts" did not like this at all. They resented common betting on their leadership stakes. They castigated me for my choice of words in the Bolton speech, "Britain cannot be governed or led by a sick septuagenarian". They said the words were unkind, selfish, distasteful, coarse, crude and many other things besides. Candour is ever anathema to Tory "stuffed-shirts". But the rank and file of the party were with me; they supported my plain speaking and the fashion I had indicated the strength of the various candidates in my betting odds.

On the last day of the Conference 12th October, 1963, Mr R. A. Butler had the great advantage of delivering the final speech, which is habitually given by the party leader. The speech, of course, added to his stature but by no means as much as it could have done. So, the conference dispersed with nothing settled. The idea of Lord Home becoming Prime Minister was still thought to be absurd. He himself was evasive when asked whether he was a candidate. Like many Foreign Secretaries, he was relatively unknown to the mass of the electorate. He was much in the public eye at Blackpool where he created the impression of being rather dated, rather fuddy-duddy, rather aristocratic, indifferent in health and altogether too well-mannered and gentle for politics in the age of Mr Harold Wilson. The mass of the electorate was, however, as usual under a delusion about its political leaders.

Personally, I was in a curious position about it all. I admired Alec Home enormously but I did not think him up to being Prime Minister. I had become thoroughly disenchanted with my original choice, Lord Hailsham, after his absurd behaviour during the Conference, although at least part of the blame for it must go to the heavy handed campaign mounted on his behalf by Mr Randolph Churchill and I imagine this was done without Lord Hailsham's consent. Thank goodness I was not on speaking terms with Randolph Churchill. I had been against the appointment of a peer, (Lord Home), as Foreign Secretary, in July 1960, and had said so in the Commons in a speech immediately before Mr Harold Macmillan's:

> Apprehensions about these Ministerial arrangements are not confined to members of the Opposition. There is, evidently, a good deal of controversy among people of all parties and of no party as to the wisdom of the present arrangements in the critical state of international affairs.
>
> I wish to ask my right hon. Friend, the Prime Minister, a very pointed question about the events of the last ten days. My political memory goes back only for about a quarter of a century, a good deal less than that of my right hon. Friend, but historical researches lead me to the conclusion that never before has there been such a precise forecast of principal Ministerial offices before their announcement by the Prime Minister. Number 10 Downing Street, today looks like a very leaky colander.
>
> I thought it quite incredible that the *Guardian*, about ten days ago, could have reliably forecast the name of the present Foreign Secretary. Indeed, that forecast was received with incredulity by the majority of my hon. Friends and myself. But, as time went on, more and more newspapers got used to it or confirmed that it was correct, until, last week-end, we had the extraordinary situation of the names of nearly all the new holders of Cabinet offices appearing, reliably published in national newspapers.
>
> Was it a coincidence that a distinguished former member of the Establishment, Sir William Hayter, wrote an article in last Sunday's *Observer* lauding the principle of having the Foreign Secretary in another place? I am not fond

of arrangements of that kind. I believe that forthcoming Ministerial offices should be safeguarded with the same privacies and secrecies which are applied to, for example, a Budget statement. I hope that next April we shall not have my right hon. Friend the Chancellor of the Exchequer dropping a few inspired leaks to test public opinion or trailing a coat to find out what would be public reaction. I deprecate what has been said and done in the last few days, for I believe that the Ministerial changes should have first become known, not only to the House of Commons and to the House of Lords but to the whole world, when the Prime Minister decided to announce them officially. As to the position of my right hon. Friend the Prime Minister, it would be a stupendous impertinence on my part if I did not confess at once that the sole prerogative rests with the Prime Minister as to who his Ministers shall be, but I am sure that he would not expect me to refrain from commenting adversely upon a decision as to the holder of a particular portfolio, when I consider it not to be a judicious appointment. There is no constitutional objection—I do not use the word 'constitutional' literally, for there is no British Constitution—to the Foreign Secretary sitting in the House of Lords, but, in present circumstances, I gravely doubt whether it is politically desirable. I am quite confident that the constituents I represent in Kidderminster, a marginal seat—it was held by the party opposite between 1945 and 1950, it is not a safe Conservative seat—My constituents are not very happy about this. What they are unhappy about—and I have every right to report the views of my constituents—is that the Foreign Secretary cannot sit where my right hon. Friend the Prime Minister is sitting at this moment and be rigorously and relentlessly cross-examined by myself on his policies and decisions. (Laughter). I am sorry that that should be greeted with hilarity. Surely what I have said is of the essence of Parliamentary democracy.

I am concerned only that the Foreign Secretary should be a man of the greatest stature who is available from our midst in either House of Parliament. I have said that, in my opinion, it is politically undesirable that he should be a Member of the House of Lords. But if it is the Prime Minister's view that there is no equal to Lord Home in diplomacy and in international negotiations and affairs, I bow at once to the superior wisdom and perspicacity of the Prime Minister. I would not, of course, question his judgement. I can only express my own view. My own view is that the Treasury Bench is strewn with much greater talent which could be called upon.

It has been written in national newspapers such as the *Observer* that the Foreign Secretary is so over-burdened with work that he must be relieved of constituency responsibilities and day-to-day House of Commons' affairs, by sitting in another place.

What is the logical conclusion to be drawn from a statement of that kind? Surely, it is not suggested that the work of the Foreign Office in the next few years will get less. If the work of the Foreign Office is so onerous today as to require the Foreign Secretary to be relieved of his constituency responsibilities by sitting in another place and relieved of day-to-day Parliamentary tedium, the successors of my right hon. Friend the Prime Minister will call this precedent in aid for posterity and say that, for ever and a day, the Foreign Secretary shall sit in the House of Lords. That is a state of affairs that is anathema to me. I do not believe that the Foreign Secretary, the Home Secretary or the Chancellor of the Exchequer should at any time be members of the House of Lords.

I make this additional comment in winding up. My right hon. Friend has made this decision and it is irrevocable. This evening's Motion is a Motion of no confidence in the Prime Minister. It is nothing else. Parodying my right hon. Friend the Home Secretary, I take the view that the present Prime Minister is the best Prime Minister we have.

If I construed the present situation about the Foreign Secretary as anything but a temporary aberration on the part of my right hon. Friend the Prime Minister, there might be some sort of excuse for my taking the Opposition view about this.

I shall vote this evening as if this were a Motion of no confidence in the Prime Minister. I have every confidence in my right hon. Friend, subject only to this one matter, and I propose this evening to vote with and vote for my right hon. Friend the Prime Minister, to whom the sobriquet 'Mr Mac-Wonder' has been applied on many recent occasions.[1]

Lord Home remained Foreign Secretary from that day until he became Prime Minister, sitting in the House of Lords and dealing through a deputy Mr. Edward Heath, with Members on the floor of the House of Commons. Apart from his office, it explains why he was relatively little known in 1963, by comparison with Mr Butler, Mr Macleod and Mr Maudling, who were on their feet daily in the House of Commons. The week after the Conference, on 19th October, *The Economist* concluded at the end of an appraisal of Lord Home as a possible Prime Minister:

The blunt truth is that if he were designated it would be because the Conservatives were frightened of the qualities, not of the defects, of the other contenders in the field.

Mr Harold Macmillan's chosen successor was Lord Hailsham but he had lost faith in him and by the time the scene and centre of action moved from Blackpool back to London, the situation was so confused that the

[1] *Hansard*, 28th July, 1960, cols. 1989–92.

inner party hierarchy had decided that elaborate soundings of opinion would have to be taken in every section of the party. Opinions were collected in the following way:

THE CABINET	polled by	The Lord Chancellor, the Rt Hon. Lord Dilhorne.
CONSERVATIVE MPS	polled by	The Government Chief Whip and Patronage Secretary, the Rt Hon. Martin Redmayne, DSO, TD, DL, MP; and the Chairman of the 1922 Committee, Major John Morrison.
CONSERVATIVE PEERS	polled by	The Captain of the Honourable Corps of Gentlemen at Arms and Government Chief Whip in the Lords, the Rt Hon. Earl St Aldwyn.
CHAIRMEN & EXECUTIVE COMMITTEES OF ALL THE TORY CONSTITUENCY ORGANISATIONS.	polled by	The Joint Chairman of the Conservative Party Organisation, the Rt Hon. Lord Poole, CBE, TD; the Chairman of the National Executive Committee of the Conservative Party, the Rt Hon. Lord Chelmer, MC, TD; the Chairman of the Conservative Women's Associations, Mrs Margaret Shepherd, CBE.

When I was asked my choice of leader by Mr Martin Redmayne, the conversation ill-advisedly took place over a long distance telephone line because I was in Liverpool and Redmayne in London. Forgiving Quintin Hogg his absurd behaviour in the belief that it was an aberration which would in no way affect his chances of being a first class Prime Minister, I named him. So my order of preference was . . . Quintin Hogg (1), RAB Butler (2) and Iain Macleod (3). Redmayne then fired a devious supplementary question . . . "and would I accept Alec Home if none of the three I named could secure a clear majority?". I replied, "Yes, if it is the will of the majority. I am sickened by public brawling". Redmayne agreed and rang off.

Much later, on 17th January, 1964, after refusing to serve under Alec Home as Prime Minister, Mr Iain Macleod, by then Editor of the *Spectator*, branded the whole affair as the result of the machinations of the old Tory establishment, led, insofar as it was led at all, by Major John Morrison now Lord Margadale, then the Chairman of the 1922 Committee. Macleod claimed that neither he nor Maudling had any idea of how far

Home's candidacy had advanced until the news of his "emergence" began to circulate within the Party. Nor had I. None of this was endorsed by Mr Randolph Churchill who wrote in his book *The Fight for the Tory Leadership*:

> Never in the history of the Tory Party, or indeed of any other political party, have such full and diligent enquiries been made in the selection of a new leader. This was no decision made in a 'smoke-filled room'. Everyone in the party had had an opportunity to make his or her views felt, and the result of the canvass had been decisive. There was no election, no precise counting of noses. It was Tory democracy in action.

And the reception given to Lord Home in the country was typified by the *Economist* of 26th October:

> The major national misgiving must be that this accession could retard the progress of modern Conservatism as a radical innovating force. To say this is perhaps to invite misunderstanding. It is unlikely that Sir Alec's administration is going to be blackly reactionary or feebly ineffective; abroad (including in Africa and the United Nations) as well as at home Conservatism is likely to go forward in much the same way as Sir Alec thinks it has been going forward hitherto. And one evident guarantee against feebleness is that Sir Alec is a man with an undoubted aura of natural authority; Labour may well make a bad mistake by underestimating this. The new Prime Minister also claims to be by nature a Tory radical. He has in the past defined this himself—in a revealing phrase—by saying that he sees change as a fact of life, not merely to be recognised but welcomed. But he has not so obviously seen change as something he should strive to initiate and bring about. And herein lies the great divide, one which liberal Conservatives like Mr Macleod are right to emphasise and which at least some of those who have sponsored Lord Home's appointment still seem loth to understand.

It was for these reasons that Mr Macleod and Mr Enoch Powell, who also refused to join Sir Alec's Government, regarded the outcome of the leadership contest as unsatisfactory.

As Lord Home went to the Palace, I responded to a Press invitation to comment on the new leader and I said:

> Any man who has been President of Pop, Keeper of the Field and Captain of the Eleven must command my admiration. And a good Foreign Secretary as well.
>
> Evidently the next General Election will be won on the playing fields of Eton.

Because right up to the last moment, we did not know whether it was to be Lord Home or Mr Butler for Prime Minister, I prepared a comment on Mr Butler as well, and though it did not see the light of day at the time, I reproduce it now:

> Though Mr Butler was my second choice, I shall serve under him with enthusiasm and devotion.
>
> At the Bolton Town Hall, on 9th October, I called Mr Butler . . .
> 'Donnish,
> Dignified,
> Dull.'
> Dull he is and my duty now will be to try and liven him up, for I want to be supporting a Prime Minister NOT a Leader of the Opposition.

I must record that now, after five years of Mr Harold Wilson, I would regard as virtuous indeed any Prime Minister who is "donnish, dignified and dull".

3. *The Tory Leadership: The Rt Hon. Sir Alec Douglas-Home, KT*

Lord Home renounced his peerage on 23rd October, 1963, just fourteen days after my speech at Bolton Town Hall in which I had conspicuously failed to name him as a candidate for the leadership. In my defence it may be said that nobody else had either. Because both Lord Home, as Prime Minister, and Lord Hailsham, as Lord President of the Council and Minister for Science, had renounced their peerages, they were in the extraordinary position of being Ministers who were Members of neither House of Parliament. Seats had to be found for them in the Commons. In order to minimise this temporary anomaly, the opening of the Parliamentary session was postponed for two weeks and both of them delayed actually renouncing their peerages until the very last moment before nominating themselves for their respective by-elections.

Lord Home was the third successive old Etonian Prime Minister, after Eden and Macmillan and, like Eden, he had also been at Christ Church, Oxford. After renouncing his peerage, he elected to call himself Sir Alec Douglas-Home, KT, and under this name contested the by-election at Kinross and West Perthshire, which was vacant following the death of Mr Gilmour Leburn in the previous August. The by-election, not surprisingly, attracted candidates from unusual places. Sir Alec won the election on 6th November with a majority of nearly ten thousand and 57·4% of the poll. The Liberal was second and the Labour candidate was a poor third with 15·2% of the poll. The gallant and honourable Douglas-Home thus re-entered the Commons with this encouraging evidence of support north of the border, the Scottish Nationalist candidate at Kinross having achieved less than 10% of the votes. And William Rushton, a member of the BBC Television satirical team "That was the week that was", polled a derisory figure, lost his deposit and demonstrated what the public thinks of television satirists.

As to Lord Hailsham, now Mr Quintin Hogg, QC, room was conveniently made for him in the Commons by calling to the House of Peers a former England Rugby Football Captain, Sir Wavell Wakefield, Tory MP for St Marylebone, a copper-bottomed Tory seat, since 1945. "Wakers" had been in Parliament for twenty-eight years, having sat for Swindon for ten years before moving to St Marylebone, where his majority in 1959 had been nearly fifteen thousand. On 5th December, 1963, Mr Quintin Hogg retained the seat with a majority of 5,276. Anyway, both Home and Hogg were safely restored to the Treasury bench in the Commons by the end of the year, after absences of twelve and thirteen years respectively. My prophecy of many years earlier in connection with the Wedgwood Benn affair and the return of Home and Hogg to the Commons, had come to pass. And a tremendous shot in the arm they were to the Tory Party after the year of scandal, failure and disunity, in 1963.

Sir Alec Douglas-Home was Prime Minister for rather less than a year before the dissolution of Parliament in the autumn of 1964 and the General Election held on the last date constitutionally possible, 15th October, 1964. Throughout this short Premiership, he was under the greatest possible pressure from Mr Harold Wilson, Leader of the Opposition. The opinion polls showed Labour continuously in the lead, even though by the time of the election, the margin had become very small. Sir Alec's behaviour throughout this exacting period was quite wonderful and an inspiration to his party. In the event, instead of Labour winning by the large majority which the pundits had almost unanimously forecast, they scraped home by a whisker:

Labour	317	Mr Speaker	1
Tory	303	Total	630
Liberal	9	Overall Labour majority 5.	

'Heavens be praised! The Captain's got to the bridge in the nick of time!"

THE FIGHT FOR THE TORY LEADERSHIP, *Daily Express*, 9th November, 1963. Matelots L. to R.: Rt Hon. Quintin Hogg, MP, Rt Hon. Reginald Maudling, MP, Rt Hon. R. A. Butler, CH, MP, Rt Hon. Henry Brooke, MP, Rt Hon. Edward Heath, MP, Rt Hon. Selwyn Lloyd, CBE, QC, MP. At the wheel: The Prime Minister, Rt Hon. Sir Alec Douglas-Home, KT, MP. The Spectator (Rowing Boat): Rt Hon. Iain Macleod, MP. At porthole: Sir Gerald Nabarro, MP.

So Sir Alec Douglas-Home became Leader of Her Majesty's Opposition and continued as Leader of the Conservative Party, until he resigned on 22nd July, 1965. Snide press and party comment forced him to do so. He was said to come over badly on television but that point is debatable. He had served his party superbly well and I had much to say about his personal achievements when contributing the leading feature article to the *News of the World*, forty-eight hours after the General Election of October 1964. I wrote:

Through many a day of darkness,
Through many a scene of strife,
The faithful few fought bravely
To guard the Nation's life.

This ought to be Sir Alec Douglas Home's epitaph. His achievement in such a short Premiership was truly remarkable.

He rallied and led a dispirited Tory party from an adverse Gallup Poll signifying a Labour majority of 150 in the House of Commons, to a near dead-heat.

He did this despite a snide Mr Butler, sitting on the side lines. He did this despite two petulant Tory leaders, Mr Iain Macleod and Mr Enoch Powell, refusing to serve under him.

He did it despite the garrulous indiscretions of Mr Quintin Hogg, such as the 'adulterers' speech at Plymouth and Labour voters 'bonkers' a few days later.

I hail Sir Alec's achievement, but it was not good enough. It is to be the 14th Mr Wilson after all.

Compared with Mr Harold Wilson, Sir Alec's image was dull, stodgy and dated. Those silly bags behind a shotgun going off on Scottish moors, all reminiscent of a past age, did the Tory character and spirit in the eyes of the unaffiliated voters, no good at all.

And the imputation which stuck, that Sir Alec could not do economic sums without matchsticks, at a time when economic crisis threatened, with a huge balance of payments deficit reported for several consecutive months, made poor showing for the Tories, compared with Mr Harold Wilson's sharp, bright grasp of economic facts and figures.

Remember, Mr Wilson was once a top statistician and can use a slide-rule faster than practically any man alive. He knows how to interpret figures and economics, and therefore business and industrial trends and international trade. Patently Sir Alec does not. We are a great trading nation and the Tory image suffered thereby.

Sir Alec's integrity is irreproachable and everybody knows it; his conduct is impeccable and everybody knows it. He is utterly the gentleman in the Etonian tie, and everybody knows it.

But on the hustings he is not a patch on Wilson, who conducted a campaign all over Britain with consummate skill and precision, which carried him to a photo-finish victory—aided by Mr Herbert Hill of Hardy Spicer.

Both sides made mistakes in the campaign, and the Tories have suffered much more from Liberal intervention than Labour.

For example, two Tory seats at Stockport, Cheshire, switched to Labour only as a result of Liberal intervention. These were Tory seats even in the Labour landslide in 1945.

In many constituencies, Liberal voters gave the election to Mr Wilson, albeit with a totally unworkable Parliamentary majority.

These Liberals have contributed towards the ending of thirteen years of progressive Conservative rule. They have substituted instability and danger, without advantage to their country or to themselves, save only the exultant crowing of Mr Lubbock at Orpington, who expresses delight that the gaggle of Liberal members will hold the balance between the main parties.

Every losing party at a General Election proclaims it will be a responsible Opposition without fractious obstruction. I do not believe it in the next few months.

The Tories WILL go flat out to precipitate another General Election. Their policy WILL be to kill off the Government with its majority of four.

Endless late nights, something Tories are much better at than Labour, will soon put a few elderly Government members on their backs.

There are only two Tories over seventy years of age, but twenty Labour members: the latter will be the first casualties.

Then we shall have the dismal spectacle of the Government carrying their stretcher cases and pushing their wheel-chair incumbents through the Lobby to sustain their majority. Then defeats as in 1950–51, and finally collapse.

I predict another General Election within eighteen months. Neither Labour nor Liberals will hurry because they have no money.

At any General Election within eighteen months the Liberal candidates will inevitably diminish by about 100.

The Tories will be the chief beneficiaries, but the Tories will only win next time if they drastically reform their top leadership.

Sir Alec Douglas-Home (Eton), Duncan Sandys (Eton), Peter Thorneycroft (Eton), Christopher Soames (Eton), Michael Noble (Eton), Lord Dilhorne (Eton), Lord Blakenham (Eton), Quintin Hogg (Eton), Sir Edward Boyle (Eton) and many more, are no advertisement for competitive efficiency in a technocratic age.

This battle will not be won on the playing fields of Eton. A new leader with

drive, determination and sheer ability on television, radio and public platform is needed to restore Tory fortunes among millions of younger voters.
That leader and his henchmen must be drawn from Macleod, Maudling, Heath, Powell, Redmayne, the men who came to the House of Commons in 'the finest Tory vintage in history' (as Mr Aneurin Bevan put it), namely the famous 1950 vintage.
They should be the Tory leaders of the early future and the sooner the better for me.

I was not the only commentator to be shaken by the outcome of the 1964 General Election after thirteen years of unbroken Tory rule. Mr Frank Cousins (General Secretary of the Transport and General Workers Union), Mr George Woodcock (General Secretary of the TUC), Lord Boothby and myself were retained by BBC Television, at Wood Lane for twenty-four hours from 9.00 pm on polling day, 15th October, 1964, to comment on the results as they came in. At 10.00 pm on polling day, just before the first results were declared, we were asked to speculate on the final results. This is what emerged:

Mr Frank Cousins	Labour majority 150
Mr George Woodcock	Labour majority 120
Lord Boothby	Labour majority 80
Sir Gerald Nabarro	Dead heat

Next afternoon, my companions were shocked. My forecast was very nearly exactly correct but I lost a thousand guineas at Ladbrokes, having backed the Tories to win and I also lost a "mixed double" on Worcestershire to win the County Cricket Championship and the Tories to win the General Election. Worcestershire just did: the Tories just didn't, but only just.

What I love most and greatly admire in Sir Alec Douglas-Home is his absolute sincerity, integrity and honesty. It shone through in the preface to a little book of his speeches, *Peaceful Change*, published from 10 Downing Street in June, 1964:

> My purpose in each speech was to try and put into plain words the need for policies which will strengthen the moral and material fibre of the nation and enable our country to play a leading role in establishing order and justice in a peaceful world. I hope they will strike a chord in the hearts and minds of many of my countrymen.

That's my politics too; though I don't wear silly bags, blow off on grouse moors, or count with matchsticks.

4. The Tory Leadership: The Rt Hon. Edward Heath, MBE

MR EDWARD HEATH became leader of both Her Majesty's Opposition and of the Conservative Party on 27th July, 1965. He had been in the House since he won Bexley from Labour with a tiny majority in 1950. He entered the Commons for the first time along with Maudling, Macleod, Powell and ninety other new Tory Members, including myself. Four months after taking the oath, he made a somewhat belated maiden speech, and, events casting their shadows before them, it was in support of the motion on the Schuman Plan, precursor to the European Economic Community:

> That this House requests His Majesty's Government in the interests of peace and full employment to accept the invitation to take part in the discussions on the Schuman plan subject to the same condition as that made by the Netherlands Government, namely that if the discussions show the plan not to be practicable, freedom of action is reserved.[1]

The Schuman Plan proposed the creation of a High Authority to dispose of coal, iron and steel, for France and West Germany and any other West

[1] *Hansard*, 26th June, 1950, col. 1907.

European countries who cared to join. Mr Anthony Eden, shadow Foreign Secretary, said:

> I begin by submitting to the House that it is an essential British interest that the Schuman proposals should succeed, and to enable them to do so Britain should take part in them.

And later,

> We cannot fail to recognise the trend among democratic nations throughout the post-war years to make all arrangements among themselves touching very nearly this question of sovereignty.[1]

The Common Market was to be at the centre of British foreign policies in the sixties. Mr Edward Heath made his maiden speech on the Schuman Plan and he was the architect of Britain's first attempt to enter the Common Market, ten years later. The difference in view between Mr Heath, a dedicated European, and many of his not so dedicated colleagues appeared as early as this in the history of his generation in Parliament. At the end of the debate on the Schuman Plan, the Conservative Chief Whip, Mr Patrick Buchan-Hepburn, MP for Beckenham and later Lord Hailes, put on a three-line whip which was disobeyed by a small group of Tories who considered that the threatened loss of sovereignty inherent in the Schuman proposals was premature. These Tory dissentients sat publicly on the benches during the division. They included Mr Enoch Powell, the newly elected Member for Wolverhampton, South-West. Eighteen years later, following Powell's notorious immigration speech on 20th April, 1968, Heath sacked him from the shadow Cabinet in which he was shadow Minister of Defence. Also abstaining with Powell were Air-Commodore Sir Arthur Vere Harvey, MP for Macclesfield and now Chairman of the 1922 Committee, Sir John Mellor, MP for Sutton Coldfield and the inimitable ex-Major of the Blues, Sir Harry Legge-Bourke, MP for the Isle of Ely. I abstained as well and that was my first brush with the Whips. However, I was in good company.

At that time I had never spoken to Enoch Powell. Similarities in view on certain aspects of foreign policy brought us together then and have done so since from time to time, but I am not and never will be his political disciple.

On Saturday 1st July, 1950, I justified my defiance of the Whips to my constituents at Alfrick, a village in my Kidderminster constituency.

[1] *Hansard*, 26th June, 1950, cols. 1909–10.

I thought that I was unheard by the Press. Not so, for on the following Monday afternoon back at the House a Government backbencher, Mr Hector Hughes, KC, MP for Aberdeen North, congratulated me on the comment in that day's *Daily Express* "Opinion" column (3rd July):

> Mr Gerald Nabarro, MP for Kidderminster, explains to his constituents why he defied a three-line Tory Whip and refused to vote in favour of the Schuman plan. He says: 'I do not believe you sent me to Westminster to support a motion in which the Germans and the French would have a control in our coal and steel. Neither did you elect me to make a contribution to the weakening of the British Empire. I believe I was sent to the House to uphold the strength of our Commonwealth.' Mr Nabarro is right in his beliefs. The sooner his Tory colleagues realise that they too were sent to the House in order to uphold the strength of the Commonwealth, the sooner a Tory Government will be returned to power.

It was the first time a leader in a national newspaper had referred to me. I reckoned that it was worth the painful castigation for disloyalty, insubordination and insolence which I received from the then Chief Whip, Mr Patrick Buchan-Hepburn.

During the Fifties, Edward Heath really had remarkably little experience of Government, outside the Whips' Office. He first went to the Whips' Office in February, 1951, a year after his election. There he toiled and was not heard, except at an occasional party meeting, until 1955, when he became Chief Whip. He saw Eden, Macmillan and the party through all the turbulence of Suez; he gradually increased his majority at Bexley from 133 in 1950 to nearly nine thousand in 1959; he was an industrious but unremarkable Minister of Labour from 1959 to 1960; and then Lord Privy Seal, number two to Lord Home as Foreign Secretary and charged with special responsibilities to negotiate Britain's entry into the European Economic Community. In that summer of 1960 I had thought that he would be made Foreign Secretary; I did not anticipate Mr Macmillan's preference for a Member of the House of Lords. At that time I was temporarily writing the "Straight Talking" column in the *Sunday Graphic*. On 24th July, I took the opportunity of speculating about the imminent Cabinet reshuffle. On one of the rare occasions I have known Edward Heath thank anybody for anything, he said thank you to me in the Lobby for what I had written about him:

> As the outsider, long odds for the Foreign Office, the tough, imperturbable Edward Heath (Ted to all his hosts of friends, and he has more than practically any other politician I know): ex-Tory Chief Whip, ex-Balliol organ scholar,

the prodigy who held the Tory Parliamentary ranks together in Premier Macmillan's acute post-Suez Party troubles—and never, never does this Premier omit to reward loyalty.

Though Heath had special responsibilities for European affairs and spoke in the Commons on behalf of Lord Home after he became Foreign Secretary, Mr Macmillan ostentatiously left him behind on a visit to Bonn shortly after the appointment was made.

Edward Heath failed to take Britain into Europe. The new policy that Mr Macmillan had relied upon to revive his fortunes lay in ruins as he left office in 1963. Heath was a long way from the top among possible successors to Mr Macmillan by the autumn of 1963, after the Common Market failure. He had lost ground and looked far less promising than he had done a year before. At Budleigh Salterton, on 11th August, 1962, I had said that "Edward Heath is now regarded as the best future Prime Minister we have": so he was at that time. However, Sir Alec Douglas-Home rewarded him with a new portfolio and from October 1963 until the General Election a year later, he was President of the Board of Trade and Secretary of State for Industry, Trade and Regional Development. At Bexley, his majority was halved in both 1964 and 1966. I went down to speak there on his behalf in 1966 and was not surprised to learn that his constituents love him.

For his first nine months in Opposition, October 1964 to July 1965, Edward Heath was shadow Chancellor of the Exchequer under Sir Alec Douglas-Home and he led his shadow Treasury team with consummate skill in opposition to the abstruse and compendious 1965 Finance Bill. On the downfall of Sir Alec Douglas-Home in July 1965, the succession was decided for the first time by the votes of the Parliamentary party. The figures were:

Rt Hon. Edward Heath, MBE	150
Rt Hon. Reginald Maudling	133
Rt Hon. Enoch Powell, MBE	15

I was temporarily out of the House because of illness, so I had no vote. On the eve of the poll, 26th July, I was cross-examined for some time by Robin Day on "Panorama". I described Heath as "very professional, dedicated, assiduous, incisive" and the best of the three candidates at handling people. I said that Maudling was "big, shambling, amiable" and would do most to improve the Party's image. I said that it was a matter of opinion who would make the best Prime Minister, but I implied that

I thought Heath would win by announcing that I had put 100 guineas on him at evens at Ladbrokes. The wily Day saw through all this and the following exchange took place at the end of the programme:

DAY: Finally, Sir Gerald, who would be your choice if you were an M.P.?
NABARRO: I cannot answer that question in present circumstances. I say to you however that I am not myself a candidate, though tipped at five hundred to one at Ladbrokes as a dark horse outsider. But I have put a hundred guineas to win at evens, very good odds, I consider, a hundred guineas to win on Mr Edward Heath.
DAY: But that might indicate what you think the result will be, as opposed to what you think it ought to be.
NABARRO: You're exactly correct, sir, with your analytical mind.

The election of Heath was accepted with fortitude but with remarkably little enthusiasm by most of the Conservative Party. *The Economist* judged realistically two days later (31st July) when it said:

> Taken all round (and not forgetting Bonar Law), Heath is the biggest departure from the Tory leadership norm since Disraeli. If he is as big a risk as Disraeli seemed in the 1850s, he also holds the potential to be as big an influence.
>
> Life with Ted Heath may well be very uncomfortable. The art of running a party has three rules: to give a clear lead, to make sure that your lead is being followed, and to arouse enough loyalty so that your chaps will back you up even when you make the inevitable boobs. Mr Heath will certainly match up to the first, and probably the second: the doubt is whether he has the personal charisma to win devotion. It may sound odd about a man who is always being photographed looking jolly, but the Tory party is littered with people still nursing bruises from some Heath brusquerie. The reason is that he does not suffer fools gladly and by his fairly exacting standards there are quite a few of them still around.

The article allowed him considerable originality of mind, but continued:

> The trouble is that hardly anyone reads his speeches. During all his years in politics, he has hardly coined a single memorable phrase. Even the word most associated with him, 'modernisation', drops into the nation's drawing rooms with the dynamism of lead. In private he can be sharp and witty, in the Commons he can be effective by sheer brute force, but on the public platform and on television, the only places where the voters see him, he is competent but rarely inspiring. There is every chance that he will produce the right policies for the nation: what he has to find is his own new language to explain them.

Passing from Mr Heath personally to his significance for the party, *The Economist* said:

> For the first time in three years the Conservative Party has no leadership crisis to nag at it. This is what is really new in British politics. For the first time since Mr Macmillan's star began to dim in the heavens the Tories have a man who is confident in himself and in whom they have confidence. They were right to pick Mr Heath. They were right to pick him quickly. . . . It would be flattering the Tories to say that, at a stroke, they have announced themselves to be a liberal, modernising party, anxious to have a grammar school boy at their head. They are not: or at least, not yet. Mr Heath certainly carries radical hopes in his baggage. But in electing him the Tories have primarily shown their instinct for power. They picked, by a narrow majority, the man they reckoned most likely to bullock their way back into power. They will remain united behind him just as long as his pursuit of power looks promising. If it does not, then the Tories, like the Labour party in the 1950s, or any party in prolonged opposition, will be liable to fall apart in fractricidal struggles in which the leader becomes exposed to every punch that can be thrown. Mr Heath has been elected because the Tories expect him to fight Mr Wilson. He has been elected because, such has been the Tories' admiration of Mr Wilson the politician, they have opened their arms to the best potential Mr Wilson they could discern. There were other motives: but this was the decisive one. The success symbol of British politics today is to be a Mr Weath or a Mr Hilson. So be it.

How true. If there had been a General Election in the month after Edward Heath's election as leader, the Conservatives would have returned to power with a majority approaching one hundred, but from September 1965 onwards there was a steady decline. It was already becoming clear that Mr Heath had to be driven from behind in order to make an impact. On the Sunday before that year's Party Conference at Brighton, I had an opportunity to make the point in the *News of the World* of 10th October:

> Mr Heath has to demonstrate, and be seen by the nation to demonstrate, that he is Mr Wilson's superior as leader, as strategist, as tactician and as saviour of Britain.

As usual, the Party Conference was a success from the point of view of improving the party's rating in the opinion polls. But the country quite obviously did not take to Mr Heath or his brand of Toryism for long. At the General Election on 31st March, 1966, Mr Heath was crushingly defeated and together with the Conservative Party was condemned to five years in Opposition. The results were:

Labour	363
Conservative	253
Liberal	12
Republican Labour	1
The Speaker	1
Overall Labour majority	97

I returned to Parliament as Member for South Worcestershire after an absence of seventeen months. I had clear ideas of why the Tories had lost the General Election and I was able to give them in public in the *News of the World* of 3rd April, 1966, forty-eight hours after Polling Day, in exactly the same way as I had held a post-mortem forty-eight hours after the 1964 Elections. I said:

Nationally, this 1966 election is noteworthy for six reasons. First because it more closely resembled than ever before a Presidential contest between two men, Wilson versus Heath.

Second, the effect of opinion polls which gave the trends correctly but grossly overstated Labour's majority.

For example, one national newspaper gave Labour an eleven per cent lead on the morning of the polls, thus forecasting a majority of 175.

Actually the swing to Labour has been three per cent and their majority 97, only half of what the opinion polls gave them.

The depressing effect of the polls on the Tories was matched by the bookies. Huge sums of money were wagered.

Ladbrokes quoted for my constituency: Labour 400-1 against, Liberal 400-1 against, Tories 1000-1 on.

Betting was on a prodigious scale and Ladbrokes alone took £1,600,000, finishing with odds of 16-1 against a Tory win and Labour 66-1 on.

But the opinion polls and the betting had done their dirtiest; by depressing the Tories, exhilarating Labour, they had a profound influence on the outcome of the polls. We have copied the Swedes with an Ombudsman: shortly there may be clamour to copy them by prohibiting opinion polls during an election.

I DO NOT DOUBT WHY LABOUR WON.

Mr Wilson proves a Titan among party leaders. Never before in peacetime has any single politician gained such ascendancy over his party. After all, when Mr Gaitskell died a few years ago, Mr Wilson won the leadership of the Labour Party from Mr George Brown.

Had the position been reversed, the Tories would have won this General Election. I believe that Mr Wilson's personal performance and character, matching Presidential standards in America, have been a decisive factor in Labour's big majority.

Moreover, Mr Wilson demonstrated that he could govern for $17\frac{1}{2}$ months with a majority of three, which all the pundits said he could not do. He walked a tightrope between left and right in his party.

Bad though the Tories consider his measures to be, he steered them through the House of Commons with consummate skill. He was seen to do all this and was admired for it by the unaffiliated voters.

They have now given him five years tenure of office and absolute security, with the parliamentary majority to match the Tories' in 1959. Mr Wilson's victory in 1966 is almost exactly the Tory victory of 1959 in reverse.

Third, the three-quarters of a million deserting Liberal voters (as I forecast in this column on March 6th) went two thirds Labour and one third Tory. In other conditions they might desert the other way round. The Liberals have gained nothing from this election, only roughly the status quo.

Fourth, this Common Market business.

I have often been called a Tory super-salesman. Whether I am or not, I cannot easily convince the unattached voter that he will be better off (which is what he thinks about when he polls) mixed up with a bunch of French, Germans, Italians and the remainder.

All these unattached voters leaned more to the Attlee and Wilson line of extreme caution before 'crawling into Europe' and 'abandoning our Commonwealth'.

I support European policies but have failed to persuade many waverers. Incongruous though it may seem, the great majority of deserting Liberals voted Labour against the European theme; it is all paradoxical.

Fifth, it has proved nearly impossible in an atmosphere of wage-packet prosperity and over-full employment to persuade the industrial worker that Britain is living on borrowed time and borrowed money.

Sixth, the Conservatives fighting on their manifesto 'Action not words' have been monumentally unspecific. Elections should be won by specific propositions.

Questions about the rate of income tax, corporation tax, capital gains duty, lands tax, went unanswered. Specious replies came over that it would depend on the economic position when the Tories returned to power.

That is not good enough. Something much more precise is needed today by our sophisticated electorate.

Last, a word on the Tory Party leadership and Mr Edward Heath. He started slowly, warmed up and in the last week was in cracking good form. I reckon he outpaced Mr Wilson during the 96 hours before polling day, but the verdict had been decided in advance.

I am for Edward Heath. Six years ago, in the halcyon days of Mr Harold Macmillan's Premiership, I tipped Mr Edward Heath as a future Tory Prime Minister. He has fought a magnificent, sustained election campaign basing his policies on real relevant live issues. There will be no 'night of the long knives' in the Tory Party.

Britain gets the Government she deserves. Britain has asked for Labour and got it. Five years is the tenure of office with an impregnable majority.

Mr Wilson's Left wing complains that he has governed for eighteen months as a Tory Prime Minister.

Now his big Socialist majority will promote real Socialist measures and stiff nationalisation medicine in big doses.

I doubt whether the nation will take this kind of thing for long; neither will the foreign bankers lend more money to support Socialist shiboleths. Look out Mr Wilson, your financial nemesis is near.

I shall put the case of the Conservative Opposition loud and clear in the Commons, on television and on radio, on public platforms and in the Press, as will my 252 colleagues.

Democracy demands one party in power and the other in Opposition.

THE TORIES WILL BE BACK.

Throughout his period as Party Leader, Edward Heath has had three major disadvantages. They are:

1) Heath has never been Prime Minister and thus lacks the authority which any ex-Prime Minister commands when forced into Opposition.
2) Heath has no wife. The Tory Party does not readily take to bachelors and at constituency level, the party is dominated and activated by women. Home life, family, wives, children, dogs and all the other trappings of domestic life are aspects of their political leaders which the British electorate likes to see. Stan and Lucy, Winston and Clemmy, Anthony and Clarissa, Harold and Dorothy, were all paragons of this vote-winning marital devotion.
3) Heath is prosaic, unexciting and unpersonable. So many electors, particularly the women, say that he lacks warmth and charm and that he does not have the ability to "communicate" instantly and naturally with the mass of the people by way of the television.

The tragedy is that in private he has all these qualities, massive intelligence, strength of character, sincerity and dedication: but, while in the public opinion polls the Conservative Party often leads the Government by unprecedented margins, Heath has consistently dragged behind Wilson. His rating on the question whether he is a "good leader" has even descended at times below 30%. With the leader apparently "on the floor" in public esteem, the lack of enthusiastic support from some of the Conservative front bench has not helped; neither has the row with Powell over immigration.

Accordingly in 1967 when I returned from a tour of Canada and the United States, I decided on arrival at Southampton, in the *Queen Elizabeth*, to raise the Tory leadership matter. I chose my words with care during the voyage, so that when I got back home to Worcestershire on 23rd September, I made the following statement:

> I do not favour a change in the Tory leadership but the Conservative party is deeply apprehensive.
> I believe it is my public duty to say loud and clear that Mr Edward Heath's personal popularity as our leader must be caused to match our increasing popularity as a party, in the country.
> I have been musing on the paradox that Tory popularity in the country increases, but so does the unpopularity of the leader.
> Mr Wilson is now so widely mistrusted that I reckon his party may chopper him this winter.
> And if the Labour party change their leadership and the Tory party do not, it could well result in an entirely new pattern in the political situation, especially if the popularity of the Tory leader continues to decline.
> The riddle is: Who goes first, Wilson or Heath?
> Therefore, unless Mr Heath can personally capture majority acclaim and support in the country it may imperil Tory chances of winning the next General Election.
> If Labour changes its leader and the Tories do not and Mr Heath does not recover, Labour will lead again.
> Thus fickle are politics.

This statement was given the greatest publicity by every medium on the following day, a Sunday. The noise was terrific because a Tory private member had dared to voice the fears of the rank and file of the party. In interviews for "The World this Weekend" and on "Panorama" with Edward Heath, I was obdurately consistent in stating that I wanted no change in the leadership but that I wanted to engender unanimous

"DAMN'D PEDESTRIANS!" Garland, *Daily Telegraph*, 25th September, 1967.

On the evening of 25th September, 1967, Sir Gerald Nabarro, MP, presents Road Safety Awards at the Pump Room, Bath.

support within the party and to see Heath acclaimed by the public as a credible alternative to Harold Wilson as Prime Minister. This was my conviction and I stuck to it throughout the ensuing row.

Meanwhile, Heath did take action and his action was to jettison the popular and proven Edward du Cann, appointed Chairman of the Party by Sir Alec Douglas-Home in January, 1965, and to put in a complete Heath man, Mr Anthony Barber. Naturally this gave rise to widespread and unfavourable criticism. On 17th October, *The Times* said in a leading article:

> Mr Heath did make a mistake in appointing Mr Barber Chairman, not because he is a bad Chairman, but because he is too like his leader, like him in attitude, in energy, in experience, in lack of public appeal. The tricks Mr Barber takes Mr Heath could take already; he should have chosen someone who could win support that he could not win himself.

And *The Observer*, on 17th September, had examined the strains in the Tory party created by the removal of Mr du Cann:

> Mr Wilson seemed to be heading straight for the trough of his political misfortunes last week-end. Unemployment was rising; adverse trade figures were on the way; one, very possibly two of this week's by-elections looked likely to be lost. His party conference was about to assemble, coldly hostile to his policies.
>
> Then that same week-end, his opposite number, Mr Heath, made a complete Charlie of himself. 'Damned lies', he said of a *Daily Express* report which spoke of a coming showdown with Mr du Cann, the party chairman. Within two days, Mr du Cann was no longer chairman. Mr Anthony Barber, his holiday in Bermuda cancelled, was serving in his place.
>
> Mr Heath's appalling sense of public relations will not make Mr Wilson's winter any warmer. But it must enormously increase the confidence with which the Prime Minister looks forward to the spring, when, with luck and good management, he expects the economy to take an upturn. If that is how the leader of the Opposition behaves when he has the ball at his feet, what will he do when he's up against it?
>
> The du Cann incident, trivial enough in itself, tells us something about Mr Heath and something about his party set-up. It shows Mr Heath less at ease than he should be, lacking in self-confidence. He is game enough. He works immensely hard. He hardly ever lets up. Yet the spark obstinately refuses to fly. He has little gift for a phrase. Without it, his arguments about the economy are wearisome, repetitious and puddingy.

Of course, the real reason for the replacement of du Cann by Barber was that du Cann thought we should break off our Common Market application, whereas as Barber would slavishly obey every whim and dictate of his dedicated and effusive Common Marketeer leader, Edward Heath. And du Cann is a successful banker, Unit Trust pioneer and company director, whereas Barber has nothing but his record as a good House of Commons man and junior minister to commend him. The lobbies buzzed with assertions that only men in the image of Heath were admissable in the new Tory order.

Leading articles in *The Times* always command the attention of politicians, especially since Mr William Rees-Mogg became Editor. There was much chuckling over the opening paragraph of the one which appeared on 17th October, 1967, under the title "Not a cosy leader":

> Sir Gerald Nabarro, who has made himself known on the subject of the Conservative leadership, now says that his views represent his affection for Mr Heath and his loyalty to the Conservative Party. It is a comfort that the ancient British profession of humbug should still have qualified modern practitioners.

And within hours of this, Mr Edward Heath was largely endorsing my view about projecting himself as leader in a "Panorama" interview:

> JAMES MOSSMAN: Can a man in your position simply say: I will not be tailor-made by the public relations men; I'll go my own way; I'll stamp my image on the party; I'll be myself?
>
> EDWARD HEATH: I believe in being myself. As you know, I have always objected to the word 'Image' because this implies that a politician ought to try to show he is something which in fact he isn't. If you like to say, as Sir Gerald Nabarro was saying, that I ought to project myself better, very well: let us have a go at doing that.

Not only *The Times* made an ass of itself in this Heath leadership controversy. I had been asked by Colonel Sir Tufton Beamish, MC, MP for Lewes, to address a meeting during the Conservative Party Conference at Brighton, in Lewes Town Hall on 19th October, 1967. A fortnight before this date, the Chairman of Lewes Division Conservative Association, Mr David Campion, supported by Sir Tufton, wrote to me in the following terms:

> We were all immensely pleased when you accepted our invitation to come and speak on Thursday, 19th October in Lewes and were very much looking forward to the meeting. However, in the light of your recent comments

"IF YOU CAN KEEP YOUR HEAD WHEN ALL ABOUT YOU . . ." *Daily Telegraph*, 17th October, 1967.
Tories at Brighton.

"Very well, Sir Gerald — you tell us. What sort of image should a Tory Leader project?"

Punch, 18th October, 1967.

> about the leadership, I feel sure that you will not be surprised that the Constituency Association Executive Committee on the unanimous recommendation of their officers feel obliged to withdraw this invitation.

Mr David Campion arranged for all the newspapers to have the information and in fact his letter was first read to me by a newspaper man. Later, Mr Campion failed to secure selection for the Pavilion division of Brighton as their prospective Conservative candidate: Mr Julian Amery was selected. Mr Quintin Hogg, MP for St Marylebone, ex-Party Chairman and shadow Home Secretary, took my place at the Lewes meeting and was suitably censorious of me in his opening remarks.

Needless to say, I was not pleased when the Lewes invitation was withdrawn. But next day another letter arrived, this time from the Chairman of the Worthing Young Conservatives:

> We were sorry to hear the decision of the Lewes Constituency Association since we feel that in a democratic party criticisms of policy or observations on the public attitudes to them should not be stifled. We would therefore be grateful if you could accept our invitation to address Worthing Young Conservatives on Thursday, 19th October, 1967. This would give us an opportunity to hear a good speaker: and yourself the opportunity to restate your case or enlarge upon it. We feel that both would be in the best interest of the party.
>
> signed, Peter Moseling
> Vice-Chairman, Worthing Young Conservatives.

Worthing is the next-door constituency to Lewes. I accepted the invitation. The Press and television representatives at the meeting outnumbered the Young Conservatives. Large numbers of them could not get in. Hogg's loss was my gain. I re-stated my views to Worthing Young Conservatives on the Tory leadership, in the following terms:

> Many self-indulgent Tories at Brighton are preening themselves prematurely, about by-election successes. The heady, strong air of Brighton is causing hallucinations.
>
> I point to the realities of the depressing Public Opinion Polls. Only this morning the *Daily Mail* National Opinion Poll again swings against the Tories and puts:
>
> i) Labour ahead by a couple of points.
> ii) Mr Wilson's personal popularity rating alarmingly high.
> iii) Mr Heath's unchanged and undeservedly low.
>
> Contemporary troubles could hardly be worse for Mr Wilson as witness:
>
> a) Protracted dock strikes ruining our export performance.

b) Communist anarchy on building sites.

c) Dreadfully and ominously poor trade figures in September, with prognosis of even worse economic troubles ahead.

BUT STILL, I repeat STILL, the Tories are not ahead of Labour.

What is wrong? It is an indictment of Tory opposition tactics.

Mr Heath's team is manifestly not rough enough and not strong enough. Why not include three additional and powerful Privy Councillors in his Shadow Cabinet? I name the redoubtable Sandys, Boyd-Carpenter and Marples—all dedicated Tories and magnificent, trenchant debaters. We do not want only Heath images in every post.

Also, full Tory strength in the country will never be harnessed to defeat Socialism, until definitive Tory policies are clearly enunciated.

EXPANSIVE CAPITALISM is the mood of the country today, not pale pink, turgid, quasi-Socialist drip.

Please do not tell me that you must not publish Tory policies because the wicked Socialists might pinch your clothes before the next General Election.

Do you really think Mr Wilson would pinch EXPANSIVE CAPITALISM when his Government stands for the precise antithesis—RESTRICTIVE SOCIALISM?

Largely, Mr Heath's trouble, and I want to help him mend it, is that the country does not know what the Tory party stands for today. Until you tell them, Mr Heath, your personal rating and that of the Conservative Party, will not improve.

My campaign to gain more support for my elected leader continued in greater detail in my article in the *Sunday Express* on 15th October, 1967, under the title of "What is Mr Heath's Future?":

I am not myself a candidate for the leadership of the Tory Party. I am just a Tory back-bench Member of Parliament, sitting in a Worcestershire seat where I have spent all my political life since 1945.

Thus I am a dispassionate party observer of circumstances and events. I claim for myself only one party dedication, that the Tories should win the next General Election.

With passion, I believe it will be disastrous for Britain if Mr Harold Wilson wins again. That, and that alone, is why I slog round the country addressing public political meetings, broadcasting, televising, writing, propagating what I conceive the Tory alternative should be to Socialist mediocrity and misery.

In these peregrinations I have learned one thing recently. All is not well in the Tory camp. There is deep apprehension.

Why?

Because though the party popularity has risen and Tories are ahead of the Labour Government in electoral appeal, as witness the sweeping gains in local-government elections in the spring and the Labour seats won by Tory candidates at Pollok, Cambridge and West Walthamstow, and no doubt more to follow at Gorton, Leicester and Acton, the personal popularity rating of the Tory Party leader, Mr Edward Heath, remains depressingly and persistently low.

Mr Wilson's rating is higher. Even between the third week of September and the first week of October, four points were added to the unpopularity of the Opposition leader in the National Opinion Polls.

Now, my proposition is simple and unequivocal. It is this.

Surely it is truly paradoxical that the popularity of the Tory Party in the country steadily rises, whereas the personal popularity of the leader, Mr Heath, steadily declines.

And the corollary?

The Tory Party cannot win the General Election if these trends continue.

I say that all political history shows that the personal popularity rating of the leader must be right up with the popularity of the party. The Tories will lose unless these logistics are complied with—and I am dedicated to winning.

Some Tories go further than I. They say that the leader ought to be ahead of the party rating to win.

This is not the first time I have been blunt and forthright with Mr Heath. That is the privilege of being his friend and supporter, which I am. I quote just two examples of what I have said about him in recent years. In 1960, five years before he became the Tory Party leader, I wrote:

> 'As the outsider, long odds for the Foreign Office, I tip the tough, imperturbable Edward Heath (Ted to all his hosts of friends, and he has more than practically any other politician I know).'

Five years later, the night before Mr Heath won the election for the party leadership, I went on BBC television, interviewed by Mr Robin Day in the 'Panorama' programme, and backed Mr Heath to win. Then, a few days later, I wrote:

> 'For myself, I prophesy that Mr Edward Heath will be the first bachelor occupant of Downing Street for 60 years—since Mr Arthur Balfour. Personally, to make the man and the image complete, I would like to see him carry a beautiful bride over the threshold to share his occupancy with him.'

Then, in October 1966, I wrote after the Party conference:

> 'Now stop all the chuntering about Ted.'

My views have not changed. I do not want to change the Tory leader. Mr Heath is the democratically elected leader of the Tory party, but his public image is bogged down, lacking the personal magnetism so critically important to success.

Sir Winston Churchill had it, that quality of personal extrovertism, even idiosyncrasy; Mr Stanley Baldwin had it; Sir Anthony Eden had it; Mr Harold Macmillan had it; two Harrovians and two Etonians I name.

Could it be that the Tory Party is trying too hard to present Mr Heath as a grammar school cloth-cap, a sort of poor man's Harold Wilson? If that is the intention, then they are wrong. Likewise, if the electors want Socialism, they will vote for it, not a bogus, watered-down, pale-pink version in the guise of Toryism.

What Mr Heath wants for his own image is much more extrovertism, much more raciness, much more bounce, much more showmanship.

The *Daily Telegraph*, on September 25th, 1967, in a leading editorial appropriately entitled 'Worcester Sauce' called me an 'expert and dedicated publicist'. They thought they were being rude to me: on the contrary, I was delighted. I regarded it as a compliment. Why? Because unless a politician is expert at publicity he cannot attract the ears and the minds of the electorate to enunciate his views to them.

No good being the finest politician in the world talking to an empty hall. And unless the image is good the reception is bad.

I wish Mr Heath were an expert and dedicated publicist. His personal rating in the polls, with his blazing sincerity, his fluency of speech, his boundless integrity, his shining honour and character, would then be much higher.

I blame very largely the Tory Party, its central office machine, its followers, workers and supporters. They do not project powerfully enough, favourably enough, or assiduously enough the image of the Tory leader in the country.

Not that I want an American Presidential system or anything like it. Neither do I recommend detergent salesmanship. But the fact remains that unless Tories everywhere, from members of the Shadow Cabinet down to the humblest party member, hammer out everywhere and on every occasion, that not only is Mr Edward Heath a credible alternative Prime Minister, but would make a better Prime Minister than the one we have got, the Tories will not win.

Whoever heard a speech by Woolton, by Eden, by Lyttleton, by Stanley, or any other Front Bench spokesman, between 1945 and 1951 when the Tories were fighting under Sir Winson Churchill to regain the reins of Government, which did not extol the merits and virtues of their leader, Sir Winston, as well as his policies?

Whoever reads reports of the present leaders of the Tory Party, the Opposition front bench, Maudling, Macleod, Hogg and Powell, to say nothing of the Tory backbench Privy Councillors, Sandys, Marples, Boyd-Carpenter, Selwyn Lloyd, Geoffrey Lloyd, extolling the merits of the leader with his policies? I do not.

But perhaps I read the wrong newspapers. Perhaps they do extol. If they do not, they ought to. Because their party leader is as important as their party's policy: the leader's image and the party policy are indissolubly mixed together. You cannot have one without the other if the Tories are to win at the polls next time.

After the last war Sir Arthur Salter, MP, later Lord Salter, don and author, diplomat and Minister wrote in a book called *Personality in Politics* these pregnant words:

> 'He was tough and wiry in mind and body; physically and morally courageous; seeing clearly what was within his range of vision, exceptionally insensitive to what was outside it, with both the strength and the weakness of a concentrated purpose and a limited imagination. He had intellectual integrity, a disciplined and orderly mind and untiring industry. He was precise and punctilious; pertinacious and authoritarian; courteous without geniality; respected and feared but without the magnetism, sympathy and inspiring quality that make the greatest of leaders.'

This was written of Mr Neville Chamberlain, Prime Minister, 1937–40. He was described by Mr Lloyd George as a good Lord Mayor of Birmingham in a lean year.

I hope none of this will be Mr Edward Heath's epitaph. Then there would be no hosannas for Heath.

The *Daily Telegraph* emerged ingloriously from the controversy with a series of contradictory arguments and opinions. On 14th September they were making much the same point as I was but by the time of the leader entitled "Worcester Sauce" on 25th September, they counselled Mr Heath not only to "ignore Sir Gerald" but to "stand more aloof from Tory debates and wrangles, to be more of the chairman and less of the drill sergeant in handling his Parliamentary supporters", while on 27th October, Anthony Lejeune wrote in the *Weekend Telegraph*:

> Sir Alec Douglas-Home resigned, not because he was unfit or thought himself unfit, to lead the Party, but because he knew there would be no peace in it until he went. Suppose Edward Heath now did the same, and for the same reason. Suppose he stood up one day and said: 'In the present desperate situation we need a special sort of leader to confront the scoundrel Wilson. Not necessarily the best economist, not necessarily the best administrator, just a shiningly straightforward and honourable man, a gentleman, someone who stands for the traditional virtues of this country. I have therefore asked Sir Alec Douglas-Home to resume the leadership of our Party, and I will gladly serve as his second-in-command.'
>
> There wouldn't be a dry eye in the house. The cheers would echo from Land's End to John o' Groats. . . . Alas, I'm afraid this is too imaginative to

hope for. We must accept and try to build on the prosaic fact that Conservative policies do show some glimpses of new grace, and that a Heath Government would be sensible and amiable and infinitely preferable to the Wilson regime.

But, oh, for a Party, for a leader, who could command our hearts as well as our heads!

What did all this controversy achieve? For a few weeks it had the effect I had aimed at, and Edward Heath's personal popularity shot up. The *Daily Telegraph* in publishing a Gallup Poll on 26th October showed that Heath's personal popularity rating had risen by eight points, while Wilson's dropped by seven points. But the *Daily Telegraph*, whose interpretation of these polls is more remarkable than the consistency of its editorial opinion, sombrely pointed out:

> Mr Heath registered a similar rise in popularity immediately following the Conservative party conference last year.

However, I was delighted and I immediately sent Edward Heath a telegram at Albany:

> Good work Ted. Well led. Just what I said.
>
> Gerald Nabarro.

And he punctiliously replied by letter:

> Dear Gerald,
>
> Thank you for your telegram.
>
> Yours,
>
> Ted.

But of course, it did not last. Ted's personal popularity was soon on the floor again.

The idea of bringing back Sir Alec Douglas-Home did not end with the article by Anthony Lejeune which I have quoted. In April, 1968, Heath sacked Powell from the Shadow Cabinet and that action illuminated some of the conflicting shades of opinion within the Conservative party. Sir Arthur Bryant, popular historian and a high Tory, argued in the *Sunday Express*, on 29th September, 1968, that the condition of the party resembled "that which split the Conservatives when the cautious Balfour was leading them and the more radical Joseph Chamberlain was advocating Tariff Reform. So long as Lord Salisbury, with his immense prestige and wisdom had remained at their head, their position was impregnable. After his retirement, electoral disaster followed." The Lord Salisbury referred to here was Prime Minister until 1902, although he had been in that office twice before. Curiously enough, he and Sir Alec are the only peers who have been Prime Minister this century, although there may well be more now that peerages can be renounced. However, the message was clear in Sir Arthur Bryant's mind and he did not hesitate to pass it on at the end of his article:

> There is one man who could do so (reconcile both sides of the Party)—the elder statesman who four years ago, against all expectations, so nearly led the party to victory and then resigned rather than endanger its unity. By that act of self-abnegation and the good sense and wise judgement he has since shown on every issue, Alec Douglas-Home has immensely increased his public stature.
>
> A great gentleman, as shrewd as he is fearless, he is trusted by both friend and foe. No one is so well aware of the dangers facing the country or better qualified to restore its faith and unity. If he could be persuaded, for his country's sake, to resume the leadership, he could win adherents from every section of the community.
>
> Both he and Heath are men of flawless loyalty—to one another and their colleagues. Many believe that the latter may one day make a great Prime Minister.

This was before the party conference at Blackpool in 1968. At about the same time, the ex-Party chairman, Mr Edward du Cann, again enlivened the issue by calling for an end to what he called "pat-a-cake policies". *The Times* reported:

> The nation, he (Mr du Cann) said, demanded competent leadership and 'our party's preoccupation with the so-called middle ground of politics has led us too often to fail to present to the nation our themes in a sufficiently distinctive form'.
>
> Yesterday Mr du Cann disagreed with any interpretation which suggested he was arguing for a change in the Tory leadership. He said he did not blame Mr Heath for the lack of enthusiasm for the Conservative Party; he blamed the whole party, and 'I have merely said in public what many people say in private'.
>
> Speaking earlier in Somerset he had introduced the theme of 'pat-a-cake politics' by pointing out that prominent supporters were leaving the Labour Party, but people were still not turning to the Conservatives with enthusiasm.
>
> 'The country has every reason to expect leadership and inspiration from the Conservative Party, and I hear it too often said that this has been conspicuously lacking in recent months', he said.

TEST TOYS BEFORE BUYING. *Daily Telegraph*, 3rd December, 1968.

Consumer Protection against dangerous imported toys. Teddy Bear: The Rt Hon. Jeremy Thorpe, MP; Rocket: The Rt Hon. Enoch Powell, MBE, MP; Jack-in-a-Box: Sir Gerald Nabarro, MP; Rattle: The Rt Hon. Roy Jenkins, MP; Balloon: The Rt Hon. Edward Heath, MBE, MP; Doll: The Rt Hon. Barbara Castle, MP.

> If that is not intended as a judgement of Mr Heath alone, it has no political meaning other than a judgement on the Shadow Cabinet, who set the tone and terrain for the Tory fight at Westminster and the campaign in the country.
>
> The timing of the speech is also significant: as Mr du Cann said, the Tory conference in Blackpool next month provides a brilliant opportunity for the party to put over to the nation a clearer and distinguishable alternative to the present administration.

Thus Mr Edward du Cann was yet another voice calling from within the party for a more vigorous statement of the Conservative alternative. I commented on du Cann's speech, restating what I had first said over a year before, I felt confident that the combined demands of Enoch Powell, Edward du Cann and myself would be echoed by the party rank and file at the Blackpool conference. So they were, but the conference produced little of substance beyond controversies on Powellite racial and immigration matters and these are but a tiny fraction of party policies as a whole.

Sir Henry d'Avigdor-Goldsmid, DSO, OBE, MC, TD, JP, MP for Walsall, South, went off like a damp squib when he wrote to *The Times* on 10th September:

> 'Damn with faint praise, assent with civil leer,
> And, without sneering, teach the rest to sneer;
> Willing to wound, and yet afraid to strike.'
>
> These lines from Alexander Pope epitomize more effectively than any words of mine the attitude of my colleagues, Edward du Cann and Sir Gerald Nabarro (your report, September 9th), towards the leader of our party, Edward Heath.
>
> The time for equivocation is past: if these distinguished gentlemen seek to replace Mr Heath with a candidate of their own choosing, let them speak up, stand up and be counted.
>
> If, on the other hand, they wish to row in on our party's current successes in local government elections and parliamentary by-elections, let them give a modicum of credit to the leadership under which these astounding victories have been and are being won, and pipe down.

Nobody took the least notice of him because it was all beside the point. It is widely understood that critics of the leadership in the Tory party are all dedicated to creating more dynamic leadership and clearer policy statements of what the party is going to stand for in the seventies. Not to change to party leadership before the next General Election.

Anyway, every well-conducted business has trained and competent successors to the Chairman and Managing Director. God forbid that Mr Heath should be the victim of some natural disaster. Were any calamity to occur, the Tory MPs would democratically choose their new leader from among, say, Home, Maudling, Powell, Macleod and others.

It would be idle to speculate further.

I am never idle.

Now that the mantle of office is about to descend on the Rt Hon. Edward Heath, MBE, MP, Leader of Her Majesty's Opposition, his Parliamentary and public stature grow. Throughout the summer of 1969, Edward Heath has become increasingly bellicose at the Commons Despatch Box, relaxed and confident, smiling and urbane. Gone is the rather tetchy demeanour displayed in earlier years when Wilson scored one of his vicious party or debating points in their almost daily exchanges on the floor of the House.

Moreover, Edward Heath begins both to look like and sound like a Prime Minister. When he enters that office at the onset of the seventies, with twenty years' superb Parliamentary and Ministerial experience behind him, I am confident that he will be a Premier of better than average quality.

My desire will be to help him in the House of Commons and in the constituencies, on television and on radio, to become yet another great Tory Prime Minister.

5. *Parliament: On Being Selected*

VERY properly, in a vigorous democracy, large numbers of people want to go into Parliament. Few have the least comprehension of what is entailed, how difficult it is to get in and how difficult it is to stay in. Except for the favoured one or two, or the lucky, the road to Westminster is hard and treacherous. Generally, it takes a good conscientious Parliamentary aspirant ten years to get there. Since 1945 there have been eight General Elections, if one includes the one expected at the end of the Sixties. That means that post-war Parliaments have lasted on average about three years and two months each. Serious Parliamentary candidates generally have to wait three Parliaments before being elected. Of course, some never get in at all, even though they may run six, eight or ten times. Some get in first time, more often because of exceptional luck than ability. Such men rarely make good members. Far better to have got in the hard way as I was advised by a tough old Tory MP when I first ran in 1945. . . . "Go to the Potteries or the Black Country and fight a couple of elections there, to learn how very rough politics can be."

Thus Mr Aubrey Jones, now Chairman of the Prices and Incomes Board, contested South-East Essex unsuccessfully in 1945 and a by-election at Heywood and Radcliffe in 1946, before being elected for Birmingham, Hall Green, with a majority of nearly four thousand, in 1950; thus Sir Harmar Nichols, who was adopted for Nelson and Colne in 1938 but because of the war did not have an opportunity of fighting it until 1945, when he was defeated by the late Sydney Silverman. At a by-election at Preston in 1946, he was defeated by Edward (now Lord) Shackleton and in the same year was adopted as prospective candidate for Peterborough, which he won after a recount in 1950. He has held the seat ever since with some very small majorities, including one of three in 1966 after seven recounts. This record is unique. At no time since the Reform Act has any one person retained an unchanged Parliamentary seat through six elections over twenty years with so many recounts—nine in all. My friend Dr Donald Johnson had the following extraordinary record:

1935 Bury (Liberal) Beaten
1937 Bewdley (Liberal) Beaten
1943 Chippenham (Liberal) Beaten
1945 Chippenham (Liberal) Beaten
1955 Carlisle (Tory) Elected
1959 Carlisle (Tory) Re-elected
1964 Carlisle (Independent Tory) Beaten, lost Deposit
Total: Seven elections. Won two, lost five.

Mrs Margaret Thatcher, MP for Finchley since 1959, has had her record complicated by eight years *hors de combat* while having her family, but before that she had fought Dartford unsuccessfully in both 1950 and 1951; Peter Walker fought the same Labour stronghold in 1955 and 1959, before getting in at Worcester at a by-election in 1961.

It is reckoned to be twenty times or more as difficult for a woman, Labour or Tory, to be selected as it is for a man. The reason is simple: women are catty about voting for a woman and men do not much want to be represented by a "skirt". There were only twenty-six women elected in 1966 out of the eighty who ran. Labour women seem to be more acceptable and there are nineteen of them compared with seven Tories and, sadly, no Liberal lady Members, although the delightful Lady Megan Lloyd-George sat for Anglesey as a Liberal for over twenty years before she joined the Labour Party and returned to the House as Member for Carmarthen, which she represented until her death in 1966. Lady Members are formidable beyond their numbers and there are eminent examples in both main parties. The present Parliament has been impressed by the arrival of two more, in the shape of Mrs Winifred Ewing (Scottish Nationalist, Hamilton) and Miss Bernadette Devlin (Independent Irish, Mid-Ulster). But as a general rule, it is a regrettable fact of life that selection committees do not go for the ladies.

Getting selected as a prospective Parliamentary candidate is invariably more difficult than getting elected.

High in the Cotswold country near Broadway, Worcestershire. Sir Gerald Nabarro, M.P. and Lady Nabarro with their dogs.

A garden view of The Orchard House (*circa* 1602) Broadway, in the Parliamentary Constituency of Worcestershire South: home of Sir Gerald and Lady Nabarro.

"ON THE BOX"
As millions see him: B.B.C. 1 Television, March 1969.

"Early Days:"
Family group for the 1951 Election Address. Mr. and Mrs. Gerald Nabarro, Rupert (6 years), Jeremy (5 years) and Sarah (15 months), in the garden of Dawn House, Winchester.

Elected for the second time as Tory Member of Parliament for Kidderminster by a majority of 5,158 votes: Declaration of Polls outside the Kidderminster Town Hall, October 1951.

Left to Right, on the steps:

Labour Candidate	The Town Clerk	Tory Candidate
Mr. Jack Williams	John Evans Esq., M.A.	Mr. Gerald Nabarro

The white rabbit held by Mr. Nabarro was the mascot presented to him on adoption as Tory Candidate.

60th RIFLEMEN IN THE 1950–1951 PARLIAMENT "THE RHODESIANS"

Left to right: Sir Gerald Nabarro, M.P. (Con. Kidderminster 1950–1964 and Worcestershire South from 1966); Rt. Hon. Nigel Birch, O.B.E., M.P. (Con. Flintshire 1945–1950 and Flintshire West from 1950); Rt. Hon. Sir Anthony Eden, K.G., M.C., M.P., Earl of Avon (Con. Warwick & Leamington 1923–1957 Prime Minister 1955–1957); Brigadier Sir Charles Howard, K.C.V.O., D.S.O., Sergeant-at-Arms; Rt. Hon. Sir Toby Low, K.C.M.G., C.B.E., D.S.O., T.D., M.P. (Con. Blackpool North 1945–1963) (Lord Aldington); Rt. Hon. William Deedes, M.C., M.P. (Con. Ashford from 1950); Rt. Hon. Richard Wood, M.P. (Con. Bridlington from 1950)

"In April 1940, detachments of Rhodesians joined the 1st Battalion and by the end of the month a Rhodesian platoon had been formed in the Battalion, receiving reinforcements from Rhodesia, and were later on formed into a Rhodesian Company, one of the finest companies in the Regiment."

(Page 81: A Brief History of the King's Royal Rifle Corps, 1755–1948. 3rd Edition.)

ELECTED FOR THE FOURTH TIME AS TORY MEMBER OF PARLIAMENT FOR KIDDERMINSTER BY A MAJORITY OF 9,343 VOTES: Declaration of Polls on the steps of the Kidderminster Town Hall, at 1.15 a.m. on 9th October 1959. Over Mr. Gerald Nabarro's shoulder can be seen Mrs. Nabarro and to the right of the picture the Labour Candidate, Councillor Mrs. Joan Tomlinson of Birmingham.

The General Election of 1955: when Mr. Gerald Nabarro was elected for the third time, as Tory Member of Parliament for Kidderminster, by a majority of 8,224 votes: Mrs. Nabarro pins on her husband's blue and white election winning rosette, at the first of 68 public election meetings, beginning and ending in the Kidderminster Town Hall.

Let me deal with the three parties and dispose of the Liberals without ado. Anybody reasonably presentable can obtain a Liberal candidature by paying his or her own expenses. Whatever else the Liberals have, the one thing they do not have is money. Another is prospects. They won't win a General Election this century, nice likeable chaps, intelligent and reasonable, though their leaders are—the Rt Hon. Jeremy Thorpe, the Rt Hon. Jo Grimond and such Liberal peers as Lord Byers and Lord Gladwyn. The Liberals have no future and so their candidates are rarely serious Parliamentary contenders.

In the Labour Party, the selection of candidates is quite as democratic as in the Tory Party. Competition is very fierce and as many as three hundred men and women come forward when a safe seat is vacant. They are understandably anxious to win the candidature for the majority party in that constituency. But only a handful offer themselves for the minority party in a safe seat and for the most part they are beginners in search of nursery training.

Constituency selection committees in the Tory Party are awesome. Usually consisting of twenty-four people, they are supposed to represent men, women, young Tories, Tory trade unionists, Tory teachers, middle "Cs"—that is the thirty to forty year olds—and any other party pressure groups, national or local. The Monday Club is not yet known to be officially represented.

For all the Committee members, especially in a safe Tory suburban seat, selecting a Parliamentary candidate is their moment of power. They know it. In a good county constituency the Committee will want a man aged between thirty and forty. He should have a good family background, with a Tory tradition; he should have served in the armed forces and made progress in his chosen occupation; he should be on the Tory Central Office list of approved candidates; he should have a nice wife, who should offer herself decorously and demurely for the selection committee to look over; three to four children, also dogs, are desirable; and wife driving, "à la Attlee", a substantial, but not too showy, car. Of course, the candidate must be personable and resident in or near the constituency. When it comes to the confrontation with the selection committee, well-cut clothes, old school, college, sporting or regimental tie, and wife in a tailored suit with matching regimental brooch, are all helpful. Fluency, self-confidence and thorough political knowledge are said to be universal among Tory Parliamentary aspirants.

Eton and Christ Church is a helpful background for a Tory, pace Sir

Edward Boyle and Mr Quintin Hogg; and generally unhelpful to a Socialist, pace Mr Reginald Paget—Eton and Trinity College, Cambridge and now Master of the Pytchley—and Mr Ben Whittaker—Eton and New College—who unseated Mr Henry Brooke in Hampstead.

Of course, party images and the composition of parties change over the years and not always for the better. The Labour Party, fearful of too much Keir Hardie, Clause 4, clothcap Socialism, heavy watchchains and Trade Unionism, have over-played the bias towards academics and the parliamentary party now contains all manner of pedagogues and prosaic theorists who look down their elegant noses at the horny-handed sons of toil who made their party in the first place. The pendulum has swung too far towards the intellectuals and away from the working men.

So also with the Tories in the image of Edward Heath, who was the nearest thing to Harold Wilson, in terms of parentage and background, that the Tories could knock up at short notice. And, for a while, though not for long, an aspiring young candidate had to be grammar school, redbrick university, non-U, non-county and left of centre, in short "a Teddie boy", to make sure of adoption as a Tory Parliamentary candidate in a good seat.

For myself, I have gone through the last twenty-five years following my nose and seldom taking advice from my elders and betters on constituency selection matters. I have been selected four times:

1945 Eddisbury, Cheshire:	selected 33 to 1.
1945 West Bromwich, Staffordshire:	selected 47 to 1.
1946 Kidderminster, Worcestershire:	selected 31 to 1.
1965 South Worcestershire:	selected 87 to 1.

At Eddisbury, a constituency now abolished and absorbed into the Northwich seat of Tory Sir John Foster, QC, I had entered my name mainly as a lark, shortly before the end of the war. It was a safe Tory seat but had recently been won from a Churchill Coalition candidate by a Commonwealth Member. I had hardly started work on winning it back, when I was telephoned by the General Director of Conservative Central Office, Sir Robert Topping, and told that the Liberal National leader, the Rt Hon. Ernest Brown, Member for Leith, had thrown in his lot with Sir Winston Churchill, the Tory Leader, and that seats which had been Liberal National in 1940, of which Eddisbury was one, were not to be contested by Tories. At the time I was most depressed by all this but the seat disappeared in the re-distributions which took place in 1949 and

Sir John Barlow, who had won it comfortably in 1945, had to wait until 1951 before he got another seat, at Middleton and Prestwich, which he lost in 1966. With hindsight, I count myself well out of Eddisbury.

Just before the 1945 Election, I was lunching with a friend in London and I was introduced to Colonel Sir Harold Mitchell, Vice-Chairman of the Conservative Party and MP for Brentford and Chiswick. He told me that West Bromwich was unexpectedly without a Tory candidate. I was on the train that evening, booked into the Midland Hotel at Birmingham and went to the Conservative headquarters at "The Elms". Forty-six other hopefuls did too. I got the nomination. The runner-up was a young officer from the Welsh Guards, Captain David Llewellyn. He went off to contest Aberavon, Glamorgan, where he lost by nearly twenty thousand votes. I was nearly as badly beaten in West Bromwich:

John Dugdale (Labour)	27,979
Gerald Nabarro (Tory)	12,028
Labour Majority	15,951

all of which deflated me, somewhat.

But I was "blooded". Winston Churchill was beaten after the 1945 General Election. The "Red Flag" had been sung in the House of Commons by a huge Labour majority. Overwhelmingly, the officers and men in the armed forces had voted Labour, swallowing propaganda that Winston Churchill would keep them in uniform, whereas the liberal and liberalising Socialists, building a new Jerusalem in technicolor, would demobilise without delay. Then, Conservative Central Office appointed me, subject to election later on, Chairman of the newly formed Young Conservative movement in the West Midlands. I was responsible for the City of Birmingham and Warwickshire, Shropshire, Herefordshire, Worcestershire, Gloucestershire and Staffordshire. In the autumn of 1945, there were fifteen Young Conservative branches in this area and when I gave up the post in 1948, in order to become President, there were two hundred and sixty-nine. In two and a half years I made more than three hundred Young Conservative speeches and my adolescent, soap-box oratory brought me to the notice of the Kidderminster Conservatives who had lost their seat to Labour in 1945, for the first time in history. As Young Conservative Area Chairman, hand held by a dynamic Central Office Agent, Lt Col R. J. W. Ledingham, OBE, MC, I fell in at Kidderminster with thirty others seeking the nomination, including quite a number of defeated MPs from the 1945 General Election. I won the nomination and on 24th March, 1946, I was adopted as prospective candidate before thirteen hundred cheering Tories in Kidderminster Town Hall. Forty-seven months later, after more than a thousand speeches and functions while nursing the constituency over this long period, I won the seat from Labour with a majority of 3,805. Tory MP at last, I represented Kidderminster in the House of Commons until I was forced to give up my seat there, seriously ill and anguished at being chucked out of Parliament, not by the electors, which I could have borne, but by the doctors.

The 1964 General Election is the only one I have missed since the war. I sailed to South Africa with my wife and returned at Christmas 1964 to learn that:

(i) Mr Harold Wilson, the Socialist Prime Minister, had a majority of only three seats and evidently could not gasp along for many months longer without a General Election.
(ii) My local MP, Commander Sir Peter Agnew, Bart (Tory, South Worcestershire) at the age of sixty-five felt that he ought to retire and because the General Election could not be long delayed warned the Chairman of his Constituency Association that he would not contest the seat again.
(iii) The doctors signed me off, subject to light duties for two years.
(iv) Eighty-seven people had applied for Sir Peter Agnew's seat in South Worcestershire, including a score or more 1964 Tory casualties.
(v) The eighty-seventh applicant, Mr Geoffrey Johnson-Smith, who had lost Holborn and St Pancras at the General Election, had been adopted at East Grinstead on 27th December, in the room of Lady Emmett, who had been ennobled.

I put my name down in place of Geoffrey Johnson-Smith. I was desolate and lonely out of Parliament and was prepared to take risks with the doctors.

By elimination before the Selection Committee, the eighty-seven became twelve, mostly ex-MPs; the twelve became four and all of them have since entered or re-entered Parliament:

Mr Maurice Macmillan	Farnham. Since 31.3.66
Mr Peter Tapsell	Horncastle. Since 31.3.66.
Mr Jerry Wiggin	Weston-super-Mare. Since 27.3.69
Sir Gerald Nabarro	South Worcestershire. Since 31.3.66.

The press had a feast for the final selection at the Royal Three Tuns Hotel in Pershore on a bitter January night, in 1965. The television wanted to get in on it as well but Mr Maurice Macmillan and I agreed that it was a private meeting and that even though the selection had attracted unusual general interest, to have it conducted in front of the cameras would be thoroughly undesirable. "Cross-Bencher" was a great help to me when he wrote in the *Sunday Express* on 17th January, the day before the Final selection:

> In a drowsy West Midland townlet this week-end excitement grows. Plum-growing little Pershore (pop. 5,181) is suddenly all-alive-o.

" HEY, GERT — GUESS WHO WANTS TO COME BACK TO THE HOUSE OF COMMONS — ! "

Birmingham Mail, 19th January, 1965.

For there tomorrow the top Tories of South Worcestershire assemble to take a decision of high public interest:
Whether to put one of the most zestful, roistering politicians of our time back on the road to Westminster.
Sir Gerald Nabarro.
At 7.45 pm sharp the 175 members of the divisional executive council will be called to order at the Three Tuns Hotel.
For the next two hours they will listen to speeches by Sir Gerald and his three rivals for the candidature.
At 9.45 they will be handed ballot slips for a secret vote.
At 10.15 the result will be announced.
Of course, you may well think that Sir Gerald is bound to win.
Before illness forced him to resign last October, he held next-door Kidderminster for fourteen years.
His parliamentary record is one of ability, wit and conspicuous achievement.
He has lived in the South Worcestershire division for twelve years.
He formed its first Young Conservative branches at Malvern and Evesham.
Last July, a sick man, he came forth to make his only major speech of 1964—in support of Sir Peter Agnew, its sitting member.
And tomorrow he will be looking at a sea of familiar faces. Virtually all his 175 judges know him.
Is it, then, to be a walkover for ex-LCC schoolboy Sir Gerald?
Do not be so sure. Consider the other hopefuls.
Mr Peter Tapsell, ex-MP for Nottingham West, may perhaps be regarded as the outsider.
But Mr Maurice Macmillan, former Treasury Minister, and local farmer Mr Jerry Wiggin share a special qualification.
Both went to Eton.
Is this so important?
It could be. The Tories of Worcestershire seem partial to the Grand Old School.
Two of the county's present four Tory MPs wear its tie: Mr James Dance (Bromsgrove) and Sir Tatton Brinton (Kidderminster).
And there will be those at the Three Tuns tomorrow who would not mind seeing the percentage raised from 50 to 75.
My final comment on the battle of Pershore?
Cross-Bencher is as impartial as always.
Good luck, I say, to all four contestants.
Particularly to Sir Gerald Nabarro.

I won the nomination.
My adoption meeting was at the Winter Gardens in Malvern on 8th

February and was attended by fourteen hundred paid-up members of the South Worcestershire Conservative Association. For just over a year I nursed this gorgeous constituency and on 31st March, 1966, I returned to the House of Commons.

I had beaten the bodily ills. I had voted for myself at 0.700 hours on the morning of polling day in my own home village of Broadway, in the Parliamentary Constituency of South Worcestershire.

My cup was brimful of happiness.

6. *Parliament: On Being Elected*

I HAVE contested six General Elections since the end of the Second World War, with the following results:

4th July 1945	West Bromwich	defeated by 15,951
23rd February 1950	Kidderminster	elected by 3,805
25th October 1951	Kidderminster	elected by 5,158
26th May 1955	Kidderminster	elected by 8,224
8th October 1959	Kidderminster	elected by 9,343
31st March 1966	South Worcestershire	elected by 11,084

Now the professional pundits, psephologists and scholars will tell you that the character, ability and personal attributes of the candidate count for next to nothing; only five hundred votes one way or the other they will say. Also, that public meetings are an anachronism; only television and broadcasting matter today. Neither proposition is correct.

Perhaps it is true that when there are three candidates, Tory, Labour and Liberal, none of whom has ever contested the seat before and all of whom are relative strangers to the constituency, then a good, personable candidate—leaving aside matters of party and policy—may only be worth five hundred votes more than a bad, unpersonable candidate. But this does not apply in the case of a sitting member who, over a number of years, has observed the five golden rules of conduct towards his constituents:

(1) Complete accessibility to constituents by carefully planned constituency "surgeries", so that no voter can ever say that the Member cannot be reached.
(2) Meticulous attention to constituency correspondence, however trivial, or irrelevant, the case may be. Handle it, and where appropriate, be seen to handle it.
(3) Televise, broadcast and write in newspapers as often as possible. Idiosyncrasies of style, voice and features are always helpful.
(4) Speak in the House a good deal and if the Chair is discouraging, then proceed by committee work and Parliamentary questions, where the opportunities are boundless. Local constituency newspapers, which are always sympathetic to good Members of Parliament, should be encouraged to publish the relevant parts of *Hansard*, or a paraphrase of them.
(5) Establish and maintain an ubiquitous constituency organisation. In my case, this consists of a Conservative working committee in almost every ward and parish of a big county constituency.

Given decent policies and provided the candidate is tolerably presentable, this is the basis on which election successes are assured and the reason why the winning candidate's majority goes up, even when the tide is running against his Party. Two splendid examples of this are experienced Labour campaigners. Both managed to increase their majorities in 1955, even though there was a national swing to the Conservatives of 2.15%:

		1951	1955
Sir Geoffrey de Freitas (Lincoln)	maj.	3,560	5,222
Mr Anthony Greenwood (Rossendale)	maj.	1,670	2,911

Of course, both Sir Geoffrey de Freitas, now Member for Kettering, after a period out of Parliament as High Commissioner in Kenya, and Mr Anthony Greenwood, are Members of great distinction and ability.

For twenty years, I have relied on the five rules I have described, as election winners. On the first Saturday of every month, the constituency newspapers (five of them when I sat for Kidderminster and four in South

Worcestershire since 1966), carry a double column advertisement with a photograph of myself and some such caption as: "NABARRO IS ACTION—LET HIM ACT FOR YOU", followed by a list of places, dates and times. For almost fifteen years at Kidderminster, I used three town halls in the mornings of my peregrinations, at Bewdley, Stourport-on-Severn and Kidderminster, and ten villages on a three monthly cycle in the afternoons. Thus I covered the town halls twelve times each and the thirty villages four times each in the course of a year. My working day lasted from nine in the morning until seven in the evening. Nowadays, still on the first Saturday in every month, I visit five centres in South Worcestershire for the interviews, at Malvern, Upton-on-Severn, Pershore, Evesham and Broadway, twelve times a year. The tour lasts from nine in the morning until two in the afternoon. The round trip is seventy-five miles, which is twenty-five miles less than it was, on average, in Kidderminster. These constituency tours are immensely important. Constituents value them and the Member is refreshed by them. There is no danger that any elector can say at a General Election that his Member of Parliament is out of touch or inaccessible. This way the Member hears "the lot", as he ought to, if he is to be effective.

Then, the correspondence. I average three hundred letters weekly or, say, fifteen thousand annually. Often a constituent's case involves twelve letters before it is settled and the voter is nearly always grateful for the help. Attention to constituency letters is a sound vote winner and over the five years of a Parliament, many unattached voters can be attracted in this way.

It is even more true of frequent participation in television and broadcast programmes. Every constituent, irrespective of his political sympathies—with the exception of the most bigoted and diehard opponents—likes to see or hear (or both) his MP on the air. That is why there is such friction in the House of Commons when some Members participate so much more often than others.

Speeches in the House of Commons and Parliamentary Questions are equally important. Copies of the relevant *Hansard* extracts should be sent to editors of local newspapers who seldom have either Lobby Correspondents or the service of the Press Association.

The Member should report himself to his constituents, especially on their local interests, whether carpets in Kidderminster or asparagus in the Vale of Evesham, open-cast coal mining in Worcestershire, the closure of railway stations or branch lines, effluent from power stations, the price of electricity and gas, road accidents, motorways and planning consent refusals. The conscientious Member must act and be seen to act and in doing so should use every medium at his disposal. The greatest omission and error as Party Politician is to fail to be reported.

Finally, there is the Constituency Party organisation. Labour are very bad at this and Mr Harold Wilson's "penny farthing" jibe after the lost election of 1959, is even more true today. The Socialists are woefully lacking in working committees at constituency level and their supporters are eternally squabbling among themselves. Organisation is not everything. The candidate's party and the way he puts policy across is obviously the main thing but the constituency organisation is invaluable in doing so effectively and is worth a good many votes. Personally, I think that after five years' work in South Worcestershire I have one of the best constituency machines in Britain. There are more than sixty committees at work within the South Worcestershire Conservative Association. About £8,000 a year is raised, of which about £2,000 goes to Central Office to help candidates in marginal seats. There are literally hundreds of social events of every kind each year and I make scores of speeches annually. I live at Broadway, in my constituency, and this ensures that I keep in close touch with the full-time and highly experienced agent and his staff as well as the thousand or more committee members spread over an area of 172,000 acres. Were an election called at the shortest notice, the whole machine would slide smoothly into action and produce a dynamic campaign. It is called, facetiously, "The Nabarro Band-Waggon". I don't mind. I built it. The purpose is to win elections. That is what it does. My opponents are merely envious and conscious of their own deficiencies.

Do not let those long-haired intellectuals, journalists, television men and the like, tell you that the late twentieth century has no place for the public political meeting. On the contrary, there is no substitute for an election candidate doing his stuff in the flesh, delivering his speech, answering the hecklers in kind and dealing with questions. Paradoxically, television has increased the popularity of public meetings and in both 1959 and 1966 I found the halls packed for every meeting. During an election campaign, I do three or four meetings a night, at intervals of three quarters of an hour. This allows for a speech lasting twenty minutes, followed by fifteen minutes of questions and then ten minutes to get to the next meeting. For travelling on these occasions, I need a car in front of me, to show my driver the way and another one behind, in case I get a puncture; and for the actual meetings, a speaker to warm up the audience before I arrive and another one to cool it down after I leave. Here is the 1959 programme of public meetings, when I held the seat by 9,343 votes:

Friday, 18th Sept.:	8.00 pm.	Adoption Meeting: Kidderminster Town Hall.
Saturday, 19th Sept.:	7.00 pm.	Lower Broadheath, The Bell Inn.
	7.45 pm.	Stanford-on-Teme, The School and the Shelsleys.
	8.45 pm.	Lindridge, Eardiston Village Hall.
Monday, 21st Sept.:	7.00 pm.	Kyre, The School.
	7.45 pm.	Tenbury, St Michael's Parish Hall.
	8.15 pm.	Rochford, Church Hall.
	9.00 pm.	Clifton-on-Teme, Memorial Hall.
Tuesday, 22nd Sept.:	7.00 pm.	Shatterford, Village Hall.
	7.45 pm.	Wribbenhall, Parish Room.
	8.45 pm.	Stone, The Dog, Harvington.
Wednesday, 23rd Sept.:	8.00 pm.	*Gloucester*, The Guildhall.[1]
Thursday, 24th Sept.:	7.00 pm.	Rushock, The School.
	7.45 pm.	Blakedown, The School.
	8.45 pm.	Wolverley, Sebright Room.
Friday, 25th Sept.:	7.00 pm.	Crown East, The School.
	7.45 pm.	Grimley, The Peace Hall.
	8.45 pm.	Rushwick, Parish Hall.
Saturday, 26th Sept.:	7.00 pm.	Upper Arley, The School.
	7.45 pm.	Trimpley, The School.
	8.45 pm.	Kidderminster, St Oswald's Hall.
Monday, 28th Sept.:	7.00 pm.	Holt, Village Hall.
	7.45 pm.	Shrawley, Parish Hall.
	8.45 pm.	Arley Kings, Parish Hall.
Tuesday, 29th Sept.:	7.00 pm.	Knightwick, The Talbot Hotel.
	7.45 pm.	Leigh Sinton, The School.
	8.45 pm.	Hallow, Parish Hall.
Wednesday, 30th Sept.:	7.00 pm.	Far Forest, Village Hall.
	7.45 pm.	Stourport, Wilden Village Hall.
	8.45 pm.	Chaddesley Corbett, The School.
Thursday, 1st Oct.:	7.00 pm.	Broadwas-on-Teme, The School.
	7.45 pm.	Wichenford, Memorial Hall.
	8.45 pm.	Martley, The Chantry.
Friday, 2nd Oct.:	7.00 pm.	Pensax, Village Hall.
	7.45 pm.	Astley, Parish Room.
	8.45 pm.	Cookley, Village Hall.

[1] Helping in a marginal seat.

Saturday, 3rd Oct.:	7.00 pm.	Rock, Village Hall.
	7.45 pm.	Mamble, Village Hall.
	8.15 pm.	Knighton-on-Teme, The School.
	9.00 pm.	Tenbury Wells, The Royal Oak.
Monday, 5th Oct.:	7.00 pm.	Bayton, The School.
	7.45 pm.	Bliss Gate, Gorst Hill Village Hall.
	8.45 pm.	Kidderminster (Franche) Primary School.
Tuesday, 6th Oct.:	7.15 pm.	Abberley and Great Witley, St George's Hall.
	8.30 pm.	Stourport-on-Severn, Town Hall.
Wednesday, 7th Oct.:	7.15 pm.	Bewdley Town Hall.
(Eve of Poll)	8.30 pm.	Kidderminster Town Hall.

The great send-off at the beginning is of course the adoption meeting. My wife is with me on every election platform. If she is about to have, or has just had, a baby, the anticipation or the accomplishment of such a happy event is a great vote winner. My wife's family planning arrangements have been superb. I am full of admiration. It has all made electioneering so much easier, especially in my earlier and more exacting campaigns.

In 1950 my wife saw me elected by 3,805 votes and winning Kidderminster back from Labour. It has been Tory ever since. Cheering me on, all the women knew my wife was expecting. No more politics until the summer for my wife, and then a baby girl, christened at the Crypt Chapel of St Stephen's at the House of Commons on 6th September, 1950, six months after I had first entered the House. Little did I think that this lusty infant, Sarah Penelope, god-daughter of Sir Tatton Brinton, who succeeded me as Member for Kidderminster in 1964, would be the cover girl of the Oxford University Conservative Association programme for Hilary Term, 1969. Thus, Tory women are made. I show the child Sarah, "muling and puking" in her mother's arms in Palace Yard, Westminster, a few minutes after her baptism, and now in 1969, torrid, trousered and with-it, groomed for her course at the London School of Economics.

So too in 1955. My wife then preceded the General Election by a couple of months. My second daughter, Dinah Jane, was born on 18th March, 1955, and Sir Anthony Eden called the General Election on 26th May. Walking the new baby through Broadway village at the beginning of the campaign, wags affixed "Nabarro Again" car stickers to the perambulator. A picture of this event appeared in newspapers all over the world and the Kidderminster Labour Party accused me of levity and of failing to treat election matters with the seriousness demanded by contemporary troubles. Because so many Kidderminster ladies attached "Nabarro Again" stickers to their perambulators, the Labour Party levelled against me the further grave charge of moral laxity. However, we won by a record majority of 8,224 and Dinah Jane undoubtedly contributed substantially to this success.

Every Member seeking re-election, especially if he lives in or near his constituency, should include on his election address a picture of his wife and children, if he has any, and his dogs: especially the dogs. There is deeply engrained in the minds and hearts of British electors, the belief that a Member of Parliament with children and dogs: a man who has reared a family, a man who keeps a decent home and has suffered all the trials and tribulations of domestic affairs, is far better able to represent ordinary men and women, than a Member who lacks children and dogs. It was with this in mind that I wrote of Mr Edward Heath in the *News of the World* on 1st August, 1965:

> For myself, I prophesy that Mr Edward Heath will be the first bachelor occupant of No. 10, Downing Street for sixty years: since Arthur Balfour. Personally, to make the man and image complete, I would like him to carry a beautiful bride over the threshold to share his occupancy with him.

Certainly, he would do much better with children and dogs; and many well-known politicians are notably philoprogenitive. For example:

Mr Robert Mellish	(Labour, Bermondsey)	Five sons.
Mr Quintin Hogg, QC	(Tory, St Marylebone)	Two sons and three daughters.
Mr Robert Maxwell	(Labour, Buckingham)	Four sons and four daughters.
Viscount Lambton	(Tory, Berwick-on-Tweed)	One son and five daughters.
Mr Hugh Fraser	(Tory, Stafford & Stone)	Three sons and three daughters.

Any connection between the size of family and party political activities is entirely circumstantial. But no politician is complete without vigorous progeny and a happy home life.

7. *Taxation: The Scourge of Britain Today*

LOTS of naïve people think that General Elections are won or lost because of this or that party's policy on housing or education, or social services or welfare, or roads or trade, or the United Nations or foreign affairs.

The fact is that the most powerful single influence on how people vote is taxation and promises by the parties to reduce particular forms of taxation.

In the twenty years since 1950, the Labour Party has been in office for about seven and the Tories about thirteen years. Labour has demonstrated that it is the party of increased and increasing taxation and the Tories the party of reduced and reducing taxation. Nowhere has this been more clearly demonstrated than in the principal forms of direct personal taxation, Income Tax and Surtax, and in Purchase Tax. The Tories, when they returned to power in 1951 inherited the standard rate of income tax at 9/6d in the £; when they went out in 1964, it was down to 7/9d in the £ and all allowances for wives, children, age relief and so on had been greatly increased. The hated Schedule "A", or Landlord's Property Tax, had been abolished, thus relieving nearly seven million owner-occupiers of houses. The iniquitous Development Charge under the Socialist Town and Country Planning Act of 1947 had been abolished; the starting level of Surtax had been raised from £2,000 per annum to £5,000 but sadly and illogically not for those people living on unearned income derived from savings and investments, whom both Tory and Socialist Governments seem to regard as socially undesirable: monstrous I call it and equality of treatment for Surtax payers on earned and unearned income is long overdue.

The Labour Party, as soon as they returned to power in 1964, put all this into reverse immediately, by raising the standard rate of Income Tax to 8/3d in the £, reintroducing their tax on land development, but calling it a Betterment Levy, and hitting every consumer by vicious increases in every form of indirect taxation, including motor-car vehicle licences, petrol duty, general increases in Purchase Tax and taxes on gambling. Moreover, they have introduced three new taxes: Selective Employment Tax, Corporation Tax and Capital Gains duty, although the Tories had stupidly shown the Labour Party the way to tax gains on stocks and shares held for under six months on realisation, and on land held for less than three years.

Never has public expenditure and related taxation grown so fast as in the five years between the autumn of 1964 and the autumn of 1969. Whether judged *ad valorem* or as a percentage of Gross National Product, the rise represents:

(1) A massive disincentive to hard work.
(2) An incentive for many of our best brains to emigrate.
(3) An intrusion and an assault on personal liberty and freedom.
(4) An incitement to tax fiddling, which is now a national pastime at all income levels.
(5) An encouragement to gamble, for winnings are taxed, if at all, at rates much below work earnings. Premium Bond winnings are tax-free, and Gilt Edge gains are tax-free.
(6) A discouragement to savings and capital formation which aie so essential to growth.

These factors, which condemn an abstruse and often incomprehensible taxation system, represent a major reason for our appalling slide into foreign debt—about £3,600m contracted since 1964. Unless the taxation system is simplified and reformed and the present penal rates of direct taxation are reduced in order to restore incentives to work and save, the calamitous trends of recent years will continue.

Here are the figures which demonstrate our profligacy:

TAXATION, GOVERNMENT EXPENDITURE AND THE GROSS NATIONAL PRODUCT

Year	Taxation Total £ million	% of GNP	Government expenditure Total £ million	% of GNP
1913/14	255	10	324	13
1925/26	903	20	1,424	32
1930/31	950	21	1,491	33
1935/36	1,024	23	1,391	31
1938/39	1,220	23	2,053	39
1946/47	3,488	39	4,969	55
1950/51	4,509	37	5,264	44
1955/56	5,279	33	7,038	41
1960/61	7,355	32	9,685	42
1961/62	8,190	33	10,689	43
1962/63	8,573	33	11,102	43
1963/64	8,853	32	12,055	44
1964/65	9,888	33	13,075	44
1965/66	11,142	35	14,481	46
1966/67	12,067	36	15,974	48
1967/68	13,331*	39	18,125*	53
1968/69	15,100*†	42	19,000*	53

* — Estimated.
† — Not including November, 1968 increases.

Tory estimates now show that taxes are costing each family an average of three pounds per week more than five years ago.

It is, therefore, no exaggeration to say that taxes are a dominant election issue. No speech on the hustings can be complete without full reference to the tax policies of the two major parties, Conservative and Socialist. Thus, throughout twenty-five years of party political warfare in the House of Commons, in the constituencies, on television, radio and in the newspapers, I have been embroiled in the continuous and continuing row about our taxation arrangements: and all that is so dreadfully wrong with them.

In brief and simple terms I set down broad lines for fiscal reform in the *Weekend Telegraph* on 31st May, 1968. The article received widespread, powerful and popular support from every section of the community:

Our penal rates of taxation and excessively complex and fiscal Statutes frustrate any prospect whatsoever of dynamic economic growth.

Why are these words axiomatic in contemporary Britain? First, because direct taxes are much too high, thus militating savagely against the creation of new wealth (call it growth if you like)—our most urgent need. Tax laws are so difficult to interpret correctly that hordes of lawyers, accountants and otherwise perfectly honest and law-abiding citizens now occupy countless hours every year searching for means of tax avoidance and evasion. Nothing is more calculated to slow down growth and shrivel and stultify economic performance.

Secondly, the proliferation of rates of indirect taxation has created a jungle of fiscal incongruities. For what good reason, logical, economic or financial, should the following extraordinary disparities and discriminations occur in Customs and Excise duties?

Commodity	Usual retail price	Tax	Tax as % of retail price
Whisky: per bottle	54/5	40/–	71
Beer: per pint	1/11	10¼d	40
Petrol: per gallon	6/–	3/11	67
Cigarettes: packet of 20	5/7	4/4	78
Lipstick	6/4	1/7	25
Diamond ring	say £184	£50	27
Savile Row suit	say £81	£7	9
Colour TV set	say £341	£63	18*

All are sumptuary; all contribute to exports; all give gainful employment; why therefore, the diversity of tax rates and proliferating anomalies and inconsistencies? Why is whisky deemed three times as luxurious as lipstick, cigarettes three times as luxurious as a diamond ring, and petrol, the life blood of 12 million motorists, seven times as luxurious as a Savile Row suit? Expediency piled upon expediency over thirty years has created this fiscal nonsense.

* Since the compilation of the above table, taxation was raised in November, 1968 by £250m and in April, 1969 by £340m. Allowing for these further advances in taxation, the revised figures are:

The Statutes for direct taxation are no better. Every situation in business, every venture in private life, every new enterprise, everywhere in Britain, is judged on taxation treatment: rightly so, when the best brains pay 91¼% marginal rate on their top earnings, and 'close-companies', director-controlled, pay, by Treasury ordinance, four-fifths of their earnings in taxation.

These penal rates stifle personal incentive, enterprise and initiative. Meanwhile, the economy stagnates.

Finance Acts, 1965/67, reveal a disgraceful record. They total 183 new sections or 436 pages of incomprehensible gibberish. This year's finance Bill (1968) adds another 56 clauses, 20 schedules and 111 pages. Small wonder national treasure diminishes, and lawyers and accountants suffuse the industrial community. Political parties in opposition promise platitudinously to reform our taxation system. In office, they do nothing. If we are to survive, it is urgently necessary to clean up the fiscal chaos. Simplicity is imperative: simplicity of structure, of assessment, of collection. Here are the three emergent taxes that are required:

PERSONAL (Direct Tax): To replace Income Tax, Surtax, Capital Gains Duty, Estate Duties, Betterment Levies. The top rate for both earned and unearned income would be 13/4 in the pound. Income of spouses and children would be non-aggregated.

Footnote cont. from p. 98

Commodity	Usual retail price	Tax	Tax as % of retail price
Whisky: per bottle	58/5	44/–	75
Beer: per pint (i)	2/0	11¼	47
Petrol: per gallon (ii)	6/7½	4/6	68
Cigarettes: packet of 20 (iii)	6/1	4/9	78
Lipstick	7/11	3/2	40
Diamond ring	say £234	£100	43
Savile Row suit	say £82/14/–	£8/14/–	10
Colour TV set	say £370	£84	23

Notes : (i) Lower range of estimated public bar prices. (ii) Price of five star (B.P.) petrol in London. (iii) 20 standard, full size, non-tipped.

Sources : Scotch Whisky Association;
Brewers' Society;
Shell-Mex and B.P.;
National Union of Retail Tobacconists;
Customs and Excise Intelligence Department.

SUMPTUARY (Indirect Tax): An Added-Value Tax, as evolved in France and West Germany, totally rebated on exports. It should be spread on a broad base, replacing all present Customs and Excise duties, Selective Employment Tax, Purchase Tax, Betting Duties and Road Fund Licences. It would be a flat rate tax and un-cognisant of so-called luxury. It would raise more than present indirect taxes, which would allow a reduction of direct personal taxation. Lower income groups not paying direct taxes would be compensated through social welfare benefits and pensions, for any increased living costs caused by the Added-Value Tax.

CORPORATION: This would be levied on companies alone, and revised to remove the exceptional tax burden on our great companies trading overseas (eg. Rio Tinto Zinc and Shell) who contribute so much to our national well-being.

These fiscal reforms would re-establish the desire to create new wealth; swing the emphasis from taxation of earnings to taxation of spending; encourage thrift as the true basis of private investment; liberate untold energies, latent at present, discouraged by the sheer weight and complexity of our taxes. Thus we would strike the most powerful blow for resumption of economic growth, an end to personal lassitude and the recovery of our national strength.

Of course, the rates of indirect taxation have gone up even more since this article was published and the more prices inflate, the more purchase tax inflates.

The most preposterous of all taxes in Britain is Purchase Tax. Of its origins, I wrote in the *Liverpool Post* on 10th March, 1958:

We cannot remain forever the prisoners of Purchase Tax. It is a shocking hangover from the direst and darkest days of the war, and was introduced eighteen years ago deliberately to depress to subsistence levels consumer demand in Britain for manufactured goods of every description in order to free for the national war effort—the 'blood, toil, tears and sweat' of Winston Churchill—every possible square yard of factory space, plant, machinery, transport and manpower. Today the requirements of our economy are exactly the opposite: an expanding economy is the purpose and policy of the Conservative Government, based on skill and craft, enterprise, efficiency and powerful unfettered salesmanship.

Purchase Tax penalises skill and craftsmanship, damages progressive design, obstructs expansion of exports, discriminates arbitrarily and generally unfairly between trade and trade, product and product, dissipates time and money for assessment and collection of the tax and thus raises costs and sterilises capital in business and commerce.

I had launched my first one hundred Parliamentary questions, three every Tuesday and three every Thursday, all addressed to the Chancellor of the Exchequer on the subject of Purchase Tax anomalies. It was a campaign designed deliberately to ridicule the Treasury. A further three hundred were to follow in the ensuing years. In retrospect I may claim some success, for when I started there were seven rates of the tax—the hangover from the days when the late Sir Stafford Cripps was at the Treasury and the Rt Hon. Douglas Jay, MP, was his Financial Secretary—from 90% at the top to 5% at the bottom, whereas four years and my four hundred Parliamentary questions later, there were only three rates, 25%, 15% and 10%.

In the *News of the World* on 5th April, 1959, the Sunday before the Budget, I wrote:

> The ridiculous purchase tax, inflationary, unfair and still riddled with anomalies, should be dealt with. Last year, seven rates with the top at 90% were reduced to four rates ranging from 5% on many essentials, to 60% on cars, radio, television, cosmetics and gramophone records. The tax on records is particularly offensive. Books are not penalised. Nor should records be. This is a tax on culture.
>
> This year further progress should be made towards a single flat-rate tax by reducing to only two rates, 30% and 15%. Prices in the shops would plummet down, exports would be boosted and employment would be further strengthened.

The campaign on Purchase Tax caused lots of eyebrows to go up. It was not done to rag the establishment: it was disloyal to assault Derick Heathcoat Amory, Etonian, Devonian and gentleman, twice a week at question time; no good would come of it for trade and commerce; that Kidderminster cad; the rotter; the swank-pot, that charlatan masquerading as a Parliamentarian. Those were the sort of epithets passed around by the stuffed-shirts in Club Smoking Rooms. Not so in the real world outside: the general public loved it. When Mr Heathcoat Amory resigned and joyfully permitted himself to be called to the House of Peers as Viscount Amory of Tiverton, "Publius" writing in *Achievement* in August 1960, said:

> If you see a lonely figure with the air of a philosophical countryman wandering about the corridors of Westminster, the chances are that it will be Mr Heathcoat Amory. A year ago he was the favourite of the gods but now he walks like the First Grave Digger.

There may have been academic reasons for putting up the Bank Rate, but the economy was vibrant and everyone was happy. The feeling at Westminster is that the Chancellor was like the nurse who sends someone to find out what the child is doing and tell it to stop.

But there were good men available to take his place when he resigned. Selwyn Lloyd, for example, had earned a rest from Foreign Affairs.

Who else was available for the Treasury? It may seem an odd suggestion but my choice would have been that incredible Tory, Gerald Nabarro. In this quiet Parliament here is a man who draws MPs from the smoke room and the Terrace when his name goes up on the ticker tape. Mr Nabarro is a character, or what Arnold Bennett would have called 'a card'.

He has handle-bar moustaches which literally wave in the breeze. In fact he looks like one of Bairnsfather's Old Bill drawings, and he has a booming voice that can almost be heard on the Terrace. In private life he is a successful industrialist.

I would not have been surprised if Harold Macmillan offered him the Board of Trade. It would be a heartening change to have a Cabinet Minister who wears a Board School tie.

The Purchase Tax Questions were a mixture of custard pie, pawky humour, good clean fun and pure hilarity. My difficulty was less in preparing them than keeping a straight face during question time. The facts were checked almost throughout by trade associations and their help was indispensable. Here are one or two which have already found their way into many Parliamentary manuals and standard works on both sides of the Atlantic. *The Times* had this to say on 11th February, 1958:

In the last financial year Purchase Tax netted £458m for the Exchequer. It is without doubt one of the most peculiar taxes ever imposed on British consumers, falling as it does with such markedly uneven severity. For example, 90% on cosmetics, 60% on a mirror or a suitcase, 30% on a stainless steel watch, 10% on a top hat, 5% on a rabbit fur coat and nothing on caviar. It is, indeed, as full of anomalies and inanities as would be expected of a tax which was originally imposed in order to discourage consumption altogether and has since been adapted by successive Chancellors of the Exchequer for influencing particular forms of consumption, channelling goods into the export trade, raising revenue, or whatever has been fancied as a special need of the moment. Naturally the task of defining the classification for tax has been difficult and the boundary lines are apt to become lunatic fringes. Mr Nabarro has made some palpable hits with his baskets which undergo a drastic change in their taxable capacity by moving in or out of the back door and his telephone directory covers which move in or out of the taxable class from one volume to another. Doubtless he will make many more.

A few days earlier, under the title "First victory for Mr Nabarro", *The Times* had written:

> Mr Nabarro, the Conservative Member of Parliament for Kidderminster, is nothing if not a tryer, and during the past two vain months of his single-handed campaign against the anomalies of Purchase Tax the august Treasury has come nowhere near to breaking his spirit.
>
> Tuesday by Tuesday, Mr Nabarro has fired his three allotted questions at the Chancellor of the Exchequer. Tuesday by Tuesday he has had to retire defeated. But on the Commons Order Paper his choice cullings of absurdity from Purchase Tax lists still stretched, three by three, far away into eternity.
>
> What happened yesterday will fortify him afresh. For at last he scored a palpable hit against the Treasury. Why, he asked, was a telephone directory cover entitled 'Telephone Directory, London E—K' not charged with tax although a similar cover marked 'London Telephone Directory' had to pay 30% tax?
>
> This, if ever, was a moment for the new Chancellor, Mr Heathcoat Amory, to nibble his handkerchief, as he does when he plunges deep in thought. 'The ruling that this directory cover was taxable', he rose to confess to a delighted House, 'was mistaken and has been reversed.' Then he added ruefully: 'I have no doubt that the hon. Member will feel encouraged—but I hope not too much encouraged.'
>
> Mr Nabarro, rich in a sense that 'my modest researches are now reaping their just reward', seemed to be looking through the arches of the future into a sunlit new day. The Treasury were on the run. Now for next Tuesday when he has baited for the Chancellor some mouse and rat traps that have to pay 30% Purchase Tax.

Then followed door knockers and nut crackers, on 13th February, 1958:

> Mr Gerald Nabarro (Con. Kidderminster) asked the Chancellor of the Exchequer whether he is aware that in view of the fact that a nut cracker is liable to Purchase Tax at 15%, whereas a door knocker over five inches in length is free of tax, there is an increasing practice of supplying nut crackers with screw holes that could theoretically be used as door knockers, with the result that with such modifications these nut crackers became free of tax; and what instructions have been issued to the Customs and Excise staff with regard to this matter?
>
> Mr Jocelyn Simon (Con. Middlesbrough, West), Financial Secretary to the Treasury: No. I do not think Customs staff need instructions to help them distinguish a nut cracker from a door knocker.
>
> Mr Nabarro: Why this invidious distinction between door-knocking nut

crackers and nut-cracking door knockers? This is a perfectly well-known device practised by many factories. This kind of ridicule, which occupied a leading article in *The Times* on February 11th, is bringing the whole of the Purchase Tax schedules into disrepute. Is it not time the matter was drastically overhauled by the abolition of Purchase Tax and the substitution of a sales turnover tax, at a very small uniform rate, over the whole field?
Mr Simon: I am tempted to reply in the words of the conductor Richter, to the second flute at Covent Garden: 'Your damned nonsense can I stand twice or once, but sometimes always, by God, never.'

The following evening at Plymouth, the "Any Questions?" panel, consisting of the late Lady Violet Bonham Carter, Mr Dingle Foot, QC, MP, (now the Rt Hon. Sir Dingle Foot, QC, MP), the late Arthur Street and myself, debated it all over again to the delight of millions of listeners.

From there, I moved on to blinds:

Mr Gerald Nabarro (Con. Kidderminster) asked the Chancellor of the Exchequer why blinds fitted with three-inch circular peepholes were free of tax, while those without peepholes were not.

The Chancellor of the Exchequer, Mr Derick Heathcoat Amory, said a 15% tax was charged on blinds for domestic and office use. "I am advised by the trade that blinds with peepholes are only used in shops."

Mr Nabarro: "Does not this fiscal discrimination encourage the sale of blinds with peepholes, and as the presence of these peepholes is an incitement to offences under the Justices of the Peace Act, 1361—that is the Peeping Tom Act—will you not remove Purchase Tax from all these blinds, so as to give a modicum of comfort to law-abiding citizens?"

Mr Heathcoat Amory: "Your knowledge is encyclopaedic. I had no idea you were an expert on peephole blinds among other things. I will naturally take into account what you say and look up the reference. It is unlikely it is a ground for adopting your proposal."

And from blinds to chin and ankle straps. It was discovered that straps for supporting double chins and caps for projecting ears were taxed at 90% while wrist and ankle supports were tax free. Women's stockings were taxed at 5% but stocking substitute liquid was taxed at 90%. Australian opossum, if undyed and sold in strips not more than nine inches long and not more than one inch wide was exempt from tax, but if it was longer and wider it was subject to the 50% Purchase Tax charged on all other furs. Anomalies of this kind were endless.

On 25th February, 1958, I asked Mr Heathcoat Amory whether the exemption from Purchase Tax already extended to celestes, clavichords, harpsichords, pianofortes, spinets, virginals, pipe organs, electronic organs and reed organs, might be extended to all musical instruments, and how much it would cost. Mr Amory replied: "The cost of exempting musical instruments, excluding gramophones, radio-gramophones and record players, would be rather less than £1m per year. I feel sympathy with your interest in music and I should hate to put any obstacle in the way of your acquisition of a trumpet of your own."

Piggy banks raised the important issue of small savings:

"Pursuing his relentless campaign against Purchase Tax, Mr Nabarro today turned his attention at question time to 'Piggy Banks'."

"He did not obtain any real satisfaction from Mr Heathcoat Amory, the Chancellor of the Exchequer.

"Mr Nabarro pointed out that a pottery piggy bank used for saving was subject to Purchase Tax at 30% as a toy, but if painted with the words 'razor blades' it paid 15% as a salvage receptacle. He asked that all should be relieved of tax to help small savings and salvage of steel.

"Mr Amory replied that the distinction arose out of Parliament's decision that toys should be taxed at a higher rate than domestic hardware. Mr Nabarro could not expect him 'in such a vital matter to anticipate his Budget statement.'

"I do not underestimate the importance of encouraging small savings, particularly when it has a rural bias. If you fill a piggy bank with spare razor blades it is difficult to extract the blades for salvage without permanent damage to the bank!'" (*Daily Telegraph*, 26th March, 1958).

In the Budget on April 15th 1958, there was a crumb of comfort for me over Purchase Tax reform. Mr Harold Wilson, as shadow Chancellor of the Exchequer, had this to say during the Budget debates:[1]

> The Chancellor of the Exchequer can be sure that we shall be ready to make constructive proposals to add to and improve what he is doing about Purchase Tax. He has streamlined and simplified the chaotic Purchase Tax tangle which he inherited from his predecessors and has reduced the seven rates of tax to four. In 1951, when the Lord Privy Seal (Mr R. A. Butler) took over there were only three rates and I should say that my Right Hon. friends managed to achieve that without any help from Kidderminster.

Up to a point Mr Harold Wilson was right. When Labour left office in 1951, there were only three rates of Purchase Tax, but the top rate was 90%. Under the Tories, the number of rates had grown to seven, thus

[1] *Hansard*, 16th April, 1958.

vastly complicating the tax and creating thousands of the anomalies on which many of my questions were based. After my first hundred questions, the Chancellor reduced the number of rates to four in his 1958 Budget, but, more important, he abolished the 90% rate, which applied mainly to cosmetics and the 50% and 10% rates. He retained the 60%, 30%, 15% and 5% rates, the last being on clothes and furniture. It was a step forward and greatly encouraged, I plunged into my second one hundred questions, which came up between the end of December, 1958 and the 1959 Budget in the following April.

Musical instruments have always yielded a rich harvest of anomalies, especially since Mr Butler as Chancellor of the Exchequer abolished Purchase Tax on pianos to save the trade from extinction by German competition. Among my 1959 questions I launched into the 30% Purchase Tax remaining on other musical instruments, as *The Times* reported on 6th February:

> Mr Gerald Nabarro (Con. Kidderminster) asked the Chancellor of the Exchequer whether he was aware that a horn regarded as a wind musical instrument was subject to Purchase Tax at 30%, whereas a musical motor car horn did not attract Purchase Tax even if used occasionally for theatrical performances; what rate of tax was applicable to a hunting horn and to a child's toy trumpet; what particular considerations guided his decisions as to the rate of Purchase Tax applicable to particular horns; and to what extent he was influenced in his decision by the volume or by the melodious quality of the noise produced.
>
> Mr George Chetwynd (Socialist, Stockton-on-Tees): On a point of order, should not the hon. Member declare his interest, since he is always blowing his own trumpet?
>
> Mr Nabarro: Further to that point of order, is an opprobrious comment of that kind, in view of the reference to musical instruments, notably the French horn, in order?
>
> The Speaker: Two horns are mentioned here, the hunting horn and a child's toy trumpet. I do not know that either of these apply to the hon. Member.
>
> The Economic Secretary to the Treasury (Mr F. J. Erroll): The answer is yes; 30%; the tax schedule and common sense. The answer to the last part is 'not at all', but personally I rate quality above volume, even in Parliamentary questions.
>
> Mr Nabarro: Is it not a fact that a motor car horn makes a harsh, raucous and unmelodious noise; and having regard to the fact that a 30% Purchase Tax is placed on musical instruments, including the French horn, which make melodious noises and music and contribute to the arts and culture, why should the Chancellor of the Exchequer be depressing the arts by this vicious impost

MR GERALD NABARRO, MP, Menu Cover for Mr Nabarro's address to the Authors' Club on taxation, 15th March, 1961. Drawing by Norman Mansbridge, Esq.

and encouraging raucous noises by removing the instruments which make them from the Purchase Tax schedule? Is there any equity in that?
Sir Godfrey Nicholson (Con. Farnham): Are not the Treasury on the horns of a dilemma?

The Budget following the second hundred questions was on 7th April, 1959. Mr. Heathcoat Amory said of his new four-rate Purchase Tax, inaugurated in his 1958 Budget:

Certainly a year's experience has revealed no basic defect in the new structure. It is significant that my Hon. Friend the Member for Kidderminster (Mr Nabarro) only found scope this year for 199 questions on this tax.[1]

[1] *Hansard*, 7th April, 1959, col. 54.

"AND DON'T WORRY, MR JONES, THE CHANCELLOR WOULD HAVE TO GET UP EARLIER THAN MR NABARRO TO CATCH ONE OF MY CLIENTS WITH HIS TAX."

Daily Herald, 11th April, 1962.

And in the Budget he took the Purchase Tax off replacement television tubes and commercial vehicle chassis. The latter had been the subject of a long and arduous campaign by Mr Donald Stokes, Sales Manager of Leyland Motors (now Lord Stokes of Leyland) and myself, ever since Sir Stafford Cripps when Chancellor had blundered by putting the Purchase Tax on commercial vehicle chassis in 1950, the only item of industrial capital equipment to pay the tax. But, these Purchase Tax reliefs were worth a significant £81½m in the full year. Things were still coming my

THE BUDGET, 1958 by Cummings, *Daily Express*, 16th April, 1958.

way so at the end of 1959, in readiness for the Budget of 1960, I launched my third one hundred Purchase Tax questions.

Fiscal absurdity abounded:

Thursday 11th *February*, 1960.

Mr Gerald Nabarro (Con. Kidderminster) to ask the Chancellor of the Exchequer whether he proposes to dispose of the anomaly whereby toilet requisites for animals such as forceps, tweezers and brushes are charged to Purchase Tax at half the rate at which similar equipment for human use is charged.

Thursday, 18*th February*, 1960.

Mr Gerald Nabarro (Con. Kidderminster) to ask the Chancellor of the Exchequer what decision he has reached concerning the undertaking he gave on 3rd March, 1959 that he would consider the desirability of introducing equality in the field of Purchase Tax on mouse traps, rat traps and fly swatters, at present applied to such devices only when used for domestic purposes; and whether he will undertake at an early date to ensure that all such devices for the destruction of verminous insects and rodents will be free of tax in the same way as rabbit traps and snares.

Wednesday, 2*nd March*, 1960.

Mr Gerald Nabarro (Con. Kidderminster) to ask the Chancellor of the Exchequer, why babies' plain teething rings consisting solely of a shaped piece of bone, plastic or rubber, are not chargeable to 25% Purchase Tax under group 20 whereas babies' teething beads, which can alternatively be used by the child as a rattle, are subject to such tax; and what would be the effect on the revenue of extending to all babies' teething equipment the same Purchase Tax treatment as is given to plain teething rings.

Wednesday, 9*th March*, 1960.

Mr Gerald Nabarro (Con. Kidderminster) to ask the Chancellor of the Exchequer when he last reviewed the case of bird cage fittings which are chargeable to Purchase Tax at 12½%, and bird cage novelties chargeable at 25%; and when such novelties are regarded as established and normal bird cage fittings and so eligible for the lower rate of tax.

Monday, 21*st March*, 1960.

Mr Gerald Nabarro (Con. Kidderminster) to ask the Chancellor of the Exchequer, why eyelash curlers are liable to Purchase Tax at 50%, whilst eyebrow combs are chargeable at 25%.

After winning a General Election with an overall majority of one hundred in 1959, I expected the Conservatives to bring in a reforming and progressive Budget. We got nothing of the kind. In spite of buoyant economic conditions, the Budget was a "standstill". I refused to vote for its resolutions on 4th April, in spite of a Three-line whip. I tell the story elsewhere.

By 1961 I had spread the base of my questions on tax. Mr Selwyn Lloyd had become Chancellor of the Exchequer in July, 1960 and his first Budget the following April contained no Purchase Tax reliefs. In 1962, Mr Selwyn Lloyd broadened his base and for the first time brought confectionery, soft drinks and ice-cream into the Purchase Tax schedules at a new rate of 15%, to bring in £50m in a full year. Mr Lloyd said:

> As the father of a small daughter, I expect some trouble on the home front myself, but I shall brace myself to meet it.[1]

However, we were now down to four rates—45%, 25%, 15% and 10%. Mr Selwyn Lloyd fell in the "purge" of July, 1962 and Mr Reginald Maudling took over as Chancellor of the Exchequer. On Guy Fawkes Day, 1962, he lowered the rate of Purchase Tax on cars—the biggest revenue yielder of any item liable to Purchase Tax—to only 25%. Two months latei, on 1st January, 1963, Mr Maudling killed the 45% rate, so that there were only three rates left.

I was very pleased because when I started campaigning against Purchase Tax in 1958, there were seven rates, ranging from 90% to 5%. When I finished, just over four years later, there were only three rates—25%, 15% and 10%. Had the Tories reigned a little longer, we should have had a flat rate of say, 12½% of wholesale prices, or 1½d in the shilling: very sensible compared with today's incalculable muddle of 55%, 36⅔%, 22% and 13¾%, which divides exactly into no known currency denominations. Thus Mr Jenkins and the Treasury bedevil traders everywhere. Their arrangements are the deliberate antithesis of fiscal efficiency.

Purchase Tax has always been only one of my topics within the field of taxation reform. By 1963, I had become immersed in another taxation campaign for the abolition of the Landlords Property Tax, or Income Tax Schedule 'A', paid by nearly all the 6,600,000 owner-occupiers of houses.

It was Sir Anthony Eden in the fifties who had coined the phrase "a property-owning democracy" and it had become enshrined in Tory housing policy in the 1955 and 1959 General Election manifestoes. Personally, I had always considered that policy and Schedule "A" tax to be incompatible. How could people be encouraged to own their homes, generally bought on a mortgage in the first instance, if they were then subject to this house-ownership tax, which was not paid by council house dwellers? So the private owner had to subsidise the council house not only through his rates and general taxes but also through this pernicious tax scaled according to the assessed value of his owner-occupied house. All this I decided was militating against the spread of home ownership. Moreover, I learned that less than one in ten owner-occupiers was aware that all the costs of house repairs and maintenance were allowable as a charge

[1] *Hansard*, 9th April, 1962, col. 990.

against the assessment of Schedule "A". Thus the Inland Revenue were collecting millions of pounds annually to which they were not entitled. I wanted to know why lurid notices were not publicly displayed in post offices and elsewhere telling all owner-occupiers to claim what was properly their due. The silence of the Inland Revenue was deafening. The print about maintenance claims for home owners was very, very small indeed.

This was the basis for my campaign against Schedule "A" Tax which I launched in the House on 21st June, 1960. Of course, I was defeated. I divided the House against my own party. The Labour Party abstained. I acted as teller accompanied by Mr Roy Wise, then Conservative Member for Rugby. Seventeen stalwarts came with us and their names ought to be engraved on the porch of every owner-occupied house in Britain, for it was their action which led shortly afterwards to the abolition of this detested tax. Here are the nineteen:

Tellers:	Mr Gerald Nabarro.	(Con. Kidderminster)
(2)	Mr Roy Wise.	(Con. Rugby)
Labour:	Mr William Baxter.	(Stirlingshire, West)
(5)	Mr Fred Bellenger.	(Bassetlaw)
	Mr Francis Noel-Baker.	(Swindon)
	Mr Ellis Smith.	(Stoke-on-Trent, South)
	Mr Percy Wells.	(Faversham)
Liberal:	Mr Clement Davies.	(Montgomery)
(5)	Mr Jo Grimond.	(Orkney and Zetland)
	Mr Arthur Holt.	(Bolton, West)
	Mr Jeremy Thorpe.	(North Devon)
	Mr Donald Wade.	(Huddersfield, West)
Tory:	Mr John Biggs-Davidson.	(Chigwell)
(7)	Mr Anthony Fell.	(Yarmouth)
	Mr Reader Harris.	(Heston & Isleworth)
	Dr Donald Johnson.	(Carlisle)
	Capt. Harry Kerby.	(Arundel & Shoreham)
	Mr John Magginis.	(Armagh)
	Mr Paul Williams.	(Sunderland, South)

I had said in my speech on 21st June: "I have never paid a penny in Schedule 'A' Tax in my life."[1]

[1] *Hansard*, 21st June, 1960, col. 249.

The next morning most of the national newspapers telephoned me with the simple question: "Please tell our readers how to 'fiddle it'." I chose the *Daily Mail* and with the help of their splendid feature writer, Mr Vincent Mulchrone, the following article appeared on 23rd June, 1960:

NOW . . . ABOUT THE TAX ON THIS HOUSE OF MINE

I own a house. It is called the Orchard House, at Broadway, Worcestershire. And I live there happily with my wife and four children.

There are 6,000,000 other owner-occupiers in this country just like me.

And, just like them, I receive every year one of those wretched, buff envelopes from the tax inspector with a demand to pay property tax, dignified by the name 'Schedule A Tax'.

Strange to say, only 600,000 of them, or one in ten, seem to know what is their fiscal right and privilege under the income tax laws, namely to claim as an offset against their annual Schedule A Tax assessment the net cost of any repairs they may carry out to their home in the course of the year, or maintenance of the structure of the building.

The other nine out of every ten, either through ignorance or idleness, or fear of the bureaucracy as characterised by the local tax inspector, fail to make a claim and thus abate their Schedule A charge.

A man is a fool not to maintain his property decently and I believe the overwhelming majority of householders do keep their property up to scratch—quite apart from such things as calling in the plumber when a pipe bursts in frost.

What are these repairs?

I have searched through my own receipted bills for the past few years and the repair charges which the tax inspector has allowed for my Schedule A tax relief.

I do not maintain my property inordinately well. I just keep it in good order. And the list of such repair items is impressive when put together and viewed in retrospect.

Here are some of them:

Unstopping and removing a soil pipe to a W.C. which was broken through age—cost £2.6s.

One of my small children dropped a pot on the lavatory basin and smashed it. The basin is a fixture and the pot is not. So the smashed basin, which cost (including the plumber's labour) £19.5s.9d. to replace went into the claim and was allowed.

Then, the interior of the water tanks had to be repainted with bituminous preservative and the ball valves regulated, and that cost £11.17s.6d.

I have a hard tennis court in the garden. I sometimes play on it on Sunday afternoons, but mostly it is used by my children. The surface became worn last year and a cavity developed which required filling. The bill came in for £8.4s.7d.—which was allowed.

A local electrician was called in to put some new fuses into a switch box to remedy a blackout while I was at Westminster. My wife paid him 15s.6d. and got a bill, which was duly allowed as a repair.

Door handles were repaired for 10s.5d. An oak lintel in the dining-room had to be renewed at a cost of £11.13s.

Window panes repaired, new draught excluders fitted to the doors, chimneys rodded and repaired, some paving stones replaced outside the nursery—all these items have been allowed.

Periodically, rooms have to be repainted, and every good householder paints his house externally every four years—and all these go into my claim as well.

And when the gravel on the garden drives becomes dispersed, the cost of rescarifying and re-gravelling comes into the claim, including the cost of both materials and labour. I do not want you to think that I live in a broken down house in need of a lot of repair. These are routine repairs over a number of years.

And the law provides that the taxpayer may take a five-year average of all repairs and maintenance to his property—strictly excluding any improvements, which are not allowed—and set these repairs off against his assessment. Of course, the wily taxpayer must do a little manipulation of the charges for repairs, seeing to it that the charge which falls into each year ending April 5th, produces a correct average over five years to offset the amount of the assessment.

This may sound very complicated, but I give all taxpayers a little gratuitous advice—for I am not myself a qualified accountant.

They should go to an accountant for advice and pay a small fee, taking with them any receipted bills. Any competent accountant will arrange their affairs for them in such a way as to attract a minimum tax liability—which to any taxpayer is a happy and desirable state of affairs. Be careful how you go about things. You must not do the repairs yourself, because your own labour would not be accepted as a charge for relief. You must have receipted bills.

But, of course, you can employ your wife to do the work or your son or daughter, pay them and get a receipt and put it in your claim.

If all the 6,000,000 home owners in this country did as I advise, then the Inland Revenue would be submerged in paper, and very quickly their lamentations would find their way to the ears of a reluctant Chancellor of the Exchequer, who might then view with a little greater benevolence my claim in the House of Commons on Tuesday that Schedule A tax is illicit.

If all these 6,000,000 house owners knew the ropes and claimed their just tax

> deserts, the Chancellor of the Exchequer might well find himself without any revenue at all from this iniquitous levy.
>
> Finally, a look at the politics of it all. The Tory Party, if they stand for anything, believe in a property-owning democracy. Their ticket, in four General Elections since 1950, has been to encourage ordinary people to own their own homes. And, let it be said, they have done extremely well.
>
> They have swept away building controls, lightened stamp duties on conveyances, reduced the standard rate of income tax from 9s.6d. to 7s.9d. in the pound, and arranged for loans up to nearly 100% on mortgages.
>
> It is the more surprising, therefore, that the Tory Government does not unequivocally accept the need for yet further encouragement of thrift and home ownership by putting an end to the penal system of collecting tax on the notional rent of a house which the owner himself occupies.

This article gave the matter a thorough public airing. By 1961 Mr Selwyn Lloyd was Chancellor of the Exchequer and during the Committee stage of the Finance Bill, I said that Schedule "A" was "fiscal prostitution"; that the Chancellor was "living immorally on the earnings of Schedule 'A' owner-occupiers" and that he "ought to be appropriately ashamed of himself for doing so". Mr Selwyn Lloyd's reply was pretty sympathetic but I insisted again on dividing the House, and at 2.7 a.m. on 21st June, 1961 the Division took place, with the Labour Party *again* abstaining. The Tories, of course, backed the Chancellor and seventeen members followed me:

Tellers: (2)	Mr Gerald Nabarro	(Con. Kidderminster)
	Mr Donald Wade	(Liberal Huddersfield)
Labour: (1)	Mr Victor Yates	(Birmingham, Ladywood)
Liberal: (2)	Mr Jo Grimond	(Orkney & Zetland)
	Mr Arthur Holt	(Bolton, West)
Tory: (12)	Wing Cdr Eric Bullus	(Wembley, North)
	Sq. Ldr Frederick Burden	(Gillingham)
	Mr Leonard Cleaver	(Birmingham, Yardley)
	Mr Harold Gurden	(Birmingham, Selly Oak)
	Mr Philip Hocking	(Coventry, South)
	Mr John Hollingworth	(Birmingham, All Saints)
	Mr T. L. Iremonger	(Ilford, North)
	Mr Gordon Matthews	(Meriden)
	Mr Fergus Montgomery	(Newcastle, East)

Mr Graham Page	(Crosby)
Mr John Talbot	(Brierley Hill)
Mr Roy Wise	(Rugby)

Rather a mixed bag, thirteen Tories, three Liberals and one Labour; but not too bad, considering that the time was after two o'clock in the morning; and the Tory Whips could only muster 110 to vote us down. Publicity mounted, as did the maintenance claims on the Revenue. Owner-occupiers were beginning to assert their rights. Eventually the Revenue became saturated, and groaning, deplored my ungentlemanly behaviour. Owner-occupiers everywhere accepted my advice and submitted maintenance claims for everything down to the humblest nail, screw and washer.

Next year, 1962, in his Budget statement, Mr Selwyn Lloyd announced that he would legislate the following year for the abolition of Income Tax Schedule "A" for nearly 7,000,000 owner-occupiers. He was denied the opportunity of making the announcement himself to abolish Schedule "A" but his successor, Mr Reginald Maudling, said in his Budget statement on 3rd April, 1963:

> I propose now to abolish Schedule 'A' altogether. In the case of owner-occupiers of residential property, I propose that Schedule 'A' shall be brought to an end in one operation this year. They will not be asked to pay again.[1]

And so it was. The detested tax on owner-occupied houses disappeared before the Tories left office in 1964. My campaign, start to finish, had occupied just above three years. It had involved me, as with the Purchase Tax campaign, in much fierce controversy with my Party leaders. Tories in the House liked it little: home owners in the country loved it. To this day, ordinary men and women walk up to me in the street and thank me. It was all very satisfactory and the Labour Party's abstention in the voting makes clear for all to see, their antipathy to home ownership. The contemporary manifestation of this antipathy is their opposition both on Local Councils and in the Commons to the Tory policy of selling council houses, with mortgages, to sitting tenants.

[1] *Hansard*, 3rd April, 1963, col. 457.

8. *William Barkley, Francis Boyd and Gerald Nabarro*

NO ONE has underlined the power of the back-bencher to stir up turgid Ministers or deflate pompous bureaucrats more than two great journalists of the post-war years. William Barkley of the *Daily Express* (he died in 1968 loved by politicians of all parties), and Francis Boyd of the *Guardian* (still with us in the Lobby). Both have helped me over the years and as a tribute to them and because it confirms what a back-bencher can do, I reproduce here, verbatim, newspaper reports by both of them.

The most appropriate tribute and expression of admiration felt by Members of Parliament for William Barkley, was voiced by the present Speaker of the House of Commons, Dr Rt Hon. Horace King, when he said that he was proud to testify on behalf of us all that William Barkley "served democracy, served Britain, with industry, with devotion, with fearlessness, with kindliness and with utter integrity". This was part of Mr Speaker's address at the Memorial Service to William Barkley at St Margaret's, Westminster on 13th November, 1968. It is such a splendid appraisal both of the man and his profession, that it deserves to be reproduced:

> I am honoured that the Parliamentary Press Gallery and Mrs Barkley have invited me to join in this tribute to a great British Parliamentarian.
>
> I use the word Parliamentarian advisedly. Parliament is 630 Members of Parliament. Parliament is the Clerk of the House and his highly skilled staff.

Parliament is the humblest policeman who stands on duty and who must know every Member. Parliament is the team of *Hansard* reporters faithfully setting down every word—immortal and not so immortal—uttered in the Chamber. And Parliament is in its own special way the Press Gallery—the men and women who, day by day, convey the Parliamentary scene to the British public, selecting, commentating, according to the exigences of space, the policy of their papers and their own idiosyncrasies, but sharing with the Prime Minister and the Leader of the Opposition the task of preserving, not a party policy, but Parliamentary democracy itself.

Let me then begin by paying on behalf of the House and on behalf of the Press Gallery a warm and sincere tribute to William Barkley who maintained, and indeed helped to enhance, the finest traditions of Parliamentary reporting. Not for him the urbanity of Lucy or the objectivity which some of you here perhaps display in your morning column. He was a fighting man, who wrote what the Western films call 'fighting words'. But, strangely enough, although he wrote for the *Daily Express*, not a party-man. If he belonged to any party—it was the Barkley Party.

Here is a quote:

'If they get Socialism from the Socialists and Socialism from the Tories, what hope have they?'

Or this one:

'I like Ernest Bevin. His tongue is rough. He is at least cut out of old English oak, with all the knots and gnarls. . . . You know where you are with a man like that.'

And you knew where you were with a man like William Barkley.

He wanted lower income tax and no State ownership. But beyond that he wanted and he loved free Britain.

I thought that today I might ask him to speak to you some of the words he loved to write. 'Dictated' (these are his words) 'on the telephone to relays of men who take it down as fast as I can speak, in seven copies on silent type-writers'. I think that few people realise the enormous strain and speeds under which Parliamentary journalists work.

Here then is a great Parliamentary reporter speaking:

'The most splendid moment in my memory is of Mr Churchill defeated in his hour of supreme triumph, making his first speech in Opposition last year. He found it in him to say that it was the glory of the Parliamentary institution that it could strike down the most powerful people if it chose. His theme was to trust the people, however much he may have thought them mistaken. That Churchill incident transcends for me all high moments of debate or decision or passion or ceremony.

'It is to Parliament in its day to day vigilance that the people look for their protection.

'If it cherishes the individual then the House of Commons will be doing much, even when it may appear to be doing little.'

On his simple political programme in a few pungent words:

'Soak the speculator. Back the earner. That seems a good line even if it cuts out a bit of the song and dance in our life and emphasises reward for merit only.'

Reward for merit only was surely the dream of political philosophers from Plato and Aristotle to the man who wrote through the night for the *Express*. He was a good hater. He hated the planners, and parodied Swinburne when he wrote:

'Thou hast conquered, O ruddy Teuton
Old England grows planned at thy breath'

Barkley hit hard. Here are a few headlines:

'Wanted. More ladders for the young men'
'If you can't be sacked will you still work hard?'
'Cut the PAYE and soak the speculator'
'I won't sell my conscience for a piece of Gold'

I seek the Higher things—which headed an article on kindliness, in which he wrote 'Kindliness to one another is the essence of the congenial atmosphere. If we once lost the qualities of toleration and mutual appreciation, we might be a wealthy nation again, but never a happy one'.

For William Barkley was a kindly man. A fair man. He hit hard, but never below the belt. When he attacked persons the attack was political not personal. He wore his heart on his sleeve, and it was a great British heart. He told us with pride of the birth of his son in 1935. He told us of temporary deafness in the same year, and of the joy of regaining his hearing.

He wrote, 'Your ear drums are about the size of your finger nails, or less. But with them you can hear the music of the spheres'—words sadly prophetic of the man as he grew older and sat in his favourite corner seat in the Gallery with a hand cupped to his ear.

He was incorruptible and prided himself on this.

He wrote:

'Relations between the Politicians and the Press should always be bad. That is a good working formula.' He at once commented on this profound halftruth, 'Like all maxims it is not of universal application.'

He was stating his conviction that it would be a bad day for Britain if reporters were under the thumb of politicians.

He was proud of his profession, and boasted that he did his job without fear or favour, 'acting with an almost mystical sense of responsibility to the readership, and making immense exertions in the cause of accuracy.'

This conception of the high nature of his office he lived up to, and in doing so set an example to his younger colleagues and to all of us.

Years ago, William Barkley and I became friends in Parliament and outside it. We shared a common hobby—a desire to reform English orthography, under the leadership of a distinguished friend, Sir James Pitman. Mr Speaker can no longer commend any reform—political or linguistic. But we enjoyed many precious hours of fellowship in this scholarly field and watched with common enthusiasm the progress of Pitman's ITA.

I know how his colleagues in the Press Gallery loved and esteemed Mr Barkley, as he became with advancing years, a father figure. When the Gallery in 1947 said good-bye to an old colleague, Mr William Burton, they inscribed his presentation plate with the words 'To our wellbeloved friend and counsellor.' And Barkley wrote that day, with kindly panache:

'Kindliness and mutual helpfulness abound where I have lived in these last twenty years in the home of the thoroughbreds of Fleet Street, the Press Gallery, the Reporters Gallery of the House of Commons, Westminster, London, England.'

That kindliness William Barkley himself helped to create, helped to foster, helped to extend.

Democracy is assailed today almost as never before. We owe its preservation to men who gave limb or sight or even life that we might have a free Parliament and a free Press.

Whether it is to continue depends on the quality of free men—among them Parliamentarians of all kinds, Members and reporters.

Today I am proud to testify on behalf of all of you that William Barkley served democracy, served Britain with industry, with devotion, with fearlessness, with kindliness and with utter integrity.

Let the last words today be from the author for whom we shared a common love.

'His life was gentle
And the elements so mixed in him
That nature might stand up
And say to all the world
This was a man!'

Here, then, is an example of the William Barkley Mr Speaker was talking about, taken from the *Daily Express* of 22nd June, 1960:

NABARRO: I COULD BE CHANCELLOR

Or Premier? M.P.s ask

In the words of an old soldier who wrote: 'Dear Mother, I am sending you a ha'penny, but not today,' owner-occupiers may hope to get Schedule 'A' income tax reduced or abolished next year. But not this year, said Mr

Heathcoat Amory, the Chancellor of the Exchequer, in the Commons last night on his Budget Bill, because it would cost the Treasury £45,000,000 a year.

But Mr Harold Wilson (Lab. Huyton) perked up and said: 'But according to the Press you will not be here next year. You tell us that you may think of this, but we have not heard who will replace you. It may be Mr Gerald Nabarro.'

Mr Nabarro, brown from the sun at Cap Ferrat, and thumbing scarlet braces—retorted: 'I have always been ready to take that position.'

Mr Wilson: 'I am aware that you have realised this possibility, but few of us have.'

Mr Austen Albu (Lab. Edmonton): 'There is a leaflet going around saying, "Nabarro for Premier".'

Mr Nabarro: 'One thing is perfectly certain: that whoever succeeds Mr Heathcoat Amory, it will not be you'—with a finger stabbing at the very heart of Mr Wilson.

Mr Wilson turned the point of this attack in the most subtle way by saying: 'As for the suggestion of Mr Nabarro for Premier, I am one of those who hold the view that it would be an improvement.'

Imagined scowl on the face of Mr Harold Macmillan, who holds that position.

It appears to be accepted in the Commons that Mr Heathcoat Amory will get out as fast as he can once the Finance Bill embodying this year's standstill Budget is passed. As Chancellor of the Exchequer, he is largely rubbed out.

Tories massed on their back benches yesterday demanding abolition of Schedule 'A' tax on owner occupiers, as one party conference after another has urged.

It was a Labour MP, Mr John Cronin (Loughborough) who opened an attack on the wrongfulness of taxing a man for owning a house.

He moved that owner-occupiers should be exempted from tax up to £15 a year. This was defeated by 259 votes to 195.

Mr Nabarro had a different proposal—that Schedule 'A' be abolished altogether on owner-occupiers.

He denounced this tax as illicit inasmuch as no well-advised owner-occupier would ever pay a penny of it. He claimed all he could on the upkeep of his property.

Mr Jack Diamond (Lab. Gloucester) interrupted: 'That is unfair. Many people get the statutory allowance for maintenance although they do not spend that amount.'

Mr Nabarro: 'You well know that there is nothing exceptional about me'—snapping his scarlet braces twice. 'I have never paid a penny of Schedule 'A' tax in my life.

'I maintain my property in such a way as to make quite certain that I do not pay Schedule "A".'
A Labour MP: 'Tax dodger'.
Mr Nabarro, striking one hand against the other: 'It is not being a tax-dodger. It is my right. That is what the law says.'
Mr Heathcoat Amory said that this issue was all very complicated. 'The decision is not an easy one.
'To abolish this tax would be to discriminate against the man who rents a house.' (Protests from Tories.)
'There may be arguments in favour of that discrimination.' (Loud cheers from the Tories.)
It finished with the Chancellor saying that if it came to a balance of arguments he would favour discrimination for owner-occupiers against renters.
'But not this year.'
Mr Wilson gestured with both arms to Tories to get up and cheer, but they were silent.
'It must be a profound disappointment to you,' he said.

Next Year came the announcement of cancellation and in 1962, the end of the hated Income Tax Schedule "A" Tax for owner occupiers.

Comparable to William Barkley in journalistic skills, vivacity and parliamentary and political erudition is Francis Boyd of the *Guardian*. In his column "Aspects of Politics" he wrote under the title of "Candid Friend".

Mr Gerald Nabarro, the Member for Kidderminster, is making himself one of the most valuable back-benchers in the present Parliament. He can blow away, in a sentence or two, the clouds of words which Ministers generate to conceal plain facts. One of these plain facts is the variety of treatment which individual taxpayers receive under the law, as it now stands.

The Government announces solemnly that it cannot afford to abolish Schedule 'A' tax on property: Mr Nabarro says that he so manages his own affairs that he never pays Schedule 'A'.

The Government announces solemnly that club subscriptions cannot be treated as business expenses and relieved of tax: Mr Nabarro says that his subscription to the Carlton is allowed as an expense because as a politician he must have good political talk. (I am reminded of a confession once made to me by the late J. W. Dulanty, High Commissioner and later Ambassador from the Irish Free State and later Republic. He said he had chosen as his London club the one place in which he was certain never to be asked: 'When will Ireland rejoin the Commonwealth?')

Mr Nabarro is a sound Conservative. He is a convinced private enterprise

Daily Mirror, 1st January, 1963.

Worcester Evening News and Times, 19th January, 1965.

News of the World, 10th October, 1965.

Dundee Evening Telegraph, 1st April, 1966.
GENERAL ELECTION RESULTS.

man. He is not shy of welcoming the Chancellor's relief to surtax payers. He represents a large body of opinion among the Conservative rank and file. And he says what he thinks and boasts of what he does. He is very much in the position of Disraeli when that great man began his attack on Peel for abandoning the Corn Laws. Disraeli, addressing Peel in the House, said (1945):

A great many of his supporters were elected on the hustings under very different circumstances to those under which they sit here. . . . I admit that

I for one was sent here by my constituents to sit on this side. He may object to me, although I think he has no great occasion to object that I am sometimes in a different lobby to himself; but I was sent to swell a Tory majority —to support a Tory Ministry. Whether a Tory Ministry exists or not I do not pretend to decide: but I am bound to believe that the Tory majority still remains and therefore I do not think that it is the majority that should cross the House, but only the Ministry.

Mr Nabarro must feel that the present Chancellor, Mr Selwyn Lloyd, is learning the secrets of Conservative finance quite creditably and will have mastered them if, in addition to his surtax relief, he stops wage claims. Yet there is an ambiguity in the Government's presentation of its case that obscures the Government's goal. Mr Nabarro is not yet content with the Ministerial treatment of purchase tax and the financing of nationalised industries.

Mr Lloyd himself boasts of his own enterprise in putting into the hands of the Chancellor two new economic regulators. They may well be needed: but what would he have said if a Labour Government had taken such vast new power? Labour, for certain, will not forget what a Conservative Chancellor can get away with.

It is a pity that Mr Nabarro's candour has been limited so far to financial and economic affairs, and that no student of foreign affairs on the Conservative side, with the possible exception of Lord Lambton, has matched his power to pierce the wordiness of the Government. This situation is a challenge to Opposition members, too, but in the nature of the party battle they cannot shock the Government so much as a critic from the Government benches who is expressing widely held Conservative opinion.

The *Guardian*, 11th January, 1961.

So much for the backbencher in the British House of Commons. I believe in him. He is not suborned. And I consider William Barkley of the *Daily Express* and Francis Boyd of the *Guardian* two of the outstanding Parliamentary journalists of the last two decades.

9. *"Floreat Etona"*

The Right Honourable Sir Anthony Eden, KG, MC, MP, 60th Rifleman and diplomat to his elegant finger tips, thrice Her Majesty's Principal Secretary of State for Foreign Affairs, became Prime Minister and First Lord of the Treasury, in succession to Sir Winston Churchill, in April 1955. Debonair, splendidly good looking, member of Parliament for Warwick and Leamington since 1923, darling of Tory ladies and married to Clarissa Spencer-Churchill; almost universally admired, here in Britain and throughout the western world, Sir Anthony had every obvious attribute of a successful Prime Minister. Moreover, he was seen to be the epitome of honour and chivalry.

He had resigned as Foreign Secretary in Neville Chamberlain's Government in 1938 rather than appease the fascist dictators Hitler, Mussolini and Franco. On the outbreak of war, being out of office, he had immediately returned to his Regiment but was very soon recalled to political office and served again as Foreign Secretary under Churchill. His years at the Foreign Office—1935–38, 1940–45 and 1951–55—probably longer than those of any other incumbent in history, gave him unique experience and stature in international affairs. At any rate, they provided the foundation of his three unique volumes of memoirs: "Full Circle", "The Reckoning" and "Facing the Dictators".

I loved him as statesman, as politician, as friend, soldier and colleague. I hated the manner of his departure at the height of the Suez crisis, chronically sick and reviled by many who should have been his friends.

Some years later I fought a long and bloody libel action on his account, defending myself against Mr Randolph Churchill. When I lost, Anthony Eden, who later became the Earl of Avon, sent me this message which I treasure:

Fyfield Manor,
Pewsey,
Wiltshire.
29th October, 1960.

Dear Nabarro,

I want to write to you these few lines to say how sorry I was to read the result of your case. My wife and I are most grateful to you for your good wishes.

Yours sincerely,

ANTHONY EDEN.

Of course, he filled his administration with Etonians. His preference was always for the upper crust, the ultra "U" members of his party, and he taught his successor, Harold Macmillan, how to do it. When the Tories were returned to power at the General Election on 26th May 1955 with a majority of sixty, 56% of Sir Anthony's Cabinet were old Etonians, that is to say ten out of eighteen members, as follows:

Prime Minister and First Lord of the Treasury	Sir Anthony Eden, KG, MC, MP	Eton and Christ Church
Lord President of the Council	Marquess of Salisbury, KG	Eton and Christ Church
Secretary of State for Foreign Affairs	Mr Harold Macmillan, MP	Eton and Balliol
Secretary of State for Scotland	Mr James Stuart, MVO, MC, MP	Eton
Lord Privy Seal	Mr Harry Crookshank, CH, MP	Eton and Magdalen
Secretary for Commonwealth Relations	Earl of Home	Eton and Christ Church
Minister of Housing and Local Government	Mr Duncan Sandys, MP	Eton and Magdalen
President of the Board of Trade	Mr Peter Thorneycroft, MP	Eton and RMA Woolwich
Minister of Agriculture, Fisheries and Food	Mr Derick Heathcoat Amory, MP	Eton and Christ Church
Minister of Pensions and National Insurance	Mr Osbert Peake, MP	Eton and Christ Church

The best Harold Macmillan could do seven years later was eight old Etonians out of a Cabinet of twenty-one, that is 38%; but in both Cabinets the hard core were members of the Cecil-Churchill-Cavendish clan.

Gravy for Etonians: thin gruel and skilly otherwise. The rest of the Eden Cabinet, with the exception of the Mancunian Lord Woolton, were almost as well born. Woolton was already seventy-two and had an impressive record first as Minister of Food and then as Minister for Reconstruction in Sir Winston Churchill's war-winning coalition; later he was the best party chairman the Tories ever had, from 1946 to 1955. But he was rather too old for heavy ministerial service. There was not a single industrialist, business man or leader of trade in the higher echelons of Eden's Ministry.

It took seven years before Mr Harold Macmillan recognised this and made sweeping changes in what I dubbed the "Westminster abattoir" of July 1962. By then it was too late, and the Tories were firmly established in the popular mind as a party dominated by blue-bloods and run by aristocratic patronage. It made the electorate all the more receptive to the bunkum of Mr Harold Wilson in 1964, with his "white heat of technological revolution". Mr Edward Heath has been warned.

Sir Beverley Baxter, a former Editor-in-Chief of the *Daily Express* and Tory MP, first for Wood Green, 1935–50 and then for Southgate, 1950–64, a total of twenty-nine years in the House of Commons, put it all fairly and squarely in a contribution to the magazine *Everybody's* on 25th June, 1955, one month after Sir Anthony Eden's great General Election victory:

IS THERE ONLY ONE OLD SCHOOL TIE?

It is not unnatural that some eyebrows were raised and that some ink-wells erupted when Sir Anthony Eden announced the personnel of his first Government. Not only was Waterloo won on the playing fields of Eton but so was the struggle for office in the present administration at Westminster.

Floreat Etona! As for Harrow there is now a special significance in its school song: 'Forty years on'.

Personally, I have the greatest respect for politicians who take on ministerial tasks. By comparison with commercial life they are badly paid, they have no security of tenure, and they must defend themselves daily at Question time—unlike company chairmen who only have to defend themselves once a year. They are sniped at by the political commentators, hammered in the leader columns and seldom flattered by the gossip writers. All of which is to the good. Except at election time we do not want too much fraternising or unity of spirit between Parliament and the Press.

What then is the case against the Etonians? Kipling expressed it in sardonic terms when he said that some day we would lose India because it would be Stinky's turn. The inference was that a Prime Minister, at a difficult moment, might send his old school fag to be Viceroy because he was due for promotion —and not because he was the best available choice.

Certainly the public school engenders the team spirit and only a cynic would deny its value. But there are times in war and peace when team spirit can be a form of timidity. The courageous man is he who defies his colleagues if the issue is more important than the preservation of unity.

I recall that exciting day in February 1938 when Foreign Secretary Anthony Eden and his Parliamentary Under-Secretary, Lord Salisbury, came to the House of Commons to resign. Instead of speaking from their accustomed place at the Front Bench they sat three rows back as private members.

Eden made no attempt to dramatise the situation nor render the position of Prime Minister Chamberlain more difficult. Instead he paid tribute to Chamberlain's sincerity and tireless energy but said that he could no longer support the appeasement of the dictators.

Lord Salisbury, although a Junior Minister, spoke as we would expect from the titular head of the Cecil family. So persistent has been the influence of that family from the sixteenth century onwards that MPs often used to refer to the House of Commons as the Hotel Cecil.

It is of no importance, but I was (and still am) a supporter of Chamberlain's policy, but I respected the sincerity of the two Etonians who had the courage to resign. The sneer that they were getting out from under, and thus assuring their political future, was utterly unfair. Chamberlain had an enormous majority and if he had saved the peace, Salisbury and Eden would have walked in the wilderness.

But what about the present old Etonian who presides over the fortunes and misfortunes of the Foreign Office? Is not Harold Macmillan a man who has relentlessly backed the winner and now earned his reward?

I met him first in unusual circumstances in 1918. Somewhat unnecessarily I was invalided from France as a junior officer and eventually ended up late at night in a bedroom in Lord Bathurst's house in Belgrave Square, which had been taken over as an officers' nursing home.

It was completely dark, about midnight, but I could sense that there were others in the room. Then just as I was falling asleep I heard a strange, calm and slightly affected voice say: 'Have you any ideas on Parliamentary reform?'

As no one answered I said: 'Are you speaking to me?'

'You will do,' was the languid response. Then after about two minutes silence the voice said: 'The only chap who ever had a workable plan for Parliamentary reform was Guy Fawkes.'

Yes, it was Harold Macmillan who, while serving with the Brigade, had been cruelly wounded. He suffered greatly and he never complained.

But when he became a Tory MP in later years was he not just another hide-bound Etonian traditionalist whose only concern was to maintain esprit de corps and prosper under it?

The very contrary was the case. He was an out and out radical who made war on privilege and became such a nuisance that finally he renounced the party Whip. This was in the piping days of peace, of course, when he saw that great reforms were necessary to bring about better conditions for the people.

In fact not until war came again was he given office, and then he did a grand job in North Africa. Nor can we forget his services as Minister of Housing in the 1951 Tory Government.

'Any fool could build 300,000 houses in a year,' said Aneurin Bevan.

'I know one fool who didn't,' drawled Macmillan. It sounded exactly like that strange night in the nursing home.

Since we are being entirely realistic in this article I admit that part of the technique of Parliamentary life is to choose your moment to rebel. But I claim that in the case of Eden and Macmillan the motives were not only sincere but that both of them risked their future in politics.

But is it not a fact that the Old Etonians stick together closer than brothers? Well, what about Captain Harry Crookshank (Leader of the House in the last Parliament) who also served with the Guards in the first war and was buried alive by a shell burst in the front line trenches?

Now he is probably to be buried alive in the House of Lords. There is no office for Harry. Yet, after a doubtful start, he was an admirable leader of the House. But, as I say, he has been dropped from the first eleven. On the other hand Duncan Sandys, who not only married Sir Winston Churchill's daughter but became a successful Minister of Supply, was continued in that office when the Eden Government was announced.

By his marriage into the Churchill family Duncan might be said to have dallied with Harrow, but actually he is an Etonian.

Which seems an opportune moment to ask what has gone wrong with Harrow? It cannot be said that famous school on the hill is no breeding ground of politicians. Any school that can produce Winston Churchill, Stanley Baldwin and Pandit Nehru must have high claims to political fecundity. Yet Harrow has knocked up a very small score in the match against Eton at Westminster.

Well—the Prime Minister is the boss and he has chosen as his ministers men of ability and experience. And there is no reason, if he thinks they were the best available, that they should have been passed over merely because they wore a morning coat and topper at school in their early teens.

Yet with respect I suggest that if Sir Anthony carries out a reshuffle of Ministers before Parliament adjourns for the long summer vacation, he should consider three or four Tory MPs who would add strength to any Ministry.

For example take Gerald Nabarro who sits for Kidderminster. He is a tough bird and has a voice that booms o'er Eden, to say nothing of Attlee. He was educated at an LCC school and understands fuel, power and carpets. In fact he has a first class brain and possesses the common touch despite his habit of wearing a topper in Parliament on State occasions. I'm all for the Nabarro Boy.

Then think what an admirable Secretary of State for Scotland Sir Robert Boothby would make. Bob, although an Etonian, is a romantic idealist. His 'herring folk', whom he represents in Parliament, adore him. He is a brilliant debater and he would fight for Scotland with no mercy for the Sassenach.

And let Sir William Darling be the chief Scottish Under-Secretary. Darling was a splendid Lord Provost of Edinburgh and he commands the ear of the House when he addresses it.

But there—I am being seduced from my original theme which is: 'Are there too many Etonians in the Government?' For the health of Parliamentary democracy there are probably more than are strictly necessary, but if the Prime Minister believes that those whom he has appointed to office are better than the available material on the back benches then he should stick to his team, or even replace his present Etonians with better Etonians if they turn up.

Thus I have performed the considerable feat of supporting the Prime Minister's appointments with absolute loyalty while suggesting that the introduction of some rougher individualists might add strength to the brew.

Therefore in a climax of metaphor I now declare the rest is silence.

Rougher individualists, indeed. We are still looking for them, 15 years later.

10. *The Journey from Navarre*

The Right Honourable John Freeman, MBE, has had a varied and highly distinguished career. Indeed, a model career, characterised by extraordinary diversity.

Born in 1915, and educated at Westminster and Brasenose College, Oxford, he had hardly embarked on his chosen career as an advertising consultant before the Second World War enveloped him. He joined the army, saw much active service and in 1945 was demobilised as a Major in the Rifle Brigade. He immediately entered Parliament as Socialist member for Watford, Hertfordshire. After several junior Ministerial appointments, he resigned from Mr Attlee's second administration in the Spring of 1951, along with Mr Aneurin Bevan and Mr Harold Wilson, preferring welfare to arms for the Korean war. In October 1951, after only six years, he left Parliament and Watford reverted to a Tory seat, which it remained for the next thirteen years.

John Freeman then became one of the most illustrious televisers and broadcasters of our day. Among many well known programmes, his "Face to Face" on BBC Television and the radio equivalent "Frankly Speaking", became top ratings of their time. On "Any Questions?" he was superb. Personally, I reckon one of the best radio programmes I have ever participated in, owed its spark and inspiration to Freeman. It was in January, 1963 from Berkeley Nuclear Power Station in Gloucestershire, with Miss Joyce Grenfell and Professor Bronowski and, of course, Freddy Grisewood as Question-Master. At the same time, and throughout the fourteen years before he took to professional diplomacy, Freeman was on the editorial board of the leading Socialist and Fabian weekly, the *New Statesman*, as assistant Editor, then as deputy Editor and finally, from 1961–1965, as Editor. Throughout, he had a fine and close intellectual affinity with Mr Harold Wilson. Bevan, Wilson and Freeman were the foundation of the Bevanite schism that kept Labour out of office for thirteen years after Mr Attlee ran for cover in October 1951.

Now, Mr Harold Wilson never forgets his friends and accomplices. Within months of becoming Prime Minister, Mr Wilson had plucked Mr John Freeman from the Editor's chair of the *New Statesman* and appointed him British High Commissioner in New Delhi. Personally, I had thought that Mr Wilson would give him a Life Peerage and a senior post in the Government. The Indians liked Freeman's brand of Socialism and he was a great success in New Delhi. Much more perilous was the appointment that followed in 1968, as British Ambassador in Washington, after all the snide and wounding things that Freeman had said about the new Republican President, Mr Richard Nixon when, with every medium of mass communication at his disposal, Freeman had wallowed in Socialism.

I do not myself think that Freeman will fail to make the grade in Washington. Given a Labour Government in Britain, he is the best available man for the job. Freeman may well become to President Nixon what David Ormsby-Gore, now Lord Harlech, was to President John Kennedy. Anyway, I believe that Freeman is big and statesmanlike enough to sublimate political prejudice to professional diplomacy.

As a journalist, Freeman was superb. I count this article which appeared in the *New Statesman* on 25th July, 1959 and attributed to the then Deputy Editor, as one of the best political profiles I have ever read. I should be extra critical, for the profile is of me. So assiduous was Freeman's researching that he knew more about me than I knew about myself:

> From Navarre to Kidderminster is a long Sephardic journey which has taken four and a half centuries. Some of the Nabarros have appeared in that time, no less distinguished as doctors and jurists than once they were in Spain. Mr Gerald Nabarro, still the bearer of the orthodox family name of Nunes, has crossed over to a different tradition. If Disraeli seemed an ibis who had lost the way in the Buckinghamshire woods, Mr Nabarro seems rather like a rhinoceros who, having wandered into a Tory Business Men's Club, has successfully adopted himself as its pet.
>
> The trumpeting voice, the trampling manner, the tough hide and the horn

permanently cocked, might at their first appearance seem as rebarbative to Conservatives as to Socialists. (Was it an ostentatious tribute to the acquisitive society or to Number One that made him register his car as NAB 1? Or was it a piece of unconscious atavism? For 'nabi' means 'prophet'—see Proust's frequent references to the artistic group 'les Nabis' and King Edward VII's well-known remark, 'quelques-uns de mes meilleurs amis sont des nabis'.) But Mr Nabarro has both stamina and intelligence, two qualities which in time have won the hesitant respect first of his opponents and then of his colleagues. There have been few since 1945 in the House of Commons who can think so effectively on their feet as this self-made business man, party-machine man and churchman.

Orphaned at an early age, Mr Nabarro began life in conditions which were more arduous than those of most of Labour's front bench. From his LCC elementary school, he went to sea for nearly a year before enlisting in the regular army. After nine years of soldiering, he retired with the rank of staff-sergeant-instructor and went into industry, still in the non-commissioned ranks, as a charge-hand and foreman. With the war, Mr Nabarro, now a 25-year-old officer, entered a new heritage. The Navarrese tradition belonged to history; Nabarro, the New Man in the opportunity democracy, would make his ancestors descend from him.

In 1943, he married the elder daughter, an ATS officer, of Colonel B. B. von B. im Thurn, DSO, MC, of Dawn House, Winchester and laid the foundation of a happy family life in Broadway, Worcestershire—which he has enriched with two sons, one now at Harrow, and two daughters. By 1945, he was a Parliamentary candidate, by 1946, chairman of the West Midlands Young Conservatives, by 1950, a director of companies and the member for Kidderminster. Mr Nabarro had arrived.

With his exaggerated moustaches, his popping eyes and his megaphonal voice, he seemed all set at first to join the parliamentary eccentrics. To the Socialists, he seemed wholly bogus. They knew where they were with a Tory gentleman who had been to Eton and Magdalen; or with a Tory trade unionist like Mr Mawby. But Mr Nabarro was obviously neither one nor the other, although he wore a Bevis Marks top hat on Budget Day and chose to make speeches on industry. When Mr Nabarro, who really has a very loud voice, shouted 'Utterly ridiculous' or 'Incomprehensible' or 'Bloody non-sense!' or 'Another instance of Socialist extravagance'—remarks which in report of others might be thought to be remarks-we-doubt-were-ever-shouted—the Opposition either laughed, invited him to shut up, or, probing his armour with its bludgeon, used to call out: 'Nabarro-boy!' Many a time was the former Tory Chief Whip's pallid face seen to flush as Mr Nabarro rushed thundering, uninvited, into some sophisticated exchange between the Prime Minister and the leader of the Opposition.

THE JOURNEY FROM NAVARRE. A profile in the *New Statesman*, 25th July, 1959.

Our hero remained unabashed by the scowls in front of him or the frowns behind him. Within a few months of his arrival at Westminster, he had achieved his first objective. He had been noticed. From the centre of their nepotic circle, Prime Ministers might choose to overlook him; but he couldn't be ignored. An unhappy incident in 1956 when he was stopped for speeding by a policeman whom he called half-witted and insolent, and who alleged that Mr Nabarro, after knocking his note-book out of his hand, 'seemed to be impressing upon everyone his own importance', resulted in a fine of £10 for careless driving and £2 for exceeding the speed limit. This was more than a blow to a man who belonged to 20 automobile clubs and carried 21 badges on the radiator of his car. It suggested—the worst offence in a Member of Parliament—that he was throwing his weight about.

But Mr Nabarro is a quick learner. When a National Coal Board official described him a little later as 'a carpet-bagger and political hoodlum', he airily waved away the suggestion that he could raise the matter in the House as a breach of privilege. 'MPs,' he said, 'ought not to be too tender, and I don't like privilege'. The country applauded and took his side against the chinovnik who was being beastly to him.

After a year of impressing his image on the party—an image as vivid as that of a neon-lit factory on the fringe of a village at dusk—Mr Nabarro was ready for his second objective, a pew among the hierarchs. This has proved more difficult. Preferment in both main parties depends either on the patronage of the leaders or on the leader's need of patronage. Great bodies of power such as the landed aristocracy, the FBI, the trade unions and the co-ops have titles to office for their parliamentary representatives, however dull personally, which are stronger than those of any unsupported individualists, however brilliant. Mr Nabarro recognised this early, and just as he worked hard within the party machine, so now he worked inside the parliamentary party till through assiduity and knowledge he became vice-chairman of the important Atomic Energy Committee.

While others paired, Nabarro burrowed. And, suddenly both the Government and the Opposition heard themselves listening attentively to a well-informed and fluent expounder of fuel policies, not in the least eccentric, not in the least like the jargon of the heckler, but enterprising, bright with new ideas, not flashy but sober. It is true that he was often in conflict with the Minister of Fuel and Power and even resigned from the secretaryship of the Fuel and Power Committee of the Conservative Party because of his differences of opinion. It is true that in debate he used to speak of 'my fuel policy. . . .' But these disputes were on matters of substance. His arguments were those of an expert. This was Nabarro, Mark II.

In January 1955 he opened his campaign for clean air by having his parliamentary letters franked, 'Gerald Nabarro's Clean Air (anti-smog) Bill

RHINOCEROS. With apologies to Sir Laurence Olivier's "Rhinoceros" at the Royal Court Theatre, London, *Evening Standard*, 10th May, 1960. Treasury Bench, left to right: The Rt Hon. R. A. Butler, MP (Lord Privy Seal, Home Secretary and Leader of the House of Commons), The Rt Hon. Harold Macmillan, MP (Prime Minister), The Rt Hon. Derick Heathcoat Amory, MP (Chancellor of the Exchequer), The Rt Hon. Iain Macleod,

Second Reading—Friday, Feb. 4th, 1955.' Before long he had become the only man of this century to have brought through his own initiative three measures on to the Statute Book—the Clean Air Act, a new Coroners' Act and an act for the insulation of new factories. In each of these cases he combined persuasion with attack. The unpopular boy at Greyfriars, ragged and ducked in the first chapter, who in the last chapter carries off the cup, to the cries of 'Good Old Gerald!', had nothing on Mr Nabarro in his moment of triumph. His demeanour was modest. The braggart manner had mildened. He had fought for a limited but worth-while cause and established himself as a more hard-working and productive Member than most of those who had tried (partly, let it be said, with his assistance) to make of him a buffoon.

Mr Nabarro's House of Commons manner is, of course, that of a jester rather than of a wit. His alliterative insults ('Meddlesome Matty' for Miss Elaine Burton) are as simple in their humour as fifth-form puns. His oratory, like that of Sir Winston Churchill, Mr Aneurin Bevan and other self-educated men, is polysyllabic. His pronunciation of certain long words makes the listener feel that Mr Nabarro has read them more often than he has heard them. For all that, there is no one like Mr Nabarro to retain command of an elaborate supplementary question, full of participial and dependent clauses, undistracted by cries of 'Speech!' 'Sit down!' and 'Not again!' Who else but Mr N. could ask a supplementary like:

> Is my Hon. Friend aware that his answer seems to suggest that he has not read with his customary avidity the evidence given by the North of Scotland Hydro-Electric Board chiefs themselves to the Select Committee on Nationalised Industries, which made it perfectly clear, in the words of those chiefs of the Hydro-Electricity Board, that pumped storage schemes worked in conjunction with base-load nuclear power stations were by far the most economic means, both in capital cost and in terms of operation, for future electricity generation in Scotland?

—and get away with it?

But Mr Nabarro knows his rights. 'Mr Speaker, sir,' he says, with a haughty look at his interruptors and a pause for the silence which may or may not come. Then the Voice starts its emphatic question that seems to spell itself out in hexameters, until the interruptors begin to fade and at last Mr Nabarro, enchanted with his own powers, can be seen in full possession of the House. 'He knows his stuff,' a Labour voice will grudgingly admit. Nor do the Tories disdain the uses of a hoplite who is always ready for the heat of the battle.

There have been times, of course, when Mr Nabarro has stepped very effectively on the toes of his own generals. Apart from his fuel activities, he has caused great irritation to his Ministers by his 200 questions dealing with purchase-tax anomalies, as when he asked why should toothbrush holders that are personal to the owner be taxed at 90% when other toothbrush holders only pay 30%? Why are false beards and moustaches taxed at 30%? Why are blinds fitted with peepholes free of tax, since peepholes are an incitement to offences under the Peeping Tom Act? Small wonder that Mr J. E. S. Simon, Financial Secretary to the Treasury, once exclaimed in the words of the conductor Richter to the second flute at Covent Garden: 'Your damn nonsense I can stand twice or once, but sometimes always, by God never!' Yet the preparation of this campaign required considerable research, its execution great tenacity; and, although it worked by illustrations of nonsense, it cumulatively produced the effect in the public mind which Mr Nabarro desired—namely, that a lot of purchase-tax regulation is, in fact, a lot of nonsense. Mr Nabarro's pasteboard sword-play with the Chancellor was not unpopular.

If, despite these internecine skirmishes, Mr Nabarro's earthiness is on the whole an advantage to the Tories in the Chamber, it is not yet sufficient to promote him among the other earthy new men like Mr Macleod. For, unlike him, Mr Nabarro has so far shown an inability to express in public a philosophy which could be thought of as Nabarro's Toryism. Disraeli, Churchill, Macmillan, Hailsham—all have thought of Toryism as a system of ideas. Pragmatism is not enough. The most reactionary party must have some sort of ideal. And Mr Nabarro, if he is to emerge in the Tory Party as a leading figure in a race where his hurdles are six inches higher than his competitors', must before long—he is now 44—offer a comprehensive and acceptable expression of his own Tory image.

The moustache may have to be trimmed. Perhaps the carnation ought to go. And if the absurdly monocled Sir Colin Thornton-Kemsley will persist in sitting behind him on Budget Day looking like a sugar-bridegroom on a wedding cake, perhaps the Moss Bros toggery ought to go as well. If all the gimmicks disappear will anything be left? There are those who believe that, stripped of his wraps, Mr Nabarro, a courageous, intelligent and responsible man, could emerge as a considerable politician. He seems at least the equal of almost all his ministerial contemporaries.

I can say this about Freeman: notwithstanding that he is, or certainly was, a Fabian and a Socialist and I am a dyed-in-the-wool Tory, there is no man I should prefer to have with me in a tight corner than the Right Honourable John Freeman, MBE.

11. The Reluctant Peer

ANTHONY WEDGWOOD BENN has been in the House of Commons for the two decades since 1950, save only the years 1960–63 when he was disqualified owing to his succession to an hereditary peerage. His struggle to remain a commoner is a parliamentary epic which revealed him as a man of uncommon character and tenacity. I have always admired him enormously, although our party political views are poles apart. He is a Fabian Socialist; I am a Capitalist Tory.

"Young" Wedgy Benn is only forty-five and has already had a remarkable career. Son of "old" Wedgy Benn, PC, DSO, DFC, MP, who had sat in the Commons for above a quarter of a century, first as a Liberal for the St George Division of Tower Hamlets and then for Leith until 1927, when he went over to Labour and sat for North Aberdeen and then Manchester, Gorton, until his elevation to the Peerage as Viscount Stansgate, in 1942. He returned from war service in 1945 at the ripe age of sixty-eight and became Mr Attlee's Secretary of State for Air until 1946. He died in 1960, at the age of eighty-three. I appeared on "Any Questions?" with him at Eastleigh in Hampshire on 16th May 1958, when he was already over eighty and he was then as he remained to the end, charming, sincere, erudite and fluent. I used often to see him around the Palace of Westminster, arm affectionately on young Wedgy Benn's shoulder, talking earnestly to his son, arguing and gesticulating. So young Wedgy Benn had a fine political tradition in the family. I never wondered at Anthony's remarkable progress, although many of his stable-mates were jealous and showed it. As for the Tories, they unwisely wrote him off as a precocious whizz kid.

His record belied it. Westminster School and New College, Oxford; a member of the Labour Party since the age of eighteen; a charming American wife and three sons and one daughter; recreation, "staying at home with the family"; three years as a pilot, 1943–46, with the Royal Air Force Volunteer Reserve and the Royal Naval Volunteer Reserve; a fine safe Labour seat at Bristol, South-East, where he succeeded Sir Stafford Cripps in November 1950; an ex-President of the Oxford Union; Producer of BBC North American Programmes, 1949–50; televiser and television executive and member of the Labour Party executive for many years. After a host of party appointments, he was a natural for high office when Labour got in. So, from 1964 onwards he has been in Mr Wilson's Government, first as Postmaster-General until July, 1966 and then as Minister of Technology, with a seat in the Cabinet.

This is his pedigree as a politician and a very good one it is, too. But this chapter is about my extraordinary association with him in achieving the renunciation of peerages and the consequences for the Tory Party, including the return of Mr Quintin Hogg (Lord Hailsham, 1950–63) and Sir Alec Douglas-Home (Lord Home, 1951–63), to the House of Commons.

In 1958, during the passage of the Life Peerages Act, helped by my friend Lord Hinchingbrooke,[1] MP for South Dorset, 1942 to 1962, I had sought the means to bring in an amendment to allow hereditary peers to renounce their peerages and stand for election, or re-election, to the Commons House of Parliament. But the Whips got wind of it and framed the short title of the Bill so tightly as to make my intention impossible. Life Peerages were introduced and a kind of parliamentary sinecure established, whereby any long time-serving party member from the Commons could be kicked upstairs for life only, without encumbering his heirs with a peerage. After twelve years, I remain convinced that the system is a good one. One of the first to be ennobled was Lord Boothby, doyen of the political televisers, who had sat in parliament for East Aberdeenshire from 1924 to 1958. When asked by Mr Harold Macmillan whether he wanted to be one of the last of the old, or one of the first of the new, Boothby favoured the new, as a life peer, without hesitation, and in

[1] Lord Hinchingbrooke succeeded his father as 10th Earl of Sandwich in 1962 and disclaimed his peerage on 24th July, 1964, to become Mr Victor Montagu. He has not so far succeeded in re-entering the Commons.

due course emerged with the splendid title of Baron Boothby of Buchan and Rattray Head. From 1958 to 1960, I frequently broadcast with Anthony Wedgwood Benn. We discussed Lords and Commons and I commiserated with him about his inevitable departure to the House of Peers, when his father eventually died.

He said of me in the House on 31st March, 1960:

> In my opinion—I say this without flattery—the best back-bencher in the House of Commons is the Hon. Member for Kidderminster (Mr Nabarro). He is the most effective back-bencher in the sense that he puts the Government 'on the spot'.[1]

And on April Fool's Day, 1960, I wrote:

> My dear Anthony,
>
> You are very kind and generous and this short note is to thank you for the reference you made to me in yesterday's debates, col. 1555, *Hansard*, 31.iii. 1960. I am largely in agreement with you (though my approach is different) on the matter of Members of Parliament's pay, *allowances* and conditions; meantime we ought to consider a Bill to prevent you and others being translated to their Lordships' House and when you have time, why not talk to me about it?
>
> Yours ever,
>
> GERALD NABARRO.

"You and others". There were many first class parliamentarians involved, in addition to Anthony Wedgwood Benn. On the Tory side, to name just three, there were Lord Hinchingbrooke, MP for South Dorset and heir to the 9th Earl of Sandwich, Lord Lambton, MP for Berwick-upon-Tweed and heir to the 5th Earl of Durham, and Lord Balniel, MP for Hertford and heir to the 28th Earl of Crawford and Balcarres. Many more examples could be named from both sides of the House and in the opposite direction, Lord Home and Lord Hailsham.

The issue was precipitated much sooner than I had thought possible. On 17th November, 1960, old Wedgy Benn, Lord Stansgate, died. Young Wedgy Benn, the eldest surviving son, his elder brother Michael having been killed in action in 1944, immediately announced that he would neither assume the title, nor take his seat in the House of Lords. Soon the fur was flying. Sir Lynn Ungoed-Thomas[2] QC, Socialist Member for

[1] *Hansard*, 31st March 1960, cols. 1555–1556.

[2] Now the Hon. Mr Justice Ungoed-Thomas, Judge of the High Court of Justice, Chancery Division, since 1962.

Leicester, North-East, presented a petition on Anthony Wedgwood Benn's behalf, urging that his case be sent to the Commons' Committee of Privileges, which was agreed without dissent. We had put out a private all party Whip to every Member of the Commons, in the following terms:

> We are backing Anthony Wedgwood Benn for two reasons:
> FIRST: Because it is unjust to expel an elected MP from the House of Commons by reason of an inherited disqualification over which he has no control.
> SECONDLY: Because it is undemocratic to deny a constituency the right to choose anyone, not disqualified by statute, who it wants to represent it in Parliament.
> These principles go far beyond the merits of this one case and should be supported by members of all political parties.
> Signed: Barbara Castle
> Labour MP for Blackburn.
> Gerald Nabarro
> Conservative MP for Kidderminster.
> Jeremy Thorpe
> Liberal MP for North Devon.

But, four months later, the Committee of Privileges reported against allowing this "reluctant peer" to sit in the House of Commons and Mr Speaker would not allow him to plead his case at the Bar of the House, as a senior Labour Member, Mr Charles Pannell (Leeds, West), had urged. So Sir Lynn Ungoed-Thomas brought in a Private Member's Bill on 23rd March, 1961, called the Peerage (Renunciation) Bill. The sponsors, from all parties, were:

1) Sir Lynn Ungoed-Thomas, Leicester, North-East (Labour)
2) Mr Gerald Nabarro, Kidderminster (Tory)
3) Mr Donald Wade, Huddersfield West (Liberal)
4) Mrs Barbara Castle, Blackburn (Labour)
5) Viscount Lambton, Berwick-upon-Tweed (Tory)
6) Mr Arthur Holt, Bolton, West (Liberal)
7) Mr Roy Jenkins, Birmingham, Stechford (Labour)
8) Mr David Price, Eastleigh (Tory)
9) Mr Michael Foot, Ebbw Vale (Labour)
10) Mr Gilbert Longden, Hertfordshire, South-West (Tory)
11) Mr Charles Pannell, Leeds, West (Labour)
12) Mr Peter Kirk, Gravesend (Tory)

What a tough crew. Five Tories, five Socialists and two Liberals; and of course, the maximum number of sponsors for a Private Member's bill is twelve. Nine of the twelve are still in the Commons today, and Roy Jenkins, as Chancellor of the Exchequer, and Barbara Castle, as Secretary for Employment and Productivity, are in the Cabinet. Anthony Wedgwood Benn certainly knew how to pick his friends.

A couple of days later, there was a Government motion supporting the Committee of Privileges and declaring that Mr Benn was no longer a Member of the House of Commons. The matter was debated on 13th April, 1961 and as expected, the first motion to allow Mr Benn to plead at the Bar of the House was defeated. I helped to defeat it, because I knew too well the hostility of my own party towards him. He went down by 221 votes to 152. I was one of the 221, because I did not want him to destroy his own case at the Bar.

The debate following was the one that mattered. The Home Secretary, Mr R. A. Butler, had moved that Mr Benn ceased to be a Member of the House of Commons; Mr Hugh Gaitskell, as leader of the Opposition, was to move an amendment for the renunciation of peerages. Early in the debate, I clashed with Mr Butler over the setting up of a committee to consider legislation for the renunciation of peerages on inheritance:[1]

> MR BUTLER, Saffron Walden (Con.) Home Secretary: . . . The Government have decided that it is not in the interest of the body politic at the present moment to set up such a joint committee. That is the answer to my hon. Friends who placed the Amendment on the Order Paper. (Hon. Members: 'Why?') We have decided that and I am stating—
>
> MR NABARRO, Kidderminster (Con.): I hope that my right hon. Friend does not think me discourteous if I say that I feel that a statement of that kind is somewhat arbitrary. Is he not aware that a substantial volume of opinion in the Conservative Party believes that a reform of the House of Lords is long overdue? How can we decide the form which such reform should take unless advised by an inter-Parliamentary committee with all-party participation?
>
> MR BUTLER: My hon. Friend's intervention is appropriate, because I was about to deal with that question. The Government do not exclude the possibility of future reform of the House of Lords. Indeed, during the debate on the Life Peerages Bill—I introduced the second reading—it was mentioned both here and in another place that such a possibility was not remote but was indeed a definite possibility. All we are saying here is that we do not consider that this matter of the petitioner's case should itself be referred to a joint Committee of both Houses.
>
> We have come to that conclusion, and it is so much better that I should

[1] *Hansard*, 13th April, 1961, cols. 570–571.

state so frankly to my hon. Friend the Member for Kidderminster (Mr Nabarro), so that he knows the position which the Government take in this matter. It would be a great pity if we had any misunderstanding and any belief that we proposed to do it. It is not our intention so to do.

VISCOUNT LAMBTON, Berwick-upon-Tweed (Con.): Perhaps there is some misunderstanding of what my right hon. Friend said. Is he saying that it is not the intention of the Government in the immediate future to set up such a Committee?

MR BUTLER: That is what I said. It is not our intention to set up a joint committee to deal with the problem arising out of this case.

MR NABARRO: I want to be precise about this because it dominates my future action in this case. Is it not a fact that there is a marked difference between dealing with the matter in the specialised atmosphere of the Wedgwood Benn case and the general proposition enshrined in the Amendment to be moved shortly, I hope, on the reform of the House of Lords? Is it not a fact that the Conservative Party seems to be of opinion that a committee to inquire into general reform of the Upper House is what is needed?

MR BUTLER: This is a matter upon which I must reserve the Government's position. It is possible that we would consider that possibility. All I am dealing with here is that we cannot set up a joint committee to deal with this particular case. If that is any help to my hon. Friend, I give him that assurance.

My Speech followed.[1]

MR GERALD NABARRO: I do not dissent from many of the conclusions reached by the Committee of Privileges, and to define my position clearly at the outset I want to say, of the summary of conclusions listed in paragraph 29, that I agree with the Committee in conclusions a, b, c, d and f, but disagree with conclusion e, which reads:

> 'They do not recommend the introduction of a Bill to enable Mr Wedgwood Benn to remain a member of the Commons House of Parliament.'

It will be recalled that that conclusion was the subject of a deadheat on a vote. My hon. Friend the Member for Carlton (Sir K. Pickthorn) voted with the four Labour members of the Committee.

SIR KENNETH PICKTHORN (Carlton): They voted with me. It was upon my motion that we voted, and my reason for it was not the one which my hon. Friend the Member for Kidderminster would approve, but the opposite one. I wanted no reference whatever to the possibility of legislation.

MR NABARRO: I can only draw my conclusions from the printed precis of the conclusion which I quoted. I apologise to my hon. Friend for saying that he

---

[1] *Hansard*, 13th April, 1961, cols. 595–603.

DINAH JANE NABARRO

1955 election child born, 18th March 1955. The picture that went round the world: the "Nabarro again" perambulator. Mrs. Gerald Nabarro walking the new baby Dinah Jane: with Sarah Penelope, age 4 years and golden retriever dog "Peter" age 3 years.

"SARAH PENELOPE NABARRO—1950 Election Child." Born 17th July, 1950. Christened in St. Stephen's Crypt Chapel beneath Westminster Hall, 6th September 1950.

As Cover Girl, age 18 years, Oxford University Conservatives' (O.U.C.) Programme, Hilary Term, 1969.

"Kidderminster: 1946–1965". Presentation to Sir Gerald Nabarro of his portrait in oils by Mr. Edward Halliday, President of the Portrait Painters Society of Great Britain and a Churchill Vase for Lady Nabarro: the portrait and vase subscribed to by a large number of Kidderminster electors.

Centre: Lieut. Col. J. D. H. Butcher, O.B.E., who served in the Worcestershire Regiment in two world wars: Chairman of the Kidderminster Division Conservative Association 1948–1956 and President 1956 onwards. *Left:* Sir Gerald Nabarro. *Right:* Lady Nabarro.

At the Royal Three Tuns Hotel, Pershore, Worcestershire, 19th January 1965. Final Selection for the Worcestershire South, Conservative candidature; Sir Gerald Nabarro chosen from 87 seeking nomination:

Left to Right: Mrs. Peter Tapsell, Mr. Peter Tapsell: now M.P. for Horncastle, Mr. Maurice Macmillan: now M.P. for Farnham, Mrs. Maurice Macmillan, Sir Gerald Nabarro: now M.P. for South Worcestershire, Lady Nabarro, Mrs. Gerry Wiggin, Mr. Gerry Wiggin: now M.P. for Weston-Super-Mare. Thus the Worcestershire South, Selection Committee Short Listed *Four*, all future Tory M.P.s

The Member's wife: Lady Nabarro with senior lady citizens at Malvern, Worcestershire, 1967.

The General Election of 31st March 1966: Sir Gerald Nabarro, Tory Candidate for Worcestershire South, discusses the farm price review with farmers at Longdon, Worcestershire.

"The General Election of 31st March 1966". Sir Gerald Nabarro, Tory Candidate for Worcestershire South, with the girls of St. James's at a Malvern public meeting.

Mr. Gerald Nabarro, M.P., and Mrs. Nabarro, as Pearly King and Queen at the Eve of St. Valentine's Conservative Fancy Dress Ball, at Tenbury Wells, Worcestershire, 1959.

THE WEDGWOOD BENN AFFAIR: SUMMER 1961, *Sunday Times*, 14th May, 1961. Cartoon by Norman Mansbridge, Esq. Nanny: The Rt Hon. R. A. Butler, CH, MP (Home Secretary). Little Lord Fauntleroy: Mr Anthony Wedgwood Benn. Pugilists: The Rt Hon. Harold Macmillan, MP (Prime Minister), Mr Sydney Silverman, MP. Skipping: Mrs Bessie Braddock, MP. Urchin: The Rt Hon. Hugh Gaitskell, CBE, MP (Leader of Her Majesty's Opposition). Members playing Marbles: Mr Gerald Nabarro, MP; Mr Richard Crossman, OBE. In their Lordships' House: The Most Hon. The Marquess of Salisbury, KG.

supported four Socialist Members. In fact, four Socialist Members supported him, though their arguments may have been, and evidently were, entirely different in view from his interpretation of the position.

My position on this matter has for many years been patently clear. I worked with Mr Wedgwood Benn on this problem from the days before the Life Peerages Bill was brought to this House. I then told him, and said publicly on radio, on television and elsewhere, that I wanted three simple reforms.

They were all of substantial moment but simple in character.

The first was that a Peer of the realm should have a vote at Parliamentary elections. The second was that a peer of the realm might offer himself for election to the Commons House of Parliament. The third was that in the event of his election to the Commons House of Parliament he should renounce his peerage for himself, his successors and heirs. In other words, that peerage should be extinguished.

Though I was largely in agreement with the Peerage (Renunciation) Bill, a Private Member's Measure which is still before the House and which was introduced by the hon. and learned Member for Leicester, North-East (Sir Lynn Ungoed-Thomas), and I was the first Conservative sponsor of that Bill and my name still appears on it, during the Committee stage I would have sought to amend it, had it reached Committee upstairs, so that any renunciation of a peerage would have had to be a complete renunciation and there could not have been an arrangement whereby there was a sort of family battledore and shuttlecock, with father renouncing the peerage for his lifetime and seeking election to the House of Commons and becoming a Member, and then later, on father's death, his son, with no interest in party politics, taking the oath and sitting in the Upper House. I would find a position of that kind quite intolerable and in supporting the Bill I would have sought to make that important Amendment to it.

In the course of his interesting speech, my right hon. Friend the Home Secretary referred to the year 1626, and the right hon. and learned Member for Montgomery (Mr C. Davies) defined the position of the peerage by saying that it was settled by custom and that there was no Statute Law. In fact, the origins of the defined position of the peerage in the case quoted by my right hon. Friend the Home Secretary in the matter of the Earldom of Oxford was when Mr Justice Dodridge in 1626, said that a peerage:

'. . . is a personal dignity annexed to the posterity and fixed in the blood.'

I have a certain amount of respect for the hereditary system, but it is limited. When I read drivel of that kind, written 340 years ago, it substantially weakens such little respect as I have for the hereditary system.

Would anybody dare to suggest that my blood is less luscious, less rich, less red, coursing through my veins as it is at this moment—(Hon. Members: 'It is blue.')—On the contrary, it is very unblue. Here appears the contradistinction between my noble Friend the Member for Dorset, South (Viscount Hinchingbrooke), and myself. Am I, in 1961, really to subscribe that my noble Friend's title rests upon the quality of his blood and that he will succeed to the Earldom of Sandwich on account of an antiquated decision given by a long-dead judge? That kind of thing is drivel and is manifest nonsense, which I absolutely reject.

MR DAVID PRICE (Eastleigh): I support my hon. Friend, but will he point out that that learned judge gave his opinion in the reign of Charles I, at a time when the divine right of kings was the popular doctrine of sovereigns, which ended up on the scaffold and the block and when the decision was taken by this House in a somewhat unconstitutional way, not to support the divine right of kings?

MR NABARRO: I am most grateful to my hon. Friend for his support and succour. We are evidently at one on this matter.

I am not ashamed to say that there is a substantial number of my hon. Friends, approximately of my generation and who have been here for up to fifteen years, who take the view which I am now endeavouring to express, about hereditary matters though subscribing in part measure to the retention of hereditary peers in the Upper House.

MR PETER KIRK: (Gravesend) My hon. Friend the Member for Kidderminster refers to the retention of the hereditary principle. I am the elder son of a peer and the peerage goes back to 1542. My father[1] is dead and I did not succeed to the peerage because it was one of the original peerages attached to the office and not to the man. All peerages in the Middle Ages were so attached. The hereditary principle is a modern abortion which was introduced in the sixteenth century—'abortion' is perhaps an unfortunate word in this connection. My hon. Friend should not say that the hereditary principle is annealed into the House of Lords.

MR. NABARRO: I agree. That emphasises some of the incongruities of the peerage. It is evidently the fact—I learn this from page 6 of the Minutes of Evidence of the Committee of Privileges—that peerages were regularly surrendered prior to 1678.

The right Hon. Gentleman the Leader of the Opposition spoke of five of my hon. Friends being affected by the present arrangements and eventually, on the death of their fathers, having to go to the House of Lords. But the number is considerably larger than that. The unfortunate aspect of the case of Wedgwood Benn is that he is the second son and, due to the death in action in the last war of the elder brother, who would have succeeded to the peerage, it devolved upon the second son.

Taking into account both first and second sons who might possibly accede

---

[1] Bishop of Oxford, 1937–54.

to the peerage, there are in this House my noble Friend the Member for Hertford (Lord Balniel), my noble Friend the Member for Dorset, South (Lord Hinchingbrooke), my noble Friend the Member for Berwick-upon-Tweed (Viscount Lambton), my right hon. Friend the Member for Oswestry (Mr Ormsby-Gore), my hon. Friend the Member for Oxford (Mr Woodhouse), my hon. Friend the Member for North Fylde (Mr Stanley), my hon. Friend the Member for Glasgow, Hillhead (Mr Galbraith), who is Joint Under-Secretary of State for Scotland, my noble Friend the Member for Edinburgh, North (The Earl of Dalkeith), my hon. Friend the Member for Cirencester and Tewkesbury (Mr Ridley), and there are others.

Public support is very widespread for the views so cogently expressed by the right hon. Gentleman the Leader of the Opposition this afternoon. He made a magnificent speech—magnificent in that it was enthralling in its application to constitutional problems as ordinary men and women understand them today. There is no doubt that the bulk of public opinion is with the views expressed by the right hon. Gentleman the Leader of the Opposition and the views that I am endeavouring in a much more humble fashion, to express from these benches.

I want to quote this evening only two of these expressions of opinion. I regard the *Daily Telegraph* as the principal Conservative daily newspaper. In its leading article this morning it said, under the heading 'Conscript Peer':

> 'It would be a pity in such matters to take any stand that smacks of formalism, and it was quite unnecessary that the Committee, by the smallest possible majority, should have advised against legislation. The argument seems to be that this case should not be dealt with apart from a general reform of the second chamber.'

I commend the following words to my right hon. Friend—

> 'Surely that excuse is a trifle hoary. It is almost exactly half a century since the Prime Minister of the day—'

a Liberal Prime Minister—

> 'proclaimed that reform of the House of Lords "brooked no delay". Now it seems to brook nothing except delay. There has recently been a bit of tinkering about with its composition. One of the last acts of Labour in Office was further to curtail its powers.'

It goes on with these significant words in the context of the Wedgwood Benn case:

> 'But is there any reason why anybody should be compelled to accept such membership, if he does not want to? Why should an heir be able to discard any part of an inheritance except a peerage? Many may think it strange to prefer the electoral dust to the undisturbable dignity described by Lord Morrison. . . . But provided the choice is confined to the

individual, there is no reason why it should not be free. The case has already received so much publicity'—

and, as a Conservative, this rather makes me squirm—

'that it is surely superfluous to allow the person concerned"—

Mr Wedgwood Benn—

'to plead at the Bar of the House of Commons.'

SIR PETER AGNEW (South Worcestershire): Hear, hear.

MR NABARRO: My hon. Friend the Member for Worcestershire, South (Sir Peter Agnew) says 'Hear, hear' too soon. The leading article continues:

'But this is superfluous only because the arguments in his favour are already crystal clear.'

I hope that my hon. Friend will say 'Hear, Hear' again.

I now pass to an equally authoritative journal, which generally commands the attention of hon. Members in all parts of the House, namely, *The Economist*. On 8th April it wrote these words, under the heading 'Common Peers':

'The Commons will be well advised, when it debates the privileges' committee's report on the Wedgwood Benn petition next Thursday, to resist the temptation to indulge in a general splurge on reforming the House of Lords. Everybody has his pet scheme for that, but this is not the time to discuss it. The immediate reform that is needed is in the Commons, and it is a minor one at that. The issue affects the political career of less than half-a-dozen individuals at any time, and it should be treated on its own merits.

The Economist shows less than its usual accuracy in saying that less than half a dozen individuals are affected, but the purpose is there.

My right hon. Friend talked about 'pulling bricks out of the structure of the Constitution'. Also, he talked about 'tinkering with it'. The measures of reform proposed in the Peerage (Renunciation) Bill, reinforced this afternoon by the motion in the name of the Leader of the Opposition, are at least as substantial as the life peerage innovation. Neither would this proposal weaken the House of Lords by denying a passage upstairs to many of the most illustrious Members of this House. Surely it would do the opposite. Surely what would happen is that reinforcement of the House of Lords would come inevitably from additional life peerages—and that brings me to the critical point of the reform of the Upper House.

I am now placed in the happy position of having at least something slightly more than intangible to probe my right hon. Friend the Home Secretary upon during the months ahead. He has taken a slow and faltering step in the direction of my hon. Friends and myself in suggesting that at some time in the future we might have an inter-Parliamentary committee to go into the question of the reform of the House of Lords. (Interruption) Before my hon.

Friend the Member for Worcestershire, South (Sir Peter Agnew) snorts too loudly—I am sorry; I apologise to him. He was evidently thinking.

SIR PETER AGNEW: What my hon. Friend described as a snort was the result of my recollection of the long hours spent by Members on both sides of the House in just such a Committee, which, unfortunately, foundered in its results because of a failure to achieve reforms with both sides of the House agreeing to them. I am not very optimistic that such a Committee would produce fruitful results just now.

MR NABARRO: My hon. Friend has not noted the progress in political and Parliamentary thought during the last thirteen years. He was missing from the House between 1950 and 1955. I welcome him back because he is my own Member of Parliament, and I live in his constituency. But, obviously, he has failed to observe that we have made progress in the matter of thought upon reform of the House of Lords, as witness life peerages.

I say to the House this evening that I do not want the total abolition of the hereditary system. The kind of second Chamber I have in mind would endeavour to be as representative as possible on a complementary basis and not competitive with the House of Commons. It would comprise approximately eighty hereditary peers elected in each Parliament by an electoral college of nine hundred peers, but only eighty hereditary peers would take the oath and sit there. There would be another eighty life peers and approximately forty bishops, judges and lords of the defence forces. There would be forty university representatives. A total of two hundred and forty legislators in the upper House. No two men would ever agree on the exact composition, but a committee of the kind I am describing could surely achieve the highest common factor of agreement. It is that kind of representative assembly which should be aimed for, and in the months ahead I shall press my right hon. Friend for this inter-Parliamentary committee of inquiry. The final point I wish to deal with is a practical one. It concerns the position into which the Conservative Party now puts itself by a refusal to take any action upon the Wedgwood Benn case. There is no doubt that Mr Wedgwood Benn, Lord Stansgate—I ride both horses, as the BBC has done ever since this controversy began by referring to Mr Anthony Wedgwood Benn, Lord Stansgate—will offer himself as the Labour Party candidate for the Bristol, South-East constituency—(Hon. Members: 'Hear, hear') I am glad to note the 'Hear, hears' from my hon. Friends. I hope to call on many of them to accompany me to Bristol, South-East in support of Mr Wedgwood Benn's case, to remain in the Commons. This is a constitutional issue of great importance. I hope that the Conservative Party will not put up a candidate against Mr Wedgwood Benn. The Liberal Party has already said that it will not.

I know that my right hon. Friend thinks that this is really a bit much, but, of course, it is a bit much. The Liberal Party has already said it is not going to put up a candidate against Mr Wedgwood Benn and I hope that my party will not put up a candidate. I hope that Mr Wedgwood Benn is either returned with a huge majority over a splinter candidate—I am told that there may be an independent candidate—or that he is returned unopposed. He will come to the Bar of the House and the Government will be in the ridiculous position of being compelled to take steps to disqualify him.

MR SILVERMAN (Nelson & Colne, Lab.): And the hon. Gentleman has been refusing to hear him.

MR NABARRO: I should not want to hear him.

MR SILVERMAN: The hon. Gentleman voted against him.

MR NABARRO: I should not want to hear him because he would have been heard quite adequately in the Bristol, South-East by-election.

If he is returned again as the Member, what is the position of the Government? Are they to have him disqualified? And suppose he offers himself again, are we to go on for months on end with no Parliamentary representative in Bristol, South-East? Is this constituency to be permanently disfranchised? All this arises because of the refusal by some hon. Members of my party to recognise that in certain circumstances a Member of this House, if he succeeds to a peerage, may renounce the privilege of sitting in the Upper House with the safeguards I have described.

I say to the Home Secretary, who enjoys the unique position of being Chairman of the Conservative Party, that not only is disrepute being brought upon the House of Commons by the inevitable course of events in the next few months, but opprobrium is being brought on the Conservative Party, to which I belong and that is nearly as serious, in my opinion. I represent the young and progressive element in the Conservative Party. I believe in the Amendment set down today on the Order Paper by the Leader of the Opposition is the closest to my own desires in this matter. I shall therefore vote for that Amendment in the Lobby tonight and urge the other Members of the younger and progressive element in the Conservative Party to vote with me.

At the end of the day, fourteen Tories joined me in voting with the Opposition:

Lord Balniel (Hertford)
Humphry Berkeley (Lancaster)
Christopher Chataway (Lewisham, North)
Julian Critchley (Rochester & Chatham)
Reader Harris (Heston and Isleworth)
John Hollingworth (Birmingham, All Saints)

Peter Kirk (Gravesend)
Lord Lambton (Berwick-upon-Tweed)
Charles Longbottom (York)
Robert Mathew (Honiton)
David Price (Eastleigh)
James Prior (Lowestoft)
Peter Tapsell (Nottingham, West)
Sir William Teeling (Brighton, Pavilion)

Of these Lord Balniel and Lord Lambton were, and still are, heirs to peerages. Although we were beaten 207 to 143, the fifteen Tories who had voted against their party and the large number of deliberate abstentions convinced the Cabinet that Anthony Wedgwood Benn had much Conservative support. Gallantly, Benn nominated himself for the Bristol, South-East by-election four days after the debate, handed in his papers on 24th April, 1961 and on 4th May, romped home:

Wedgwood Benn	(Labour)	23,275
St Clair	(Tory)	10,231

Both candidates prepared for legal proceedings and Mr Speaker Hylton-Foster gave Benn permission to use the House of Commons Library while preparing his defence. But on 28th July, 1961 the Electoral Court ruled against him and when St Clair arrived to take his seat three days later, several Tories joined me in stalking out of the Chamber as a demonstration of our disgust. However, the Tory dissentients had already done their job because the Cabinet had relented and formed a Joint Committee, to consider the reform of the Lords, on 26th April.

I was in constant touch with Benn throughout this period. He had written to me on 6th March, 1961 when his fortunes were their lowest:

My dear Gerald,

Can you advise me on the best tactics in the next stage of the peerage battle? I gather the Privilege Committee report will come out in about three weeks and on the point of law involved (am I disqualified or not) it is pretty likely that it will come out against me. It may or may not add a recommendation that the law should be changed.

The really key point will be the debate in the House on the Committee's report. I guess that RAB Butler will be very sympathetic but will not feel able to pledge a new Bill. Everything will, therefore, depend on whether there is sufficient goodwill to persuade some of your chaps to vote for a resolution calling for legislation to amend the law and whether others would be likely to abstain from opposing it.

I know that the usual channels[1] are totally blocked by the current battles but hope that on this occasion it might be possible to get a resolution backed by Members on both sides. We can't draft it until after the report is published, but it seems that the best bet would be one along these lines:—

1. that the present law governing this matter is ancient, uncertain and unsatisfactory.
2. that new legislation to clarify the law should include provision to abolish hereditary disqualification from the Commons and
3. that meanwhile no one should be disqualified on these grounds.

One would then urge the appointment of a Joint Select Committee of both Houses to get on with the job of preparing the necessary legislation, which should not take long.

Do you think that there would be many of your people willing to join in the support of such a resolution? If so, who do you think they would be and how do you think would be the best way of going about approaching them?

Sorry to trouble you with all this but I would immensely value your help. I think a list of sympathetic names would be the first thing to work on and then try to build it from there.

Perhaps we can have a talk about this at Konigswinter?

Ever yours,

ANTHONY WEDGWOOD BENN.

And I had replied on 13th March, 1961:

My dear Anthony,

Yes, I will certainly help in the sense suggested in your letter of 6th March, 1961, and privately I propose to endeavour to ascertain from my friends in the Conservative Party, what measure of support there might be for amendment of the law, in the event of the report of the Committee of Privileges going against you (i.e. disqualifying you from sitting in the House of Commons.)

During my earlier enquiries, I am sorry to say that the majority of Conservative Members with whom I talked, were opposed to my doing anything at all to assist. They believe in the House of Lords and that heirs to peerages should take their seats there, exactly in accordance with tradition and the pretty long history in this matter. They are anti-reform, in this sense.

I shall be at the House almost continuously until commencement of the Easter recess, say, 29th March, and I hope we can have a chat together.

---

[1] "Usual Channels"—Parliamentary jargon for Communications Between Government and Opposition Whips.

Would you please give me forty-eight hours notice or so, of the publication of the report of the Committee of Privileges, as that is the time for me to endeavour to enlist support?

Yours ever,

GERALD NABARRO.

On 27th April, 1961 I wrote to him again and by this time I had developed a strong enthusiasm for the cause:

My dear Anthony,

I was gratified to hear Mr Butler's statement yesterday in the House of Commons to the effect that a Select Committee of both Houses is to be established to enquire into the composition of the House of Lords. Undoubtedly this Committee must consider closely all the provisions of the Renunciation of Peerages Bill, of which I am the first Tory sponsor.

Many of my friends on the Government benches have worked with me in the House of Commons for a long while past to secure reconsideration of Lords' Reform, and as you will know, I have consistently spoken and voted in a fashion to denote my full support for renunciation of peerages, when personally desired by the holder, eligibility, subject to safeguards, for peers to sit in the Commons if elected at a Parliamentary election and votes for peers at elections.

Peers are neither felons, lunatics nor bankrupts and should have the same prerogatives and privileges as other adults within universal suffrage.

I am confident the Select Committee will recommend these reforms and my friends and myself will continue to work towards that end.

I expect you will secure a majority of votes at Bristol (South-East) by-election next Thursday. It seems to me that the law in its present unsatisfactory state will then cause you to be disqualified from taking your seat in the Commons House of Parliament. The position becomes even more farcical now that it is reported that your Conservative opponent at the by-election is also heir to a peerage.[1]

The law is an ass.

But, before this Parliament is over, we all hope to have the law changed.

In that event, you would be legally eligible to offer yourself again for the Commons, where so many of us, though not accepting your political philosophy, have admired your Parliamentary ability and pertinacity.

In all these circumstances, I feel no useful purpose would be served by my speaking at Bristol, particularly as the establishment of the Select Committee represents to me achievement of the first objective in my campaign for Lords Reform.

---

[1] Malcolm St Clair, heir-presumptive to his kinsman the 17th Baron Sinclair, MVO, York Herald of Arms, 1957–68.

Please use this letter for any purpose you wish, and with warmest personal regards to your wife and yourself.

Yours ever,

GERALD NABARRO.

Immediately after his re-election, albeit illicit, I sent him the following telegram:

Congratulations upon well deserved and magnificent victory. Hope to continue to help towards reform of existing law to facilitate renunciation of peerages. Warmest regards. Gerald Nabarro.

When he was finally declared disqualified, I joined Lord Attlee, Lady Violet Bonham Carter, Jo Grimond, Sir Harold Nicolson and many others in contributing to the Bristol Fund to help with Wedgwood Benn's very heavy legal expenses. This was at the end of July 1961, when the cause looked very bleak indeed.

My dear Anthony,

Last Friday, the Court upheld the hereditary principle in our legislature, and though this may be right in law, it is my opinion that it is in flagrant defiance of all democratic principles of Government.

I deplore the decision and send you my deepest sympathies. As the first Tory signatory of the Renunciation of Peerages Bill, I would like you to know that I will continue to work in the House of Commons, for Lords' reform and indeed, only last Thursday, I was pressing the Leader of the House, Mr R. A. Butler, for a full debate on Lords' reform before the end of this session, (see col. 608 *Hansard*, 27th July, 1961). Personally, I hope the Labour Party will co-operate.

Anyway, the Government having driven a 'coach and four' through the hereditary principle in the Lords, by creating Life Peerages, should legislate in the next session, with or without official Labour and Liberal support, to allow renunciation of peerages by holders, should they so desire: and, in perpetuity.

My wife and I wish to be associated with Earl Attlee, Lady Violet Bonham Carter, Dr Bronowski, Sir Harold Nicolson, Mr Grimond and others, who have established the Bristol Fund to help you with your heavy legal costs, and we have pleasure in enclosing a cheque for twenty-five guineas. Principles apart, it is intended as a manifest of our sincere admiration of your gallant struggle. Eventually, you will succeed, and I hope I may be one of the first to greet you back, albeit as a doughty political opponent, to the

Commons House of Parliament, where men of spunk and spirit are always welcome.

With warmest regards to your wife and yourself.

Yours ever,

GERALD NABARRO.

It was entirely characteristic of Wedgwood Benn to send my donation back seven years later, when it was all over and he was a Cabinet Minister. I was gratified to have backed the winner.

At the end of 1961, Woodrow Wyatt, Socialist Member for Bosworth, Leicestershire, Katherine Whitehorn of *The Observer*, Anthony Wedgwood Benn, then right out of politics, and myself, met for a BBC television programme before a large audience of American servicemen at Sculthorpe Bomber station in Norfolk. Afterwards, on 6th December, I wrote to Benn:

My dear Anthony,

It was delightful to see you at Sculthorpe, and I am now writing as promised to say that:

(1) negotiations through the usual channels, i.e. between Front Benches are far advanced, for the establishment of the All-Party Committee for the Reform of the Lords, and it is likely that it will be linked by wider terms of reference to an increase in House of Commons Parliamentary pay, and payment of Peers, as advocated in certain quarters. There should be an announcement before Christmas.

(2) The papers from Hinch are sent herewith, notably the One-Clause Disqualification Bill.

Would you please give your comments on the above two matters and return the papers. Of course, if the all-party motion does appear on the order paper of the House of Commons we should let it run, as it would be a mistake to try and bring in the Disqualification Bill, while the Committee is deliberating, as I expect you would agree?

Yours ever,

GERALD NABARRO.

and Benn replied on 12th December:

My dear Gerald,

Many thanks for your letter. I am glad to hear the talks are going well and must just hope for the best. Macleod has agreed to see me next week and I may know a little more after that.

Hinch's Bill has the merit of great simplicity and, of course, were it to be passed I should take advantage of its provisions with the profoundest gratitude.

There are, however, some snags about it which he might want to consider.

1) Under this Bill any peer can move from the Commons into the House of Lords at any time simply by applying for his Writ of Summons. This might be considered to confer too great a privilege upon such a person.
2) The Labour Party view tends to be that a man who wishes to enjoy the rights of a commoner should renounce his title completely, either for life or for himself and his descendants.

For this reason I think it unlikely that you would get Labour sponsors for Hinch's Bill. Indeed some Tories might object to it as well.

I am now working on a brief memorandum setting out various alternatives which would meet the point and when it is completed, perhaps I could let you have it. If there is to be a hope of success we must try to get the widest volume of support.

One point keeps cropping up and does deserve a moment's attention. People say that whatever Bill is introduced could not possibly be retrospective and would consign me affectionately to the dustbin with the comforting addition that I would have achieved victory for those who come after. This, of course, is absolute nonsense. The only valid objection to retrospective legislation is to protect people from being punished for something which was lawful when they did it and subsequently became retrospectively unlawful. No such consideration could apply in this case. In addition, it should be pointed out that there is no need for retrospective legislation if the legislation is properly drawn.

For example, if the legislation follows Hinch's pattern, I would be eligible to sit in the Commons since I have not applied for my Writ. Or, alternatively, if it is laid down that any peer may renounce his title, it would not have to be retrospective for me to enjoy this right. If this point does come up, perhaps you could help clarify it.

I am so grateful for your continuing interest and friendship, which I value immensely.

Ever yours,

ANTHONY WEDGWOOD BENN.

To which I replied on 19th December:

My dear Anthony,

Yes, I will do exactly as you say in the penultimate paragraph of your letter to me on 12th December, 1961, and I am glad to have your views on Hinch's proposal for a One Clause Bill.

Personally, I think it would be a mistake to do anything further at this particular moment, because I am informed privately that the discussions 'through the usual channels' and notably between the Leader of the House,

Iain Macleod, and Hugh Gaitskell, are now well advanced for the establishment of the all-Party Committee for Lords' Reform. Perhaps linked as well, subject to expiration in due course of the pay pause, to the question of salaries and allowances for Members of the House of Commons.

My private information is that there will be a statement on this matter in the last week of January or first week of February, and therefore I propose to put my papers on one side, and your interesting letter of 12th December, until then.

My wife joins me in sending warmest regards to you, and greetings for Christmas and the New Year. May you make further and successful progress in your arduous and gallant struggle in the New Year, and I need hardly tell you that I will continue to do all I possibly can to assist, though I am deeply conscious of my own inadequacies in that regard.

Yours ever,

GERALD NABARRO.

In the spring of 1962, there was a debate on the Lords Reform Committee motion and shortly before it, on 23rd March, Benn wrote to me:

My dear Gerald,

Is there any chance at all of your being able to speak in next Wednesday's debate on the Lords Reform Committee motion? Months have now gone by and there are rumours that it may not even be put right before the next General Election. It is already seven years since the Lord Mayor, Aldermen, and Burgesses petitioned both houses under the Great Seal of the City and on that occasion Lord Kilmuir spoke of the necessity for 'full, frank and free consideration of all its implications'.

After all the struggles of the last eighteen months, I am naturally hoping we don't have to go through the whole thing again. If you press for a speedy conclusion and even some sort of semi-pledge of action, it would make all the difference in the world.

Thanks again for all your help.

Ever yours,

ANTHONY WEDGWOOD BENN.

I was able to offer some reassurance in my reply to this letter on 28th March and the timetable I had prophesied turned out to be accurate, with the exception of the General Election date:

My dear Anthony,

The apprehensions in your letter of 23rd March, 1962 are not very well founded in my view: we shall get our Committee, within a few weeks, and I would expect very roughly that the time-table might run out as follows.

May, 1962 .... Committee formed: membership announced.
May/December, 1962 .... Committee deliberates and reports early January, 1963.
Autumn, 1963 .... General Election.

It will be the duty of my friends and myself on the Conservative side of the House, aided, I hope, by a large number of Socialist and Liberal Members, to urge the Government, within the last session of the present Parliament, commencing at the end of October, 1962, to legislate in the sense we have in mind.

The only thing which would upset the above time-table in my judgement, would be a couple of fractuous or obstreperous fuddy-duddy Tory Members who do not want reform of the Lords at all, or alternatively, non-progressive Socialist representatives who want total abolition of the House of Lords: both extremist elements are equally dangerous: but, if we have none of them on the Committee, or if they are a tiny minority, I would confidently expect that the above programme could broadly be followed out.

Jo joins me in sending love to your wife and warmest regards to yourself.

Yours ever,

GERALD NABARRO.

and on June 24th:

My dear Gerald,

How very kind of you to have written so soon after your return to London. I do appreciate your continuing interest in my exile and undoubtedly Hinchingbrooke's case does create a situation which is favourable to both of us.

I have thought very carefully about your suggested question this Thursday in the House. The only anxiety I have is that the Government might say 'No' without thinking about it and it would be harder to get them to reconsider it later on. The Committee is in fact making very rapid progress and if you were to ask Macleod anything it might be better to confine yourself to one narrow point:

> Would my Right Honourable Friend consider asking the Joint Select Committee to make an interim report before the end of July on the narrow point of MPs who inherit peerages and have not applied for their Writs of Summons so that the Government can prepare legislation to deal with this single issue for early in the new session.

It might be that the best thing of all would be just to drop Macleod a line about this including this suggestion and urging them not to hurry on the by-election in South Dorset which will be an infernal nuisance to the Party. If the law were changed before the by-election was held Hinch could stand again as a qualified candidate. The Government might be prepared to consider this idea privately. But if it were put to them publicly they would be bound to turn it down for fear that they might be criticized for giving more favourable treatment to one of their own colleagues than they gave to me.

If anyone raises a query about the undesirability of leaving South Dorset without an MP for so long the answer is very simple. Bristol, South-East had no MP in the Commons from November 1960 to July 1961 while the Committee of Privileges and the Election Court were untangling the legal complications. It would therefore be perfectly reasonable that South Dorset should be in the same position while the Legislation goes through until say next Easter. And no doubt *they* would rather have Hinch—even if it means waiting for him—than have a by-election they don't want and a new MP. they don't want sooner.

Thanks so much for sending me the cartoon which I will have photographed and returned to you.

All the very best to you both from us both.

Ever yours,

ANTHONY WEDGWOOD BENN.

We lost Hinchingbrooke from the Commons. He became Earl of Sandwich, took his seat in the upper House and then renounced his peerage to become Mr Victor Montagu. Sadly this fine parliamentarian never got back into the Commons, where he was loved by all parties. I replied to Benn's letter on 26th June, 1962, enclosing a draft of my proposed question for the following Thursday:

My dear Anthony,

I arrived back in London a few minutes ago, and the car bringing luggage from my home also has on board the framed cartoons by Norman Mansbridge. Accordingly, in spite of your letter of 21st June, which I have only this minute seen, I am sending the framed cartoons to you, and please have your publishers extract the original for block making and then send both the cartoons back to me, dis-mantled if you wish, from the frame: I have a tame picture-framer in Chester who does this work for me, and he could put the thing together again in a few minutes, without any trouble at all to yourself or to myself.

I am devastated about Hinch and because I have been abroad for three weeks, have not yet seen him. I shall start things on the lines you suggest in the next week or two, trying to hurry up the Committee, and I thought of seizing the opportunity on the Business Question on Thursday afternoon, to put something like the attached to Iain Macleod, as Leader of the House? If you have any brighter ideas and you are so much better at this sort of thing than I am, please tell me by return of post.

Jo joins me in sending love to your wife and warmest regards to yourself.

Yours ever,

GERALD NABARRO.

The question was:

On business: having regard to the demise in a House of Commons sense of our Noble Friend, Lord Hinchingbrooke, or Lord Sandwich (I am not sure which title I should give him) and the urgent need to keep such magnificent characters in the House of Commons, thus avoiding the embarrassment to my Rt Hon. Friend of a by-election, in his capacity as Chairman of the Conservative Party, would my Rt Hon. Friend make a statement next week, denoting progress made by the Select Committee on Lords Reform and whether the findings of that Committee may be presented to this House before we rise for the summer recess?

By December 1962, I was beginning to think about the issue in relation to the future leadership of the Conservative Party and I wrote to Benn:

My dear Anthony,

I should certainly play it 'Softee, Softee, Catchee Monkee', if I were you. There is much vicious party politics in Lords Reform and a lot of Members of both parties do not like you personally, as indeed so many of them dislike me personally. They regard us as extroverts, swank-pots politically, and lots of other nasty things which we are certainly not, but they think we are.

Therefore, your public reaction when the Committee Report is published, should be in my judgement, to express mild gratification and say . . . 'of course, I am delighted that I may be able, once again, to offer myself on some future date for election to the Commons House of Parliament where all democratic power resides and resume the role, I hope, of offering my services to the community'. That is what I would say, if I were you, suitably embellished of course!

THERE WILL BE OPPOSITION FROM THE TORY SIDE TO THE PROPOSED REFORMS: THE MACMILLAN SUCCESSION, COUPLED WITH THE REPORT OF THE COMMITTEE, AS WE SUPPOSE IT TO BE, MAY ADMIT MY LORDS HAILSHAM AND HOME AS FUTURE TORY PRIME MINISTERS: AND THEY ARE BOTH LIKELY CANDIDATES BECAUSE, DUE TO THEIR SEATS IN THE RAREFIED ATMOSPHERE OF THE LORDS REMOVED LARGELY FROM THE TAINT OF UNPOPULAR GOVERNMENT POLICIES, THEY EXCITE PUBLIC FANCY AND CONSERVATIVE ADULATION, THE LATTER ALWAYS LOVING A LORD!

Yours ever,

GERALD NABARRO.

And immediately the House reassembled after the Christmas recess:

My dear Gerald,

I gather that about now the Government are deciding what line they will take on the Select Committee Report on my case, and any help you can give in pushing for early action will be most appreciated. I hate to trouble you in this way but am so grateful for your past help.

Yours ever,

ANTHONY WEDGWOOD BENN.

My dear Anthony,

When I reached the House yesterday for the Hugh Gaitskell tributes I had your kind letter of 18th January and I shall be talking to our friends a good deal during the next ten to fourteen days. I hope to get into touch with you by telephone after your return from Eastern Europe, about the second week of February.

Yours ever,

GERALD NABARRO.

And after the death of Hugh Gaitskell:

My dear Gerald,

Many thanks for your letter. I look forward to another talk when I get home again on February 7th.

The enclosed is based on various memoes I have prepared for Hugh Gaitskell in the past. Though a bit more radical than your views it shows that interest in Lords Reform is not limited to your side of the House.

Yours ever,

ANTHONY WEDGWOOD BENN.

On 31st May 1963 the Peerage Bill was published. It included provision for the renunciation of peerages and became law on 30th July 1963. Mr St Clair, the unhappy Tory Member for Bristol, South-East, resigned his seat at once.

The following day I wrote to Wedgwood Benn:

My dear Anthony,

Thank you so much, and your lady wife as well, for a delightful party at the House last Monday afternoon, and I am honoured to have been included among your friends and guests. Also, for the first time, I had the pleasure of meeting Mrs Dora Gaitskell and found her perfectly charming, all of which made it a memorable occasion for me.

I am writing finally to give you my warmest congratulations. The Bill is through to the Statute Book and the Royal Assent given. St Clair has resigned his seat in your old constituency and I shall exert the utmost pressure at Conservative Central Office to get you returned unopposed, thus avoiding all the expenditure and trouble of a needless by-election.

I shall greet you opposite me in the House in the next Session, as friend and opponent. Jo joins me in sending love to your wife and warmest regards to yourself, and congratulations to you both once again.

Yours ever,

GERALD NABARRO.

And he replied on 6th August 1963:

My dear Gerald,

How very nice of you to have written about the end of the campaign. I SHALL NEVER BE ABLE TO THANK YOU FOR YOUR CONSISTENT ENCOURAGEMENT AND SUPPORT OVER THE YEARS EVEN WHEN THINGS WERE VERY BLACK WHICH THEY OFTEN WERE. I LIVED ON OPTIMISM AND WHEN MINE RAN OUT OCCASIONALLY A TRANSFUSION FROM YOU WAS ALL THAT WAS NECESSARY.

We were delighted that you could come to the party and I hope you didn't feel too isolated. My constituents were so pleased to see you as they know how much you have done.

I look forward to seeing you again when Parliament meets in October.

All the very best.

Yours ever,

ANTHONY WEDGWOOD BENN.

The by-election at Bristol, exactly as I had wanted, was NOT contested by a Tory candidate and on 20th August, 1963, Benn defeated all his other opponents:

Wedgwood Benn	(Labour)	20,313
Martell	(Nat. Fellowship)	4,834
Mrs P. Lloyd	(Ind.)	287
G. Peart	(Anti-Soc. L-C)	44
	Labour majority	15,479

And so Benn took his seat again on 21st September, 1963.

Later, on 6th November, 1963, Sir Alec Douglas-Home (formerly Lord Home) took his seat in the Commons as Prime Minister and Member for Kinross and West Perthshire, and Mr Quintin Hogg, QC. (formerly Lord Hailsham) as Member for St Marylebone, on 5th December, 1963.

Had those fifteen dissident and rebellious Tories, under my leadership, not defied the Home Secretary, the Rt Hon. Richard Austen Butler and the Tory Whips on 13th April 1961, the Committee to reform the House of Lords would never have been established. The renunciation of peerages would never have been realised and Home, Hogg and Benn would never have returned to the Commons. Thus was the course of history changed.

Anthony Wedgwood Benn's determined and gallant struggle, to which I was privileged to contribute, both for him and for my Tory friends Home and Hogg, should carve Benn's name on the annals of Parliament, along with those of Hampden, Pym, Wilkes and Burke.

After the fall of Harold Wilson, I reckon Anthony Wedgwood Benn a possible successor, as leader of the Labour Party.

12. *Budgets: Particularly the Budget of 1960 and the Tory Chancellor, Heathcoat Amory*

THERE have been ten Chancellors of the Exchequer during the two decades, 1950 to 1970, and thus their average tenure of office has been two years apiece. Six of these Chancellors have been Tories and four Socialists:

Sir Stafford Cripps,	1947–50.	(Winchester)	Socialist.
Mr Hugh Gaitskell,	1950–51.	(Winchester)	Socialist.
Mr. R. A. Butler,	1951–55.	(Marlborough)	Tory.
Mr Harold Macmillan,	1955–57.	(Eton)	Tory.
Mr Peter Thorneycroft	1957–58.	(Eton)	Tory.
Mr Derick Heathcoat Amory,	1958–60.	(Eton)	Tory.
Mr Selwyn Lloyd,	1960–62.	(Fettes)	Tory.
Mr Reginald Maudling,	1962–64.	(Merchant Taylors)	Tory.
Mr James Callaghan,	1964–67.	(Elementary & Portsmouth Northern Secondary Schools)	Socialist.
Mr Roy Jenkins,	1967–	(Abersychan GS)	Socialist.

The best post-war Chancellors have been Butler and Maudling; the worst, Amory and Jenkins. Butler was outstanding because with calm and

The *Daily Telegraph*, 4th February, 1969.

deliberate individualistic intent, he retrieved the near bankruptcy inherited from Attlee and Gaitskell, who in 1951 had fled to the country after only twenty months in office. Butler put the economy on an even keel, restored incentives, reduced taxation and almost abolished consumer rationing in just four years, 1951–1955. Prosperity grew at an astonishing speed during his four years at the Treasury and the electors felt it because they gave the Tories a much bigger majority in 1955.

Maudling largely retrieved the errors of his predecessors, especially Amory, and in 1964 almost won the General Election for the Tories. He was expanding fast, without undue inflation and given just a little more time would undoubtedly have pulled it off. I rate big, shambling Reggie a very good economist indeed and a first class financial mind. He has spent his years in Opposition not only as Deputy Chairman of the Conservative Party but also as an executive director of Kleinwort, Benson, one of the largest of our merchant banks, which is some evidence of his financial stature.

In contrast: Jenkins. This Socialist Chancellor has done little to commend himself either to the electors or to economic observers since he took office in 1967. In his first year at the Treasury, 1968, he brought in two Budgets, the eleventh and twelfth of the Socialist administrations in just under five years, and raised taxes by £1,200m in a single year. In 1969, he budgeted for sixteen and a half million thousand pounds—say, £16,435m—or nearly double the Tory figure of five years earlier. Jenkins is a big spender, a big inflater, a fervent Socialist who believes that he can tax the nation back to prosperity.

In the early months of 1969 I had an altercation with Mr Roy Jenkins about the Road Fund Licence for motor cars. I said that he intended to raise the amount from an excessive £25 per annum to an exorbitant £35. Following the disturbance and a Select Committee, Mr Jenkins decided to take my advice. In his April, 1969 Budget, he left the Road Fund Licence alone at £25 and put a modicum on petrol. Thus, I had won. Mr Jenkins was very cross and even said that he had written a Treasury minute four months earlier deciding not to raise the Motor Tax. I regarded him as a latter day Ananias and pregnant with expectation I await 1999 A.D., when the Treasury minute is made public, thirty years on.

I rate Jenkins the biggest flop as Chancellor since the end of the war and too much the bureaucrat. But then Jenkins is a Socialist and running true to form.

There was no such excuse for Mr Derick Heathcoat Amory, now

The War of Jenkins's Ear was in 1739.

I.

This form should be used for licensing a motor car (see Note 3) on initial registration and subsequently if any change of ownership since the issue of the last licence and/or any changes made to the vehicle or in its use affecting taxation class or duty payable have not been recorded in the Registration Book. However, changes of colour, type of engine or propelling fuel may be notified on form VE.1A and this full declaration form need not, in such limited circumstances, be used.

The completed form, accompanied by

(i) *the duty payable,*

(ii) *a certificate of insurance (not the policy) or security in respect of third party risks, valid on either the day on which the licence is issued or the first day of the month during which the licence comes into force, whichever is the later (see Note 4 (ii)).*

	12 monthly rate £	s.	4 monthly rate £	s.
First registered before 1st January 1947 and not exceeding 7 h.p. / Electrically propelled	18.	0	6.	12
All others	35.	0	13.	3

(iv) the rate of duty appropriate to any vehicle is entered in the Registration Book. The rate is liable to change from time to time and changes usually become effective immediately. This means that any licence taken out after a change having immediate effect has been announced, will be subject to the new rate. T[illegible] includes a licence taken out within 14 days of the expir[illegible] previous one.

The Flea in Jenkins's Ear was in 1969.

Viscount Amory, KG, a sedate Devonian and a splendid Minister of Agriculture before Harold Macmillan moved him on to the Treasury in 1958. In April, 1959, he reduced taxes by £360m and won the General Election in October of that year with a much increased majority for a grateful Prime Minister and Party. It was the third General Election win in a row for the Tories and Budgets played a prominent, if not predominant, part in the outcome of all of them, demonstrating what I have always expounded, that taxes are the first consideration in the minds of the electors, when voting. Thus:

1951:	Labour majority of 8 becomes Tory majority of 16.	Tories gain 24 seats.	Big tax increases in Korean War Budget of Mr Gaitskell, April, 1951.
1955:	Tory majority of 16 increased to 59.	Tories gain 43 seats.	Tax reducing Budgets of Tory Chancellor, Mr. R. A. Butler.
1959:	Tory majority of 59 increased to 100.	Tories gain 41 seats.	£360m off taxes in Mr Heathcoat Amory's 1959 Budget.

Later, on 4th April, 1960 when Mr Amory brought in his first Budget after the General Election of the previous autumn, it was generally expected that it would be a full-blooded Tory-Capitalist Budget to encourage enterprise, foster thrift and promote industrial growth, expansion and exports. The country was bullish, world trade good and in Britain a climate of confidence reigned supreme.

Amory blundered. Economically and politically, he shocked the majority of the Tory Party. At the end of his Budget speech, there was stony silence from the packed Tory benches and jeers and derisive, ironical cheers from Mr Gaitskell, Mr Bevan, Mr Wilson and the Socialists opposite. Mr Gaitskell said:[1]

> There is certainly for many people a great deal of disappointment in this Budget. It has disappointed many hopes, particularly of those who voted for the Conservative Party at the last election. It also surprises them, though it did not surprise me because in fact this Budget is of a pattern that we recognise from previous experience—the pattern that, when the Conservative Party is in power and a General Election is impending, we always have an easy

[1] *Hansard*, 4th April, 1960, col. 76.

Budget, with plenty of tax concessions, but, as soon as the election is over, then the Chancellor of the Exchequer gets tough with the taxpayers and tough with the country.

A group of Tory friends and myself refused to support the Budget and the next day, 5th April, 1960, I launched my assault on it in the House of Commons. I was lucky to be called after dinner, at 8.35 p.m. The House was expecting my speech, the benches and the Press Gallery were packed

BUDGET DAY: 7th April, 1959. Treasury Bench, left to right: The Rt Hon. R. A. Butler, MP (Lord Privy Seal, Home Secretary and Leader of the House of Commons), The Rt Hon. Harold Macmillan, MP (Prime Minister), The Rt Hon. Iain Macleod, MP (Minister of Labour and National Service), The Rt Hon. Derick Heathcoat Amory, MP (Chancellor of the Exchequer), and as Parliamentary Private Secretary to the Chancellor of the Exchequer (behind), Mr Gerald Nabarro, MP (Con. Kidderminster).

and from my corner seat on the second bench below the gangway I gave the Chancellor the full treatment. The *Daily Express* report of the speech the following day was written by William Barkley under the headlines:

Tax-cuts champion Nabarro makes devastating attack on Chancellor.

BUDGET REVOLT EXPLODES

Amory goes pale as Tory rebel wades in.

Tory fury with the 'bad Budget' crashed from the secret committee room out on to the floor of the House of Commons last night when Mr Gerald Nabarro (Tory, Kidderminster) perhaps more in sorrow than in anger, delivered the most devastating attack on Mr Heathcoat Amory that any modern Chancellor had had to take from his own side.

He denounced him for inaccuracy, for political turpitude, for disgraceful political action.

And he accused him of making a 'mendacious' claim.

Mr Nabarro announced that he and a group of back-bench Tories will reserve their position to vote against specific issues in the Committee stage of the Finance Bill incorporating the Budget.

'Our group are the unofficial Opposition in this House', he declared, and when Labour members shouted 'Nabarro boys' and 'the Nabarro band', he retorted amid many cheers from the Tories: 'I claim we are much more effective than the official Opposition.'

Dark, picturesque, flamboyant Mr Nabarro leaned only a few yards away from the contrasting figure of the Chancellor.

Mr Heathcoat Amory, who shrank down on his Front-Bench seat with his feet on the table, affected at first to be amused and to smile.

But the smile was wan and grew sicklier as the 50-minute sizzling attack continued.

At one point Mr Amory was scribbling on a pad on his knee, and Mr Nabarro paused with a broad smile to say: 'You are drawing such an elaborate doodle in front of me that I hope you will now draw that addled egg laid on your window-sill.'

Mr Amory obliged and in a moment held up a sheet with a pencilled egg on it.

Mr Nabarro began by saying that in his most charitable mood he could agree with the Budget only in its abolition of entertainment duty, its modest tax reliefs and its action against tax avoidance.

'There I part company with the Chancellor of the Exchequer', said Mr

The *Evening Standard*, 21st March, 1960. Left to Right: Mr J. Enoch Powell, MP (Con. Wolverhampton, SW), The Viscount Hinchingbrooke, MP (Con. Dorset South), The Rt Hon. Peter Thorneycroft, MP (Con. Monmouth), Mr Gerald Nabarro, MP (Con. Kidderminster), Lord Beaverbrook, The Rt Hon. R. A. Butler, MP (Lord Privy Seal, Home Secretary and Leader of the House of Commons), The Rt Hon. Harold Macmillan, MP (Prime Minister).

Nabarro, who dramatises every phrase with all the more effect as he can quote figures and weave his argument together with never a note in his hand.

'I disagree with you in the fundamentals on which your Budget is based.'

He recalled that in 1955, after the Tories were re-elected on a ticket of continuing reductions of taxation, they slapped up taxes in an autumn Budget. He found it painful then not to vote against the Budget because he had stumped the country promising tax relief.

'I am dismayed that there has been a repetition of these events in the last few weeks.

'We were returned last October and my assessment of the Tory victory would be that the principal contributory factor was the Prime Minister's assurance that there would be continued reduction in taxes.

'In this Budget the Chancellor has increased taxation very considerably.

'I thought once in 1955 was bad politically. I think twice in five years is disgraceful politically.'

And he added amid great shouts from the Opposition: 'It is an act of political turpitude. That is why for the first time in at least two decades as many as twelve Government supporters yesterday spontaneously abstained from voting on the resolution.

'We did it as a protest against what we consider to be an appallingly bad Budget, the worst Budget from a Conservative Chancellor since we returned to power in 1951.

'We have been called rebellious and mutinous. I do not believe that adherence to the political principles which one has espoused all over the country is a matter of mutiny or rebellion.'

Last year, he said, Mr Amory reduced taxation by £360m. And what was the result?

'You won the election!' shouted Labour M.P.s.

Mr Nabarro: 'Never before in the history of this nation, until last year, have we increased production by 10%, increased the volume of exports by 14% and personal savings by 15%.

'I believe passionately that all these desirable results have flowed from the policy of last April of drastic reduction of taxes.'

He recalled that Mr Amory, in his estimates last April, predicted a revenue surplus of £102 million and got £386 million; he predicted a capital deficit of £751 million and got £314 million.

His surplus was four times as large as he had budgeted for, and his overall deficit less than half of his estimate.

'When the Treasury achieves margins of error and inaccuracy of that kind, my faith in Treasury advice is destroyed. I have no confidence in Treasury budgeting after reading such wildly inaccurate figures.'

He predicted that the Budget will not curb spending but merely reduce savings. 'There is room for very substantial tax relief this year. Tax relief would stimulate savings and provide the incentives so necessary for continuing the rise in production.'

To the accompaniment of bursts of cheers from the Tories, Mr Nabarro said that this year's Budget should have taken threepence off income tax, abolished Schedule 'A' tax, raised the surtax starting point to £3,000 and scrapped the profits tax along with the allowances which largely offset it.

As for Purchase Tax, he recalled that on November 10th Mr Amory had said in the Commons that he had made reductions of £120 million. Mr Nabarro recited the yield of Purchase Tax over the last four years as £494 million, £498 million, £501 million and £535 million, and said:

'All you have done is progressively to increase Purchase Tax but to claim mendaciously to the House and the country that you have reduced it.'

There was silence and then some protests, and the Chairman of the Committee, Sir William Anstruther-Gray, checked him saying, "mendaciously" is not a proper word to use'.

Mr Nabarro said: 'I substitute "gross inaccuracy" '. The Chancellor's claim on Purchase Tax is very nearly as wildly inaccurate as his budgeting last year.'

Mr Nabarro concluded by saying to Mr Amory: 'You have been very provocative. You will reap your due reward.'

'Long after the Finance Bill is finished you will be constantly in trouble', he said, 'unless you have regard for the careful advice given you by a group of Conservative Members and myself that there must be much stricter control of Government expenditure.

'Otherwise we shall face a series of Tory Budgets from Chancellors practising Socialism, and a return to the dreariest period of the post-war years characterised by Butskellism.'

To give the widest publicity to the claims of my Tory friends and myself that the Budget had gravely misjudged the requirements of the economy and the genuine expectations of the electors who had given the new Tory Government such a great majority in the House, I said candidly to Mr Heathcoat Amory that "Tory Chancellors should not produce Socialist Budgets" under the heading "Budget Blunders and Why—a case for widespread modest tax cuts", in the *Daily Telegraph* on 6th April, 1960:

Last year's Budget, with £360m of tax reductions, was nectar. This year's Budget, with substantial tax increases, is porridge—and porridge with salt to rub into Conservative wounds, not sugar.

Cynics will point to the analogy between 1960 and 1955.

In May, 1955, the Conservatives got back under Sir Anthony Eden with a majority of sixty seats, immediately following the April Budget, which substantially reduced taxes. In a supplemental Autumn Budget the "pots and pans" Budget, the Conservative Chancellor raised taxes.

The Conservatives got back in October, 1959, with an even better majority of 100 seats, largely on the ticket of Mr Macmillan's 'continuing reductions in taxation,' and in the first following Budget taxes are again raised. This may widely be interpreted as political turpitude.

Moreover, Conservative Chancellors of the Exchequer are expected and indeed reputed to be logical in their fiscal policy, and to show continuity of theme year by year. Beer and 'baccy go together. Last year, before the Election, the Chancellor surprisingly took 2d off a pint of beer. Then, with a majority of 100 behind him in the House of Commons, he slaps it on the 'baccy—2d on 20 cigarettes and more still on an ounce of pipe tobacco. The conclusion is inescapable.

Rather disingenuously, the Chancellor proclaims that his sins are not very great as he has raised taxes by only £72m in a full year.

This he achieves by neatly omitting in his Economic Survey and in his Budget speech any reference to the unloading of expenditure by Central Government on to local councils, which is causing rates to go up all over the country; for example, at Wrexham the increase is 1s 8d in the £. There may well be as much as £50m extra taxation through the local rates, and it is significant that Mr Amory was silent on this point; otherwise, he should properly have confessed that he is really putting the taxes up not by £70m but by £120m.

The grave failures of the Conservative Government to control public expenditure, notably by putting a curb on the extravagances of nationalised industries, is the primary cause of Mr Amory's fiscal bathos, which he is pleased to call 'a cautious and unexciting Budget'. The proper riposte to that is that 'If you go in for Socialist spending, you can expect a Socialist Budget.' Let us go back to the Budget of 1959, with record tax reliefs of £360m, and study what flowed from it. Ten per cent increase in production in a single year and 14 per cent increase in the volume of exports are extraordinarily fine achievements, judged by any standards. Earnings reached the highest level in our history, with stable prices for nearly two years. Real values were established. It was also remarkable to see an increase in personal savings of all kinds amounting to 15 per cent, and in National Savings the increase was 20 per cent.

Even the Chancellor, in the House on Monday, habitually miserly in his praise anyway, referred to the splendid record during the year. Unemployment fell and the numbers employed rose. A part of the slack in the economy was taken up during the year, following the big tax reliefs, but not all of it, and exports rose by 14 per cent in volume, with the pound strong abroad and a weakness developing in the balance of payments position only towards the end of the year. This last symptom was probably largely due to stock-piling in industry, a tendency which may well tail off in the early future.

The lesson to be learned from the 1959 Budget with the big tax reliefs was the following year of real gains, the nation buying more, earning more and spending more, and under-written is the maintenance of price stability. Thus the Chancellor's axiom 'to consolidate and fortify our present prosperity'. The controversial question is, how best to consolidate and fortify?

Surely not by a return to Butskellism and the dreary philosophy which says that immediately a sign of strain develops anywhere in the economy, including the prospect of wage inflation, the way to tackle it is to put the taxes up. On the contrary, the remedy is to offer further and powerful incentives for increased production and productivity by tax reductions, and equally powerful incentives for saving.

The latter should have a dual objective: first to furnish the sinews of new capital formation and industrial investment, and secondly to act as a strong counter both to wage increases and the growing hire-purchase debt. It is notable that last year, after accounting such items as dis-saving as the hire-purchase debt, personal savings reached the huge figure of £1,449m compared with £885m in 1955, an advance of nearly two-thirds.

The Chancellor's Budget on Monday offended all these principles. Far from restraining spending, as he intends, by 2d on cigarettes and higher profits tax, it is probable that spending will be at the same level or higher, and that savings will suffer.

Also, if the Chancellor really means what he says about splendid results of National Savings, he should match his words by splendid opportunities. Formerly, the limit for the 10th issue of National Savings was 1,000 certificates worth £750, becoming £1,000 after seven years. This issue had sold almost to saturation before the last Budget. Now all the Chancellor does is to raise the maximum by 200 certificates to 1,200 and at the same time he fiddles about with Premium Bonds, making some of the prizes bigger and altering others, evidently in an effort to compete with football pools.

The Chancellor should have had an 11th issue of National Savings Certificates, on a slightly less advantageous tax-free interest terms, allowing everybody to buy a further £750, not £150 worth. Now the temptation will be to maintain spending, not saving.

Budgets are always a matter of individual judgement. The Chancellor evidently wants to de-fizz the economy, retreating from the prosperity he himself has created. Last year, having Budgeted for an 'above-the-line' surplus of £102m, he came out with a surplus of £386m. Then, having Budgeted for an overall deficit of £721m, he came out with an overall

President, The Worcester Locomotive Society at the controls of ex-Great Western "Manor" Class steam locomotive "Cookham Manor" No. 7808 "Ashchurch, Gloucestershire" 1968.

Gerald Nabarro's golden rule:

"Cut down on the drink . . . go in for the women." Sir Gerald Nabarro, M.P., receives at the Palace of Westminster and escorts on a tour of both Houses of Parliament, acting as commentator and guide throughout, members of the Evesham Branch of the Royal College of Nursing and National Council of Nurses of the United Kingdom. Lady Nabarro is President of the Branch. Here the Member for Worcestershire, South signs autographs on the terrace of the Houses of Parliament, on 2nd November 1966.

Sir Gerald Nabarro, M.P., Vice-President of the Vale of Evesham Asparagus Growers, Association, admires winning exhibits at the Asparagus Show at Badsey, Worcestershire, May 1969. On the left is Mr. A. Grove, Chairman of the Vale of Evesham Asparagus Growers' Association.

"Redundant British Eagle air stewardesses lobby Sir Gerald Nabarro, M.P. (Conservative, Worcestershire South) about their grievances,"
20th November 1968.

"THE BELOVED SIR ALEC"

Left to Right: Mrs. Peter Jones: wife of Chairman, Kemerton Branch, South Worcestershire Division Conservative Association, Sir Gerald Nabarro, M.P. (Conservative, Worcestershire South), Lady Nabarro, Rt. Hon. Sir Alec Douglas-Home, K.T., M.P. (Conservative, Kinross and West Perthshire), Mr. Peter Jones, Chairman, Kemerton Branch, South Worcestershire Division Conservative Association, Lady Douglas-Home, Major R. D. Unwin, Chairman, Worcestershire, South Division Conservative Association, in 1967 during Sir Alec's visit to South Worcestershire.

Judging the Beauty Queen "Miss Harlech" at Longleat House, Wiltshire, September 1968.

After Mr. Enoch Powell's Birmingham speech, 20th April 1968, London dockers strike in sympathy with his policies and march on Westminster.

Sir Gerald Nabarro, M.P. (Conservative, Worcestershire, South), received dockers outside the House of Commons and urged: (1) Return to work; (2) Non-violence.

Thoresby Pit, 1955. East Midlands coal field, *4th from Left:* Mr. Gerald Nabarro, M.P., Conservative, Kidderminster, *5th from Left:* Mr. Harold Neal, M.P. (Labour, Bolsover).

deficit of £314m. So much for the major inaccuracies of the Treasury. It is to be hoped that this year's inaccuracies will be less large.

The Chancellor should have continued the policy of last year, relying on further production and productivity gains and massive savings to keep prices stable, sustain exports and yield revenue which would have given an even better surplus above the line than last year, notwithstanding the increase in Government expenditure, the vicissitudes of deficit financing in nationalised industries, and associated problems. There should have been a deliberate and calculated policy of widespread though modest tax relief.

Income tax reduction should have included 3d off the standard rate and the abolition of Schedule A tax for owner-occupied houses. This latter relief could not conceivably affect the balance of payments and is an illicit collection by the Inland Revenue anyway, because nobody who knows how to make a maintenance relief claim and does all the usual repairs to his house needs to pay the tax. To scrap it would cost only £34m and would benefit 7m home owners.

There should have been further consolidation of the purchase tax, on lines not dissimilar to those of 1958 and 1959, compressing the rates and keeping the lowest level at 5 per cent.

A few weeks ago the Chancellor boasted in the House of Commons that he had reduced purchase tax by £120m. How false that statement is may be judged by the fact that in 1958 purchase tax raised £494m, in 1959 £498m, in 1960 £501m and in 1961 will probably reach £535m. These figures may be compared with steel de-nationalisation, which started in 1951 with a State stake in steel of £251m which will shortly be £360m, thus representing the antithesis of denationalisation. Treasury words are seen to be worth little.

Finally, there should have been 'a bonus for brains' and an attempt to prevent many of our best scientists, technicians, doctors, teachers and professional men emigrating in large numbers to the Commonwealth and foreign countries, where tax rates are lower, by raising the commencing level of surtax from £2,000 per annum to £3,000.

Tax reliefs of this kind would have stimulated industry and taken up the remaining slack, countered inflationary tendencies, and provided yet further incentives to every class in the community to earn and to save. It is doubtful whether the Chancellor would have lost anything in revenue by such tax reductions, because of the higher output and greater personal savings engendered.

Politically, he would have behaved like a Conservative Chancellor, practising what Mr Macmillan preached at the last General Election, that the nation under the Conservatives would enjoy continuing reduction in taxation, instead of a poor and unimpressive imitation of Mr Harold Wilson, the Socialist 'Shadow' Chancellor.

Briefly, if the electors want Socialism they will vote Socialist, not Tory, to get it. Our Tory insurrection had some little effect. In the next three years Surtax came down: rates of purchase tax fell to 25%, 15% and 10%; income tax allowances for children and dependents rose and generally the Tories managed to lop a lot off taxes. But, they never again achieved the dynamic created pre-1955 and pre-1959 General Elections, especially the latter which led to the unequalled growth in production, exports and personal savings, quoted in my speech in the House of Commons and repeated in my *Daily Telegraph* article. I repeat again those oft-derided and mocked words I used in the House on 5th April, 1960:

> I believe passionately that all these desirable results have flowed from the policy of last April (1959) reducing drastically the level and incidence of taxation.[1]

Also, it illuminates the deep and fundamental cleavage in political and fiscal policies between Mr Jenkins and his Socialist colleagues, who believe that sackcloth and ashes, the hair shirts and even bigger tax bills for the citizens of Britain, encourage hard work, expansion and growth: and the Conservative Party, which believes the opposite.

Moreover, the student of Politics and economic affairs will not fail to perceive that whereas the periods 1945–51 and 1964–70 show huge increases in taxation, the intervening thirteen years 1951–1964 show a progressive decline in rates of taxation, while maintaining steady increase of wealth throughout the community, notably large accumulations of personal savings, and growth of overseas investments.

An impartial observer would then be right to deduce that:

The Labour Party is the Party of increased and increasing taxation.

The Tory Party is the Party of decreased and decreasing taxation.

I have never been slow to point this out on the hustings, which invariably makes the Socialists squirm; and so they should. It is a nice, simple, solidly-based approach, which has great appeal to the mass of the voters; and that is the stuff of which propaganda is rightly made. I am a dedicated political propagandist, as I said later, and in another context.

But I should not leave the memorable Budget of 1960 and the inglorious role of Mr Derick Heathcoat Amory without recording two significant interpretations of it all. The first is from "Essence of Parliament" in *Punch* on 13th April, 1960:

> 1846 AND ALL THAT? The beginnings were pure comedy. The Chancellor was only just in time to hear his own speech and had the greatest difficulty in

[1] *Hansard*, 5th April, 1960, col. 304.

finding a seat to hear it from. After a lot of pushing and pulling they shoved Sir Edward Boyle off on to the floor and Mr Amory was just able to squeeze on to the front bench. Then he looked around him and caught sight—of all improbable sights to catch—of Mr Abse, the Socialist Member for Pontypool, in a grey top-hat. What was the meaning of that I cannot imagine. The pigeons laying eggs in the Treasury were as nothing to its improbability.

Is this 1846 all over again with a Conservative Government supported only by the applause of its Opposition, with Mr Nabarro as Disraeli and Lord Hinchingbrooke as Lord George Bentinck? It is tempting to think so. There is something attractively appropriate about the casting. In the Carlton Club the Tadpoles and Tapers were muttering about 'this damned Socialist Government'. White's Club though that they were in the White Highlands and had been sold down the river, and it is certainly true that as far as the speeches went the Government had a rough ride from its supporters, beginning with Mr Cooper, the first back-bench speaker, and running right through the debate, and it is also true that the twelve bold abstainers registered their protest from the first. It is true that Mr Narbarro's attack was far from knockabout and far from merely genial. It bristled with statistics and it bristled with good full-throated abuse. Yet I cannot quite see Mr Nabarro as a king-murderer. Would Sir Robert Peel ever have fallen if Disraeli had had a handle-bar moustache? To stage a successful revolt it is necessary to be fanatical, humourless, intense—to enjoy being hated. Mr Nabarro, with all his high qualities has two fatal defects as a politician, he is a nice man and he has a sense of humour. He tries to be a fanatic, but with him as with Dr. Johnson's Edwards, cheerfulness is always breaking in. There is always that fatal twinkle in the eye, the suspicion that he is calling attention to himself because he likes attention and not because he thinks himself the Messiah. Also he made his speech too soon and before the end the Chancellor's supporters were beginning to hit back—notably the Cromwellian Mr Cyril Osborne, prepared to out-Cripps Cripps without apology. Lord Hinchingbrooke might try to raise the temperature again towards the end by complaining of the Chancellor's "waspish, donnish way", but the Chancellor had only to answer that he had "a great respect and affection for Lord Hinchingbrooke but he was sorry that he could not subscribe to his economic views," and this "Pekinese Parliament", as Mr Peyton called it, was apparently content. Indeed it was too content, for amid all the talks about personalities and lower taxes not enough has been said about the dangerous risk that in future we are to pay in accordance not with the letter of the law but with the Government's intention. That way indeed is the road to slavery.

THE THORNEYCROFT STAKES. Mr Enoch Powell evaded controversy by taking refuge in history and philosophy. But there is of course an alternative leader for revolt. No one has a better excuse for heading one than Mr Thorneycroft.

The *Evening Standard*, 8th April, 1960. Left to Right: (Extreme left) Mr J. Enoch Powell, MBE, MP (Con. Wolverhampton S.W.), fifth from left Mr Gerald Nabarro, MP (Con. Kidderminster), The Viscount Hinchingbrooke, MP (Con. Dorset South), The Rt Hon. Peter Thorneycroft, MP (Con. Monmouth).

> He has a seniority of status over the other dissidents. He has behaved admirably since his resignation—has not factiously attacked his colleagues—has borne in silence some unworthy press jeers and has now lived to see the warnings through which he resigned, largely justified. His was an able and honourable speech—an accusation that neither of the parties really intended to bring expenditure under control—without such control, inflation was inevitable—that Governments should at least tell the truth about their intentions—that the Chancellor was nearer to catastrophe than he realised. Was this perhaps then the banner of the clans?
>
> THE TWO MUSKETEERS. The reason why it was improbable was given in the next speech by Mr Anthony Crosland. Mr Thorneycroft's revolt, he showed, was quite different from that of Mr Nabarro. Mr Nabarro thinks that taxation can be reduced here and now. Mr Thorneycroft thinks that it cannot be reduced. Was the real doctrine of Tory revolt then being preached from the Socialist benches by Mr Crosland and Mr Roy Jenkins? Stranger things have happened in this confused world, and since for all their persuasiveness there is clearly no remotest chance that the death-wish beetles on the Socialist benches will adopt the policies offered by these two gay Musketeers, why should not the Conservatives adopt them and they end up as the rising hopes of the stern unbending Tories? After all, they must end up somewhere, and that seems as good a place as another. But there are two obstacles in the way of the Up-Jenkins Gospel of more money for investment. The one is that, as Sir Edward Boyle brought out, the rest of their party have made it clear that if ever they lay their hands on more money they are going to give it out in pensions. The other is then when they contrast the increase of production on the Continent with its lag in Britain they never clearly explain why it is that the Continent has increased its production by following policies quite different from those which they are recommending.

All prophetic words indeed, because, of course, the Two Musketeers have been President of the Board of Trade (Mr Anthony Crosland) and Chancellor of the Exchequer (Mr Roy Jenkins) in the Socialist Government of recent years.

On 10th April 1960, the columnist "Peregrine" in the *Observer* wrote engagingly about my friends and myself, embattled for our Conservative principles:

> The chief fascination in the small Tory group that would like to dance on the grave of Heathcoat Amory's Budget is the close association between Nabarro and Hinchingbrooke. The more rustic Conservatives already regard Gerald Nabarro as their own Aneurin Bevan. And Lord Hinchingbrooke has been called the Crossman of the Right.

THE BUDGET DEBATES, 1960 by Cummings, *Daily Express*, 8th April, 1960. Left to Right: Mr Gerald Nabarro, MP (Con. Kidderminster), The Rt Hon. Peter Thorneycroft, MP (Con. Monmouth), The Rt Hon. Iain Macleod, MP (Secretary of State for the Colonies), The Rt Hon. Harold Macmillan, MP (Prime Minister), The Rt Hon. Derick Heathcoat Amory, MP (Chancellor of the Exchequer), The Rt Hon. Hugh Gaitskell, MP (Leader of Her Majesty's Opposition), (Taking cover) The Rt Hon. R. A. Butler, MP (Lord Privy Seal, Home Secretary and [illegible])

Hinchingbrooke, intellectual and austere, stiff-necked but kind, a Conservative by blood and conviction, yet an interested and not unsympathetic visitor to European Communist countries, seems a strange companion for the brash and brainy Nabarro, with his trade-mark moustachios and his well-publicised cars, licensed from NAB 1 to NAB 4. Nabarro, the self-made man (Educ.: LCC Elementary School until fourteen), revels in the friendship.

Nabarro is able to tell you about the making of Nabarro ('Couldn't afford a commission in the Army. Product of the managerial system, I suppose') without being offensive or boring—which is quite an achievement. He and Canadian Ted Leather are the only two of the rebels who made it in what is popularly considered the hard way. (Recently six of the group met at dinner; there were five Old Etonians—and Nabarro.)

Hinchingbrooke can rebel with impunity; he may suspect that Nabarro may not take revolt to the ultimate limits. But Nabarro is now so far from the Tory inner circle that he, too, probably has nothing to lose. He has said that he will vote against the Budget if his amendments are not accepted. The dozen or so Tories for whom he speaks are a mixed bunch, but they are quite united in contempt for Heathcoat Amory. Nabarro admits that his attack on the Chancellor was partly personal, because he thinks Amory is no good as Chancellor. In numerical terms the rebels can hardly worry the Conservative leadership. But it must be disconcerting to know that among the solid, sterling worth of the Conservative back benches, where facts and figures do not often count when inconvenient, there is the restless, rather shamefaced feeling that that bounder Nabarro has got something.

Personally, for myself alone, I value the advice of two great soldiers:

"The important thing is not how people get into the House of Commons, but whether they are fit to be there"

(*The Duke of Wellington*)

"An educated democracy is one in which it is unprofitable to lie at elections. We are still a long way from this ideal"

(*Field Marshal Lord Wavell*)

I wish that more politicians today had learned to observe these axioms, especially in fiscal matters.

13. *A Conversation Piece with Lord Snow*, *CBE, PhD, Hon.LL.D, Hon.DSc, Hon.D.Litt, Hon.DHL, FRSL*

Reprinted from *King* magazine, April, 1967.

BOTH of the participants in this month's conversation came from humble homes. Both, in their own way, have scaled the heights through a tireless amalgam of ambition and ability.

Lord Snow, knighted in 1957 and created a life peer in 1964, is best known as C. P. Snow—a name which has appeared with distinction on the title-pages of a dozen novels and the marquees of five West End plays. Born in Leicester sixty-one years ago, "C.P." showed brilliant promise at school and won a scholarship with consummate ease to Christ's College, Cambridge. He began his adult life as a professional scientist, but in 1935 returned to his alma mater as a tutor. For ten years he was one of Cambridge's best-known personalities. Then, in 1945, he forsook the academic life for a post with the Civil Service Commissioners—the "corridors of power" he was later to immortalise as the title of his best-selling novel. Since then, he has divided his time between the political, cultural and scientific worlds with dazzling success. In addition to a regular output of novels, plays and articles, he was Rede Lecturer at Cambridge in 1959, Godkin Lecturer at Harvard in 1960. This latter appointment led him to a close association with the United States, and he currently holds honorary degrees at a host of American universities including Dartmouth, Bard,

Temple, Syracuse and Pittsburgh. In Britain, he holds similar appointments at Leicester, Liverpool and St Andrews, where he was Rector for three years from 1961. In 1964, when Labour came into power, he was appointed Parliamentary Secretary to the newly established Ministry of Technology, a post he admits he found "frustrating" and has now somewhat thankfully given up. Married since 1950 to novelist Pamela Hansford Johnson, he has one son and lives in a pleasant but unpretentious house in Kensington.

Unlike Lord Snow, Sir Gerald Nabarro first found success in the rough and tumble of business life. Born fifty-three years ago, he was educated at a local LCC school which he left at fourteen. At seventeen he enlisted in the Regular Army, but left it seven years later to take up a succession of labouring jobs in the engineering and sawmilling industries. By his early thirties, he had worked his way up to managing director, and this in turn led to a consuming interest in politics. After failure at the hustings in 1945, his ambitions materialised in 1950 when he was elected member for Kidderminster. Almost immediately he established himself as one of the Conservative Party's most consistently outspoken backbenchers. In 1964, when ill-health forced him to resign, political correspondents mourned the departure from Westminster of one of its most flamboyant personalities. They had reckoned without Nabarro's energy and determination. Eighteen months later he was back—this time as MP for South Worcestershire.

KING: A question we should like to put to both of you, as men intimately involved with the government of this country, concerns the power of the Prime Minister. It's been said just recently that his power has increased to such an extent during the last quarter-century that he now closely resembles an American President in personal prestige. Would you agree?

SNOW: I certainly wouldn't accept that the Prime Minister has assumed all the Presidential powers. But I would agree he has almost complete powers of appointment, which is tremendously important. Of course, the Prime Minister has always had this power, but the way it has been used by Macmillan and Wilson is much more complete than in the case of, say, Asquith.

NABARRO: Even so, his powers are still very incomplete. Take that massive demonstration by sixty-two Labour men who abstained from a three-line Whip over the Defence Estimates. That was a method of expressing the view "less money on armaments, more money on social services". Or interpreting it in Hitler's famous phrase "less money on guns, more money on butter".

KING: But to what extent does the Prime Minister have to take notice of them?

NABARRO: Quite a lot. I have no crystal ball, but I would hazard a guess that Harold Wilson will be very, very careful how he handles his annual conference in October. No Prime Minister can ignore sixty desertions, even with a hundred majority.

SNOW: Of course not.

NABARRO: Let me give you another example. In 1957, a Bill appeared before the House of Commons on the question of Life Peerages. All the Conservative leaders knew that I led a lobby in favour of reforming the Lords. I tried to get written into the Life Peerages Bill votes for peers at General Elections, and also the renunciation of hereditary peerages. The Government knew what I was up to, and tried to draw up the Bill so tightly that it couldn't be amended in the way I wanted. So I had to wait until the Wedgwood Benn case. Then I whipped up a lot of feeling on my side of the House, and took quite a large number of Tories with me into the Lobby against the Home Secretary, demanding that a top-level committee should be appointed to inquire into reform of the Lords. We got our committee. And then we bombarded it with recommendations about renunciation of peerages and other associated matters, using the Wedgwood Benn case as an example. Two years later, of course, the recommendations were built into a new Bill which finally became law. What I'm trying to point out is that just a handful of Tory MPs voting against their own leadership forced a committee to be appointed, and that the course of parliamentary history was changed by a small backbench vote. Because, unless he had been able to renounce his title as Earl of Home, Alec Douglas-Home would never have become Prime Minister. And this, of course, probably had some bearing on the election result of 1964.

SNOW: Now, of course, the whole feeling in the Lords has changed. I don't believe myself that we shall ever see hereditary peerages created again.

NABARRO: I do.

SNOW: You do?

NABARRO: Yes, definitely. I went for Wilson over the Honours List, when he said he was going to change the basis for the award of honours. I went for him in particular about the proliferation of Privy Councillors. It is generally said that it is better to accept the patronage of a Privy

Councillorship than to accept a knighthood if one is a member of the House of Commons.

SNOW: I don't quite see why.

NABARRO: Well, it gives one precedence to speak in the House. If you get up in the Commons as a Privy Councillor, the Speaker isn't obliged to call you, but generally speaking he will. As an ordinary backbencher your chances are ten-to-one against being called. During the Defence debate, scores of backbenchers well versed in Defence matters were squeezed out by Privy Councillors. It's this proliferation of Privy Councillors which Wilson relies on within his Honours system. The Tory equivalent is that they give more knighthoods and baronetcies, and fewer Privy Councillorships. I certainly don't accept that the Tory Party won't revert to hereditary honours.

SNOW: After a period, I think it will be very difficult.

NABARRO: I think you may be right—in a hundred years time.

SNOW: Much sooner, I think.

NABARRO: But do you think that the life peerages system has so far worked out as we intended it to work out? It was intended to attract to the House of Lords distinguished men and women from various walks of life who could make a real contribution to the higher counsels of the nation. In fact, it seems to me that, during the last two or three years, life peerages have been given as sinecures to elderly politicians from the Commons rather than to people of distinction who have never sat in Parliament.

SNOW: I don't agree. We have several vice-chancellors and several Nobel Prizewinners, all of whom have done an extremely good job in the House of Lords. When there's a serious topic to be discussed, I think you have in the Lords the finest parliamentary debates in Europe. In the world, in fact.

NABARRO: But there are many new life peers who never seem to play a part in the House of Lords at all.

SNOW: That's true—but that's always been true.

NABARRO: I know it's always been true. The point I'm trying to make is that we were attempting to alter the situation, and it's not been altered.

SNOW: It has to a considerable extent.

NABARRO: Well, let's agree that it's a better House of Lords than it was, and leave it at that. Tell me, Charles, how important do you think television has become in the conduct of politics?

SNOW: I think that it would be very difficult to be an effective leader of either party unless you had an attractive television personality. You're lucky, Sir Gerald—you have one. A lot of people who are absolutely worthy, unfortunately don't. For instance, Sir Alec Douglas-Home, who I like as a person and respect as a man, is unlucky because his personality simply isn't projected on television. I think that Edward Heath, whom I don't know, has exactly the same disadvantage.

NABARRO: Do you think it's something one can acquire?

SNOW: No, not at all.

NABARRO: Public speaking is an extraordinary thing. When I entered the House of Commons in 1950, I made up my mind to make my maiden speech within a few days. I spoke in the first debate I thought I knew something about. I didn't write my speech: I marshalled the facts, set them down on paper, and then spent most of the night before the debate walking the streets of London committing them to memory. When I actually came to deliver the speech I was so frightened that I stood to attention throughout it. It didn't read as a very good speech, but it was hailed by the national Press as one of the best maiden speeches since before the war.

SNOW: A good speech rarely reads well. I made my first speech from the Dispatch Box, like you without notes, and that was hailed as a big success. But it didn't read particularly well. Going back to what we were saying about television, I'm quite certain that it is pure chance that one man has the gift to project himself, and another hasn't. The present Prime Minister is extremely fortunate because he has the gift.

NABARRO: Harold Wilson has many gifts. I remember being asked three of four years ago, who were the best brains in British politics today. I replied Harold Wilson and Enoch Powell—and to my mind, they're still the best brains. This doesn't necessarily mean they're the best minds. Or that a first-class brain necessarily makes a good Prime Minister. My personal view is that you don't want a first-class brain as Prime Minister. You want qualities which are rather different.

SNOW: Well, I certainly agree that Harold Wilson is a marvellously clever man. Wilson and Enoch Powell are among the men with the highest IQs I've ever known. I knew Powell at Cambridge when he was a young classical scholar. His IQ is enormously high.

NABARRO: I'll tell you something that isn't generally known about Wilson. In his early days in the Civil Service, he was the man who evolved the scheme for coal rationing and clothes rationing in the war. He even evolved a system—which, thank God, never had to be put into effect—for rationing electricity and gas. Those early exercises with statistics have produced the fast mental reactions that give him ascendancy in the Commons today.

SNOW: There's something else about Wilson that is not generally recognised. Apart from being a ruthless politician, which all Prime Ministers have to be, he is an extremely kind man.

NABARRO: I can tell you a story about that. In all the years that Wilson was shadow Chancellor of the Exchequer, and I was on the Tory back-benches, there were head-on collisions between us. To the outside world we were sworn enemies. In fact, the *Daily Express* ran a full centre-page article entitled "Wilson v Nabarro". Then in 1964, I was forced to give up my seat because of serious illness. The morning after the announcement appeared in the newspapers I got a great pile of sympathetic mail. The third letter I looked at was from Harold Wilson—written in his own hand.

SNOW: I can't say it surprises me. But I think it would surprise most people. They just see him as a ruthless politician.

NABARRO: Which he is, of course.

SNOW: Which as Prime Minister, he has to be.

NABARRO: Let me switch your agile brain to something else, Charles. What do we do about the proliferation of nuclear weapons?

SNOW: I suspect that it's too late to do much at all. I think we were wrong to make the bomb ourselves. It is valueless, and we wasted an awful lot of money. And, if we hadn't made it, I doubt whether the French would.

NABARRO: But it's a fact, surely, that the development of nuclear fission for peaceful purposes cannot be separated from the development of the fissionable material which goes into a weapon of destruction? The material you use in a nuclear power-station is equally applicable to the Bomb? So, accepting that the material is available and the secret known, how do you stop its proliferation?

SNOW: I don't think you can now. The fact is that Japan, India, Israel, Sweden, Switzerland and about six other countries—

NABARRO: Germany—

SNOW: Yes, Germany, could make these things in a matter of twelve months if they were so minded.

NABARRO: Exactly—because the engineering processes in making the Bomb are simple. The difficult and expensive part of the process is making the fissionable material. Once you've made the fissionable material you can go one of two ways: you can apply it to peaceful purposes—power-stations, isotopes and so on—or you can put it into your relatively simple engineering product and blow up half the world. That's the danger with China.

SNOW: And no one knows the answer. There may not even be an answer, in which case the outlook is pretty bleak, especially where the Chinese are concerned.

NABARRO: Unless their circumstances change. If the world is magnanimous and helpful to China, and persuades her to take the same path as Russia, the world is saved.

SNOW: Well, it may happen. But not yet. At the moment the standard of living in China is roughly equivalent to the standard in Russia in the early Twenties. That means there's a thirty to forty years gap between the two Communist ideologies.

NABARRO: What's worse, the Chinese are feeling ostracised. It was a profound mistake to keep Red China out of the United Nations. Yet, even today, if there was a vote in the Tory Party to accept or reject Red China, the majority would say "reject". I'm in a small minority.

SNOW: Yes, but an important and intelligent minority, if I may say so.

NABARRO: Of course, what we've got to do is change the American attitude before it is too late.

SNOW: Yes, but generally the Americans tend to take up their own ideological positions of extraordinary rigidity. Much as I love America, it is an ideological country, and it's almost impossible to change their views on such matters.

NABARRO: Yet, despite this, I always marvel at the tremendous quest for learning in America. I'm thinking in particular of the wife of the president of an American corporation whom I met recently. She is forty, and has just had her fifth child yet she was studying for a PhD externally at an American university. Why do we never get that sort of thing in England?

SNOW: The climate over there is different.

NABARRO: Yet there is no debarment in this country to anyone learning anything at all—if they want to learn it. The teachers are there and the State is helpful. There's no debarment or inhibition at all.

SNOW: Except the climate.

NABARRO: That's favourable.

SNOW: No, I mean the climate of opinion, of behaviour. People just don't do it over here.

NABARRO: No—yet strangely enough, the American quest for scholarship is born out of an innate sense of immaturity among Americans. There's a concept in this country which says that the education of the market-place will always defeat an academic education anyway. You are one of the few men who have had a fine academic education as well as a fine education in the market-place. There aren't many like you.

SNOW: I think there will be more as time goes on.

NABARRO: You know what I mean by "market-place"?

SNOW: Well, I've certainly heard the phrase before. You can't be in America for five minutes without hearing it.

NABARRO: It doesn't mean egalitarianism, as most people seem to think.

SNOW: No, definitely not. Egalitarianism in its crude sense is a very inhibiting thing.

NABARRO: And a very nasty thing.

SNOW: Yes, because it means—and we've seen this in our own time—that human excellence was much less regarded than it was, say, twenty years ago. Less venerated, if you like.

NABARRO: I don't think human excellence is the right phrase. I prefer "human quality": quality of brain, quality of mind, quality of experience.

SNOW: I think it's significant that no one today in the Western world is held in anything like the same regard as Einstein. Einstein was a very great man, but there are other great men living now. The respect just isn't there.

NABARRO: Who would you nominate as a great man today?

SNOW: Well, speaking off-hand, I would say Peter Medawar. He's a Nobel Prizewinner, and one of the best biologists this country has produced for God knows how long. The only person of Syrian extraction, as far as I know, who really has made a mark in the world since the days of Mohammed. This is a man of enormous intellectual gifts; but the fact that one has to explain who he is is in itself significant. One wouldn't have had to explain Einstein in, say, the early Twenties.

NABARRO: Tell me, Charles, did you enjoy your time as Rector of St Andrews?

SNOW: I enjoyed it immensely. You're not only chairman of the board, as it were, but spokesman for the students as well. And of course, Scottish students are a bit more exigent than English students.

NABARRO: You mean they threw things at you?

SNOW: Oh no. Not a bit.

NABARRO: But they do sometimes, don't they? I remember seeing pictures of RAB Butler covered in rotten eggs and flour.

SNOW: That was at Glasgow. They're really rough there. At St Andrews it's pretty gentle. Anyway, I had a detached retina at the time, so they just had to be kind.

NABARRO: They asked me to stand for election as Rector, you know. Do you know what happened?

SNOW: No.

NABARRO: Well, it was when I had given up my seat in the Commons, and was on my back. Some undergraduates from St Andrews came and asked me to run as Rector. And I said no, I'm neither a Scot nor a scholar. It then emerged that only fifty per cent of the undergraduates were Scots anyway. The rest were English or other lesser breeds. So I agreed to put my name down. As I was on my back I didn't go up there, but they ran a campaign on my behalf. But I was beaten to it by Sir John Rothenstein of the Tate. At the time I was rather sorry about it.

SNOW: Even though you were on your back?

NABARRO: Well, why not?

KING: Sir Gerald, if you were asked to name the most important lessons you've learned in life, what would your answer be?

NABARRO: Well, I've always believed that one of the two qualities needed to live a full and happy life is assiduity. The other is charity. I don't mean giving money away. I mean charity in its broadest sense, to all mankind. That doesn't necessarily mean kindness because on occasions you have to be unkind. What qualities would you choose, Charles?

SNOW: Well, if there's one lesson I've learned it's that the worst does not always happen. Occasionally you just have to stick with it. And if you do, you'll find that the results often aren't as bad as you think.

NABARRO: But that's begging the question. Those are idiosyncrasies of your own character. You are a very successful man—how have you achieved this success? That's what people want to know.

SNOW: Well, I have a clever young son aged fifteen. We were talking recently and he suddenly said "You know, you had one great advantage over me. You were a hungry boxer." I don't know where he'd picked up the American Phrase, but he meant of course that I'd come up from the lowest edge of the lower middle class. "You had a fighting class behind you", he said. "I may be as ambitious as you, I may be as talented. I don't know. But the fact that I'm not a hungry boxer is going to make it much tougher for me."

NABARRO: I don't agree with him. I think that our youngsters—your son and mine—have many advantages. Take my eldest boy. Educated at Harrow and Oriel College, Oxford, now just starting on a career. I had to say to myself: Now what do I do with you, my son? Do I give you money, do I cease helping you when you're twenty-one, do I leave you to fight it out as I had to fight it out? Or do I cosset you? That's the problem: whether a boy born with the advantages of your son and mine will match our performance if he has not got the same adversity of circumstances. One doesn't want to deny them anything. That's what one works for anyway. But if you give them too much of the best, you destroy their ambition, their fighting spirit.

SNOW: This is one of the reasons why I sent my son to Eton. I thought that was a tough enough place for anyone.

NABARRO: Charles, just before we conclude this very pleasant lunch, I am determined to ask a question of that young man who has been so assiduously tape-recording everything we say. Tell me, how does KING choose people to take part in these Conversations? Do you choose two opposites, or two people with some sort of mental affinity?

KING: Not necessarily either. We try to find two people who are good conversationalists—

NABARRO: I'm not a good conversationalist. I'm a very bad conversationalist. And I'm the world's worst after-dinner speaker. I can never remember any stories. Tell me a dirty story and it goes in one ear and out of the other. Lord Snow now, that's a different matter.

SNOW: I don't know any dirty stories.

NABARRO: I didn't mean that. I meant as an after-dinner speaker. Mind you Charles, you won't be remembered as a great speaker or as a great philosopher, or even a great writer. Your name is now indissolubly linked with one phrase—"Corridors of Power". It's used by every journalist who writes about the background to Parliament. . . . Have you ever had Boothby in this series?

KING: No.

NABARRO: He's a marvellous conversationalist. Knows a lot of good stories. Do you know Boothby, Charles?

SNOW: Yes. He's a good friend of mine. But who would you pair him with for a Conversation like this?

NABARRO: Harry Secombe. Someone vivacious like that. I don't see why comedians should be derided any more than politicians. A large part of life is laughing, after all. Secombe makes people laugh, and keeps on making them laugh. Come to think of it, so do politicians.

14. *The Right Honourable Harold Wilson*, OBE, MP

I HAVE never been in the least surprised that the Right Honourable Harold Wilson, OBE, MP, became Prime Minister. I had always regarded him as the most likely Labour Premier of the sixties, if we had to be afflicted with a Labour Government at all. And occasional changes in the ruling party are inescapable if one believes in the democratic system—one party in office and the other in opposition—in contrast to the autocratic system—one party in power and the other in prison.

Brains, professionalism and luck are the usual but by no means invariable ingredients of any successful career. It is this formula which I have observed at work in a spectacular way over the last twenty-five years in the case of Harold Wilson.

There is little dispute about his intellectual stature. His academic career is now legendary, so that it would be tedious to consider it in any detail here. What it is relevant to say is that Harold Wilson rose to the very highest level of the educational meritocracy at a time when the facilities for doing so were immeasurably less generous than they are now. From various local schools in Yorkshire and Cheshire, he reached Jesus College, Oxford, where he took an unusually good first in Philosophy, Politics and Economics and then became a Fellow of New College for one year. As an undergraduate he had been appalled by the public school Marxists of the Oxford University Labour Club and had been Treasurer of the Liberal

Club at a time when Frank Byers, now leader of the Liberal Peers, was President.

Harold Wilson's introduction to government was from an administrative rather than from a political angle. It began when he became a Fellow of University College, Oxford, in 1938 and worked with the Master, Sir William Beveridge, on problems of unemployment. It continued in the Civil Service during the War when he served in the Ministries of Supply, Labour, and Fuel and Power, and then from 1943, as Director of Economics. In this last post he rapidly became the confident of Ministers in the Coalition on the formidable problems of post-war Britain.

Thus, by the time he entered Parliament in 1945 as Member for Ormskirk, Lancashire—where he defeated Commander Stephen King-Hall—he already had considerable administrative experience. *The Times* House of Commons Book, published immediately after the 1945 election, said of him, laconically:

> Mr J. H. Wilson, the Parliamentary Secretary to the Ministry of Works, is a Fellow and Lecturer in Economics at University College, Oxford. He assisted Sir William Beveridge.

Within two years he was Mr Attlee's President of the Board of Trade and a member of the Cabinet together with Herbert Morrison, Ernest Bevin, Sir Stafford Cripps and Aneurin Bevan. He was then thirty-one and the youngest Cabinet Minister since Pitt. He was only thirty-five when he resigned from the Government in April, 1951, along with Aneurin Bevan and John Freeman, following the introduction of Health Service charges by the Chancellor of the Exchequer, Hugh Gaitskell.

In the Autumn of 1951, the Labour Party lost the General Election and began its thirteen years in Opposition during which Harold Wilson built his reputation as a political and parliamentary tactician, although it was ten years before he came within reach of the leadership and nearly twelve before he actually achieved it. His election as leader of the Labour Party in February, 1963, was rather more comfortable than Edward Heath's election as Tory leader in 1965. The other candidates were James Callaghan and George Brown and the result of the first ballot was:

Wilson	115
Brown	88
Callaghan	41

Callaghan then withdrew and on the second ballot Wilson was elected with 144 votes to Brown's 103.

I remember walking through the Division Lobby a few days before the decisive Labour Leadership ballot, and, feeling a hand on my shoulder I turned and was confronted by the Prime Minister, Mr Harold Macmillan, in his most benign and avuncular mood:

"And who, my dear Nabarro, will win the contest for the Labour Leadership?

Harold Wilson, Sir.

I am told George Brown.

I think not, Sir; I am confident Harold Wilson will win.

Does that suit us—a Wilson win?

No it does not. Brown is a clumsy, intemperate chap. Wilson is clever, very clever, far the cleverest man in the Labour Party and the most dangerous adversary we have.

"You may be right" concluded Mr Macmillan.

Though sheer brain power is only one desirable quality for effective political leadership, I have always been quite candid when asked who, in this respect, are the most impressive Members of the post-war House of Commons in replying: Wilson for Labour, Powell for the Tories. Brains apart, there is no dispute about Mr Wilson's complete political professionalism and dedication. Only once, for a relatively short while in the 1950s, did he flirt with private commercial interests, as economic adviser to the timber firm of Montague L. Meyer & Co., Ltd. He has never been allowed to forget it. Personally, I wish more Socialists were involved in capitalist enterprises because it would, without doubt, mitigate their prejudices about business, commerce and private industry, especially the City. It was in the latter area that Harold Wilson vented his spleen and earned a bloody nose over his Bank Rate leak allegations, which were found by the tribunal to be baseless. Wilson neither retracted nor apologised. Wilson wouldn't. He is utterly convinced of his omniscience and infallibility.

Moreover, he had taken the step in 1960 of standing against Mr Gaitskell in the annual election for the leader, after the Labour Party Conference at Scarborough, and had polled 81 votes to Gaitskell's 166. In other words, one Labour MP out of every three preferred Wilsonism to Gaitskellism, or, in more familiar terms, one third of Labour Members preferred the Left to the Right. In 1961 Wilson stood for the party's Deputy-Leadership against Geoi ge Brown and lost. And then in January, 1963, Gaitskell died. Save only George Brown, the field was clear for Wilson.

So to brains and professionalism was now added the third ingredient of a successful ascent of the "greasy pole"—Disraeli's metaphor for the corpse-strewn path to Downing Street—luck. Apart from the mercurial and politically intemperate George Brown, there was no obstacle to Wilson's success. Mr Gaitskell's death was, of course, the cause of the vacancy; Aneurin Bevan had died in 1961; and, more fortuitous still than either of these events, Mr Alfred Robens had been appointed Chairman of the National Coal Board in 1960. But for these three circumstances, Wilson would not have become Leader of the Labour Party in 1963 and neither—at any rate, not so soon—would he have become Prime Minister.

That George Brown and Harold Wilson neither co-operated nor coalesced for long was not unexpected by those who knew both men. Wilson is incomparably the more sagacious and sophisticated of the two and the contrast in style, character and ideology between them created strains which originated long before the issue of the leadership arose. It did not require any unusual gift of prophecy to envisage Mr Brown's resignation as Foreign Secretary in 1968 nor, given the character of the man, was the chorus of unconcealed rancour which surrounded that event any surprise either.

Like any dedicated professional who is superbly good at his job, Harold Wilson has acquired many enemies in all parties. After the 1959 General Election he was in a specially delicate position, although he was not, as things turned out, vulnerable. On 15th November, 1959, the *Sunday Times* published an article entitled "Greek gifts for Mr Wilson", which concerned Mr Gaitskell's plans to restore the party after the disaster of the election defeat. In the event, this refurbishing was done by Mr Wilson himself four years later. However, at the time it was Mr Gaitskell's intention to make Aneurin Bevan deputy-leader of the party, Denis Healey shadow Foreign Secretary and Roy Jenkins, then aged thirty-nine, shadow Chancellor of the Exchequer. The article continued:

> Mr Wilson would be presented to the party as a latter-day Herbert Morrison, an all-powerful party boss in a variety of guises—as Mr Butler's opposite number as shadow Leader of the House, general manager of Transport House (vice Mr Morgan Phillips), and possibly, as the final adornment, Mr Bevan's successor as party treasurer.

But sand got into the works:

> Mr Wilson, we should remember, is about the most sophisticated political animal in the business. He does not require anybody to spell out for him the

subtlety of political readjustment. He sniffed the bait warily and decided that it concealed slow-acting poison.

Mr Wilson has no ambition to become the forgotten man of politics; hence the ever-so-polite response to the self-appointed emissary. He was conscious of the honour, but felt he could best serve his leader by soldiering on as shadow Chancellor.

Behind the superficialities, we should recognise that some right-wing intellectuals and a number of others besides, feel that Mr Wilson should be given greater experience. To put it less delicately, they regard Mr Wilson as something of a liability as the financial kingpin, hidebound by the Socialist economics of over twenty years ago and still re-living his past as a Minister in a Crippsian era of controls, regulations and directions. And of whom could Lord Pakenham[1] have been thinking when he lamented in the Lords the other day, the prejudices which bedevil relations between Labour and the City?

Of course Mr Wilson is the most sophisticated and brainiest political animal in the business: that is what I was telling Mr Harold Macmillan in the Lobby the night before Mr Wilson was elected Labour's leader. And he proved it within twenty-four hours of his election. When he entered the Chamber of the House of Commons for the first time as Leader of his party, I was in the middle of a speech opposing the re-nationalisation of the steel industry. Mr Gaitskell had fought a long battle against Wilson and his side of the party over Clause 4 of the Labour Party constitution containing the archaic provision for nationalising all the means of production, distribution and exchange, which Gaitskell had long wanted to abandon. The country was heavily against further rash experiments in nationalisation, especially steel. The Tory Party, after twelve years in power, was unpopular and I was anxious to make Wilson declare his support for Clause 4. He obliged me and swallowed the bait:

SIR GERALD NABARRO (Con. Kidderminster): The right hon. Member for Huyton is pledged to Clause 4 of the Labour Party Constitution and to the renationalisation of the steel industry. I am delighted to see him in his place, and I congratulate him upon his election success. I shall look forward to having him as an opponent at the next General Election. At least we shall know that we are opposing Socialists, and we know exactly what their policy is. A lead has already been given by the right hon. Gentleman in the—

MR HAROLD WILSON (Lab. Huyton): I heard the hon. Gentleman muttering

---

[1] Now 7th Earl of Longford; Chairman, The National Bank Ltd, 1955–63; Leader of the House of Lords, 1964–68; Lord Privy Seal, 1964–65 and 1966–68; Colonial Secretary, 1965–66.

something about Clause 4. I am glad that he understands it, because it is the position of the whole party. Having told us that he is looking forward to opposing us at the next General Election, will he now tell us what we shall be opposing?

SIR GERALD NABARRO: In due course I will do so. I must follow my congratulations to the right hon. Gentleman by saying how pleased I am to have his acceptance of my statement that he proposes to embark on a policy of the extension of nationalisation and the bringing into public ownership of all the means of production, distribution and exchange. That is clause 4. The right hon. Gentleman has vigorously upheld it today.[1]

Thus, Labour's new leader had branded himself as a stern upholder of Clause 4 and a dedicated nationaliser within hours of his election. Given the necessary power after the 1966 General Election, Harold Wilson lived up to his nationalisation promises as I knew too well being one of the Tory Members who toiled by day and by night through 2,569 columns of Hansard opposing the Socialist majority in the Standing Committee on the Iron and Steel Bill, which produced the present British Steel Corporation and all the controversy surrounding it.

Millions of Tory Central Office leaflets (notably a leaflet called "Entitled to Know") followed Mr Harold Wilson's "Clause 4" declaration and in the course of my Party Political Broadcast on the BBC Home Service, Tuesday, 12th March, 1963, I said:

Whenever a Socialist Government has come in, in the past, confidence in sterling has gone out: the fortune and security of us all, notably millions of wage-earners in industry, depend on buoyant trade and strength of the pound.

That is why Socialist nostrums, recently mouthed by their new leaders Mr Wilson and Mr Callaghan, are so dangerous to our well-being. Not long ago in the House of Commons, Mr Harold Wilson confessed that he, and the entire Labour Party, believed in the notorious Clause 4 of their Party's constitution. This commits the Labour Party to the eventual nationalisation of all industry, all shops from Supermarkets to Barrow Boys, the Banks, Insurance, Cement and the remainder. That is avowedly their target and their ambition, but they will not say how fast they are going to move towards it, or which are to be the first victims of nationalisation: they are going to get everything nationalised by 1970, or by 1980, or will the date significantly be 1984?

All they have said so far is that they are going to nationalise steel and road haulage, water and building land, but they have also made a lot more vague

[1] *Hansard*, 18th February, 1963, cols. 106–107.

"LOOK, THAT'S HIM!"

CLAUSE 4 and NATIONALISATION ROWS, *Evening Standard*, 20th February, 1963.

and imprecise threats: what these mean and which of our great manufacturing industries would be affected, the Socialists do not tell us: are they afraid to do so? Could it be that they are frightened of what the voters would do to them at the next General Election: Nationalisation is a dirty, smelly and opprobrious word: we do not want any more Coal Boards, we have had enough of them.

This turned out to be so accurate that it could almost have been a history rather than a prophecy of the Wilson years from 1964 to 1970.

When it comes to naked party politics, no Prime Minister has ever made such an idiot of himself by flagrantly broken promises, as Mr Harold Wilson. It is unlikely that he will ever live down the following quotations:

i) "I believe we can carry out our programme without any general increase in taxation" (15th September, 1964). But taxation almost doubled in the next six years of Wilson government.
ii) "The pound in your pocket will not be devalued" (19th November, 1967). But rampant inflation followed devaluation.
iii) "You cannot go cap in hand to the Central Bankers and maintain freedom of action . . . the Central Bankers will before long be demanding that Britain put her house in order" (3rd October, 1964). But Wilson Governments have run up foreign debts of £3,600,000,000.
iv) "The first task on the Health Service will be to re-create the free service established by Aneurin Bevan" (24th March, 1961). Wilson resigned from the Attlee Cabinet in April, 1951 as a protest against his colleague Hugh Gaitskell's health charges. In the later sixties, he himself has been the architect of prescription charges and heavy imposts on spectacles and false teeth.

Some may call these miscalculations, or even aberrations. Some may denounce the flagrantly broken promises as criminal. Whichever it is, it is certain that Wilson will never, never be allowed to forget them and never be allowed to get away with anything like them again.

For myself, I do not dislike Harold Wilson. He has great personal qualities. He is erudite and lively, rational and courteous, with a mind like one of the well-ordered computers he admires so much. He has a political philosophy, Marxist in origin but none the less a philosophy, savaged by the necessities of a disordered world, but devoutly held. His faults are manifest. As a party politician myself, I should be suspect in stating them.

AND THEN GIVE THEM GREAT MEALS OF BEEF, AND IRON AND STEEL,
THEY WILL EAT LIKE WOLVES, AND FIGHT LIKE DEVILS!
—KING HENRY V, ACT III Scene VII

CLAUSE 4 and NATIONALISATION ROWS, *New Statesman*, 1st March, 1963.

The historian will doubtless delineate them as ruthlessly as those of that other great radical leader, David Lloyd George, have been. I have lived for a quarter of a century too close to Harold Wilson to attempt any dispassionate assessment of him. But I know that he is a man of outstanding kindness, charm and generosity. In 1964, he wrote inside my copy of Dudley Smith's *Harold Wilson a critical biography*:

> To Gerald, with admiration for a friendly controversialist and best wishes for the future.

And earlier, after I had announced that I would give up my seat at Kidderminster because of illness, he had written:

> Dear Gerald,
>
> I'm terribly sorry and I know I'm speaking for all our people.
>
> Whatever our political differences and they've been great, I have always felt the greatest admiration for you personally, and as one of the few Parliamentarians who brought a real breath of fresh air into our proceedings. The House is not so rich in real House of Commons characters that we can hear of your retirement without real regret.
>
> I've always enjoyed our exchanges including our very memorable broadcasts together.
>
> The very best of luck and very best wishes for a real, if necessarily slow recovery.
>
> Yours,
>
> HAROLD WILSON.
>
> House of Commons. 25th March, 1964.

Hardly the words of a Robespierre, I felt, or of any other political monster. Rather the words of a decent man addressing a colleague suffering adversity.

15. *Money and the Member*

HYPOCRISY, snobbery, self-indulgence and the underpayment of Members of Parliament are hall-marks of the British and I doubt whether they will ever change.

Especially the under-payment of Members of Parliament. They were not paid at all until 1912, when Mr Lloyd George introduced an annual salary of £400, which was raised to £600 in 1937. By the time I was first elected in 1950 it had been increased again to £1000 and this went up to £1750 in 1957 and £3250 in 1964. Together with this last rise, Members were blessed with the creation of a stingy pension scheme to which they themselves largely contribute. Thus a Member's pay, subject to taxation and pension contributions, is just over £3000 a year.

The remarkable thing is that the stingier the pay and the more squalid the conditions, the greater the number of Parliamentary aspirants. I thought that eighty-seven was a lot when I won the South Worcestershire nomination in 1965. Four years later, admittedly with a strong chance of a Conservative Government at an early date, a much less safe seat at Wimbledon, cosily close to the House, though held by Labour from 1945 to 1950, attracted three hundred and twenty-four applicants. Here is what the *Daily Telegraph* reported on 9th April, 1969:

> Nineteen former Tory MPs are among 324 contestants for one of the most sought-after seats in Parliament. They all want to take over the safe Tory-held constituency of Wimbledon that Sir Cyril Black (majority 5674) has announced he will not defend at the next General Election.

> Twenty women are in the line-up which is understood to contain a number of former Front Bench Tory MPs. But the local party is not naming anyone and has appointed a special selection committee to cut the number of applicants to an initial short list of 100.
>
> Wimbledon's Conservative agent, Mr Widney Burns, said: 'There are some really big names on the list. It's almost like a miniature Who's Who, but it would be wrong to name any of these applicants'.

So, the more depressed the pay and conditions of Members of Parliament become, the greater the crush to get in. One in a hundred makes it; hence the sour grapes of the other ninety-nine, so often publicly expressed.

The British House of Commons is the worst paid legislature in the Western World. And, hold your breath, out of their pay Members have to cover all their professional expenses, including secretarial costs, postage, telephones outside London, the maintenance of a second home in London, a parliamentary office and so on. The more closely one compares the £3,250 a year of a British Member of Parliament with the pay and allowances of his counterpart in almost any other civilised country, the more apparent its scandalous inadequacy becomes. In West Germany, for example, the figure is £3,150 which is £100 less than here but not only is it tax free but there are also tax free allowances of £104 a month to cover costs, while in Bonn on parliamentary business, and £63 a month towards office expenses. A French deputy gets about £7,900 a year, 25% of which is tax free; in Italy, an MP gets £6,500 a year and £80 a month for living expenses in Rome; and in Canada an MP gets nearly £5000 a year plus a non-taxable allowance of £2,350 a year and one secretary provided at the expense of the Government. In other words, MPs in most of these countries get more in allowances than a British MP does in taxable income.

Of course I declare, and always have declared, that I collect all my Parliamentary salary free of tax. Why? Because I prove to the Inland Revenue that I spend a sum in excess of my Parliamentary salary wholly, exclusively and necessarily in connection with my Parliamentary and constituency duties. I am practically the only Member who does this and I am not proud of it, although more than half of my fellow MPs spend about two-thirds of their Parliamentary salaries in the same way. I regard this situation as a pungent indictment of a silly anachronism, and a fallacious belief that Members can perform their exacting, complex and supremely important role in penurious circumstances. Here is where my salary—and more—went in 1969:

	£ per annum
Secretarial and typing (proportion only)	1500
Postage, 15,000 letters per annum and proportion of stationery	300
Second home in London	825
Motoring 10,000 miles in my South Worcestershire constituency	500
Parliamentary office and depreciation of equipment (proportion only)	575
Total Parliamentary and Constituency disbursements	4000
Less salary, minus pension contribution, plus motor allowance (say)	3250
NET DEFICIT	£750

And then there are the many expenses which a Member of Parliament cannot avoid, such as receiving and modestly entertaining his constituents at the House, having his wife in London with him for a while during the long and exhausting Parliamentary sittings and a host of incidental expenses disallowed by the Inland Revenue. In my own case these added up to a further £750 in 1969. So my Parliamentary and constituency expenses exceeded my House of Commons salary by £1500 in a single year.

In other words, I worked for nothing in 1969 and paid my South Worcestershire constituents the sum of £1500 to represent them.

The snide, the cheap and the ignorant, notably the gutter Press and the organs of the Left, will howl like a pack of hyenas when they read this! Tell the honourable Member for South Worcestershire to sell one of his cars if he is hard-up they will jibe; tell him to eat less, drink less, send his children to State schools and the remainder. I know every taunt of these people by heart. What they never, never explain, because of course they cannot, is how a Member of Parliament, Labour, Liberal or Tory, pays all the heavy expenses which are unavoidable for an active politician and provides for a wife and family. The Member of Parliament without an income beyond his Parliamentary salary is worse off nowadays than a labourer or a primary school teacher.

Of course, one need not be a Member of Parliament. In order to be one, many Members take paid employment of some kind, full, or part-time or continue with their previous occupation in some form. I list my occupations, all of which are remunerated, as follows:

Member of Parliament
Director of Companies
Journalist and Author
Broadcaster and Televiser

I think it is desirable that I should have so many extra-Parliamentary interests, if I am to be fully informed in all commercial, political and public affairs. I confess that I am a professional businessman and an amateur politician but I am the better for it and I am at an advantage over the full-time Members of the House of Commons who are wholly immersed in party politics and insulated from the world outside the Palace of Westminster. Only Ministers of the Crown should be full-time politicians.

Nevertheless, the financial burden which Members of Parliament have to support is intolerable and every Member should be provided with a Secretary and rudimentary office paraphernalia, at least.

The British will deserve the worst if they continue to run their legislature on the cheap. This is what Ministers and Members are worth, in 1970 money values:

The Prime Minister	£30,000 p.a.	(and no tax-free allowances)
Cabinet Ministers	£20,000	Per annum
Ministers of Cabinet rank and the Law Officers	£15,000	Per annum
Ministers of State	£12,000	Per annum
Parliamentary Secretaries	£10,000	Per annum
Members of Parliament	£6,000	Per annum

Surely Cabinet Ministers at £20,000 a year are worth as much as the Chairmen of the Coal Board, the Gas Council and British Rail, whom they appointed anyway?

Why not ask Mr Aubrey Jones?

16. *Jones the Coal*

Were I asked the meaning of that nearly indefinable English word "prissy", I would reply: Aubrey Jones.

Personally, I cannot help liking dear Aubrey who is intelligent, assiduous, precise and very, very clever. All his academic and career background confirms this. But his unpleasing voice, his impeccable suavity, his infuriating gentility and an apparent difficulty in mixing with his fellow creatures, have all combined to make Aubrey rather a man apart.

Born well before the First World War, in Merthyr Tydfil, son of a coalminer when coal was Britain's first industry and the miners were the aristocrats of labour, young Aubrey hewed out a brilliant academic career for himself. Proceeding from Cyfarthfa Castle Secondary School to the London School of Economics, he won a first class degree and a postgraduate scholarship, before joining the editorial staff of *The Times* in 1937. Thence to the Intelligence Corps for six years during the War and afterwards back to *The Times* until 1948. He joined the British Iron and Steel Federation on its formation in 1949 and rose to be General Director for six months in 1955. Meantime he made two unsuccessful attempts to enter Parliament, first in 1945 at Essex, South-East and again the following year at Heywood and Radcliffe. He was elected for Birmingham, Hall Green, in 1950. Thus he joined the Tory Parliamentary Party with Heath, Maudling, Macleod, Powell and myself, and four score others, in the great vintage of 1950.

Aubrey was an atrocious Parliamentary speaker. People had difficulty in hearing and understanding him. When Sir Anthony Eden made him Minis ter of Fuel and Power in December, 1955, eyebrows went up on the Government benches. This Ministry, charged with operating the newly nationalised fuel and power industries—coal, gas and electricity—was a very hot seat indeed. It called for a political prodigy: a Tory who could make Socialist state ownership work.

During nine years since the nationalisation of the pits on 1st January, 1947, coal had increased in price several times annually. House coal was still rationed in 1956, expensive and poor in quality. Coal was at the heart of the Tory battle against nationalisation because, as the first industry nationalised, it was seen after nine years to be an expensive flop. The Tories could not denationalise the industry because nobody would buy a coal-mine. Few envisaged a profitable coal industry even after huge injected investment, a massive drain on Treasury funds and continuous price rises, pushing up the price of steel, gas, electricity and all manufactured goods. Only after the Tory programme of massive support for oil refinery construction, followed by the nuclear power programme carried through so effectively in the second half of the nineteen-fifties by Mr Geoffrey Lloyd, Lord Mills and Mr Reginald Maudling, was the coal monopoly broken and the National Union of Mineworkers cut down to size.

The onset of North Sea Gas in the sixties, called by my friend Mr John Peyton, Conservative Member for Yeovil, "the only real piece of luck we have had this decade", completed the process. From £15m of North Sea Gas landed in 1968 and £36m in 1969, it is expected to be worth £140m per annum landed by the middle seventies.

But there was no nuclear power, no North Sea Gas and, for balance of payments reasons, no easy resort to fuel oil to comfort Aubrey Jones when he took office in December, 1955, as Minister of Fuel and Power. It was "King Coal" and a powerful vested interest—the National Union of Mineworkers—that Aubrey had to contend with; and, on the Opposition benches in the House of Commons he had the Rt Hon. Alfred Robens, MP for Blyth, backed by more than forty Labour MPs who were ex-miners, members of the N.U.M., and dedicated to the fight for the supremacy of coal.

The post of Minister of Fuel and Power has changed hands twelve times since 1945, or an average tenure of office of about two years. Coal, gas and electricity involve thousands of millions of pounds of state assets. What company could succeed with a new boss every other year? Thus:

Rt Hon. Emanuel Shinwell, MP.	Socialist,	1945–47.
Rt Hon. Hugh Gaitskell, MP.	Socialist,	1947–50.

Rt Hon. Philip Noel-Baker, MP.	Socialist,	1950–51.
Rt Hon. Geoffrey Lloyd, MP.	Tory,	1951–55.
Rt Hon. Aubrey Jones, MP.	Tory,	1955–57.
Rt Hon. Lord Mills	Tory,	1957–59.
Rt Hon. Richard Wood, MP.	Tory,	1959–63.
Rt Hon. Frederick Erroll, MP.	Tory,	1963–64.
Rt Hon. Frederick Lee, MP.	Socialist,	1964–66.
Rt Hon. Richard Marsh, MP.	Socialist,	1966–68.
Rt Hon. Ray Gunter, MP.	Socialist,	April–July, 1968.
Rt Hon. Roy Mason, MP.	Socialist,	1968–

Surprisingly Erroll, now Lord Erroll, MIMechE, MIEE, was the best. Technically qualified, he could do more than just talk.

Now Aubrey Jones was the only coal-miner's son on the Tory benches in 1955. Eden was badly advised that this background would make Aubrey acceptable to both sides of the House. But it infuriated the Tories that the new Minister's policy was evidently to placate his Labour opponents, win them unlimited funds for the Socialist Coal monopoly and neglect the Tory pleas for financial solvency in the pits, coupled with a policy of lessening the nation's then almost complete dependence on coal, supported by American imports of as much as £80m in a single year. Aubrey was unhappy and querulous from the start. His Tories behind him were even unhappier that they had to contend with one of their colleagues adopting Labour policies. Even the stern whipping by Mr Edward Heath, Sir Anthony Eden's Patronage Secretary, could not prevent the inevitable explosion.

Mr Christopher Hollis, the Conservative Member for Devizes from 1945 to 1955, summed it all up in a witty book of satirical verse, copiously illustrated by Cummings, in which he wrote:

"The miners won't go mining, though the Lords of Fuel and Power,
Are determined that their ministry shall have its finest hour,
The miners won't go mining for they think upon the whole
That they couldn't do much better than with 'Jones the Coal',
And yet they must be careful for without a shade of doubt,
The Nabarro Boys will get them if they don't look out."[1]

I gave Aubrey Jones a six-month run for his money as Minister, bided my time, nagging in party committees about the maladministration of

[1] From *The Ayes and the Noes*, 1956.

Aubrey's charges, namely coal, gas and electricity, and then, on 10th May, 1956, I attacked. Aubrey had brought his Coal Industry Bill to the House on the Second Reading and asked for an increase in borrowing powers from £300m to £650m. Mr James Callaghan and his coal-mining friends on the Opposition backbenches were ecstatic. Jones talked of his innate Conservatism with a small "C": "Rather a small 'C' now", jeered the Tory Member for South Dorset, Viscount Hinchingbrooke. That night Hinchingbrooke and myself were tellers against our Tory Minister, Aubrey Jones and twenty Tories and three Liberals came with us. All the Socialists and about a hundred Tories abstained. Aubrey retired hurt. Mr Angus Maude, then Member for Ealing, South, and now for Stratford-on-Avon, castigated Mr James Callaghan and his abstaining Socialists:[1] "I regard the performance of Hon. Members opposite as being beneath contempt."

The Minister got his Bill before the summer recess of 1956: the Coal Board got its extra £350m of borrowing powers; and my friends and myself, the Tory "coal rebels" as Mr Arthur Palmer, Socialist Member for Cleveland, called us, the "Fuel Furies" as the *Daily Mail* called us, and the "Cardboard Caesar" as Mr James Callaghan called me, we got our annual investment White Paper for the nationalised industries which was what all the fuss had been about. We were blooded. Dear Aubrey did not last very long. Within a few months he was moved to the Ministry of Supply. Mr Harold Macmillan failed to give him a job after the great Election victory of 1959 and he lingered on the backbenches largely unseen and unheard until a Labour Prime Minister made Aubrey the Chairman of the National Board for Prices and Incomes in March, 1965.

Party cross-fertilisation is always fascinating because it occurs so rarely. Mr Harold Macmillan had given Mr Alfred Robens his job as Chairman of the National Coal Board in 1960 and made him a Peer. At that time, Robens had been an ebullient Labour MP for fifteen years and a Cabinet Minister from 1950 to 1951. Labour MPs regarded his acceptance of the Chairmanship of the National Coal Board as a dereliction of duty to the working classes. "The miners would have had something to grouse about if Mr Nabarro had been appointed instead of Robens", said a leader in the *Daily Telegraph*. Now a Labour Prime Minister gave Aubrey Jones £15,000 a year as Chairman of the P.I.B., on the recommendation of Mr George Brown, Minister for Economic Affairs.

[1] *Hansard*, 10th May, 1956, col. 1540.

COAL BOARD FARE—GERALD NABARRO STYLE
or COOKING THE BOOKS by Cummings, *Daily Express*,
17th February, 1960.

Of course, I had myself no great opinion of Aubrey, as "Peter Simple" observed in the *Daily Telegraph* as long ago as 22nd June, 1956:

One day, I hope, an erudite German scholar will write a treatise entitled 'Die Englische Puritanische Ethik und der geist Das Dockerismus.[1] It will describe the mid-20th century struggle waged by a handful of flamboyant personalities against the enveloping drabness of the industrial welfare state. There will also, I hope, be an appendix on Mr Gerald Nabarro, Conservative MP for Kidderminster.

Many members of his party as they grow old become remote and stately, like the people in the White Horse advertisements. A picture of Mr Nabarro would perhaps best be employed to commend the virtues of exploding cigars, whoopee cushions and other unseemly devices for deflating the self-important.

On Budget Days he sits in the House wearing a sombrely glowing top hat. On more humdrum occasions he seeks comfort in a glittering Armstrong-Siddeley Sapphire convertible, its radiator lavishly bedizened with half a hundred club badges. In case these alone should not be identification enough, its number plate is NAB 1.

Like the villain of a Victorian melodrama, he is perpetually rolling and flashing his eyes, twirling his silken moustachios and in menacing tones bidding 'me Right Honble Friend to take note that I am far from satisfied'.

The Right Honble Friend in question, Mr Jones, is a man of unassuming demeanour and excruciating gentility. In attempting to defend himself against Mr Nabarro's robust irreverence he has only Socialist cheers for support.

Week after week, the Member for Kidderminster rises in his place below the gangway to torment the Minister of Fuel. Imprisoned in Mr Jones is the shrivelled phantom of a Permanent Under-Secretary. Less strictly confined in Mr Nabarro is the life and soul of every officers' mess party.

Whenever he surges to his feet, I hear a ghostly cry of 'Drinks all round, major!'

Within hours of Tory MP Mr Aubrey Jones taking from a Socialist Chancellor of the Exchequer the appointment as Steward and Bailiff of the Manor of Northstead—an office of profit under the Crown—and leaving the Commons, in March 1965, I was addressing the annual meeting of the South Worcestershire Conservative Association at Upton-on-Severn. I said:

Doing a Robens (off the Labour Opposition benches to take a Coal Board job at £12,000 a year) is becoming fashionable. Aubrey Jones, miner's son,

[1] The English Puritan Ethic and the Spirit of Dockerism.

(ii). I.C.B.M. NABARRO by Cummings, *Punch*, 4th December, 1957.

Tory shop-window piece, has been seduced by his political opponents from the Tory benches at £15,000 a year, to run a price-cum-incomes bureau and seminar.

It is a jellyfish, without vertebrae, without muscle: only a nasty sting, in tart, official terminology, when prices or incomes rise too fast.

Anyway, will Aubrey be able to control prices and incomes without detailed control over:

1. International commodity markets.
2. Wages and salaries.
3. Interest rates and credit terms.
4. Rents and local rates (the latter up by a stupendous 13% or £140m in 1965/66).
5. Nationalised industry prices—coal, gas, electricity, transport, which rise excessively and remorselessly.

Obviously such detailed control is impossible in a free society and/or international markets.

Aubrey is not yet a deity: Conservatives should say so. Good luck, hapless Aubrey, in a hopeless assignment. Aubrey should never have joined the Brown burlesque.

I was widely reported and there was quite a storm of Left wing editorial comment, as for example in *The Sun* on 22nd March:

JUST NASTY NABARRO

Extravagant nonsense from Sir Gerald Nabarro is nothing fresh. But his sneering attack at the week-end on a fellow-Tory, Mr Aubrey Jones, is unjust and nasty.

Former MP Nabarro storms because Mr Jones is taking on a difficult job of great importance to the nation. He will head the Board being set up by the Government to keep watch on prices and incomes.

This causes Sir Gerald to blaze out that Mr Jones is a miner's son, 'a Tory shop-window piece'. He declares—unfairly and insultingly—that Mr Jones has been 'Seduced' because he has accepted this appointment from a Labour Government.

What is wrong with being a miner's son? Or a miner? Or a 'Tory shop-window piece' if you happen to be a Tory?

A parlous state of narrow-mindedness has been reached if a man cannot serve in the interests of his country, under any Government, without meanly being accused of betraying his political party.

Mr Jones will, in fact, have to give up business interests to do the job. He will be out of pocket.

Nothing could be less deserved than Sir Gerald Nabarro's outburst.

He is not the only back-biter. Tory MP Mr William van Straubenzee is another.
Theirs is the sort of claptrap that makes large numbers of people heartsick. Including the young, who are fed up with political pettiness and anxious to see Britain get on with the task of solving her difficulties.
Sir Gerald is the prospective Tory candidate for Worcester, South.
If this is the level of his political thought, Parliament would be better off if he were never again elected.'

And "Cassandra" wrote in the *Daily Mirror* on the same day:

THE GREAT BACKWOODSMAN

I am glad to tell you that Sir Gerald Nabarro, who retired from politics through ill-health, is now very well indeed.
The index of his fitness is linked directly with the liveliness and ferocity of his words.
He has just been diagnosing the ills of his erstwhile political colleague Mr Aubrey Jones, the MP who has joined the National Board for Prices and Incomes.
Sir Gerald describes Mr Jones as a 'miner's son, Tory shop-window piece', and said that 'doing a Robens off the Labour opposition benches to take a Coal Board job at £12,000 a year, is becoming fashionable'.
He added: 'Aubrey is not yet a deity: Conservatives should say so. Good luck, hapless Aubrey, in a hopeless assignment. Aubrey should never have joined the Brown burlesque.'
Yes, Sir Gerald is very well indeed.
The great backwoodsman of Tory politics has returned saying, in effect, that nobody can serve his country unless he is approved and certified by the Conservative Central Office.
Everything must be guided and coloured by party politics.
Red is red and Blue is blue and there is no place in public life for men who admit that there are other colours in the wide spectrum of the conduct of our affairs.

Yet, four years later, on 5th June, 1969, the *Daily Telegraph*, a paper which rarely endorses my views, was ragging the Prices and Incomes Board unmercifully in a leader entitled "DE MINIMIS":

When the Prices and Incomes Board was established, it was hardly contemplated that it would add richly to the comic qualities of the contemporary scene. The prices of essentials and the earnings of the larger groups would surely be the exclusive diet of this supposedly high-powered department costing currently about £1 million a year. But, it seems, no item is too inessential, no group of employees too small to escape the Board's attention. On Tuesday, the P.I.B., pronounced at length on cosmetics. Appended to this was a lecture to British womanhood on its vanity. Now we have a 25-page report on the pay of lighthouse keepers—all 436 of them.

The report contains such memorable solemnities as 'the authorities and the union should explore the possibility of consolidating the victualling allowance into a general rock allowance'. It is not, we are bound to say, a report which is likely to sell widely. It may even promote the thought among lighthouse keepers that the money spent on the report might more usefully have been paid directly to them. The governing factor in the men's pay of course is whether the employers concerned can recruit sufficient men. If they can, they will not materially alter pay and conditions because of the P.I.B.'s views. If they cannot, they will alter them, but again without much regard to the P.I.B. We would not wish by these strictures, however, to discourage the P.I.B. from investigating small groups. After all, if the Board is studying pay and conditions of saddle-makers, ivory carvers, big-game hunters, trapeze artists and other minorities, it may have less time to study, and irritate, the larger groups.

Like all campaigners in this field, I was aided from time to time, ironically, by the Left wing of the Labour Party. They strenuously opposed the omnipotence of Mr Aubrey Jones and his accomplices, slipping slowly and surely down the slope to state totalitarianism, dictation of incomes from Whitehall and the abandonment of free bargaining between employers and Trade Unions. I was gratified that my Party eventually took the same view, though not entirely Powellite. I returned to this attack when speaking at the Annual Dinner of the Bexley (Kent) Chamber of Commerce, on 5th October, 1966. The local Member, who is my leader, the Rt Hon. Edward Heath, MBE, MP, was at my elbow. I said:

Yesterday, Mr Aubrey Jones, Chairman of the Prices and Incomes Board said: 'We must never go back to the pre-freeze set-up'.
What does he mean?
Presumably, Government dictation of wages and salaries, dividends and incomes of all kinds, FOR EVER. . . .
So says Dear Aubrey.
Were that acceptable to the British people, we should be embracing the Communist State.
What folly and absurdity this is.
I reject absolutely these Socialist nostrums, whether mouthed by Mr Aubrey Jones or by Mr Harold Wilson. I am a Tory. I support competitive enterprise, which MUST include freely negotiated scales of remuneration, wages,

rewards and disciplines impressed by a free market. The Statutory Wage Freeze is grossly incompatible with a free society.

YOU MAY CALL THIS NABBERY: YOU MAY CALL IT POWELL-ISM: IT IS ALSO CONSERVATISM.

It is the antithesis of Socialist regimentation, espoused by both Mr Aubrey Jones and Mr Harold Wilson.

Yesterday, Mr Harold Wilson called me a 'political irrelevance'. I stand with my Conservative friends four-square for free enterprise against Socialist dogma and direction: against dragooning of our society by Whitehall.

More than half of our nation backs my views and Mr Harold Wilson's 'political irrelevance'.

I say we must clobber and castigate Mr Wilson's bid for totalitarian power.

Here then is the crucial issue for Tories at Blackpool next week. Also it is the crucial issue for the next General Election. If Mr Edward Heath espouses the Statutory Wage Freeze, the Tories will lose the next General Election and British citizens will lose their fundamental freedom.

The Tory Party must declaim now, unequivocally, against the Statutory determination of incomes.

Remarkably enough, Mr John Boyd, of the Amalgamated Engineering Union had declared that Mr Aubrey Jones was 'an enemy of the working classes and an enemy of the Labour Party'. So, the Chairman of the PIB was already under heavy fire from both Left and Right.

Speaking at Evesham in July, 1967, I said:

Twenty-eight months ago, I called the Prices and Incomes Board 'a jellyfish', unlikely to achieve anything worthwhile.

Today, the Trade Union Member, Mr Willis, resigns in utter frustration. Like Miss Herbison, he takes the honourable course of publicly displaying profound dissatisfaction with being a Whipping Boy of Mr Wilson's ministers.

The Government takes no heed of the Board's advice, but the Government's intention is clear—control in perpetuity of all wages, salaries and incomes from Whitehall.

There is no room in their caucus for men of independent mind such as Mr Willis. How much longer is Mr Aubrey Jones going to be the Tory fag of Socialist ministers? If he claims to be independent, which he is NOT, he should resign too.

Progressively in the House of Commons, the statutory prices and incomes policy came under heavier and heavier attack from a minority of Socialist Members and a united Tory Party. Compulsory control of salaries, wages, dividends, rents and indeed every other form of income, steadily earned the hostility and opprobrium of the overwhelming majority of the electors. At the three by-elections on 27th March, 1969, the Government Labour candidates gained only one out of every five votes recorded. The anti-Government vote was four out of five. Nothing like this has been witnessed this century.

Aubrey Jones continued to drive nails into Mr Wilson's coffin: students should help to determine the pecuniary value of their teachers and lecturers; state board bosses, in the shape of the Chairmen of the National Coal Board, the Gas Council, the Electricity Council and British Rail, should have an extra £7,500 a year, or £144 a week. The leading editorial of the *Sunday Express* on 28th March, 1969, just three years after Aubrey's appointment said:

> A cloudburst of anger has broken over the recommendation of the Prices and Incomes Board that the bosses of four state industries should have an extra £144 a week. And who can wonder?
>
> We are told that we are fighting for economic survival. The Board itself, on the precise calculation of Mr Aubrey Jones, has thrown out even a 17*s*. a week claim for farm-workers.
>
> How then can an enormous increase for the favoured few possibly be justified?
>
> The Board says that the State industries must pay the right money to get the right men. But would they ever get the right men no matter what they paid?
>
> Not under the present system whereby four hundred senior posts are distributed by political patronage.
>
> Alf Robens was no more qualified to be Chairman of the Coal Board than he was to be Grand Vizier of Baghdad. All the same, the Tories tossed the job to him.
>
> Humbly-paid trade union leaders troop into lusher pastures. Mr George Woodcock slips away from the troubles of the Trades Union Congress to a carefree £11,500 a year with the Commission on Industrial Relations.
>
> Mr James Mortimer, who was an unflagging enemy of the incomes policy, turns up on the Prices and Incomes Board at a fat £6,500 a year.
>
> Lord Carron never claimed knowledge of financial mysteries beyond his union subscription. Yet he became a director of the Bank of England.
>
> Of course, if the right men headed the State enterprises, they should be extremely well paid. But only if they have been chosen for ability alone.
>
> They would be well worth £20,000 a year, and maybe much more.
>
> As it is, most of the present bunch, far from being underpaid, get much too much.

The Sun may have been right after all. I was nasty to Mr Aubrey Jones. I apologise to him. I could not read the future sufficiently clearly. Little did I perceive that Aubrey would become the Tories' Trojan Horse. No one could have incited the majority of electors against statutory incomes control so effectively as he.

The *Daily Mirror* was nearest right, in my opinion, when it said on 19th February, 1969:

> Aubrey Jones, Chairman of the Prices and Incomes Board, has better reason than most to look ahead to the General Election with some concern about his future. If the Tories win it is virtually certain that the Board will be wound up. And with it will go the Chairman.
>
> This might not be all that disastrous for Jones but for one delicate fact. He is a former Tory MP and Minister and when he accepted George Brown's invitation to chair the newly-formed Board, he turned his back on his past; and as a state employee withdrew from active politics.
>
> The Tories, however, are not in a forgiving mood. They still claim that Jones should not have crossed the line.
>
> If any patronage is at the disposal of a Tory Prime Minister it is unlikely to go Jones's way. So he would be back to square one looking for a corner to provide for his future. But do not rule out the possibility of a 'Wilson-to-the-rescue' operation to ensure that Jones does not become the forgotten man of politics falling between the Tory and Labour stools.
>
> A life peerage before the election as a reward for public services would restore him to Westminster in the event of a Labour electoral defeat and give him a platform as well as the ermine.

With characteristic prescience Mr Harold Wilson was soon to the rescue. Sensing a Tory victory at the polls and the consequent fall of Mr Aubrey Jones, the Prime Minister offered to extend his contract as Chairman of the Prices and Incomes Board at £15,000 a year for a couple of years up to the spring of 1971, or six years after my "jellyfish" speech at Upton-on-Severn, Worcestershire. Aubrey spurned the offer. He has bigger fish to fry. He accepts from the spring of 1970 a post as an executive director and deputy-chairman of the International Publishing Corporation, the biggest publishing group in the world. The chairman, Mr Hugh Cudlipp, says that Aubrey's role will be "diversification and internationalisation". What big words and very, very portentous for dear Aubrey. But, the IPC are discontinuing *The Sun* in January, 1970, because it loses too much money and Aubrey will have to content himself, as an ex-Tory MP, with running a group which includes the *Daily Mirror*, the *Sunday Mirror* and *The People*. Moreover, he is to be deputy-chairman. The former chairman of the International Publishing

Corporation, Mr Cecil King—Wykehamist, tycoon, formerly Wilsonophile and then Wilsonophobe—was peremptorily sacked and deprived of his Rolls-Royce and sumptuous office. Without doubt, Aubrey Jones is a potential chairman of this tremendous group—a sort of plebeian Cecil King.

Anyway, Aubrey's departure from the PIB surprised nobody at Westminster, for as *The Times* observed on 16th July, 1969, "the PIB was under sentence of death when the Tories come back to power".

All this is known as having the best of both worlds. Perhaps before he goes, Mr Harold Wilson will immortalise dear Aubrey as Lord Jones of Cyfarthfa, in the County of Glamorgan. I doubt whether Jones will write such pungent leaders in the *Daily Mirror* as did Cecil King.

A splendid career. Let this be the epitaph of the Rt Hon. Aubrey Jones, Chairman of the National Board for Prices and Incomes (1965–70):

He united the British people
in the cause of freedom. RIP.

17. *Dear Constituents*

PARTY politics is the art of advocating something you know to be bad, as the only alternative to something you know to be a great deal worse.

I am no cynic in saying this. It is merely that I have noted during the last quarter of a century all the imperfections of party politicians and politics. Once they have decided how to vote, very few people ever change their party allegiance. Out of every hundred voters, excluding those who abstain, it is my experience that thirty-five always vote Tory as thirty-five always vote Labour and about ten—if they have a candidate to vote for—vote Liberal. The remaining twenty are floaters to be gathered in by a good constituency organisation or attracted by the Member of Parliament as a person who identifies himself with every aspect of community life in his constituency, religious, cultural, welfare, charitable, sporting and service. I reckon to do the lot, and also to live and vote in my constituency which creates a useful impression of local and national involvement. Any Member who does this is unlikely to be unseated by an interloping outsider, especially a carpet-bagger.

The first rule which a good constituency Member observes from the moment he is elected, is to represent and be seen to represent; to attend to and be seen to attend to; and to heed and be seen to heed every opinion of every constituent, without regard to party affiliation. Thus the pensioner who begins his letter with the ominous words "though not a supporter of your party" should always have a swift reply from the Member on the lines of the following:

> "From the moment I was elected to the House of Commons I pledged myself to serve all my constituents, of all parties and none, without fear, favour or discrimination and I am dedicated to the redress of your personal grievance."

Then, for example, when the supplementary pension has been safely obtained, the final letter to the pensioner will conclude with the splendid sentence:

> "As always, I am delighted to have been of some small service to you and I hope we shall meet in the future; with warmest regards and very best wishes to you and yours."

Often, though not always, the letter is hallowed and may well be framed and hung on the parlour wall. Anyway, it is all good constituency strategy, sound propaganda for the Member's party and evidence of his belief in the often forgotten or ignored slogan, "People Count".

An effective Member of Parliament must never, never eschew constituency trivia. Small wonder that many who would give almost anything to write MP after their name and sit as legislators in the House of Commons, shun the hustings on account of the burden of constituency work. There is hardly a subject known to man which does not appear in my Parliamentary mail in the course of a year. Pensions and matrimonial discord, maternity benefits and funeral grants, education, employment, strikes, taxation, local rates, investment, wages and prices, noise, smells and every kind of grievance and cause which arouse the paranoiac, the bigoted, the dogmatic as well as the real problems of ordinary men and women. All are the responsibility of the Member of Parliament. The wise Member deals with the lot, advises, guides, temporises and helps. All such cases are potential vote winners and they occupy two or more hours a day. That is what constituency politics is about.

With less obvious party political intent, the Member will identify himself with a wide range of other activities. I apply myself with enthusiasm to a speech to the Annual General Meeting of Barsham House, Malvern, the Worcester Diocesan Home for Mother and Child; to the North Cotswold Hunt Point-to-Point at Spring Hill, Broadway, on Easter Monday; to delivering a New Year address from the chancel steps of St Peter's Church, Malvern Wells; to addressing the National Farmers

Union of the Vale of Evesham on import levies and agricultural support; on taking the chair at the Annual Song Festival of the Salvation Army; launching appeals, donating goods at sales for charity; reading the lesson in Broadway Parish Church; distributing prizes and making the speech to children, parents and staff at any one of the three score or more schools in South Worcestershire; opening bazaars, buying thousands of raffle tickets each year and purchasing endless items off stands and giving them all away again, after a decent interval, as prizes and gifts for other fêtes, other bazaars, other raffles, other tombolas, in other parts of the constituency, for other causes.

There are four ways of earning the reputation of being "a first class constituency Member" and it is the stuff of which majorities are made:

1) Meticulous attention to every constituent's case.
2) Attending two hundred or more constituency engagements each year.
3) Belonging, with one's wife, to a large number of non-political organisations in the constituency.
4) Raising constituency issues fifty times a year or more, in the House of Commons, and doing the same when appropriate in the newspapers, on television or on radio.

Redress of constituents' grievances is both enjoyable and rewarding. I ignore the sneers of the cynical and uninitiated, who say that a Member of Parliament is merely a Welfare Officer. Maybe he is, but it is advantageous because it is the accumulated knowledge of a wide range of opinions, criticisms, problems and grievances, picked up from constituents and maturing in the Member's mind, which enables him to form a representative judgement on the countless issues on which he speaks and votes in the House of Commons. For the same reason, I never worry about my mountainous mail. I read and try to memorise the lot. My worry would be if the electorate thought me too insignificant and anonymous to write to. How I pity the Member who told me recently that he received an average of twenty letters a week. His constituents do not write to him very much, he says, because they know he does not like speaking, but prefers to work behind the scenes! Poor chap.

I have always represented a county constituency containing a number of towns and scores of villages. Peregrinations around them are routine and my minimum of a couple of hundred engagements and functions every year—only half of them political—are spread over the whole area. The political functions are, of course, Conservative. I do not attend Labour and Liberal events. These events are in many forms. Sometimes a speech followed by questions, or an "Any Questions" with myself answering all the questions, or parties of every description with speeches interspersed. The idea behind the more informal events is to raise party members and party funds. My motto is that the vote always follows the subscription and the larger the paid-up membership, the happier I am.

As for the non-political honorary offices, they are very important to me. I have scores of them, delightfully diverse and instructive. They include, for example, being President of the Broadway and District Darts League, Patron of the Malvern Opera and Ballet Club, a friend of Malvern Priory, Pershore Abbey, Worcester Cathedral and Pershore Cottage Hospital; Vice-President of the Blackminster School Silver Band Supporters' Association, Vice-President of the Vale of Evesham Asparagus Growers Association, Vice-President of the Worcestershire Marriage Guidance Council; President of Broadway Cricket Club and of Broadway United Football Club; President of the Pershore Civic Society, President of the Upton-on-Severn Chamber of Commerce and President of the Worcester Locomotive Society. There are countless others and my wife's affiliations are equally widespread and varied.

Moreover, it is a most welcome respite from the venom of party politics. It all instructs me endlessly upon every detail of the lives of ordinary men and women and the needs of 70,000 electors and their 20,000 children, who reside in the South Worcestershire constituency which I represent in the Commons, House of Parliament.

18. *Floralia Westmonasterensia*

1961

Mr Harold Macmillan succeeded Sir Anthony Eden as Prime Minister in January 1957, after the Suez débâcle when the fortunes of the Tory Party were at a very low ebb. Though the General Election twenty months before had been won with a satisfactory majority of more than sixty seats, Suez had greatly demoralised Tories both at Westminster and in the country. The Macmillan leadership was superb, and in his first two years he rapidly established a mastery over the House of Commons which has not been matched by any other post-war Premier. This was the period of "Macwonder" and unflappability, and, for Tory supporters in the country, "I'm a Mac man". With Lord Hailsham as Chairman of the Party organisation Mr Macmillan led it from the slough of despond in 1957 to the euphorious heights of the 1959 General Election, when the

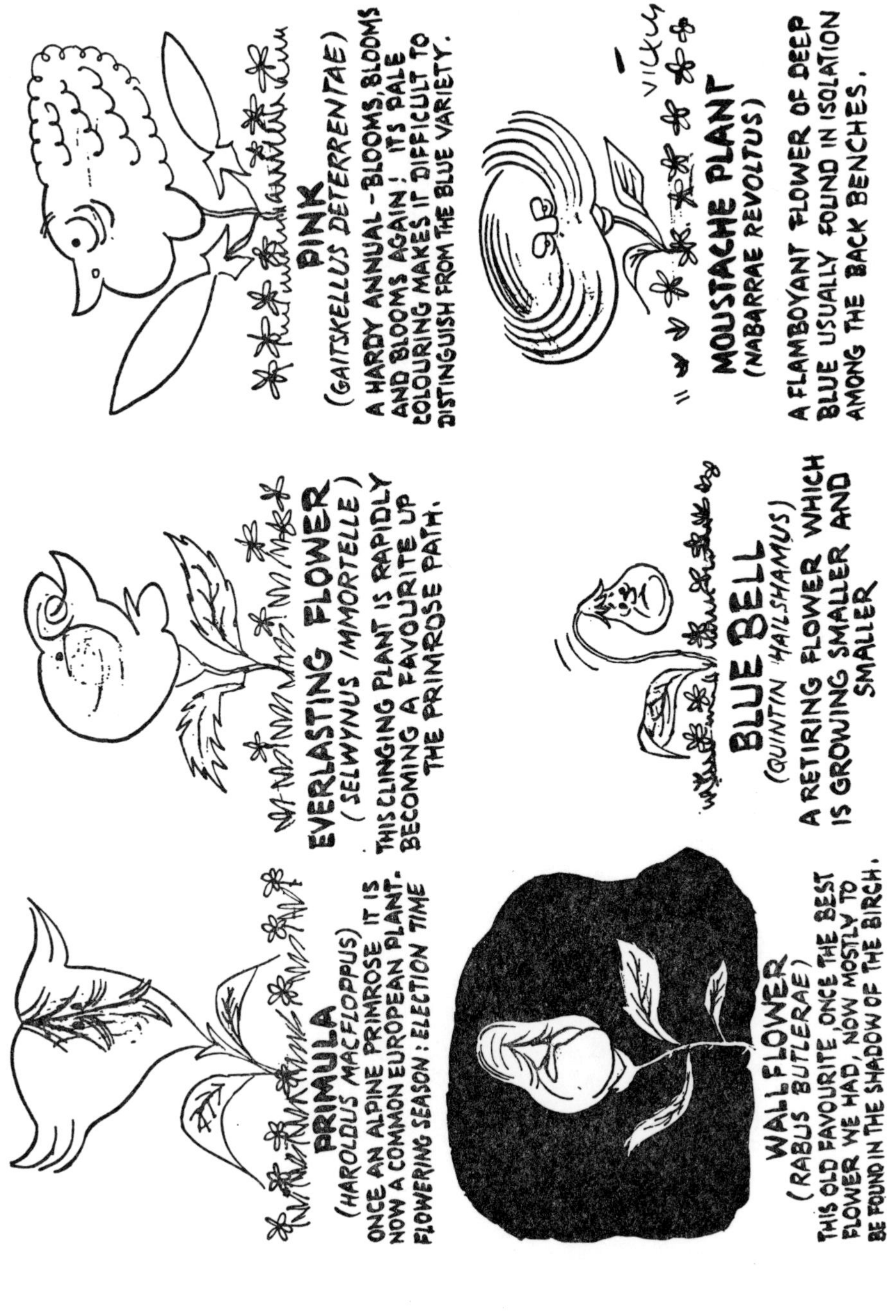

THE WESTMINSTER FLOWER SHOW, *Evening Standard*, 18th May, 1961.

Tory majority in the House of Commons was increased from sixty to one hundred. Macwonder had weathered the resignations of his three Treasury Ministers in January 1958, the Chancellor, Mr Peter Thorneycroft (now Lord Thorneycroft), the Financial Secretary to the Treasury, the Rt Hon. J. Enoch Powell, and the Economic Secretary, the Rt Hon. Nigel Birch. "A little local difficulty" quipped the imperturbable Prime Minister on the eve of his departure on his African tour. He had saved his party and pulled the country round. Both 1959 and 1960 were very good years in every way. But even then the clouds were gathering.

A "standstill" Budget in 1960 was far from the liking of millions of Conservatives who had expected true Tory measures for business expansion and increased investment. They got nothing save a prosy lecture from Macmillan's Chancellor, Derick Heathcoat Amory, and an increase in profits tax. Then the "wind of change" speech at Cape Town in February 1960, and the solicitude for Europe, although the actual Common Market application was not made until August 1961, were causing great anxiety and concern among Tory stalwarts. They apprehended a switch from Empire and Commonwealth, to Europe and continental federation. They disliked what they apprehended; so, for the most part, did the Labour Party as well.

Vicky captured it all with characteristic and uncanny skill. "Once an Alpine primrose": alpine because Macmillan had once dwelt on summits with Eisenhower; primrose because of Macmillan's self-identification with Disraeli and Disraeli's foundation of the Primrose League; and because the flora is similar, perhaps Vicky was alluding more distantly to Macmillan's crofter grandfather.

There is no doubt that Mr Macmillan was Vicky's favourite subject. For three years, 1957 to 1959, he depicted "SuperMac" and "Macwonder" and they both hit back at him like a boomerang, because the extraordinary powers attributed by Vicky to Macmillan were truly realised, and seen to be realised. The more Vicky lampooned Macmillan, the surer the touch of the Prime Minister appeared to become. Gradually the artist had to drop "SuperMac" and "Macwonder" and rather portray the Prime Minister as the grouse-shooting, Trollope-reading, tweedy aristocrat or the Edwardian con-man, or "Mac the Knife", or the fur-hatted summiteer in Moscow and elsewhere. "Common European plant" is bathos and curiously prophetic of Macmillan's declining years 1961 to 1963; the years of the Common Market rebuff, Profumo, the cancellation of Skybolt and the Westminster abattoir which destroyed seven Cabinet

Ministers who were old friends and colleagues. "Haroldus Macfloppus" was the top of the slippery slope.

The Rt Hon. Selwyn Lloyd, CH, CBE, TD, DL, QC, MP, had a greater flair for Ministerial survival than any other politician I know. He entered Parliament in 1945 and talked incessantly and well during six years in opposition until his patron, Sir Anthony Eden, took him to the Foreign Office as Minister of State in Sir Winston Churchill's second Administration. Then there followed 13 years of continuous high office:

Minister of State, Foreign Office	1951–54
Minister of Supply	1954–55
Minister of Defence	April–December, 1955
Foreign Secretary	1955–60 (including SUEZ)
Chancellor of the Exchequer	1960–62
Lord Privy Seal and Leader of the House of Commons	1963–64

In 1964 he retired on to the backbenches in opposition, a venerated figure, truly Vicky's everlasting flower. "Favourite up the primrose path", however, came to nothing. His epitaph: he survived Suez.

The Rt Hon. Hugh Gaitskell, CBE, MP, took over from Mr Attlee after Labour lost the 1955 General Election, and when Labour lost again in October 1959 by an even bigger margin, Mr Gaitskell's leadership was called in question. Vicky could hardly have forseen Gaitskell's death, in January, 1963, and the artist, who was a pacifist, astringently drew attention to the Gaitskell support for Britain's independent nuclear deterrent. Hence the "hardy annual". And, after Aneurin Bevan had contemptuously referred to Gaitskell's erudition and his faultless Wykehamist manners as a "desiccated calculating machine", Vicky, more wounding than he knew, alluded to the difficulty of distinguishing the "pale colouring" of Mr Gaitskell's policies from the Tory blue variety. "Blooms, blooms and blooms again" is a reference to the Labour Party Conference at Scarborough in 1960) when Mr Gaitskell had said:

> We may lose the vote today and the results may deal this party a grave blow. . . . But. . . . there are some of us who will fight and fight and fight again to bring back sanity and honesty and dignity.

The Pink's "pale colouring" referred to Mr Gaitskell's unsuccessful attempt to revise Clause 4 of the party's constitution, providing for the nationalisation of all the means of production, distribution and exchange which Mr Wilson embraced so fervently on the very day that he became Leader of the party in February 1963.

Vicky, far, far to the left of Gaitskell's socialism, made no attempt to include Mr Harold Wilson in his Westminster Flower Show. He contented himself with derogating Gaitskell as a crypto-Tory.

Mr R. A. Butler had been Tory Member of Parliament for Saffron Walden since 1929 and narrowly missed becoming Prime Minister in 1957. "Once the best flower we had" is a sour reference to the Butler remark about Sir Anthony Eden, the best Prime Minister we have. "Wallflower" was appropriate at the time and as it turned out was cruelly prophetic of Mr Butler's second failure to become Prime Minister when Sir Alec Douglas-Home succeeded Mr Macmillan in 1963.

Mr Butler's long tenure of the office of Home Secretary, 1957 to 1962—with which he combined numerous other duties such as Leader of the House and for a while Chairman of the Conservative Party—had many critical moments with his own party in the House of Commons, such as the reform of the Lords and the endless row over capital and corporal punishment, notably judicial birching for crimes of violence. On 11th April, 1961, five weeks before Vicky's cartoon, sixty-seven Tories had marched through the Lobbies against Mr Butler on judicial birching. But Vicky, ever cunning, gave an extraordinary double edge to the words . . . "now mostly to be found in the shadow of the birch". He was referring as well to Mr Harold Macmillan's palatial home in Sussex, Birch Grove, and the fact that Mr R. A. Butler was largely sublimated in a Parliamentary sense, to the overpowering and scintillating performances of his leader and Prime Minister. Hence "shadow of the birch" twice, the birch-rod, and Birch Grove. But RAB Butler was dignified and civilised throughout: a great and humanitarian Home Secretary.

In 1961, Lord Hailsham was tucked up in the House of Lords as Lord President of the Council and Minister for Science. He was largely in eclipse after his halcyon days as Chairman of the Conservative Party, bell-ringing, swashbuckling and contributing in his own inimitable and dynamic way to the great Tory win by over 100 seats at the General Election of 1959. In 1961, nobody could see much future for the lovable Quintin. Peerages could not be renounced and he was stranded, like a whale on the beach, in their Lordships' House. Hence Vicky's "retiring flower, growing smaller and smaller". But after the 1963 Peerage Act, which made peerages renounceable, Quintin was soon back in the Commons as MP for St

Marylebone. He quickly recovered his old form. Nothing retiring about Q.H. now.

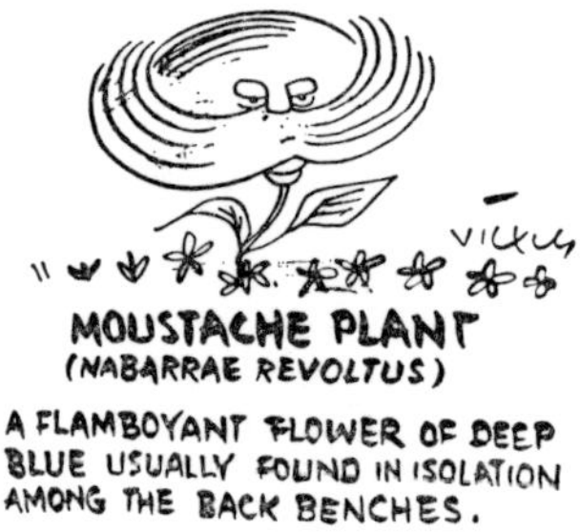

Never has any political cartoonist portrayed his subjects so succinctly and colourfully.

Vintage Vicky indeed.

GLOSSARY

Floralia Westmonasterensia	—	Westminster Flower Show.
Primula: Haroldus Macfloppus		The Prime Minister, the Rt Hon. Harold Macmillan, MP.
Everlasting Flower: Selwynus Immortelle	—	The Chancellor of the Exchequer, the Rt Hon. Selwyn Lloyd, CH, CBE, TD, DL, QC, MP.
Pink: Gaitskellus Deterrentae	—	The Leader of Her Majesty's Opposition, the Rt Hon. Hugh Gaitskell, CBE, MP.
Wallflower: Rabus Butlerae	—	The Home Secretary and Leader of the House of Commons, the Rt Hon. R. A. Butler, CH, MP.
Blue Bell: Quintin Hailshamus	—	The Lord President of the Council, Minister for Science and Leader of the House of Lords, the Rt Hon. Lord Hailsham, QC.
Moustache Plant: Nabarrae Revoltus	—	Tory Member of Parliament for Kidderminster, Mr Gerald Nabarro.

19. *Musings on Africa*

To a short list of great speeches of our time—such as those of Sir Winston Churchill, President Roosevelt and the appeal for peace by Pope Pius XII during the Second World War—I would add the speech of the British Prime Minister, Mr Harold Macmillan, to the Houses of Parliament of the Union of South Africa, in Cape Town, on 3rd February, 1960.

In thirteen years preceding that date, Britain had granted independence to India, Pakistan, Ceylon, Malaya and the Gold Coast (Ghana). In the sixties were to follow Nigeria, Nyasaland (Malawi), Tanganyika (Tanzania), Northern Rhodesia (Zambia), Kenya, Bechuanaland (Botswana), Basutoland (Lesotho), Swaziland, Sierra Leone, the Cameroons, Cyprus, Malta, Mauritius, Guyana and many Caribbean territories.

Mr Macmillan's Cape Town speech has passed into history as "the Wind of Change", deriving its name from the passage which ran:

> The most striking of all the impressions I have formed since I left London a month ago is the strength of this African national consciousness. In different places, it may take different forms. But it is happening everywhere. The wind of change is blowing through this continent. Whether we like it or not, this growth of national consciousness is a political fact. We must accept it as a fact. Our national policies must take account of it.

This was before the Congo holocaust; and, of course, nearly six years before the "breakaway" Government of Mr Ian Smith in Rhodesia, or the Unilateral Declaration of Independence (UDI) or, as it was later called by despondent Labour Ministers in Britain, the illegal declaration of independence (IDI), which dates from 11th November, 1965. Rhodesia is the only British territory in Africa not to achieve full and constitutional independence with the Mother Country's guidance and blessing. Virtually, Southern Rhodesia had been independent since 1923, when a referendum of whites had narrowly opted to remain under the tutelage of the British Colonial Office, rather than join the self-governing Union of South Africa. So, theoretically the four stated requirements of the British Government for full independence had to be met in the case of Southern Rhodesia. They were:

i) Economic viability.
ii) A working system of Parliamentary democracy, whether on the Westminster model or not.
iii) An independent judiciary and a sound system for the administration of justice.
iv) The quality which is very hard to name, but easy to see, stability, the protection of minorities, and all that connotes.

But the break-up of the Central African Federation and the failure of Lord Alport's mission in a cloud of suspicion made it exceedingly dubious that the four stated requirements for constitutional independence for Southern Rhodesia, could be adequately realised. The mouthings of Kenneth Kaunda and Hastings Banda, later to lead Zambia and Malawi respectively, and the revolutionary ardour of Mr Joshua Nkomo and the Revd Sithole in Southern Rhodesia fanned the separatist tendencies in Salisbury.

Contemporaneously, there were dramatic events in South Africa, home of apartheid, and it can be said that no true understanding of British policies for the independence of African countries is possible without detailed study of Mr Macmillan's "Wind of Change" speech and the reply of the then Prime Minister of South Africa, Dr the Hon. H. F. Verwoerd. This presaged the secession of the Union from the British Commonwealth in March, 1961, primarily on account of South African apartheid or racial segregation policies. But Mr Macmillan's speech was supported overwhelmingly by Members of both British Houses of Parliament, including myself. It was no Macmillan aberration: it was the collective will and deliberate and objective policy of the Macmillan Ministry. Of course, he strained every effort to retain South African goodwill, in spite of his thinly veiled criticism of apartheid, and I re-echo the words of the peroration of his "Wind of Change" speech:

> Those of us who by the grace of favour of the electors are temporarily in charge of affairs in my country and in yours, we fleeting transient phantoms over the great stage of history, we have no right to sweep aside on this account the friendship that exists between our two countries. That is the legacy of history. It is not ours alone to deal with. To adapt a famous phrase: it belongs to those who are living, it belongs to those who are dead and to those who are yet unborn.
>
> We must face the differences. But let us try to see a little beyond them, down the long vista of the future.
>
> I hope—indeed, I am confident that in another fifty years we shall look back on the differences that exist between us now as mere matters of historical interest. For as time passes and one generation yields to another, human problems change and fade. Let us remember these truths. Let us therefore resolve to build and not to destroy. Let us also remember always that weakness comes from division, and, in words familiar to you, strength from unity.
>
> (Rt Hon. Harold Macmillan, MP, Cape Town, 3rd February, 1960.)

On these tenets I based my beliefs in the value of policies of friendship and amity between Britain and South Africa. Millions more in the two countries felt exactly as I did. Thus it was sad that Mr Wilson, within weeks of assuming office as Prime Minister, and to satiate or placate his Party Left-wing, decided as a matter of calculated and deliberate policy to replace friendship towards South Africa by hostility and amity by antipathy.

Aboard the *Pendennis Castle*, one thousand miles and two days' sailing off the Cape in November, 1964, I became aware of the surge of indignation in South Africa, caused by the decision of the Labour Cabinet, led by Mr Wilson, to cancel the contract for Britain to supply Buccaneer naval reconnaisance jet strike aircraft for South African external defence. I was deluged with requests for Press and radio interviews immediately the ship docked at Cape Town. I gave all these and roundly condemned the highly emotional and strategically unwise decision of Mr Wilson's new Ministry. Here indeed was the absolute antithesis of the spirit and the word of the perorations of Mr Harold Macmillan's "Wind of Change" speech.

I cabled from Cape Town, on 21st November, 1964, at the request of the Editor of the *News of the World*, an article which appeared in the newspaper on the the following day under the title "HANDS OFF SOUTH AFRICA". Here it is:

> What does Mr Wilson hope to achieve by his arms ban against South Africa? Is he yielding to his extremist Left wing and taking political action against apartheid or racial segregation in South Africa?
>
> Whatever the reasons, he is likely to achieve little or nothing in the event. Certainly South Africa has a contract in Britain for sixteen Buccaneer naval reconnaisance strike aircraft and probably another fourteen to follow, thirty in all worth about £40m.
>
> But these are not aircraft for internal security use—South Africans rightly deride this suggestion.
>
> The Buccaneers are for attack in the event of war on hostile ships and submarines in the South Atlantic approaching below the radar cover and the Buccaneers would almost certainly be wearing British or other Western or Allied marks.
>
> Strictly the Buccaneer is for external sea defence of South Africa and cancellation of the contract would be utterly irrelevant to domestic apartheid policies. As for other arms, Mr Wilson appears conveniently to forget that South Africa herself produces small arms, grenades, and even armoured cars in adequate quantities for security purposes.
>
> Moreover, she can buy abundant arms outside Britain if she wants to.
>
> There is a contract between South Africa and Britain for the Buccaneers and if Mr Wilson breaks faith by refusing to supply the aircraft, then undoubtedly South Africa's Premier, Dr Verwoerd, would instantly take reprisals and denounce the agreement with Britain for the joint use of the Simonstown Naval Base 30 miles outside Cape Town.
>
> In the event of war, Britain and her allies can count on only two naval bases in the South Atlantic—Simonstown and the Falklands. Both are indispensable in the vast stretches of water where Allied merchant ships to Australia, the Middle East, Far East and South America would undoubtedly ply.
>
> Even in any major local war—for example, around Indonesia during which the Suez Canal might be closed to Western Naval forces—refuelling, repair and maintenance of ships at Simonstown would be invaluable tactical facilities.
>
> Thus, as far as naval and military necessities, Britain and America would hurt themselves far more by rupturing the Buccaneer contract and the Simonstown agreement than they could hurt South Africa.
>
> But there are even more powerful reasons for Britain's Labour Government to tread warily in condemning South African racial policies.
>
> Britain is the world's greatest international trader. Our South African trade is very large and in our present balance of payments troubles any diminution of

exports to South Africa could bring dire consequences. Last year Britain sold 5% of all her exports to South Africa, thus bringing in £195 million. South Africa sent to Britain goods, notably raw materials, minerals and foodstuffs worth £114m. Thus Britain had a huge £81m favourable trade balance on her South African trade.

In 1964 to date the favourable balance is running even higher. It is reckoned that if South Africa stopped buying from Britain—and this is a very real possibility if Mr Wilson breaks the Buccaneer contract and causes Dr Verwoerd to break the Simonstown agreement—it could lead to such a fall in British exports to South Africa, as to increase unemployment in Britain by 150,000. This is a truly dreadful prospect, but it is no idle threat.

The whole world is South Africa's oyster and she could comfortably replace imports of merchandise and manufactured goods from Britain by buying in a dozen countries, including particularly America, Japan, Western Germany and France.

Does Mr Wilson really want to give away all this huge export trade? Last year's figures for British vehicles (£26m), ships (£8½m), electrical machinery (£23m) and heavy machinery (£43m) show the vast volume and diversification of our exports to South Africa, all of which would be imperilled by any rash and provocative decision to impose an arms ban.

Anyway, arms only represent a tiny part of Britain's exports to South Africa.

It would be a different matter if South Africa were a tiny, poor country likely to be cast down by the Wilson ban.

On the contrary, it is probably the richest country in the world.

With the one exception of oil, she has everything she needs within her own boundaries to sustain a population of sixteen million.

Gold, diamonds, coal, food and sugar and grain, asbestos, copper and iron ore, steel and manganese and vanadium all abound, and there are fine roads, railways and ports.

Even if the present oil supply from the Middle East were cut off it represents only 13% of South Africa's requirements and could easily be replaced from many other sources.

I repeat—what does Mr Wilson expect to achieve by his political threats?

He won't even dent apartheid or racial segregation policies. The South African Government is strong, determined and independent, backed by a buoyant, self-supporting and vigorous economy.

All he is doing is playing politics, swanking to the Afro-Asian group at the United Nations and placating his Left wing extremists who could so easily overturn his wafer-thin majority in the House of Commons.

I say to Mr Wilson: Honour the contract for the Buccaneers.

Stop interfering in the affairs of free and independent nations abroad,

particularly our loyal friends in South Africa, who nurture enormous goodwill to, and faith in Britain.
Above all, do not impoverish British industries by threatening their hard-won market in South Africa.

Three years later, Mr Wilson was still refusing arms for external defence to our South African allies, and to mounting storms of protest in Britain, particularly after the devaluation of sterling and the continuing economic crises of Mr Wilson's second administration. At the end of 1967, Britain had the offer of an even larger export order of arms to South Africa worth in all about £200m. The Cabinet was split over whether to accept it. Those in favour were said to include such powerful Ministers as Mr Callaghan, Mr Healey, Mr Crosland and Mr Brown. But again Mr Wilson was cowed by his Left wing and the South African offer was rejected. On 17th December, 1967, I again attacked Mr Wilson's policy towards South Africa in a *News of the World* article entitled "Beggars can't be choosers, Mr Wilson". I said that "Mr Wilson's heart and emotions are ruling his head" and that the position he had taken up on the issue was obscurantist and futile. "Whom does Mr Wilson think he's fooling", I said. "His soap-box oratory in Trafalgar Square in 1963 attacking arms for South Africa is dead as a Dodo. Then Britain was rich and solvent. Then Mr Wilson was leader of the Opposition. Today, Britain is impoverished and insolvent."

A large volume of comment descended on me by letter, telephone and the remainder, and it was clear that only a small minority of the British electorate favoured Mr Wilson's policies of subjecting Britain's overseas trade to the test of approval by his Left wing of our customers' racial and social policies. Scandalous Socialist ballyhoo and hypocrisy I called it, from a Government ready and willing to supply arms to Nigeria to sustain a policy of genocide against the Ibos of Biafra in the disastrous West African Civil War.

Moreover, the intransigence of Mr Wilson in South African trade matters and the utter and abject failure of his policy of sanctions against Mr Ian Smith's Rhodesia will inevitably drive together into a shot-gun marriage, the Republic of South Africa and the Republic of Rhodesia; including South West Africa, formerly German territory, then mandated to South Africa and now absorbed into the Republic, despite United Nations protests; and also probably including the former British Protectorates of Basutoland (Lesotho), Bechuanaland (Botswana) and Swaziland, which may well make common cause with South Africa in a liberalised union; and finally, Angola and Mozambique—at present Portuguese colonial territories which might well join such a Union or Federation to create the United States of Southern Africa—U.S.S.A.—matching in wealth and affluence the United States of America. It may well come to pass before A.D. 2000 and here is great appeal for those who believe as I do, that the repressive tendencies of apartheid will gradually ameliorate; that the Transkei policies will do much to ease racial tension in the next two or three decades; and that South Africa has unparalleled opportunities. Already her Defence plans envisage the control of vast stretches of the Indian and South Atlantic oceans. Her defence White Paper of 24th April, 1969, said:

> While we are gradually succeeding in creating a reasonable maritime defence capability of our own for the protection of our sea areas, this capability also constitutes a potentially valuable international contribution to the protection of the sea route round the Cape in the event of a world conflict.

Clearly South Africa will be a great power in the twenty-first century, dominating the nodal point of sea routes in the Southern Hemisphere. Already the big tankers cock a snook at Nasser's Suez Canal, blocked and obsolescent. Britain has a huge stake already in South Africa and will have bigger investments in the future in spite of Mr Wilson's petulance and bitterness.

During 1965, on two occasions, I wrote of the developing storm clouds over Rhodesia and her deteriorating relations with Mr Wilson's Government in London. I was appalled by the clamour for armed action against the Smith regime and apprehensive that a policy of sanctions waged in desultory and incomplete fashion, notwithstanding United Nations support, would make Britain foolish and abject in the eyes of the world. All the Wilson froth about the success of sanctions in weeks rather than months has reduced us to ridicule. Why Anguilla (pop. 6,000) and not Rhodesia? chortled our detractors and Tory ex-Minister Mr Nigel Birch, MP, twitted Mr Wilson after the Anguilla adventure, about taking on someone his own size.

My first article appeared in the *News of the World* on 27th June, 1965, under the title "Britain must support this man":

> Mr Harold Wilson's first Commonwealth Conference has had abject failures, and the main one (not unexpected after the calculated omission of an invitation to Mr Ian Smith, Prime Minister of Rhodesia), was the atmosphere of acrimony in the closing stages.

It was led by President Kaunda of Zambia and backed by Dr Nkrumah and other African leaders, giving a warning that violence was imminent in Rhodesia.

Mr Kaunda even made the preposterous offer of a military base for Britain, for use against the white population of Rhodesia, who are Britons, our own people, our own kith and kin, our own flesh and blood, who have fought with us and for us against autocracy in two world wars.

It seems to me that the Commonwealth Conference ended with Mr Wilson bending over backwards to achieve a compromise communique seeking to reconcile the hostility of the African leaders to Rhodesia with the realities of Mr Ian Smith's powerful, entrenched position.

This schism, deep and largely intractable, could cause the break-up of the British Commonwealth.

Turn in more detail to Rhodesia, which until a short time ago was part of the Central African Federation along with Northern Rhodesia (now Zambia) and Nyasaland (now Malawi).

There are about 221,000 whites, all Britons and about seventeen times as many Africans.

Leaders of African states, formerly British Colonies, now demand of Mr Wilson that no independence is granted to Rhodesia unless and until there is universal suffrage for Africans—one man, one vote—or, politely expressed, majority black rule.

Now Rhodesia has never been a Protectorate or a Colonial dependency. Until 1923, it was the British South Africa Company and the local community that provided and financed the Government in Southern Rhodesia.

For the last forty years, the Rhodesians have governed themselves and balanced their Budget without any help from the British taxpayer. They are big customers of ours and their trade is in balance, not in deficit.

Rhodesia has strong armed forces, both Army and Air Force, enough food to feed all her population, British and African, and control of the railways and communications and power supply of Northern Rhodesia with its immensely rich copper belt on which the prosperous economy of Zambia so greatly depends.

The African leaders, especially Kaunda and Nkrumah, want economic as well as military sanctions applied against Rhodesia. I say that would be ruinous for Britain and disastrous for the cause of African progress.

If an attempt is made to force Rhodesia to capitulate to the demands of African extremists by introducing sanctions, it would surely require concerted action by all the trading nations of the world. History has proved that, over and over again, to be quite unsuccessful.

And how capable are these African states of taking action against Rhodesia?

They all look to Britain for annual subventions. The British taxpayer forks

"Blowing-off in Trafalgar Square." Sir Gerald Nabarro, M.P., addressing the Tory May Day Rally in Trafalgar Square, 4th May 1969. *Left to Right:* Rt. Hon. John Boyd-Carpenter, M.P. (Conservative, Kingston-on-Thames), Rt. Hon. Quintin Hogg, Q.C., M.P. (Conservative, Marylebone), Rt. Hon. Duncan Sandys, M.P. (Conservative, Streatham), Mrs. Lynda Chalker, Chairman of the London Young Conservatives. The large poster at the foot of Nelson's Column reads: "Labour Has Failed".

"Any Questions?" at Combe Martin, Devon, 17th April 1959. *The Panel, Left to Right:* Mr. Gerald Nabarro, M.P. (Conservative, Kidderminster), Rt. Hon. Patrick Gordon Walker, M.P. (Socialist, Smethwick), Mr. Jack Houghton Brown, Mrs. Mary Stocks, Question Master: Mr. Freddy Grisewood, O.B.E., Producer: Mr. Michael Bowen.

It is noteworthy that ten years later, in 1969, Mrs. Mary Stocks, now the Baroness Stocks, the Rt. Hon. Patrick Gordon Walker, now M.P. for Leyton, and Sir Gerald Nabarro, now M.P. for Worcestershire, South, are still regular participants in the programme; and Mr. Michael Bowen is still the Producer.

The Budget of 1962. Immediately after the Chancellor of the Exchequer (Rt. Hon. Selwyn Lloyd, M.P.) sat down in the House of Commons, Mr. Gerald Nabarro (Conservative, Kidderminster) and Mr. Richard Marsh (Socialist, Greenwich, later Minister of Power and then Minister of Transport in Socialist Governments) are interviewed by Mr. George Ffitch on Independent Television News.
This controversial Budget, imposing Purchase Tax on soft drinks and confectionery and creating a short-term Capital Gains Tax, is debated before millions of viewers within an hour of the conclusion of the Chancellor's speech.

"ONE PAIR OF EYES"
B.B.C. 2 Television, June 1968.

Sir Gerald Nabarro's Clean Air Bill was withdrawn at the suggestion of Mr. Duncan Sandys, Minister of Housing and Local Government, because a Private Member's Bill cannot include financial provisions. Mr. Sandys promised a Government Clean Air Bill and his assiduous support for this "Revolution at the fireside" included this Christmas card in 1954.

During the month before the Second Reading of his Clean Air Bill, all Sir Gerald Nabarro's Parliamentary letters—nearly four thousand of them—were franked in this way.

"Buckingham Palace, 5th February 1963." *Left to Right:* Rupert Nabarro, 17, Captain of Rackets, Harrow School, Lady Nabarro, Sir Gerald Nabarro, M.P. (Conservative, Kidderminster), Jeremy Nabarro, 16, Worcestershire Junior Squash Rackets Champion.

"The Right and the Left."
Knighted together: Buckingham Palace, 4th February 1963. Sir William Carron, President, Amalgamated Engineering Union. Now Lord Carron of City and County of Kingston-upon-Hull. Sir Gerald Nabarro, M.P. (Conservative, Kidderminster).

"Into the Seventies." Sir Gerald and Lady Nabarro at their home at Broadway, Worcestershire, summer 1969. *Left to Right:* Jeremy Nabarro, 23, Sarah Nabarro, 19, Sir Gerald and Lady Nabarro, Rupert Nabarro, 24, Dinah Nabarro, 14, and dogs, golden retriever "Rufus" (5), Norton terrier "Sammy" (6).

out huge sums to keep them solvent and to oppose communist infiltration from Peking.

In comparison we have Rhodesia, strong, solvent, prosperous and progressive. Premier Smith's policy is for African children in Rhodesia to be educated to take their place in a multi-racial society by evolution, not revolution; to maintain a Christian civilisation in Rhodesia for the benefit of all, irrespective of race and colour.

Leaving on one side a few extremists, the majority of Africans in Rhodesia, learning from the events of recent years in the Congo, Ghana, Zanzibar and elsewhere, have confidence that their future welfare and prosperity most largely depends on Rhodesia securing independence within the British Commonwealth, resting on the present Constitution and limited franchise with steady expansion of African voting as popular education spreads and imbues a sense of civic responsibility.

If I have to choose between African majority rule for Rhodesia or independence and the present Constitution, I shall choose the latter, led by Mr Ian Smith, supported by all his Rhodesians and by informed sections of African opinion.

For myself—and I believe millions of Britons support me—I will not accept orders to 'declare war on Rhodesia'.

Or, on a more personal note, I much prefer Mr Ian Smith to Dr Kenneth Kaunda (Zambia), Dr Nkrumah (Ghana), Dr Hastings Banda (Malawi) or any other African leader.

I believe fervently that Mr Ian Smith has the best interests of Rhodesians at heart, ardently wishes to remain in the British Commonwealth and that he and all his Britons in Rhodesia passionately love their allegiance to Her Majesty the Queen.

Four months later, on October 17th, 1965, less than a month before UDI, I again wrote in the *News of the World*, under the title "Britain cannot Bludgeon or Blackmail Rhodesia":

The heady atmosphere of a Tory Party Conference is not the best place to debate a complex constitutional and racial issue.

But to the eternal credit of the Tory Party at Brighton on Friday evening, it faced with courage and candour the responsibilities of debating before the world the explosive Rhodesian constitutional crisis.

Passions ran high: convictions were deeply held: the Party of Empire and Commonwealth did not shirk its duty.

All this was precipitated by the Marquess of Salisbury. Though often called a dynastic figure and sometimes sneered at as an 'ancient monument', he is revered in Britain and in Rhodesia.

The conference hung on every word uttered by this slender, stooping figure.

His case, shortly expressed, was that the emergency resolution of the Tory executive, proclaiming adherence to the Rhodesian Constitution, framed in 1961, and condemning any unilateral declaration of independence did not go far enough.

Said the Marquess, it would be unthinkable for Britain or the U.N. to wage war against Rhodesia by punitive sanctions, economic or military.

In the end, in a tumultuous scene, 4,000 Tories at the Conference decided against a vote on sanctions because they took the view, in sensible and matter-of-fact terms, that any unilateral declaration of independence by Mr Ian Smith was wholly bad and to be deprecated.

If mention of sanctions were dragged in at this stage it could excite less responsible elements in Rhodesia to believe that a large minority in Britain favours going ahead with UDI.

Britain's objective must be a free and independent Rhodesia within the Commonwealth.

Mr Smith as well wants to see a free and multi-racial society, but the argument will inevitably be how quickly enfranchisement of Africans is to proceed.

I liked Sir Alec Douglas-Home, winding up the debate, saying that our objective is not only to sustain the 1961 Constitution, which provides fully for progressive enfranchisement of Africans and eventual majority rule in Rhodesia, but also liberal funds available for African education. Britain would furnish the lion's share.

What would now be disastrous, having regard to the unanimity of all shades of opinion in Britain, is any UDI by Mr Smith.

Mercifully, he appears to accept that dictum and our role must be to impress upon him the need for further discussions.

The next few months will be tense and dangerous. African leaders in the emergent states of Ghana, Tanzania, Zambia and Malawi, will undoubtedly press at the United Nations and in London for physical action against Rhodesia.

Britain should stand firm against such moves because, in the first place, this constitutional controversy is nothing to do with the United Nations, and secondly, because sanctions of any kind against Rhodesia would be doomed to failure.

I give four valid reasons for that downright statement:

(1) If military measures were employed, who would carry them out? Would U.N. and if so, with what troops?
The African States are in no position, financially or otherwise, to put troops in to fight the Rhodesians, neither is India, nor Pakistan, nor even Ireland.

Even if they could, the immediate reaction would be tens of thousands of British volunteers flooding out as mercenaries to Rhodesia to fight against what would be deemed U.N. aggression.

(2) As to economic sanctions, Rhodesia is nearly independent for food and other essentials. She would probably be supported by South Africa and the adjoining Portuguese territories, which could by themselves make economic sanctions ineffectual.

(3) Rhodesia holds a lot of the aces, controlling the Kariba power supplies to Zambia and the railway system; controlling the coal from Wankie, and geographically dominating the African territories to the North.
Zambia and others would inflict more damage on themselves than on Rhodesia.
Britain would lose vastly in Anglo-Rhodesian trade and our investment there, directly and indirectly reckoned at £150m.

(4) Sanctions against Rhodesia would decimate the multi-racial Commonwealth. The Afro-Asian members would walk out, leaving only a white Commonwealth greatly reduced in influence and strength.

Our duty is to lower the temperature and take the drama out of the situation.
Both the British and the Rhodesian Governments should resume negotiations and sit at the conference table until they have hammered out the pace of African enfranchisement within the 1961 Constitution.
Certain it is that Mr Ian Smith will never, never surrender his country to Mr Joshua Nkomo or any other African Nationalist.
Mr Smith would rather go south and seek Rhodesia's union with South Africa.
I say Rhodesians are British to the core and among the most loyal of all Her Majesty's subjects.
I will not support sanctions and the humiliation they would bring.
There must be no bludgeoning or blackmailing Rhodesia into submission.
We must not, in any circumstances, be led into a declaration of war against our own kith and kin, which is what sanctions, economic or military, would mean.

In my election address to my South Worcestershire constituents before the 1966 General Election, I said:

There would have been no Rhodesian crisis had Douglas-Home been handling the negotiations. He is a statesman and a diplomat. Mr Wilson's sanctions against Rhodesia are hopeless, futile and discredited. We should talk immediately to Mr Smith, no holds barred, recognising independence, but with assurances for widening the African franchise and raising their educational and social standards with a view to eventual full participation in Government. U.D.I. may be illegal constitutionally; as bad is Mr Wilson's appropriation of Rhodesian Bank funds in London.

They gave me a very big majority to sustain these and other Conservative views. I have never voted for sanctions against Rhodesia and I never will.

Throughout the ensuing three years the wrangling proceeded interminably, accompanied by a progressive deterioration in relations, such as they were, between London and Salisbury. Talks aboard *Tiger* and *Fearless* proved abortive and if anything added to the atmosphere of mutual acrimony. Mr Ian Smith made abundantly clear the inevitable road to ultimate Republicanism, when he said in a broadcast on 20th May, 1969:

When I left HMS *Fearless*, Mr Wilson agreed with me that the only real point of difference between us was that of the appeal to the Judicial Committee of the Privy Council. However, after Mr Thomson had conferred with African leaders to the North of us during the time of our independence celebrations, this single point of difference had grown into nine non-negotiable conditions. I need hardly dwell on the cynicism of this episode. These new obstacles were unacceptable to us and so Mr Thomson returned to Britain, leaving the *Fearless* proposals, as they were called, on the table to be picked up at any time by the Rhodesian Government. Ever since, Britain has shown no desire to explore the possibility of negotiating any of these terms.

It was obvious to us that they had come to the Conference table with preconceived ideas and nothing that we could say or do would cause them to shift their position. In fact, as the last series of talks became more and more protracted, the British became more and more inflexible in their demands. Indeed, I would go so far as to say that our last two messages to the British Government were treated with indifference amounting almost to contempt.

To our message of 13th February this year we received the first reply on 11th March, which was followed by a corrected reply on the 18th March. Both of these contained a number of glaring mistakes of fact, which made it clear to us that the task had been delegated to some official who was not capable of handling the problem. To our last message of 16th April, we received a reply which made it absolutely clear that the British Government were paying very little attention and interest to the Rhodesian question. It was brief and evasive. Moreover, in the House of Commons on 5th May, the British Foreign Secretary in answer to a question said: 'We have had nothing from Salisbury which can be described as proposals or plans'. However, the record shows that our message, which consisted of five large pages of proposals and plans, had been on his desk since 16th April, for almost three weeks. Obviously they are more concerned with other problems on their home front; they are engrossed with the all important task of trying to save their own political lives.

In the end, all we have been able to get out of them is an offer to give us independence with one hand, while at the same time introducing an extra safeguard which will be tantamount to taking away our independence with the other hand.

Throughout the entire series of discussions the British have been obsessed with the question of majority rule. Everything else was subservient. The fact that Rhodesians (black and white) did not want it, was irrelevant. The fact that it would be harmful to Rhodesia was irrelevant; and so it went on, meeting after meeting, day after day. I do not believe that we could get these people to change their minds even if we lived for a thousand years.

I reflect "Plus ça change, plus c'est la même chose."

The British Government appears to have learned nothing in the last hundred and ninety-three years. In 1776, the loss of thirteen colonies and the Declaration of Independence led on to the United States of America. In 1969, the Rhodesian Republic will lead on to the United States of Southern Africa.

20. *"Any Questions?"*

ALMOST everybody who is anybody in public and political life has taken part in "Any Questions?" on BBC sound radio. The live performance is on Friday evenings and lasts for forty-five minutes, with a recorded broadcast the following day. "Any Answers?"—the written reactions of listeners to the previous week's programme—is broadcast on Thursday evenings for thirty minutes and is also repeated the following day. Millions listen to these programmes. They are among the most popular on the air. Yet "Any Questions?" was devised in the autumn of 1948 as a stop-gap for a short run of six weeks. The name was that with which the "Brains Trust" began life but that distinguished programme was always a studio production. An essential part of the character of "Any Questions?" is that it has always been held in public. Within a week of the first programme from Winchester on October 12th, 1948, it had been decided to keep "Any Questions?" going right through the winter. Now, in its twenty-second year, it is and has long been a national institution.

It is still widely suspected that the panel know the questions before the programme begins. This is completely untrue. Hundreds of questions are submitted by the audience shortly before each programme and up to a dozen are chosen by the BBC staff, led by their distinguished producer Michael Bowen. The panellist has no idea of what is coming until each questioner, seated in the front row of the audience, puts the question, generally in a querulous voice, into a roving microphone. Thus, spontaneity and topicality are ensured and these two qualities are essential to the programme's success. Major national and international events occurring only a few hours before the broadcast are often the subject of questions, so the panel, meeting together nearly three hours before going on the air, listen with care to the six o'clock news for clues to possible questions.

Personally, I have always believed in doing my homework for this most exacting of programmes. A little research on possible topics detracts nothing from spontaneity and because no subject comes up two weeks running, the field is well narrowed. For years my Secretaries listened carefully to the three programmes before each of my appearances—more than forty of them—taking note of what was asked. Then in the week before the broadcast they read ten newspapers daily, choosing issues which are likely to attract questions. As I leave for the train, the file of likely questions is handed to me. The system works like a charm and often my Secretaries produced "questimates" which were seventy-five per cent correct. These are the intelligent questions on current affairs, national and international politics, the arts, literature, sex, the young, the old, science, fashions, indeed, on every aspect of human affairs and institutions. The other questions matter relatively little, because they are trivial or nonsense questions, put in to prevent the programme from becoming ponderous or tedious.

Michael Bowen has been the producer of "Any Questions?" since 1953 and his industry, dexterity and great personality, often under delicate circumstances, are major factors in the programme's continuing success. The programme is itinerant and until recently has nearly always come from towns and villages within the BBC West Region. Many of these places have been small and some of them even obscure. I have myself appeared on the programme from such places as Middle Wallop, Hampshire (pop. 800 approx.), South Petherton, Somerset (pop. 2167), Titchfield Hampshire (pop. 2886), St Blazey, Cornwall (pop. 2571), Combe Martin, Devon (pop. 2228), Camelford, Cornwall (pop. 1849) and Beaminster, Dorset (pop. 1996), as well as from establishments like the Nuclear Power Station at Berkeley in Gloucestershire, the Atomic Research Station at Winfrith Heath in Dorset and HMS *Collingwood* at Fareham. Away from the BBC West Region, I have appeared on programmes from Leicester, Derby, Belfast, Sheffield and so on.

But of course, this most mobile of programmes requires an element of continuity and for nearly twenty years, until his retirement in 1967, this was provided by the Question Master, Frederick Henry Grisewood, OBE —Freddy to the millions for whom his name and that of the programme are inseparable. Freddy's connection with broadcasting went back to the earliest 2LO and Crystal Palace days. He was born in 1888, the son of the Rector of Daylesford, which is on the borders of my South Worcestershire constituency and close to my home at Broadway, and educated at Radley and Magdalen College, Oxford. Until the Great War, he studied singing in London, Paris and Munich and in 1913 sang the bass part in the first performance of Henschel's Requiem at the Queen's Hall. He was invalided out of the Army in 1918 after serving throughout the war in the Oxfordshire and Buckinghamshire Light Infantry and for the next eleven years was agent for the Daylesford Estate. This experience, on top of his boyhood in the same place, enabled him to become the greatest living authority on Cotswold dialect and lore. In 1934, he published "*Old Bill*" which is still the standard work on the subject. Small wonder that this man of such splendid personality, tact, humour, knowledge, impartiality and experience, the possessor of an outstanding speaking voice, should become the keystone of the success of "Any Questions?".

The major part of the producer's job is to select and balance the team so that week by week the whole spectrum of British society and opinion is represented. The teams are chosen with a view to stimulating discussion which has vigour but not rancour and so the personal dislikes and animosities of possible panellists require a certain amount of deference. With this proviso, a bellicose, cunning and fluent Left wing Socialist can be paired with a bland Tory.

Politicians, however, play a relatively small part. The programme runs for about forty-four weeks of the year, with a summer break from July to September, and politicians take part in about one programme in three. It follows that only a handful of MPs take part and many of these appear no more than once a year. The number of MPs who appear each year is about twenty, or about one in thirty of the six hundred and thirty in the House. Some appear once and never appear again because they prove unattractive in voice, radio manner or because they are flabby, verbose or culpably silent.

Although the number of appearances which any individual may make on the programme is limited, some do so very frequently including one or two who took part in the earliest programmes over twenty years ago. A short selection of these and of some others who have appeared, illustrates their diversity. The late Baroness Asquith (better known on the programme, and, indeed, everywhere else, as Lady Violet Bonham Carter), Baroness Stocks (Mary Stocks), Ralph Wightman of Piddletrenthide, Dorset (rural philosopher, agricultural journalist and smallholder), John

Arlott (doyen of cricket commentators and Liberal aspirant to Parliament), the late Arthur Street (Wiltshire farmer and author), Lord Soper, Bishop (formerly Abbot) Butler, David Frost, Lord Robens, Christopher Soames, Frank Cousins and John Freeman. Almost everybody who is anybody, as I have said, gets on to "Any Questions?" at least once. But they have to be able to perform fluently, incisively and spontaneously to be asked to appear again.

All of those whom I have mentioned so far fulfil these requirements superbly. The politicians have to come up to the same high standard if they are to appear often. One who has done so over a very long period is Lord Boothby. Boothby first entered Parliament in 1924 and served as Parliamentary Private Secretary to Winston Churchill as Chancellor of the Exchequer before he was thirty. His many appearances on "Any Questions?" included the notorious 500th edition on 23rd March, 1962. The other members of the team were Mary Stocks, Jack Longland and Ralph Wightman and it came from Liphook, the village in Hampshire where Freddy Grisewood lives.

Earlier that week the Duke of Edinburgh had publicly described the *Daily Express* as a "bloody awful newspaper". His comment, naturally enough, hit the headlines and it was not surprising that someone in the audience at Liphook chose to ask the team what they thought of the remark. Then followed some of the most expensive minutes ever known to BBC radio. Two members of the team who agreed with the Duke made statements which were subsequently alleged to be actionable (obviously they cannot be printed here). Although the entire sequence was cut from the recorded repeat of the broadcast, various writs were served and in the end the claims were settled out of court for sums never disclosed but believed to run into five figures. In all the years of its life, this was the one and only occasion, to date, on which money was paid out for alleged libel in "Any Questions?"—a remarkable record for a completely spontaneous programme, broadcast live, in which the participants are quite unaware of the questions to be put to them. There was a certain irony in the fact that because of the 500th programme, BBC top brass was present in the hall at Liphook. They were, of course, powerless to prevent this disaster. A programme which had pursued its unblemished way for so long a term without their aid had come sadly to grief in their presence. But the BBC took this costly incident in its stride, realising that none of its staff were to blame.

The importance of "Any Questions?" was pointed out to me one day in the lobby of the House of Commons by the late Walter Elliot, doctor and soldier, scholar and man of letters, Conservative Cabinet Minister and Member of Parliament for nearly thirty-five years. He used to appear on the programme often and said that he preferred it to any other Friday evening engagement in his diary. He reckoned that between a third and a half of his constituents in Kelvingrove, Glasgow, listened to the programme when he was on it. He also considered that appearing on "Any Questions?" was essential broadcasting for politicians aspiring to the Cabinet and for Ministers out of office. Incumbent Ministers, of course, are not allowed to take part.

How very right Walter Elliot was about aspiring Ministers. I have myself appeared with nearly all the Ministers who have occupied senior positions under Mr Wilson since 1964. Indeed, I have appeared with Harold Wilson himself on two occasions, at Lostwithiel, Cornwall in March, 1956 and at Holt, Wiltshire, in December, 1961. Among other present Ministers, I have appeared with James Callaghan, Home Secretary and formerly Chancellor of the Exchequer; with Denis Healey, Minister of Defence; with Anthony Wedgwood Benn, Minister of Technology and formerly Postmaster-General; with George Brown, Minister for Economic Affairs and then Foreign Secretary (until he resigned, exasperated and personally slighted); with Patrick Gordon Walker, the celebrated election loser and former Minister of Education who before the 1964 General Election was Labour's Foreign Secretary designate; with Sir Dingle Foot, Solicitor-General, 1964–67; with Richard Crossman, Minister of Housing and Local Government, Leader of the House of Commons and later Minister for Social Security; with Roy Jenkins, Chancellor of the Exchequer and formerly Home Secretary; and with Emanuel Shinwell, Labour Party veteran and former Minister.

Some of the best performers with whom I have appeared are Socialist backbenchers like Michael Foot, Hugh Delargy and Dick Taverne now a Minister and ex-Labour MP John Freeman, who is now British Ambassador in Washington. I have also appeared with Liberals such as Jo Grimond, Jeremy Thorpe, Lord Byers and Mark Bonham Carter and with eminent radicals outside Parliament such as Malcolm Muggeridge and Bernard Levin.

The discussions which take place on "Any Questions?" are seldom acrimonious, usually intelligent and occasionally very funny.

Here is an example of one which took place at Lostwithiel in Cornwall on 9th March, 1956. The team consisted of Mary Stocks (now Baroness

Stocks), John Foot (now Lord Foot), Radical and brother of Dingle, Michael, and Hugh, Lord Caradon, Harold Wilson and myself, then MP for Kidderminster. The question was on the evergreen subject of coalition governments and was asked by one Harold Liddicote, Esq.:

LIDDICOTE: When this country has been up against it, we have had a coalition Government. Now that we are really up against it, shouldn't the Members of Parliament form a coalition Government and work together for the good of everybody?

FOOT: Well, I was hoping you were going to allow the Members of Parliament to have a go first of all because I can see so little difference between the views of the Labour Party and the Conservative Party in reality—and I cannot see—

NABARRO: Oh, rubbish, rubbish, rubbish. (Laughter.)

FOOT: It seems to me that there is no difficulty about forming a coalition Government. I think it would not be a bad thing if they were to make up their minor differences—after all, they agree upon all the important matters—but if they would make up their minor differences then we should have a House of Commons in which you would have your Tory–Labour majority and we should have a healthy Liberal opposition on the other side. (Laughter and applause). But I do think that while on the surface in the House of Commons, for example, there is this difference of opinion, I think that the battle between the Conservatives and the Socialists today is very largely a sham battle. For example, today I have here sitting beside me two members of Parliament, both of whom are protectionists, both of whom are restrictionists and I don't know that I can distinguish very much between the one and the other.

GRISEWOOD: I don't think that is going to go down very well with the Members of Parliament.

NABARRO: I'm jolly sure it isn't. (Laughter.)

GRISEWOOD: Mrs Stocks?

NABARRO: Jolly sure it isn't.

STOCKS: Yes. I don't think it's true you know, at the moment, that the parties are so united. We may learn more in the course of the evening, but they are certainly disunited on the way to deal with inflation. I mean, the Labour Party believes in controls of various kinds and the Conservative Party believes in doing it through exhortation and the credit squeeze. There have recently been some differences of opinion on the Middle Eastern policy. For instance, I gather the government believes in—well—I was going to say backing our friends but we haven't got any in the Middle East, whereas the Labour Party believes in giving guarantees, oh, by the way, I'm infringing—

GRISEWOOD: Yes, I think you are, Mary.

STOCKS: I'm infringing on the fourteen day rule; we mustn't speak of these things, but anyway, let's assume there are some differences between the parties and that being so I think that a Coalition Government is a dangerous thing because it prevents any one governing group from taking full responsibility for the whole programme of government: they're always in a position to say "We can't do this", or, "We can't do that" because we should lose the support of the Party with whom we form a coalition. That is why I think that two-party government is really the best form of democracy; the most responsible form.

FOOT: Three-party . . . .

STOCKS: Two-party in effect.

GRISEWOOD: Yes, Gerald Nabarro.

NABARRO: I have been privileged to sit opposite Harold Wilson now in the House of Commons for six years. I think it is fair to say that both of us tend to specialise in economic and financial matters and in that six years I have found very, very little that I could agree with him about.

WILSON: Hear, hear.

NABARRO: Very little. He says "hear hear" at once. You heard that one. Of course, he was in the lofty position of being President of the Board of Trade, and I was a private member and the point I want to make with you all tonight is—and I think it's one of supreme importance to the future of democracy—that democracy works best when there are sharply-defined differences of view between the Government of the day, be it Conservative or be it Labour, and Her Majesty's Opposition. If there is any general identity of view between the principal parties in the House of Commons, then it leads I think to flabbiness, it leads to a general lack of drive in approach to vital matters and I am the strongest possible supporter of a virile, active and strong Opposition. I believe that the House of Commons functions very, very badly when there is an overwhelming majority on one side or the other; I think the House of Commons functioned very badly between 1931 and 1935, when the official Labour Opposition was reduced to fifty-four seats. I think it functioned very badly between 1945 and 1950, when there was a Labour majority of 200. I think the state of affairs that is best is a workable majority of forty or fifty for one party and a very virile and active Opposition. Now, I do not believe there could be a coalition today. I do not believe there is enough to coalesce about and only those people who are lacking in an appreciation of the political situation advocate a coalition and by and large they are people who, in my opinion, are mentally flabby and lazy. (Laughter and applause.)

GRISEWOOD: Harold Wilson?

WILSON: Well, Mary Stocks just now mentioned the fourteen day rule, which is a little hampering, because when you've got a Government as we have today that introduces a budget or semi-budget about once a fortnight, it means we cannot discuss economic affairs. (Laughter.) But anyone who has heard the debates over the past fortnight, whether it's economic affairs, defence, foreign affairs, will certainly not fall into John Foot's error of suggesting that there is no difference between the two parties.

NABARRO: Hear, hear.

WILSON: And for once I do agree with Gerald Nabarro, for once, in his opposition to a coalition. I think this works in wartime when you're agreed both on what you're trying to do—win the war—and, broadly speaking, on the means of doing it; but even the wartime coalition could never agree on post-war reconstruction or post-war planning. I do not think we could agree today on a Prime Minister. I gather you're having a bit of difficulty in the Conservative Party (laughter) and certainly we would have very great difficulty in accepting any of your leaders and you might not be too keen on ours.

NABARRO: I want to pull you up there. I am the strongest possible supporter of Anthony Eden. Don't you brand me as a rebel my lad. (Laughter.)

WILSON: I am delighted to hear it. Mind you don't get out of date too fast. (Laughter.) But I think in this country—I agree with what the others have said apart from John Foot—you get the best politics and the best service to the community when you have, I think, two parties fighting hard for what they believe: one in Government and the other in Opposition as long as the party in Opposition is putting up a constructive alternative. As for the Liberals, well, I think the Liberals are more likely to join with the present Conservative Party in forming a coalition than we are ever likely to do.

All this about coalitions is eternally topical. At the end of the programme, Mr Harold Wilson brought loud applause for his answer to the question, "If the team were chosen to take part in the game 'My Wildest Dream', what would be their wildest dream?" With feigned asperity Wilson snapped: "To see Gerald Nabarro as Leader of the Opposition"—

and presumably himself as Prime Minister: which he was within nine years. However, I did not myself become Leader of the official Opposition.

At Swindon, on 9th February, 1962 I found myself on the programme with my favourite Socialist opponent, that arch-radical, Mr Michael Foot, MP. He had lost the Devonport division of Plymouth to Dame Joan Vickers in 1955 by only 100 votes, in a poll of 52,000. In 1959, Dame Joan defeated him again, this time by more than six thousand votes. So, on the death of the Rt Hon. Aneurin Bevan in 1960, Michael Foot moved to Ebbw Vale which he won, even at the crest of the Macmillan Tory wave, by nearly 17,000 votes and this increased to over 20,000 in 1964 and 1966. Thus we have an Englishman—Michael Foot—sitting in a copper-bottomed South Wales Socialist seat. The panel was completed by Lady (Isobel) Barnett, gorgeous creature, Doctor, television star and accomplished debater; and Dr Mark Abrams, the Market Research Consultant.

In the course of the programme, we were asked whether we agreed that the playing of the National Anthem in cinemas and similar places was suffered in silence, rather than observed with respect. From this, the following discussion developed.

ABRAMS: I don't often go to cinemas and theatres, but when I do, what I observe is that neither of these things fits. It is neither observed with respect nor suffered in silence. Most of the people near me just get up and start walking out, unsilently. I should have thought by now there was a very strong case to be made out for dropping it completely. It has lost any real significance as a part in the lives of ordinary people, and most of them would not regard it as a loss if it were cut completely from public entertainment.

GRISEWOOD: Isobel Barnett—?

BARNETT: I would not agree with that. To me there is something very moving about hearing the National Anthem played by a good band, even if it's on a record—band of one of the Guards Regiments. I think the difficulty of having it played at the end of a performance is that so often, particularly in cinemas, the last bus goes about five minutes after the cinema performance ends, and people are faced with this considerable difficulty of do they remain in silence and respect for the National Anthem and miss their bus, or do they rush out and get the bus? Certain cinemas have compromised by having the National Anthem at the beginning of the performance and then I think it is listened to both with silence and respect. It's something I should hate to see go and I was terribly impressed two years ago when I was in Canada, where they have a possibility of three anthems that they play, "O Canada" and "The Maple Leaf" and "God Save the Queen", and when I heard that the conference would open with the National Anthem of Canada I waited for a moment wondering what was coming out and there was a real thrill in my heart when it was "God Save the Queen" that came out, so perhaps I am biased on this one. I would like it to remain and I am almost prepared to miss a bus for it. (Applause.)

GRISEWOOD: Gerald Nabarro? Gerald?

NABARRO: Of course, I thought Dr Abrams's answer was horrible and unworthy of him. The National Anthem, to most of us, I think is the epitome of deep respect and affection for the Monarchy and is exactly attuned in my mind, to the sort of thing that happened a few days ago on the occasion of the tenth anniversary of the accession to the Throne of Her Majesty the Queen, when the ceremonial battery of the Royal Horse Artillery fired off a Royal Salute in a London park. It is all part of the splendour and pageantry associated with the British Monarchy. The Union Jack as well, and very, very deeply rooted in British affairs and the British way of life. I would not change the National Anthem, nor any of the words of it and I believe it should be played on all public occasions and as frequently as possible. And if cinema audiences do indeed leave the hall before the National Anthem is finished, I deplore their doing so. (Applause.)

GRISEWOOD: Michael Foot?

FOOT: Well, I am afraid I cannot join in this devout attitude towards it. I think it is played too many times and I also must say—and this is a purely aesthetic judgement—whatever anyone may say about the Monarchy, that the tune of the National Anthem is appalling and the words are banal to a degree and I think that if you are going to have a National Anthem it is much better to have one that is really good music and that really does stir people. The Welsh, for example, have got a much better National Anthem than the British—the English. And indeed, the French have got a much better National Anthem than we have and I do not see why we should not have as good a National Anthem as anybody else. I think it would be much better, for example, if "Jerusalem" were made the English National Anthem (laughter) because you want to celebrate something that is real and there is much too much Ruritanian nonsense in this country about the Monarchy, about Royalty. The newspapers use it in order to put up their circulations whenever they have not got anything else to say and so I believe we could do with a lot less of it in this country and the place would be much healthier on that account.

GRISEWOOD: All right. We've got two for it and two against. We're evenly divided.

NABARRO: Oh, well, I notice Michael Foot refers to the Welsh; you have got to remember that he now sits for Ebbw Vale (laughter)—that was delightful, but it was for the consumption of his constituents alone, to get a bigger majority next time.

FOOT: Well, all I said was (applause)—it would hardly be possible to get it much bigger—all I was saying was that it was a better tune, and anybody who does not say that the Welsh National Anthem is a better tune than the English one, must be stone deaf and tone deaf!

NABARRO: To the Welsh. (Laughter.)

BARNETT: Well, obviously Michael Foot can never have heard the National Anthem sung by a Welsh choir, which is one of the most moving things one can possibly hear. When they sing it—

NABARRO: He is not a Welshman.

BARNETT: He is not a Welshman. (Laughter.) He must have heard them sing.

NABARRO: In the Labour Party, Isobel, they have Welshmen sitting for Scots constituencies, Englishmen sitting for Welsh constituencies—(laughter).

BARNETT: How about the Welsh?

NABARRO: What happens to the Welsh?

FOOT: What are you, a Spaniard sitting for Kidderminster?

NABARRO: But I don't (loud laughter and interruptions)—I don't think that will get you any extra votes in Ebbw Vale—

GRISEWOOD: And this is rapidly becoming a riot, so we'll go on to the next question.

Apart from his parliamentary capacity Mr Roy Jenkins has also had a distinguished career as an author and is an authority on the politics of the first two decades of the century. His two most famous books—a biography of Asquith and *Mr Balfour's Poodle*, have attracted considerable attention and praise. *The Economist* described the book on Asquith as enthralling reading and added that the style and subtlety of his authorship would have delighted the fastidious litterateurs who surrounded Asquith in his heyday. I have often appeared on television and radio with Roy Jenkins and after the Heathcoat Amory Budget of 1960, which I had castigated, we were on "Any Questions?" together at Middle Wallop on 22nd April: we were asked this question:

The masculine mind seems more prone than the feminine to enjoy the custard pie variety of humour. What light does this throw on the relative merits of the two types of mind?

The end of the discussion went as follows:

NABARRO: I confess, Freddy, that two weeks ago I did not know the meaning of the term custard pie, when a newspaper wrote it about a speech I made in the House of Commons on the Budget. It was *The Daily Telegraph* and if I recall their words correctly they said: "A magnificent speech, packed with statistics, highly censorious of the Government, but spoiled by custard pie." And I had to go and ask my wife what custard pie was. For of course, if it was a custard pie speech, the House of Commons enjoyed it because the House of Commons is overwhelmingly male, or masculine as this question says. And, in my opinion—sorry Roy Jenkins is looking at me with such disapproval, he's a serious minded politician—the House of Commons loves custard pie, Roy, doesn't it? (Laughter.)

GRISEWOOD: Oh, you'll have to come back Roy Jenkins.

JENKINS: I'm delighted that Gerald Nabarrow—

NABARRO: Nabarro. (Laughter.)

JENKINS: . . . but I am going to stick to this pronunciation now. I am delighted that in the course of a short intervention he has told us that he made a magnificent speech on the Budget—

NABARRO: No. I said custard pie. (Laughter.)

JENKINS: —a magnificent custard pie speech that the House of Commons adored because they always like custard pie: that it was a greatly masculine speech, with a great response from those who like a masculine sense of humour. And maybe this was so—I don't know. But I am beginning to think perhaps I have a rather feminine sense of humour. (Laughter.)

So much for coalitions, the National Anthem and custard pie. On 11th January, 1963, at Berkeley Nuclear Power Station, Gloucestershire, in the company of Joyce Grenfell, Dr Bronowski and John Freeman, I demonstrated my love for steam engines in answer to the question, "If members of the team had £3000 to spare, would they use it to buy a retired steam locomotive?"

NABARRO: Yes, I would spend my £3000 on this particular engine—nobody said what it is. It is Number 4472 of the old L.N.E.R., named "The Flying Scotsman".

GRISEWOOD: Yes.

NABARRO: It is a Gresley Pacific class A3 and it is one of the world's most romantic locomotives. I believe that the man who has bought it has done a great public service because it will not be broken up. It will be retained as his property for future generations to see as, I think the "wizard" product of the steam age, and certainly the most famous locomotive that Britain has produced.

Five years later in 1968, with the owner on the foot-plate, this very romantic steam engine ran non-stop with a loaded train from King's Cross to Edinburgh, Waverley, just as she used to do in her heyday. How proud her designer, Sir Nigel Gresley, would have been to have seen the BBC 2 programme in colour recording her 392 mile journey over the famous East Coast route to Scotland and later her tour around the United States of America as a splendid memorial to British steam traction.

From steam engines, to the late Lady Violet Bonham Carter, with whom I appeared on several occasions, most memorably at Plymouth on 14th February, 1958. On the previous day, there had been a by-election at Rochdale, Lancashire, caused by the death of the Tory Member, Lt-Col. Wentworth-Schofield. His majority in the 1955 General Election had been only 1590 and at the by-election the Labour candidate, Alderman J. McCann, had won by 4530 votes. The Tories finished bottom of the poll and the Liberals, with a very strong and attractive candidate, Mr Ludovic Kennedy, came second.

The team at Plymouth consisted of the late Arthur Street, and Dingle Foot, a renegade Liberal who had only gone over to the Labour party in 1956, where he subsequently reached high office, as well as Lady Violet and myself. A question on the Rochdale by-election was more or less inevitable and since I had done my homework in the manner I have already described, I was well prepared for the question, "Does the result of the Rochdale by-election indicate a revival of the Liberal Party or merely a lack of confidence in the present Government?" Naturally, Lady Violet seized on the former alternative:

BONHAM CARTER: . . . Now, I think I can't do better than to end with a short quotation from Mr Dingle Foot. I could not possibly put it better, or as well, myself, which is that there are millions of people in this country who dislike the Tory past and who dislike the Socialist present, and that is why there must be a Liberal future. I agree with every word and so did Rochdale. (Applause.)

GRISEWOOD: Gerald Nabarro, do you want to come back?

NABARRO: Lady Violet ended with a quotation against Dingle Foot.

BONHAM CARTER: Not against—in his favour. . . .

NABARRO: In his favour?

BONHAM CARTER: Entirely. . . .

NABARRO: Oh, I am sorry, I thought it was being made against him.

BONHAM CARTER: I agree with every word of it. I think they were words of wisdom.

NABARRO: Let me reply to you about the worth of Liberal candidates and prospective candidates. Take another television personality, Miss Jacqueline Mackenzie, recently adopted as the prospective Liberal candidate for Cheltenham. When asked by a national newspaper why she had gone into the Liberal fold, it was reported she said this: "I became a Liberal when I had not a thought in my head. (Laughter.) Jo Grimond was the man who really convinced me. I mean he has got something about him that Macmillan or Gaitskell just have not got. He's so sexy!" (Laughter.) Well, really, if that is the basis for Liberal candidates, God help Britain. (Loud laughter.)

Of course, Lady Violet was very cross with me because Jo Grimond was her son-in-law. So was dear Jacqueline very cross and she wrote to "Any Answers?" refuting the newspaper report. However, within a year, I had appeared on the programme with both Jo Grimond and Jacqueline Mackenzie, and we all had our money's worth.

It is good clean fun and popular debating. Small wonder that the listening public loves "Any Questions?".

Long may it continue as the best BBC sound programme.

21. Immigration, Race Relations and the Right Honourable J. Enoch Powell, MBE, MP

CONFRONTED with the position in the early nineteen-sixties that one quarter of the world's population, including the millions of India and Pakistan, could legally come and live in Britain as citizens of the Commonwealth, the Tories in power with a majority of one hundred in the House of Commons did the only possible thing: they limited immigration from the Commonwealth into Britain. The Labour Opposition howled. The Tories were accused of Fascism, Racism and everything abominable. Labour obstructed and impeded the legislation—the Commonwealth Immigrants Bill—and eventually a guillotine, or Parliamentary time-table, took the measure to the statute book against a background chorus from Labour that they would repeal the Act as early as possible.

Of course, they never did. On the contrary, from the Autumn of 1964 the Labour Governments have progressively restricted immigration from the Commonwealth into Britain and reduced it to a few thousand work vouchers annually, plus dependents, usually of earlier immigrants.

Overwhelmingly, the row is about coloured immigration, especially Asiatics because they constitute the majority of those coming in, or seeking to come in. Anything to do with this issue has become explosive in British politics. In certain areas of Great Britain, those with a high percentage of immigrants in the local population—for example, in parts of Birmingham such as Handsworth, and in Smethwick and Wolverhampton, or Bradford or Southall in Middlesex—this issue has come to dominate political discussion. Some silly-billies maintain that these matters are outside political controversy. I have myself, and most of my Conservative colleagues agree, always regarded immigration policies, together with their endless social, educational, health and housing consequences, as very much within the sphere of politics, and rightly so. Indeed, it could hardly be otherwise in view of the immensely divergent views which exist on the subject and the controversy which the Commonwealth Immigrants Act, the Race Relations Acts of 1965 and 1968 and the activities of governmental and quasi-governmental bodies have created in dealing with the problems.

The kind of heat which any discussion of race—and consequently any discussion of coloured immigration into Britain—generates, was powerfully illustrated by the reaction to some remarks I made on 5th April, 1963, at Mitcheldean in Gloucestershire while appearing on "Any Questions?". We were asked the question: "Does the team consider that the dissolution of the Central African Federation may drive Southern Rhodesia towards an alliance or even integration with South Africa?" All the replies were relatively long and comprehensive, including my own:

> Yes, I do. I think it inescapable in the passage of the next few years that Southern Rhodesia gains independence—total autonomy—I hope within the Commonwealth. But, as the electoral arrangements in Southern Rhodesia at present restrict the franchise very much indeed, and leave the white man in a position of representing the sole Government of the country, with very little contribution by the African natives, there is a condition in spirit, if not in fact, of apartheid, and in that situation and with a border running with South Africa, it seems to me that there would very quickly be a close alliance between the two. I cannot comment this evening on whether that would be a good thing or not, because I believe it is possibly some years off. I myself detest apartheid and wish that the South African Government could ameliorate their arrangements and give proper representation to the negro population. (Applause.) And South Africa leaving the Commonwealth was also in my judgement a very grievous state of affairs. I pray Southern Rhodesia does not leave the Commonwealth, but if independence is granted to Southern Rhodesia, I must say that I would have regarded it as almost impossible to avoid, a close affinity between Southern Rhodesia and South Africa, if not a full union between the two. And in the present state of affairs that would lead to a policy of apartheid. Very unsatisfactory, I think.

I am a realist, and the reason I supported Central African Federation in 1953 was that it seemed to me to be the only civilised formula for building a multi-racial society in the Rhodesias and Nyasaland. That is why I supported it, and people who have got hindsight and look back on it all and say—"Well, of course, it was an impossible proposition or formula in the first place, and should never have been embarked upon by the Government", are being unrealistic in their approach. The problem in Little Rock, Arkansas, or in Notting Hill Gate, or in Rhodesia, is one and the same. And it is a problem which has afflicted the white races and the civilising influences in the world, and the white races are the civilising influences in the world, and has been the same for hundreds of years. It is white versus black. That is all. And if anybody disagrees with that, I say to them straight away, if they are a parent, here in England: would you be happy if your blonde, blue-eyed daughter, aged 21, the apple of her father's eye, came home with a great big buck nigger and said: 'I am going to marry this man'? And you had a prospect of some coffee-coloured grandchildren. That is the problem. It is a fundamental problem; it is an ethnic problem, and we in Britain—those who supported federation, tried to steer a middle course by building a multi-racial society in Rhodesia. If we fail we should not be stigmatised or severely criticised. We tried very hard to do it, and I think it was to the eternal discredit of many Labour politicians and others that they sought at the time to break up our efforts. Though we failed, we failed honourably.

Within minutes the lines to the BBC were jammed and the matter dominated the headlines in the following morning's newspapers. The BBC cut certain passages from the repeat broadcast of the programme on the following Tuesday. Letters by the thousand deluged me, seventy to one supporting my views. I apologised at once for any offence I might unintentionally have caused to any minority and reaffirmed my complete lack of prejudice against any individual on grounds of race, colour or creed. The journalists, of course, had a feast. Mr Walter Terry of the *Daily Mail*, later to win the Oscar of Parliamentary correspondents, let his imagination run riot in this comment, which appeared on the following Monday, 8th April, 1963:

Sir Gerald Nabarro, Tory MP for Kidderminster, is in trouble over an off-the-cuff remark he made in the BBC radio programme 'Any Questions?' last Friday.

In a discussion on the Central African Federation issue, he asked: 'How would you feel if your daughter wanted to marry a big buck nigger with the prospect of coffee-coloured grandchildren?'

Immediately afterwards Sir Gerald, who normally confines himself to

ON SAFARI: HUMAN SACRIFICE IN DARKEST AFRICA, *Daily Express*, 10th April, 1963.
Left to Right: Sir Hugh Greene, Director-General of the BBC; Rt Hon. R. A. Butler, MP, First Secretary of State and Minister for African Affairs; Rt Hon. Henry Brooke, MP, Home Secretary.

domestic issues rather than Commonwealth affairs, said that the phrase 'buck nigger' was not meant in a derogatory sense.
But the damage was done. All Sir Gerald's political skill will be needed to erase the ill-effects.
Sir Gerald, knighted in the New Year honours, is normally forthright. He can be outrageous, woundingly rude, impudent in tackling his critics, triumphant on the path he sets himself.
But his mood is always well under control. He knows how far he can go . . . well, almost always.
Sir Gerald's best hope is that the remark will be forgotten as a slip-up, the kind that a politician is always liable to make no matter how careful he is.
His critics, of course, will seize on the comment.
In recent months Sir Gerald may have cherished a hope of being drafted to Conservative Central Office to help in raising Tory morale, a task for which he would be suited admirably.
Mr Iain Macleod, chairman of the Conservative Party organisation, might find such a transfer rather an embarrassment after the 'Any Questions?' remark.

From the curate of St John's Church, Kidderminster, the Revd George Erskine Morris, now Rector of Digby, Nova Scotia, Canada, came strong support for me. He is himself a West Indian born and bred and he wrote to me in the following terms on 9th April:

I have read in today's issue of the *Daily Express* that you have been censored because of words or statements which you made on the BBC programme 'Any Questions?'. I gather too, that they feel it is contrary to the well-being or relationships and that some protests have been made over the use of the words BUCK and NIGGER.

Well, although I did not hear the programme, I would like to make a comment on the subject. Why is it that people always jump to find evil and slander in what one says? I am really appalled at the action which the BBC has taken, and it is even more distressing when such decisions are made by responsible and sensible people.

I am a West Indian, a coloured man: I would not give the world to be any other than what I am. What is more, I have often used words such as BUCK and NIGGER myself and we never thought about anything sarcastic or derogatory. In this country, nearly everyone condemns racial discrimination and carryings-on. Yet what more has the BBC done, but to give to, or rather put into the minds of coloured people that you and possibly others hate them or despise them? I think, Sir, that your question was apposite and fittingly asked, and I sincerely hope that whenever you get the opportunity, that you will do the same.

In my six to seven years in this country, I have been increasingly aware of the timid way English people deal with coloured people. I see it almost as a 'creeping patronage'. As if they feel that if they make us feel good that is all that is necessary. Yet, you will agree, this is mere hypocrisy and ought to be stamped out. I would much rather them see us as Coloured, Black, etc., and respect what is good in us and reject what is bad. You put a really first class question then, and I trust the objectors as well as others will consider this.

In closing, may I thank you very much for having the courage to speak out in terms understandable for all men. And I hope that whenever possible you will do the same. I hope, too, that you will, if possible, draw it to the attention of the BBC that there is at least a few who consider their actions juvenile and unwarranted and savouring of more race hatred than the very words BUCK and NIGGER.

I circulated this letter among the many people who had written to me about the broadcast to show what mistaken views are so often expressed on matters of race. Indeed, as the Reverend Gentleman says, "Why is it that people always jump to find evil and slander in what one says?"

Later, I appeared on the Eamonn Andrews Show with Dick Gregory, the American Civil Rights leader, an able, genial lieutenant of the late Martin Luther King. Gregory had grown up in St Louis in an environment so poor that "home was a place to be when all other places were closed". After winning his way through High School and College, he had become a track star and then a leading American comedian. He is cultured, kind and rich in knowledge of life in the market place. I got on with him very well indeed, all the more so because left wing journalists had besieged him when he got off his plane at London Airport on his way to do the television show with me, and had asked him whether he knew that he would be appearing with Sir Gerald Nabarro who had been censored by the BBC for using the term "buck nigger". Gregory snapped back: "Why, I am sure looking forward to meeting the gentleman"; and he was. We had an animated and genial and constructive dialogue on race relations and many inflammatory associated problems. Before the end of the programme, Dick Gregory autographed a copy of his book and gave it to me—the first copy in Britain—for my own library. He concluded: "Dear Momma, wherever you are, if ever you hear the word 'nigger' again, remember they are advertising my book". Appropriately the book—Dick Gregory's autobiography—is called "Nigger" and in it he proclaims that he wants "to be an American citizen, first-class". As I have often said, my own philosophy allows of no second class citizens in Britain, either. And I was not slow to observe that when Gregory said "Dear Momma" he was effectively saying what my West Indian Minister of Religion had said to me about colour prejudice. Mostly it is the left wing and gutter press which seek to find mischief and calumny in these matters, where truly none need or should exist.

Then, in the 1964 General Election, the constituency of Smethwick in Staffordshire was won by Mr Peter Griffiths, a headmaster, a local man, Alderman, Conservative leader on the local council and chairman of the Smethwick Education Committee. The significance of this win was that it was against the main electoral stream in which Labour won fifty-eight seats from the Tories. There was a large concentration of immigrants in the constituency and the defeated Labour candidate was the Rt Hon. Patrick Gordon Walker, Labour's Foreign Secretary designate and only survivor of the Labour Cabinet of 1950–51. Labour fury knew no bounds. Griffiths was accused of winning the seat on an anti-colour campaign. The new Prime Minister, Mr Harold Wilson, called Griffiths " a Parliamentary 'leper'." I debated the unexpected Smethwick result with Lord Boothby on television a few minutes after the result came in. Boothby took the view that the Conservative vote had been swelled by colour prejudice, which I denied. I thought, and I still do, that this was only one factor in the Smethwick result. The well-publicised doggerel, "If you want a nigger for your neighbour, vote Labour", was not Tory propaganda. Where had it come from? demanded Boothby. "Not Birmingham England" (for the postal address of Smethwick is Birmingham, 40) "rather from Birmingham, Alabama", I replied.

Hence my detractors' reference to me as "Nabarro, the Deep South".

No, it was not so much a matter of race prejudice at Smethwick in 1964 as the poor electoral qualities of the Labour candidate, Mr Patrick Gordon Walker. After his remarkable defeat at Smethwick, Mr Wilson persisted in appointing him Foreign Secretary, even though he had no seat in Parliament. So the popular Mr Reginald Sorensen, the Member for Leyton, was given a peerage and in January, 1965, the seat became the subject of a memorable by-election. Leyton had been held by Labour since 1935 and Mr Sorensen's majority in 1964 had been nearly eight thousand. Gordon Walker lost it by 205 votes and a Tory was returned. In just three months, eight thousand Labour voters had disappeared. Nothing to do with colour at Leyton. The fact is that the electors of Leyton rose in wrath against the presumption of Mr Harold Wilson in foisting a rejected candidate on them to suit his convenience as Prime Minister. Moreover, they quite obviously did not take to the lugubrious Gordon Walker, outwardly lacking in personality and charm and possessed of a countenance often compared to a Basset Hound. So Smethwick was not won on race alone. Anyway, the Labour Party won it back in 1966 with a Shakespearean actor, Mr Andrew Faulds. Mr Peter Griffiths was an MP for only seventeen months, the victim of Mr Wilson's evil allusion to Parliamentary 'leper'. He re-entered academic life at Southampton University. Mr Gordon Walker had a second shot at Leyton and won it in 1966 with a majority of over eight thousand, thus reversing almost exactly his humiliation of January, 1965. After a brief and inglorious resumption of Cabinet office, he found himself dropped by Mr Wilson and returned once more to a backbench. So much for Smethwick. It will ever be associated in political history with racial controversy.

In the Spring of 1965, the then Foreign Secretary, the Rt Hon. George Brown, MP, was reported as saying that "we would be mad to limit coloured immigration into Britain". Thus he threw down a gauntlet to millions who thought exactly the opposite, that we would be mad not to limit immigration into Britain. I decided to publish a detailed statement of my views on the matter which I believed were a reflection of those of the overwhelming majority of ordinary voters. I did so in the *News of the World* on 6th June, 1965:

IMMIGRATION: SIX WAYS TO CLEAR UP A DISASTROUS MUDDLE

A party politician landed with a hot potato (which I define as an explosive issue) will often proclaim loftily that the matter should be 'elevated above rancorous party political exchanges'.

Tory MP Sir Peter Roberts even suggested that steel nationalisation could be dealt with on a non-party basis. As if 'Socialism versus Free Enterprise' could ever be excluded from party warfare.

And only a troglodyte would believe that coloured immigration into Britain and racial issues can be kept off the hustings. On the contrary, this particular hot potato is a biting and a bitter one.

I say that immigration and racial policies are proper subjects for the ballot box in contemporary circumstances.

Smethwick has assured just that. Here, in a Midlands industrial town, something happened last October which has made history.

A strong Labour seat for many years turned Tory and threw out the Labour shadow Foreign Secretary, Mr Patrick Gordon Walker, in favour of a near-unknown young Tory.

It is well known that the Tories in the last Parliament had clamped down on immigration, except for the Irish, and that the Socialists had voted sternly for unrestricted immigration.

Thus, the electoral message from Smethwick is loud and clear.

Parliamentary Labour in power took fright and kept on the Tory immigration controls. Lord Mountbatten has been sent round the Commonwealth to sound out the lines of future immigration policies.

I say we know the facts already and should act on what we know.

Here are the facts. There are nearly one million coloured people in Britain today, overwhelmingly immigrants in the last ten years.

At the rate they are multiplying there will probably be three million coloured people within ten years.

In spite of controls, 75,000 immigrants came here last year, the majority from Pakistan, India, West Africa and the West Indies. They come to Britain because we enjoy very high standards of living and social services and employment. Wages here are ten or more times greater than in the countries the immigrants come from. If they have no jobs when they arrive in Britain they say, what matter?: National Assistance will provide. If they fall sick, they say, why worry?: the National Health Service will doctor and nurse us.

More than 20 million coloured people in the United States of America are to have full civil rights. There is talk of a negro President in the White House within thirty years.

'Why not welcome unlimited coloured men to Britain' say the Socialist Left wingers, for are not all men equal? Why should we not take in any colour, any creed, from anywhere and in any numbers?

That is an explosive issue and cannot be kept out of General Election controversy. We are a nation of 53 millions, living on a tiny crowded island: and the population will grow to 70 million by AD 2000.

We have insufficient resources to maintain our existing and growing population. Why worsen an already difficult position?

The Government are having second thoughts about their Race Relations Bill which seeks to outlaw colour discrimination and the colour bar.

It is becoming painfully evident to theorists and long-haired idealists everywhere that men's souls cannot be changed by legislation.

Colour acceptance is a matter of patient education and toleration and can never be achieved by statutory declaration.

This year nearly 100,000 immigrants will come in, mostly coloured and unskilled. Departing from our shores will be 150,000, mostly white and skilled, including a record 70,000 to Australia, 30,000 to Canada, 16,000 to New Zealand, 15,000 to South Africa: doctors, dentists, nurses, engineers, building craftsmen, business executives and salesmen, and throughout a high percentage of university graduates.

"I'M SORRY, BUT MY OTHER TENANTS MUST BE CONSIDERED", *Daily Mail*, 16th April, 1968. Landlady at door: Rt Hon. Edward Heath, MBE, MP. Tenants: At Bottom Window: Rt Hon. Iain Macleod, MP. At Top Right Window: Rt Hon. Duncan Sandys, MP. At Top Left Window: Sir Gerald Nabarro, MP.

Why are they emigrating? Wages are better, taxes are lower, houses available, the sun shines and there is no Socialism where they are going.
So we exchange white for coloured, skilled for unskilled, high educational standards for low. Surely this is a disastrous policy for Britain?
What ought we to do about future immigration policies?
First, there must be drastic restrictions as to numbers: 10,000 immigrants a year is enough.
Second, we should take only skilled and professionally trained men and women. Potential needs for additional unskilled labour should be matched by quickening the pace of automation and mechanisation, with appropriate financial and tax incentives to do so.
Third, no immigrant should enter Britain without an official work permit and an authentic job to go to.
Fourth, every immigrant should pass a stiff medical test and their dependents too, as in the USA, Canada, South Africa. Australia and New Zealand.
Fifth, every immigrant should have proved accommodation available.
Sixth, every immigrant should have at least six months self-dependence money in his pocket.
Then we must deal with illegal entry and any immigrant in Britain now wishing to return to his homeland should be encouraged, and indeed subsidised, to do so.
None of these restrictions would apply to bona fide students with places available in our universities and colleges. We should continue to welcome students financed largely by the Governments of their countries of origin.
By all these means the immigration problem may be brought under control.
For certain, the British people will vote on immigration policies when Mr Wilson goes to the country at the next General Election.
For certain, we should reject outright Mr George Brown's recent intemperate remark that it would be mad to limit immigration into Britain.

Thirty-four months later Mr Enoch Powell, MBE, MP, shadow Minister of Defence and Conservative Member for Wolverhampton, South-West, delivered his famous and historic speech on immigration at Birmingham. "Mr Powell forces the race issue, Emotive speech", screamed the headlines of the *Sunday Telegraph* on 21st April, 1968. "Powell race bombshell sets crisis for Heath", said the *Sunday Express*. The leader in *The Times* on the following day was entitled "An evil speech" and the speech was widely described as "Highly dangerous" or as "Playing on the emotions". Other Tories regarded the speech as a direct challenge to Mr

"Fellow workers!"

The *Morning Star*, 24th April, 1968.

Heath's leadership and as a bid to secure the leadership of the Party over his head. The Liberal leader, Mr Jeremy Thorpe, added:

> "The Right wing of the Conservative Party is one of the most vicious, prejudiced and neolithic animals in British politics"
>
> (*Sunday Telegraph*, 21st April, 1968)

Not for the first time Mr Thorpe had got it all wrong. As subsequent events were to show, the majority of voters supported Powell on the reduction of the flow of immigrants to "negligible proportions". Mr Powell, of course, was well placed to comment on all the problems arising from the large influx of coloured immigrants, with a concentration of them in his constituency. Mr Powell left his Birmingham meeting to a standing ovation and is said to have stated afterwards that he had "only spelt out party policy". A Party spokesman—whoever such a faceless creature might be—said that Powell's speech was "roughly in line with other statements that had been made on the subject". However, within hours Mr Heath had dropped Mr Powell from his Shadow Cabinet. Dockers invaded Westminster supporting Powell's cause. Race and immigration controversies raged in every newspaper, in every pub and club, wherever two or three were gathered together. The *News of the World* was again my platform and after the South Worcestershire Conservative Association had declared for Powell my article appeared on 28th April 1968, eight days after the speech:

IT'S TIME TO PUT THE BAR UP

Three years ago, I wrote on this page that a party politician landed with a hot potato (which I defined as an explosive issue) will often proclaim loftily that the matter should be elevated above rancorous party political exchanges.

It was said then about immigration policies, and it is said now by the mealy-mouthed. For myself, I have always believed that the British people will insist on voting on immigration and racial policies at General Elections.

To desire immigration control or a halt on immigration into Britain is not to be racist or a racialist. Indeed, it is to be a realist and an economist.

What Enoch Powell did in Birmingham last weekend was to proclaim in lurid terms his race policies which, as far as I can see, differ very little from the official policies of the Conservative Party.

Mr Edward Heath, Tory Leader, fired Mr Enoch Powell from his Shadow Cabinet simply because:

(a) The terms of the speech were considered to be inflammatory and tending to incite racial passions.

"Sorry—with all that 'tash' and that tan, thought you were one of us ..."

The *Sunday Mirror*, 28th April, 1968.

(b) Mr Powell had consulted none of his colleagues in the shadow Cabinet —which should have collective responsibility for policies—before making his speech, and moreover, he talked to another shadow Minister's brief on Home Affairs, namely Mr Quintin Hogg, without telling Mr Hogg he was going to do so.

I do not defend the tones of Mr Powell's speech, which were unnecessarily theatrical, lurid and unrestrained. A scholar and academic such as he is, ought to have done better.

Neither do I defend his usurping his fellow Shadow Cabinet Minister's brief. On both of these points he was wrong and Mr Heath has an absolute right to fire him if he wants to, though his dismissal raises singularly unfortunate issues.

I disclaim absolutely Mr George Brown's statement in New York that Mr Powell's motive is to win the leadership of the Conservative Party. Nothing is farther removed from the truth.

Of course, Mr Brown's statement, for what it is worth, attacks Mr Powell in vitriolic terms: it was Mr Brown who, in 1965, said that it would be mad to limit immigration into Britain.

Now Enoch makes history. Dockers strike for him, Smithfield porters march for him, London airport immigration officers campaign for him and Tory constituency associations acclaim him.

Never shall I see again the extraordinary spectacle of London dockers crowding round the House of Commons applauding me as a Tory MP for supporting the substance of Mr Powell's speech.

Extraordinary indeed was the bummaree who carried a poster proclaiming:

WILSON, DICTATOR, BIGGEST TURNCOAT OF THE CENTURY—OUT.
POWELL—FREE SPEECH—IN.
HEATH—NO GUTS.

The British political scene has certainly been inverted by Mr Powell.

This brouhaha has focused public attention on immigration and racial problems. The terrific clamour supporting Mr Powell is a manifestation of English Nationalism.

We have had Scottish Nationalism, Welsh Nationalism, Cornish Nationalism and even the start of Yorkshire Nationalism in these islands in recent days. Now the Powellite eruption about coloured immigration is a mass English Nationalist movement.

It is perfectly true that the number of work vouchers for coloured immigrants into Britain in recent years has been steadily declining and is now only about 5,000 a year.

TORY TROUBLES The *Daily Express*, 29th April, 1968. Downstairs L. to R. Rt Hon. Enoch Powell, MBE, MP, Rt Hon. Quintin Hogg, MP, Rt Hon. Edward Heath, MBE, MP, Rt Hon. Reginald Maudling, MP. Upstairs L. to R. Sir Gerald Nabarro, MP, Rt Hon. Sir Edward Boyle, MP, Rt Hon. Sir Alec Douglas-Home, MP. Standard Bearer: The Prime Minister, Rt Hon. Harold Wilson, OBE, MP.

But, on what are called humanitarian grounds, ten times as many dependents of earlier coloured immigrants into Britain are allowed in so the aggregation still coming in is about 50,000 a year.

Mr Heath says there will be a drastic curtailment. I say that there should be an absolute stop on coloured immigration.

This is the one—and the major—issue. The second issue is what to do with the coloured people already settled here.

We must, of course, absorb them and integrate them into our community, treating them as absolute equals with our own indigenous white population. They must have houses, school places and hospital beds, jobs and welfare services not less favourable than those enjoyed by our own British-born population.

We must not discriminate against the immigrants settled here. But neither must we discriminate against our own people in favour of the immigrants.

The quarrel over the Race Relations Bill is whether one should try to achieve these desirable aims by legislation or without it. Personally, I think without it.

I believe a large majority of people take my view that you cannot order integration by statutory enforcement. It can be done only by persuasion and educative means.

That is why I am so hostile to the Race Relations Bill at present before Parliament, as are many of my colleagues.

Finally, some of the coloured people settled here in Britain are unhappy and wish to return to their native lands. I would subsidise them to do so, if they wish it, whether it be to the West Indies, West Africa, India or Pakistan, Malaya or elsewhere.

Certain it is that all these matters will be thoroughly debated in Parliament and in the country for a long while to come. Certainly they are major election issues and so they ought to be.

In precipitating this debate, Mr Powell has rendered yet one more great service to the British community. He is a patriot and a courageous fellow, though, like all of us, he has human failings.

This was an effective answer to many of Enoch Powell's critics including Mr David Pitt, Chairman of the Campaign Against Racial Discrimination, who had said that it was "a tragedy that a man of Mr Powell's stature should make a speech like this. It is terrible to think that it comes from a man who may hold high office if there is a change of government"; or Mr Maurice Ludmer, Chairman of the Birmingham Co-ordinating Committee against racial discrimination who had said: "We are referring Mr Powell's statement to the Attorney-General as a clear case of incitement to racial hatred"; and Mr Nicholas Scott, Tory MP for Paddington South,

TORY RACIAL POLICIES. The *Daily Telegraph*, 10th July, 1968. L. to R. 3 Black Sheep: Sir Gerald Nabarro, MP, Rt Hon. Enoch Powell, MBE, MP, Rt Hon. Duncan Sandys, MP. Little Bo Peep: Rt Hon. Edward Heath, MBE, MP, Leader of Her Majesty's Opposition. Sheepdog: Rt Hon. Quintin Hogg, M.P. (Shadow Home Secretary).

who had said: "I am saddened and distressed to see the eagerness with which Mr Enoch Powell is assuming the mantle of Governor Wallace of Alabama".

The Bill before Parliament to which Mr Powell had objected so trenchantly and colourfully in his Birmingham speech was the Race Relations Bill. Much of the subsequent criticism was caused more by the style of his speech than its substance. In particular, three short passages are often quoted against Powell and usually out of context. They are his references to "charming, wide-grinning picaninnies", "the River Tiber foaming with much blood" and "in fifteen or twenty years' time the black man will have the whip hand over the white man", words which Mr Powell attributed to one of his constituents.

The real point of the speech, in its opposition to the Race Relations Bill, came in a short passage towards the end:

> On top of this, they now learn that a one-way privilege is to be established by Act of Parliament; a law which cannot, and is not intended to operate to protect them or redress their grievances, is to be enacted to give the stranger, the disgruntled and the agent provocateur the power to pillory them for their private actions.
>
> In the hundreds upon hundreds of letters I received when I last spoke of this subject two or three months ago, there was one striking feature which was largely new and which I find ominous. All Members of Parliament are used to the typical anonymous correspondent; but what surprised and alarmed me was the high proportion of ordinary, decent, sensible people, writing a rational and often well-educated letter, who believed that they had to omit their address because it was dangerous to have committed themselves to paper to a Member of Parliament agreeing with the views I had expressed, and that they would risk either penalties or reprisals if they were known to have done so. The sense of being a persecuted minority which is growing among ordinary English people in the areas of the country which are affected is something which those without direct experience can hardly imagine.

This was yet another factor which influenced the passage of the Race Relations Bill. On the Third Reading, on 9th July, 1968, Mr Quintin Hogg, shadow Home Secretary, had a rough time in his final speech calling on the Conservatives not to vote against the Bill, for fear that such a vote would imply colour prejudice. Forty-six Tories, including Enoch Powell, were having none of it and marched through the Lobby against the Third Reading.[1] Only 184 Socialists and Liberals could be found to vote for the Bill. Thus, 230 Members expressed views on statutory determination of

[1] Division No. 274, 4.42 a.m., 9th July, 1968.

" It's disgraceful, Mr. Ram Quintin Singh Hogg! They're not wearing the regulation headgear ! "

TORY RACE POLICY 1968, The *Daily Express*, 12th July, 1968. L. to R. Rt Hon. Edward Heath, MBE, MP, Rt Hon. Quintin Hogg, MP, Rt Hon. Enoch Powell, MBE, MP, Rt Hon. Duncan Sandys, MP, Sir Gerald Nabarro, MP.

race relations in Britain. Leaving out Mr Speaker and two aides who traditionally do not vote on such occasions, 397 Members of the House of Commons declined to express their views. I wonder why? Were they undecided, or too idle, or too sleepy at twenty to five in the morning?

Anyway, Powell and myself were among the forty-six who voted against the statutory enforcement of racial harmony. I did so because the provisions of the Bill were nebulous and unworkable and unlikely to do anything towards its supposed aim. Legislation can do nothing but exacerbate a problem of this kind, for as I wrote in the *News of the World* on 14th July, 1968:

> I don't need the Civil Law to dictate interpretation
> of Christianity to me.
> I say that you cannot legislate in Parliament for
> the hearts and minds of men.

And I reaffirmed my belief that the British people wanted a complete halt to immigration, absolute equality for all citizens of this country, indigenous and immigrant, assistance for those immigrants wishing to return to their native lands and no discrimination of any kind, in either direction, between Britons of different racial origins.

The Tory Leader, Mr Edward Heath, in a speech at Walsall on 25th January, 1969, affirmed nearly everything that my friends and I had urged on race and immigration matters. Now we felt that solid progress had been made as a result. Not that this controversy will be laid within the foreseeable future. Indeed, it is now hypocrisy and humbug to deny that it is a matter which will be high on any list of electoral issues, which voters everywhere must be encouraged to discuss. As Mr Desmond Donnelly, the intelligent and articulate Independent Member for Pembroke has said: "Damn it, it is our country". He expresses in those few choice words, the views of nine-tenths of the British people.

As for Enoch Powell, he remains the most enigmatic figure in mid-twentieth century British politics. Millions of words have been written about him and it is certain that millions more will be. Some ascribe to him almost magical powers of leadership. His role in politics has been compared to that of Joseph Chamberlain and it is evidence of his stature that he would inevitably claim a very high place in any survey of contemporary politics.

But I cannot readily see him as a future leader of the Conservative Party and Prime Minister. His pale and rather frigid countenance creates an

"RACE RELATIONS", The *Daily Telegraph*, 16th July, 1968. L. to R. Rt Hon. Edward Heath, MBE, MP (Leader of Her Majesty's Opposition), Rt Hon. Quintin Hogg, QC, MP (Shadow Home Secretary), Sir Gerald Nabarro, MP (Con. Worcestershire South), Rt Hon. Enoch Powell, MBE, MP (Con. Wolverhampton, S.W.), Rt Hon. Duncan Sandys, MP (Con. Streatham).

impression of austerity, which hides his warmth and charm. He lacks ability to make an attractive impression which is an indispensable quality in any political leader today. Nevertheless, he has countless admirers and followers. Few politicians have made so many memorable speeches in recent years and Powell owes this distinction to his superb mastery of the language in spite of the fact that his speeches are usually noticeably lacking in humour.

I admire Enoch and I have done so as a friend and Parliamentary colleague since we entered the House of Commons together twenty years ago. I admire his sagacity and courage in any and every situation; his singleness of purpose; his loyalty to his friends; his plain good living and simple family life. I admire Enoch's mental discipline: his devotion to the monarchy (one of his finest speeches in Parliament was on the Royal Titles Bill fifteen years ago); his abhorrence of injustice and incompetence (another of his finest speeches was on the Hola camps); his dedication in thought and deed to every British institution; I admire his deliberate debunking of pink Tory policies and the purgatives he administers so severely to those who call themselves Tories and preach Leftist twaddle, ill thought-out concepts masquerading as progressive policies. Had the Tories no Enoch, they would have been obliged to create one. I admire his extraordinary career as scholar and soldier, which even his fiercest detractors have to accept is unmatched in contemporary times.

Enoch Powell was born in Stechford, Birmingham, in 1912. Both his parents were schoolteachers and Enoch went to King Edward's School, Birmingham, one of the most distinguished of the ancient grammar schools. From there he went on to Cambridge as a Scholar of Trinity, where A. E. Housman was still in residence at that time. He took a double first in the Classical Tripos and won every classical prize that was available, including the Craven Studentship as a result of which he spent two years in Italy. From 1934 to 1937, he was a fellow of Trinity before becoming Professor of Classics at Sydney, Australia where he remained until the outbreak of war. He was thus already a distinguished academic and on his appointment to Sydney had been the youngest academic professor in the Commonwealth. His translations of parts of Herodotus and Thucydides were published either before or soon after the War and his transcription of the laws of the tenth century Welsh King Hywell the Good—he learnt Welsh especially for the purpose—appeared in 1942. He also published three volumes of his own poetry between 1937 and 1951, and in 1968, with Keith Wallis, a book on the "House of Lords in the Middle Ages".

"Mad Mitch? As the Argylls won't need you any more, perhaps you'd come and restore discipline in my Tory orchestra ..."

THE ORGAN OF CONSERVATISM, The *Daily Express*, 17th July, 1968. Pipers L. to R. Rt Hon. Enoch Powell, MBE, MP, Rt Hon. Duncan Sandys, MP, Sir Gerald Nabarro, MP. At the Organ: Rt Hon. Edward Heath, MBE, MP (Leader of Her Majesty's Musicians).

Thus, much of his academic career was complete before the war. During the war he built a second career as a soldier, enlisting as a Private in the Royal Warwickshire Regiment in 1939 and being demobilised as a Brigadier in 1945. He served in North Africa, Middle East, South East Asia and India and in the process became an interpreter in Urdu.

From the Army, he moved on to Mr R. A. Butler's political nursery in the Conservative Research Department and became joint head, with Iain Macleod, of the Home Affairs section. He contested one by-election, at Normanton in 1947, before winning Wolverhampton, South-West in 1950. By comparison with some of his colleagues in the Research Department such as Iain Macleod and Reginald Maudling who also entered the House in 1950, his progress up the Ministerial ladder was not rapid and was further prejudiced by one resignation and one refusal to serve. From 1950 to 1955 he was an active backbencher until he became Parliamentary Secretary to the Ministry of Housing and Local Government under Duncan Sandys. A year later, when Mr Macmillan took office, he became Financial Secretary to the Treasury. He resigned along with the Chancellor, Mr Peter Thorneycroft, and the Economic Secretary, Mr Nigel Birch, in January 1958 over a proposed increase of £50m in Government expenditure. The issue was one of political faith and consistency for the Macmillan Government had previously proclaimed its opposition to further increases of this nature. At the time he said that he would never accept another post in the Government unless Thorneycroft was also readmitted. Thus, in July 1960, when Mr Thorneycroft became Minister of Aviation, Powell accepted the Ministry of Health. Thorneycroft fell in the purge of July, 1962. Powell remained Minister of Health until he refused to serve under Sir Alec Douglas-Home in October, 1963. In doing so, he remained in the company of his old colleague Iain Macleod, who also refused to serve under Sir Alec.

It is the resignation, the refusal to serve and then in April, 1968, the martyrdom at the hands of Mr Heath, that I had in mind when I referred to Enoch Powell's sagacity, courage and singleness of purpose.

There is a Powell policy for everything. Some people agree with some Powellite policies. None, so far as I am aware, agree with all of them. I am with him on immigration and against him on the total denationalisation of state industries, against him on savings and so on. He neither seeks the consensus nor accepts the compromise. He is Enoch and only his policy will prevail. That is why I doubt whether he will ever lead his party. But ever is a long time for there is a growing dislike of the grey,

" Another soccer-hooligan train ? Heavens, no ! It's the Conservative Party Special to the Party conference --- "

TORY PARTY CONFERENCE, The *Daily Express*, 7th October, 1968. Passengers Alighting L. to R. Rt Hon. Quintin Hogg, MP, Rt Hon. Edward Heath, MBE, MP, Rt. Hon. Iain Macleod, MP, Rt Hon. Reginald Maudling, MP, Rt Hon. Enoch Powell, MBE, MP, Rt. Hon. Duncan Sandys, MP, Sir Gerald Nabarro, MP. On Train: Rt Hon. Sir Alec Douglas-Home, MP.

"We had to do SOMETHING to prevent Wilson stealing all the headlines from the Tory Conference."

THE VIRUS OF POWELLISM, The *Daily Express*, 9th October, 1968. H.M.S. *Virus* L. to R. Sir Gerald Nabarro, MP, Rt Hon. Enoch Powell, MBE, MP, Rt Hon. Duncan Sandys, MP. H.M.S. *Pussycat* L. to R. Rt. Hon. Quintin Hogg, MP, Rt Hon. Edward Heath, MBE, MP, Rt Hon. Reginald Maudling, MP, Rt Hon. Iain Macleod, MP.

middle ground in politics which is increased due to the deplorable state of the country. Crisis, deep, deep crisis may project Enoch to the premiership.

Of one thing I am quite convinced. Powell has every quality of a great British statesman. Were he ever to become Prime Minister, he would be a conspicuous success.

22. *Private Legislator*

THE cynics will tell you that the Private or Back-Bench Member of Parliament is without power or influence, the creature of the Whips, the helot of the executive and that he sits in meek submission, obeying the will of his Party leaders.

It is fashionable to deprecate the role of the British Parliament and the effectiveness of its activities in legislating, administering and redressing grievances. No doubt this national mood of derogating Parliamentary institutions is born of frustration in the minds of millions of British people who have watched with dismay the failure of political leadership in recent years, and the manifest inability of the Government to solve the nation's pressing political, social, economic and financial problems. But history may well record that the frustration of the British people and their mistrust of Party politicians derives more from our abdication of an Imperial role, from the scuttle from India in 1947 to the independence of Mauritius in 1968, accompanied by a failure to determine Britain's new role in the world, than from any basic weakness in the Parliamentary system or the quality of the actual Members of Parliament, drawn from nearly every trade and profession and as representative of the nation as true democracy could devise.

Personally, I have not observed any undue submissiveness or automatic compliance on the part of Honourable Members. It would be near impossible to find a more intellectually cantankerous body of men and women. And, when Mr Harold Wilson was reported as threatening to use the ultimate sanction against his followers by withdrawing their "dog licences", he committed a cardinal error. He engendered more antipathy, not less, more party dissent and future difficulties. Mr Harold Macmillan, in his day, with the honeyed tones he reserved for party errants, knew much better than to resort to personal threats. Action of this kind is unlikely to reduce the essential independence of Members. And as for Whips, only Liberals like Jo Grimond complain about them and that is because they will never be in office this side of Doomsday. The most casual student of politics knows that Parliament needs parties and that the parties need Whips; so the sensible Member learns to live with the Whips, indeed to cultivate them.

Nothing demonstrates the independence of Private Members more powerfully than their Bills. To get a Private Member's Bill to the Statute Book is a very, very hazardous and difficult operation. A single cry of "Object" in an empty House at four o'clock on a Friday afternoon can often relegate the most worthy measure to the scrap heap. A hostile Government can delay and defeat a Bill and so can a hostile minority, irrespective of party. The debating time available is limited and religious, moral and social objections can overturn the best intentioned measures. That is why issues such as reform of the law relating to divorce or Sunday entertainment or homosexuality or abortion, have been left to Private Members to promote. Governments are afraid to sponsor such measures officially, for fear of losing votes. A Bill such as one of these takes interminable sittings to steer through the House of Commons impeded by every procedural trick such as talking out, counting out, delaying preceding Bills or just a thin House.

Theoretically, any Member can bring in a Private Bill on any topic provided he complies with certain rules of the House. Actually, the highly placed in the annual ballot for Private Members' Bills held at the beginning of each new Session are the only Members likely to succeed, together with one or two Bills brought in under the "Ten Minute" rule, a curious and most worthwhile Parliamentary device. The ballot really is a ballot, just like the draw at a Church fete. Members put their signatures at an appointed time against a number in a book and twenty-five draw the lucky places. The first half dozen are likely to get their Bills through and then only if the Government majority may be persuaded to support the measure: otherwise it will fail.

The "Ten Minute" rule procedure is much more stimulating and useful for publicity and propaganda, though less likely to initiate a measure that will reach the statute book. At the beginning of the Session, the Member reserves a Tuesday or a Wednesday. On the appointed day, at the end of Questions and Ministerial statements, he rises in his place and speaks for a maximum of ten minutes in support of his motion to bring in a Bill, for example, to prohibit coursing live hares, or otter hunting, or restoring capital punishment for the murder of policemen or prison warders, and so on. The Bill may be opposed by another Member also for a maximum of ten minutes. Then, as likely as not, there is a Division and if the sponsor wins the vote he comes up the floor of the House, presents his Bill to the Clerk, who formally reads it a first time and announces the date, prompted by the sponsoring Member, for Second Reading. Not one "Ten Minute" rule Bill in fifty ever becomes law. It is merely a device and a very good one too, for publicising a Member's legislative intent or propagating a Member's views on the need for reform and often seeking to protect the interests of a minority, all of which is laudable.

I have attempted six Private Members' Bills in nearly twenty years. Four have succeeded and two failed, which is a respectable average, thus:

YEAR	TITLE	HOW PROMOTED	OUTCOME
1953	Coroners' Bill.	Won 17th place in Ballot.	Coroners' Act 1953.
1955	Clean Air Bill.	Won 1st place in Ballot.	Clean Air Act 1956 (after government take-over).
1957	Thermal Insulation (Industrial Buildings) Bill.	Ten Minute Rule	Thermal Insulation (Industrial Buildings) Act, 1957.
1958	Thermal Insulation (Dwellings) Bill.	Ten Minute Rule	Failed.
1960	Oil Burners (Standards) Bill.	Ten Minute Rule	Oil burners (Standards) Act 1960.
1967/8	Renal Transplantation Bill.	Ten Minute Rule, 1968 and repeated 1969.	Both failed.

Often a Private Member winning a place in the Ballot has not a clue what to bring in. In 1953, as a young and inexperienced Member, I was in this position, so I asked the Whips what I should do with my seventeenth place. They advised me to help the Coroners because the Tory Government, like all Governments, had become stuffed with Bills that session and a Tory Home Secretary, the Rt Hon. Sir David Maxwell Fyfe, QC, MP, later Lord Kilmuir, had told Mr Harold Lever, Labour MP for Manchester, Cheetham and in recent years Financial Secretary to the Treasury in the Labour Government, that:

> Legislation would be necessary to increase fees paid to medical practitioners under Section 23 of the Coroners' Amendment Act, 1926, for making post-mortem examinations and I regret that I cannot say how soon it will be possible to introduce legislation for this purpose.[1]

So I decided to do it for him, lugubrious though it all was and on 18th November, 1953, I got a first reading for a Bill to:

> Amend the law as to fees and allowances payable by Coroners to witnesses, to persons summoned to attend as witnesses and to medical practitioners making post-mortem examinations by the coroner's direction or at the coroner's request.

Among my distinguished backers were Sir Harry Hylton-Foster, QC, MP, then a Tory Member and later Speaker of the House of Commons, 1959–65; Lord Mitchison, for many years a front bench Labour spokesman in both Houses; Mr Fred Willey, Labour MP and later Minister; Viscount Lambton, Tory MP for Berwick-on-Tweed from 1951 onwards; Sir Herbert Williams, Tory MP for South Croydon, who brought me into politics, and so on. I was careful to get as many Labour supporters as Tory, thus claiming all-party support. With Home Office briefing and Ministerial support, my Bill roared through and reached the statute book by 4th June, 1954. I was cordially thanked by the medical profession, who had been doomed to the 1926 scale of post-mortem fees for twenty-eight years. I did not relish my reputation as the coroners' friend. I had bigger fish to fry.

In November, 1954, I was amazed to learn that I had won first place in the Ballot for Private Members' Bills. A few weeks earlier, the committee under Sir Hugh Beaver had published their findings on chronic atmospheric pollution, including "Smog" which was afflicting large cities and industrial areas. In the great London smog of 1952, four thousand people had gone to a premature grave because of asphyxia, bronchial and heart troubles and other disorders. It was so bad that even pedigree cattle at the

[1] *Hansard*, 9th December, 1952.

Gerald Nabarro.

GERALD NABARRO, MP, THE LAW MAKER by Cummings. Thermal Insulation (Dwellings) Bill, 1958, the *Daily Express*, 30th January, 1958.

Smithfield show choked to death. The inevitable public outcry followed: hence the Beaver committee to investigate the causes and to make recommendations. It was the most extraordinary luck that the Beaver Report appeared only a matter of weeks before the ballot for Private Members' Bills, thus making quite certain that I could command the floor of the House of Commons for five hours on a Friday on this important subject of my legislative choice. For several years I had been making speeches in the House of Commons on fuel efficiency, notably the faulty combustion of bituminous coal and the consequential wastage at a time of great fuel shortage. I secured the technical help and financial support of the Smoke Abatement Society of Great Britain, drafted a Bill to give effect to all the principal recommendations of Beaver's report, included many of the provisions of the City Ordinances of Pittsburg, Pennsylvania, USA—the most rapid convert to atmospheric purity of any blackened industrial City in the world; and claiming that Britain's coal position was critical, I tabled the Bill with my coined title of "Clean Air". Never has a Private Bill had such powerful backers, limited to eleven in number by Parliamentary rule:

Rt Hon. Alfred Robens, former Labour Cabinet Minister and now Chairman of the National Coal Board.
Colonel Lancaster, Chairman of the Tory Parliamentary Fuel and Power Committee.
Rt Hon. Philip Noel-Baker, former Labour Minister of Fuel and Power.
Mr Angus Maude, Director of the Conservative Political Centre.
Rt Hon. Hilary Marquand, former Labour Minister of Health.
Rt Hon. Enoch Powell, MBE, later Tory Minister of Health.
Rt Hon. Anthony Greenwood, later Labour Minister of Housing and Local Government.
Sir William Darling, CBE, MC, former Provost of the City of Edinburgh "Auld Reekie" and distinguished Tory MP.
Dr Horace King, later Speaker of the House of Commons.
Sir John Barlow, Tory industrialist.
Mr Leslie Lever, former Socialist Lord Mayor of Manchester, one of Britain's pioneer cities in smokeless zones.

These added up to six Tories including myself and six Labour men, a half of whom were former or future Ministers, excluding Mr Speaker. We

DISTINGUISHED
PARLIAMENTARIANS
BY
Fred May.
NOW &
- THEN
FRED. MAY
SIR
GERALD
NABARRO.
CONSERVATIVE
M.P. FOR
WORCESTERSHIRE.

had a memorable time on Second Reading on 4th February, 1955. I opened my speech with an historical survey:

MR GERALD NABARRO (Con. Kidderminster): I beg to move that the Bill be now read a Second time.

In 1257, it is reported by an early English chronicler that Queen Eleanor removed from the city of Nottingham on account of fumes and the obnoxious atmosphere caused by the burning of sea coal in the city. The week before last, the city of Nottingham announced the fact that it proposed to introduce a smokeless zone. No doubt, students of the processes of Parliamentary democracy will regard the lapse of 698 years as being normal progress. In 1307, another early English chronicler reported a Royal Proclamation prohibiting artificers from using sea coal in their furnaces in the city of London, and commanding them to return to the fuel which they had originally used. There was the reported execution of one offender. Hon. Gentlemen in all parts of the House should observe that there is, in the Bill before the House today, no penalty of a capital character; we shall defer consideration of that matter until Thursday next.

In 1307, a Commission of Oyer and Terminer was appointed

'To enquire of all who burnt sea coal in the city or parts adjoining, and to punish them for the first offence with great fines and ransomes, and upon the second offence to demolish their furnaces.'

Nothing, however, of a momentous character was done, and, as late as 1578, after a lapse of 271 years, it was reported that the Company of Brewers, through one of your predecessors, Mr Speaker, in the Chair of the House of Commons, offered to Her Majesty Queen Elizabeth the First to desist from burning sea coal in their breweries and to substitute the burning of wood. In 1595, Thomas Owen from South Wales suggested that he might be allowed to transport a smokeless fuel, anthracite, to the city of London in an attempt to abate the noxious smoke. So far as my researches have been able to tell me, that was the earliest attempt made to substitute smokeless fuel for raw bituminous coal.

The most interesting historical tract on the smoke problem was probably that of 1661 by John Evelyn, Esq., submitted to King Charles II under the name of 'Fumifugium', and the following extract has particular interest, as this incident occurred a mere matter of 294 years ago. John Evelyn said:

'That this Glorious and Ancient City, from Wood might be rendered Brick and (like another Rome) from Brick made Stone and Marble; which commands the Proud Ocean to the Indies, and reaches the farthest Antipodes, should wrap her stately head in Clowds of Smoake and Sulphur, so full of Stink and Darknesse, I deplore with just Indignation.

But I will infer, that if this goodly City justly challenges what is her due,

> and merits all that can be said to reinforce her Praises, and give her Title; she is to be relieved from that which darkens and eclipses all her other Attributes. And what is all this, but that Hellish and dismal Cloud of SEA-COALE? which is not onely perpetually imminent over her head; but so universally mixed with the otherwise wholesome and excellent Aer, that her Inhabitants breathe nothing but an impure and thick Mist, accompanied by a fulginous and filthy vapour, which renders them obnoxious to a thousand inconveniencies, corrupting the Lungs, and disordering the entire habits of their Bodies; so that Catarrhs, Phihisicke, Coughs and Consumptions range more in this City than in the whole earth besides.'

> Evidently Sir Hugh Beaver was not in any way original in what he wrote in his recent report on this subject of smoke abatement (Cmd. 9322), for the quotation I have given is a description of the air of the City of London of 200 or 300 years ago.[1]

A few hours later, my friend Mr Enoch Powell, ever ready with the most apposite of quotations, said in his speech:

> Dickens described the Black Country as a place where as
>
> 'far as the eye could see into the heavy distance tall chimneys crowding on each other, and presenting that endless repetition of the same dull, ugly form which is the horror of oppressive dreams, poured out their plague of smoke, obscured the light, and made foul the melancholy air'.[2]

Mr Duncan Sandys, the Tory Minister of Housing and Local Government, welcomed the measure, a "revolution at the fire-side", but because a Private Member's Bill cannot include financial provisions, he asked me to withdraw the Bill against his assurance that a Government's Clean Air Bill would be brought in that session. In the event, Parliament was dissolved in the spring of 1955 but I had the tremendous elation of seeing *both* Tory and Labour Election manifestoes include promises for Clean Air legislation: it fell to the Tories to implement their promise to me. In 1956 the Clean Air Act was passed in much the form I had originally proposed but supported by all the necessary financial provisions.

Twelve years later, I was among the sponsors of the Labour Member for Buckingham and publisher of this book, Mr Robert Maxwell, MC, MP, in his further clean air legislation designed to strengthen and extend the original statute. Between the two, thousands of lives will have been saved, millions of lives prolonged and limitless rewards derived from greater fuel burning efficiency applied gainfully for all our people. Sadly,

[1] *Hansard*, 4th February, 1955, cols. 1422–23.

[2] *Hansard*, 4th February, 1955, col. 1479.

the noxious fumes from exhausts of motor vehicles still polute our atmosphere and hang like a pall over our congested cities. Science moves so slowly in this field and the Americans prefer to explore the moon rather than decontaminate Los Angeles.

In 1957, still pursuing fuel conservation and greater efficiency in industrial working conditions, I took through my Thermal Insulation (Industrial Buildings) Act, backed by six Labour men and five other Tories apart from myself. It was on the statute book by the Autumn and in the ensuing decade millions of tons of coal and fuel oil in industry have been saved through correct insulation to minimum standards, of the roofs of all new factory buildings. But, with the domestic equivalent—the Thermal Insulation (Dwellings) Bill—designed to replace the ineffectual collection of local authority by-laws by central government Regulations, as in Scotland, I failed to make progress and the Bill fell at the end of the session in 1958, to the intense irritation of the eleven sponsors, and myself, again drawn equally from the two main parties.

The fastest exercise ever conducted with a Private Member's Bill was the introduction of the Oil Burners' (Standards) Bill, which I initiated under the "Ten Minute" rule on 15th March, 1960. This is an extract:

> On 13th November last, at Ware, in Hertfordshire, five small children were asphyxiated and burnt to death within a matter of minutes of their parent leaving a room with an oil burner set in the middle of the floor, opening the door of the room, opening the front door of the house to go and buy groceries, crossing the road and going only a few yards away. The sudden draught which swept through the front door into the inner room caused an instantaneous fire and the death of those five children.
>
> The coroner at Ware, who conducted a detailed inquest with a jury empanelled, is to be congratulated on the thoroughness with which he dealt with this problem and his demand that the findings should be sent to the D.S.I.R., which is the cause of the train of investigations that have followed.
>
> The second accident happened sadly only a matter of ten days ago, in Nottingham, where a Jamaican left the room with an oil burner set in the middle of it, fetched a new canister of fuel and evidently sought to refill the appliance while the burner was alight. The appliance caught fire at once and notwithstanding the aid of an adult relative, it could not be removed from the room and the fire extinguished before two small children, aged two years and twelve months respectively, had been severely burned. Within 48 hours the child aged twelve months died in hospital, and the second child is still critically ill.[1]

[1] *Hansard*, 15th March, 1960, col. 1126.

My measure proposed minimum standards for portable oil burners or stoves and the sponsors were drawn from all parties, six Tories, including myself, five Labour men and one Liberal. In a few weeks it was on the statute book and Regulations were issued by the Home Secretary to require minimum standards of safety for all new heaters. The entire industry stopped to re-tool before the new heater specifications could be embodied in mass production.

But the misuse of unguarded electric fires, non-flame-proof children's clothing and portable oil fires, still cause far, far too many child fatalities especially in overcrowded dwellings and old buildings. It all needs more detailed Parliamentary attention, soon.

Worthiness of cause often has little to do with Parliamentary success. Ministerial ostracism, bureaucratic dogmatism and the supremacy of the Whips habitually prevail. In March 1967, I brought in my Private Member's measure on Renal Transplantation and secured a first reading, a second reading and a successful passage through standing committee. This is what I said when bringing in the Bill:[1]

SIR GERALD NABARRO (Con. Worcestershire, South): I beg to move,

> That leave be given to bring in a bill to permit removal from the body of a human person, duly certified as dead, any kidney or kidneys required for medical purposes, unless there is reason to believe that the deceased during his lifetime had instructed otherwise.

The entire civilised world is moved today by the medical achievement of transplanting a heart from a dead person to a living person for the purpose of saving his life. We do not know, and it is axiomatic that we shall not know for years yet, the prospects post-transplant for survival of the heart recipient. So also with prospects for transplants of other major human organs such as lungs, livers, bowels and so on.

Probably the use of plastic organs will overtake the transplantation of human organs. That will depend on medical and scientific discovery and evolution during the next few years.

Transplantation of human organs arouses deep emotions, physiological and biological, religious and social. I state my belief today quite simply. Following the diagnosis of death by conventional and accepted means, and death certified by two doctors, other than the surgeon conducting a renal transplantation, it is justified in my view, on ethical grounds, to remove a kidney or kidneys for prolongation of life of a sick human being, always provided—repeat, always provided—there should be some safeguard for persons who do not wish this to be done for religious or other reasons.

The Bill that I propose deals with kidneys alone—no other human organ—

hence the title "Renal Transplantation Bill". There is a good practical reason for this. It is that only in the field of kidneys, among all the blood-fed organs—that is, excluding corneal grafting, because the cornea is not a blood-fed organ—has there been very substantial success already achieved by doctors during the last years. At Cambridge alone, Professor Roy Calne has successfully carried out about 30 kidney transplants in the last two years. Recipients of transplanted kidneys are now living up to five years. As the supply of healthy kidneys increases—and I believe it will increase—and selection and typing of tissue the donor with the recipient, improves, the whole process will become easier and longevity post-transplant will also increase. My purpose is to seek to increase the supply of human kidneys in order to diminish the 3,000 deaths in this country alone in a single year, which are attributed to kidney disorders and diseases.

Sufficient kidneys are not, and never will be, available in the present state of the law. I paraphrase the condition of the law very shortly today under the Human Tissue Act, 1961, roughly as follows:

> (1)–(2) If any person, either in writing or at any time orally in the presence of two or more witnesses . . . has expressed a request that his body or any specified part of his body be used after his death for therapeutic purposes or for purposes of medical education or research, the person lawfully in possession of his body after his death . . . may authorise the removal from the body of any part or . . . specified part, for use in accordance with the request.
>
> (2) . . . the person lawfully in possession of the body . . . may authorise the removal of any part from the body . . . if, having made any such reasonable enquiry as may be practicable, he has no reason to believe—
>
> (a) that the deceased had expressed an objection to his body being so dealt with . . . or
>
> (b) that the surviving spouse or any surviving relative of the deceased objects to the body being so dealt with.

This, in the context of kidneys, is extremely restrictive and makes the removal of kidneys from a dead body in the overwhelming majority of circumstances utterly impracticable for saving the life of a sick person; though no blame attaches to our legislators in 1961, because at that time no successful renal transplantations had been accomplished. This branch of surgery—renal transplantation—has been largely developed in the last few years since 1961.

A human kidney, to be of use for transplantation, must be removed from the newly deceased body within one hour of death, either for immediate transplantation into the body of a sick person or for preservation under suitable conditions for future use. Preservation means that the removed kidney is cooled or refrigerated between 0 degree Centigrade and 1 degree Centigrade. Clearly, in the case of kidneys, the existing law cannot be complied with following death, for example, due to a motor accident, which is the most common case. Often the next of kin cannot be contacted by the registrar at the hospital in sufficient time. In any event, it would be callous and inhuman to expect the doctor in charge of the hospital to be obliged to telephone, say, a married woman as next of kin and say to her: 'Your husband has just been killed and is lying in the South Blankshire Hospital. May we remove his kidneys?' Yet this is what is required under the existing law. Hundreds of relatives, given time for the initial shock of bereavement to wear off, would happily have consented later to the removal of the kidneys from the dead person. But, at the time of notification, they are too grief-stricken to make the decision within one hour, which is physiologically necessary for the kidney transplant. Thus, valuable, healthy, life-saving kidneys are denied to the surgeons for saving human life and diminishing the 3,000 deaths a year due to kidney diseases and disorders to which I have alluded. Moreover, the majority of people today accept cremation as an alternative to interment. Cremation involves total destruction by fire of human remains. Most sudden deaths are subject to a coroner's autopsy, or post mortem, involving disfigurement of the body after death. Renal removal is carried out by a surgeon under conditions similar to those of an operation on a living person and involves relatively minor disfigurement of the human remains.

It is too early yet to talk of legislative reforms for transplantation of major human blood-fed organs, other than kidneys—I refer, of course, to such organs as hearts—until greater physiological progress has been made in the massive problems of tissue rejection. The conference recently convened by the Minister of Health, under the Chairmanship of Sir Hector MacLennan, President of the Royal Society of Medicine, will doubtless deal with human hearts, lungs, livers and transplants of other major organs which are, as yet, in an exploratory and embryonic stage.

I believe that unilateral legislative amendment, at once, is desirable in the case of kidney transplantation, at present largely curtailed due to shortage of kidneys arising from the existing state of the law.

I reiterate that there would be adequate safeguards in the Bill proposed, for any religious or ethical objectors.

My proposed Bill, if successful, would condition the public for wider amending organ transplantation legislation later. If permission is given to bring in this Bill today, it will have all-party support. There will be twelve sponsors of the Bill, of whom seven are Tories, four are Labour, and one is Liberal. Of the twelve sponsors, six are doctors of medicine and six are lay Members of this House.[1]

---

[1] *Hansard*, 13th March, 1968, cols. 1377–80.

After this speech, lack of Parliamentary time prevented the final stages of the Bill from being completed. In 1969 I brought in the same Renal Transplantation Bill. But the Government insist on a general Bill to cover transplants of all human organs, including hearts, livers, kidneys and so on. I believe, for the time being, in proceeding only in the field of proven success, namely kidney transplants.

Indeed, I sigh: the path of the Private Legislator is often hard and stony.

23. *A Tory May Day*

I HAD always wanted to address a large crowd at a political gathering in Trafalgar Square but for twenty years I mistakenly had the idea that the Tories were too genteel by half to participate in such boisterous party politics. Rather, I had thought that they would permanently surrender such activities to the Left, the Socialist Party, the Trades Unions, the Co-operatives, the Communists and all the other organisations and bodies purporting to represent the proletariat. Certainly, the sanctity of May Day had always been a particularly ridiculous Socialist shibboleth on both sides of the Iron Curtain. The hallowed character of the day goes very deep into English history but its political associations are more recent, although as long ago as 1833, Robert Owen appointed 1st May as the day for the commencement of the millennium. But apart from that instance, the political observance of the day cannot be traced any earlier than 1889, when the first Congress of the Second Socialist International at Paris selected the day for international celebration. Labour Day celebrations were not held in Great Britain until 1892 and since then have usually taken the form of a great rally of members of the three main constituents of the Socialist movement—Labour Party, Trades Unions and Co-operatives—in Hyde Park, together with peaceful processions accompanied by hundreds of banners, signs, devices, emblems and an occasional band, though not to keep the marching throng in step or any kind of formation.

In the United States and Canada Labour Day is an official national holiday—though not necessarily on 1st May—in which workers of all classes, employers and employees, managerial and manual, participate. Thus the North Americans allow no distinction or discrimination in their laudable acclamation of the nobility of labour. All who toil, by brain or by hand, or by both, to earn their daily bread are workers. In Britain, Labour Day is observed on the Sunday nearest to the first of May, although in 1969 certain sections of the working population rather unnecessarily observed both days. It is a day when all those whose political inclinations are to the Left attempt to demonstrate the fraternity engendered by their opinions.

I fervently believe in the French maxim "Il n'y a pas de sal métier". I seek, as a Conservative politician, to represent all those who work and their families. Over the years, I have succeeded in attracting the support of the majority of the workers in both the constituencies I have represented. It was Lord Woolton, then Chairman of the Conservative Party, who observed in the last dying days of the immediate post-war Labour Government, that three out of eight Trade Unionists were voting Tory which was a rude awakening for those pundits who had imagined that the affiliation of a Trade Union to the Trade Union Congress was a manifest of a monopoly of Labour voting strength. Today it looks as if the proportion of Trade Union members voting Tory has gone up to something like a half and the remainder must include some Liberals and certainly some Communists.

All of which shows that the cleverest thing about the Labour Party is its name; and that one half of the alleged supporters are good voting capitalists, supporting the party they think will bring the greatest prosperity to the country, their families and themselves by capitalist methods and the equitable division of rewards from the profits legitimately earned in highly competitive industry and trade. Harold Macmillan's "Middle Way" in the thirties, Anthony Eden's "Property-owning democracy" and Butler's Education Act of 1944, have all played a considerable part in gathering Tory Trade Union votes over the last twenty years.

That is why I was so pleased to be associated with the enterprise of the Rt Hon. Duncan Sandys, MP for Streatham, former Cabinet Minister and a stalwart leader of the Tory Right wing, who, with great élan and perspicacity, booked Trafalgar Square on Sunday, 4th May, 1969, for a "Tory May Day Rally". Never before had the Tories indulged in anything so vulgar and never had they perpetrated such a blatant theft of the Socialists' clothes. The Prime Minister was relegated to the Royal Festival Hall, on the South Bank, where a depressing fifteen hundred bought the modestly priced tickets for admission to a closed Labour Meeting. The vast Labour procession was compelled to make its way around the edge of Trafalgar Square on its way to Hyde Park along a route lined by several hundred Metropolitan Policemen. The Tory posters proclaimed their message "LABOUR HAS FAILED—REBUILD BRITAIN WITH THE TORIES" from the base of Nelson's Column behind the platform facing the National Gallery, where the twelve speakers sat surrounded by television cameras and pressmen.

The Tory faithful arrived early. They had been well trained. Here are the instructions to the marchers from North Paddington, a seat strongly held by Labour:

> RALLY—The Rt Hon. Duncan Sandys is arranging a Conservative Mass Rally in Trafalgar Square on Sunday, 4th May. This date is traditionally Labour Day, a time when the Socialists are out in force. The Conservative Party felt that they too should make a showing, and were fortunate enough to book Trafalgar Square before the Socialists! We want all the support we can get, it is up to us to make the Socialists look small! The Young Conservatives are arranging to walk from Winston House, where everybody is going to meet at 11 a.m., to the Square. They hope to amass at least a hundred people to join them in this: members who feel fit enough to walk all the way will be encouraged to do so: others can travel part of it by bus or tube. The important part is to have a large gathering outside Winston House at the start of the march and to arrive in force in the Square. Members are advised to take something to sit on in the Square, a newspaper or groundsheet, as there may be a wait before the speeches are due to start. We hope that refreshments will be available.

It didn't rain. The pigeons dropped the lot all over everybody's clothes during the two hours or more of exposure. The National Front screamed "We want Enoch"; the Young Socialists chanted "Fascist Beasts"; the more extreme Right wing elements went off to deal with the unruly students at the London School of Economics, leaving the Young Conservatives from that seat of learning, one of whom, Mr Francis Dobbyn, was among our speakers, to applaud their leaders in the Square but the police frustrated disturbance in Malet Street. The galaxy of banners and placards in the great crowd demonstrated the endless grounds for opposition to Mr Harold Wilson's Government:

Wilson OUT
Ted for No. 10
NAB for Transport Minister
Nationalise means paralyse

Socialism is out of date
Support Rhodesia
Labour has failed
Don't knock Enoch
Save the Argylls
Free Radio—vote Tory
Swing to the Right
Tories for Freedom
Ahead with Ted
Lower Taxation—more incentives
Britain First
We want Enoch
Rebuild Britain with the Tories

and many more.

Duncan Sandys had chosen his speakers very carefully to represent every section of the Tory Party, ranging from the Monday Club and Mr Patrick Wall, MP, to the present Shadow Cabinet, represented by Mr Peter Walker, MP, Shadow Minister of Housing and Local Government and Mr Quintin Hogg, QC, MP, former Chairman of the Party and Minister of Education in Mr Macmillan's government. The other former Ministers, apart from Mr Sandys himself, were Mr Julian Amery and Mr John Boyd-Carpenter. Tories outside Parliament ranged from the Chairman of the London Young Conservatives, Mrs Lynda Chalker, to the Leader of the Greater London Council, Mr Desmond Plummer and Colonel Colin Mitchell, "Mad Mitch" of the Argyll and Sutherland Highlanders. There was even a student speaker from the London School of Economics.

Duncan Sandys and Quintin Hogg began and ended with speeches of about ten minutes each and the rest of us were allowed about six minutes each. I was amazed when the crowd quietly dispersed: that there had been no rough house, and no confrontation between Tories and the National Front and the Young Socialists. Of course, there were various minor altercations between individuals in the crowd but these, together with a few obviously experienced and highly articulate hecklers, smartened up the parade.

On the following day (5th May), "Peterborough" wrote in the *Daily Telegraph*:

As the large and orderly trade union procession, moving west through Trafalgar Square just before the Duncan Sandys rally began, reminded us yesterday, Labour are more solid and experienced Sunday marchers than the Tories.

The Tory affair, with a dozen hustings speeches in 90 minutes, was admirably organised and presented, less impressively supported. The National Front, whose banners blocked out everyone's view of the platform, was too much in evidence. Conservative organisations too little.

Most of Mr Sandys' team proved adept at the specialised brand of speech 'belting' which Trafalgar Square demands, none more so than Mrs Lynda Chalker, Chairman of the London YCs, who got it exactly right.

Education and taxation raised little excitement, housing only a little more. One of the biggest cheers greeted Julian Amery's reference to the TSR2. That and the ovation for Col. Colin Mitchell and the Argylls hinted that defence may loom larger in the public mind than some politicians think.

It is perfectly true that the loudest cheers went to Colonel Colin Mitchell and the loudest of all to his reference to cleaning up the Crater district of Aden and to Julian Amery's reference to the most advanced military aircraft ever built in Britain, the TSR2, scrapped by the Socialist Government in favour of American aircraft which were later cancelled as well: the youngsters in Trafalgar Square appeared to feel real apprehension about our naked national defences.

In a note afterwards, I said to Duncan Sandys that I was painfully aware we had attracted only four thousand people, whereas the capacity of Trafalgar Square is ten thousand. "Only two cheers for Duncan", I said. I was pleased with his reply saying "You must have been delighted with the tremendous reception which the crowd gave you".

Indeed I was: I went to my bed at the Carlton Club that night, happy that a baker's dozen of Tories in Trafalgar Square had made history that May Day, and properly established their identity with the toiling masses.

24. *Private and Personal*

GENERALLY, a Member of Parliament does not live in his constituency and I never intended to do so myself. I had always preached that the Member should live in the same County, fairly close to his constituency but far enough away to obviate the professional underdog, the perpetual chip-on-the-shoulder and every other kind of inveterate scrounger proving too much of a pest at close quarters. I had been warned of the council house waiting list, knocking on the door on Sunday evenings, the abusive telephone calls, the hoaxes, the short of cash, the improvident and the ne'er do well who invariably try their luck with soft-hearted Members of Parliament.

So, in 1950 when I was elected by a small majority for a Worcestershire seat, Kidderminster, I started house-hunting south of Kidderminster on the London road, so that when my week's work finished, late on Saturday night after a full day of constituency chores, I could drive to my home and save thirty or forty miles of my Monday morning journey to Westminster.

I came to rest in England's most beautiful village, Broadway, just inside Worcestershire and thirty-six miles to the south of Kidderminster. Not only was it well placed for my far flung constituency but I had found and bought my dream of a house which was ideally suited for my family and such political image as I had then succeeded in creating, at thirty-seven years of age.

I immediately renamed my new home the Orchard House and abandoned the historic name, Orchard Farm, to forestall nasty Labour Members accusing me of hobby farming. This sturdy farmhouse was built in

1602. It nestled at the foot of the Cotswold escarpment at the southern entry to the village of Broadway. It stood on the old coaching route from the Royal City of Worcester, along the Vale of Evesham and through the ancient Borough of that name; then from Broadway itself to Moreton-in-Marsh, Chipping Norton, Woodstock, Oxford and thence to London. From my front door at Broadway to Palace Yard at Westminster is ninety miles. Now that I sit for my own home constituency of South Worcestershire which includes Evesham, a Tory seat since the beginning of time, I record in my foreword to a recent publication, these words:

> All this Parliamentary business, so treasured by Britons everywhere, hallowed and sanctified by seven centuries of usage and copied throughout the world, was begun by Simon de Montfort, killed in 1265 at the Battle of Evesham in the constituency of Worcestershire, South which I represent today in the Commons, House of Parliament. During all those years, Knights of the Shires and Burgesses have gone to Westminster, to champion causes. Humour has been among their greatest weapons. Parliament and wit are inseparable. So it will be, to the end of time.[1]

I love living with my wife and four children in a great stone Cotswold house in the gorgeous countryside on the Worcestershire and Gloucestershire borders where so much of English history was made. The Domesday village of Broadway is filled with fine buildings and noble inns and is a great centre of tourism, especially for those Americans who seek endlessly to establish their genealogical links with the Broadway families who sailed in the *Mayflower* in 1620. Broadway, England, is one of the most lucrative of all dollar earners in our tourist industry, and deservedly so with hotels of the quality of the Lygon Arms which I unhesitatingly call England's finest country hotel. My house is besieged by the tourists as well, although I only open it once a year under the National Gardens Scheme for my favourite charity, the Retired District Nurses Benevolent Fund. We have many, many visitors to see the house, the garden, seven acres of it, to hunt autographs and to see the politician. I do this only one day a year and otherwise I am "ex-directory" save only to the local telephone supervisor who knows how to get me in matters of life and death. Constituents in trouble are told to come to my surgeries, which are copiously advertised, or to write to me at the House of Commons, or both. Thus, on the one or two days a week I am at home, I can enjoy reasonable privacy and peace.

[1] Foreword to *The Wit of Westminster* by Adam Sykes and Iain Sproat.

The immense prosperity of the Cotswolds was founded in the Middle Ages on wool and this continued throughout the sixteenth and seventeenth centuries. The wool merchants were comfortable men and able to build solidly in the conservative tradition of the area. My house was a farm-house of about a dozen rooms with a large, high barn set at right angles to it. Orchards lay on three sides, and behind were the superb Cotswold hillsides, which are today National Trust Land. During the eighteenth century the property fell from grace and was divided, one half to become a village shop and the other to become two dwellings for agricultural labourers. In 1899, Lady Maud Bowes-Lyon, daughter of 13th Earl of Strathmore, and thus an aunt of Queen Elizabeth the Queen Mother, bought the Orchard Farm because of the splendid landscape and views surrounding it. Much was required to restore the neglect of the previous century and the celebrated Edwardian architect, A. N. Prentice, was commissioned to carry out a complete renovation and to make substantial additions to the building. The great barn was made part of the house and its roof raised to allow bedrooms to be built aloft. Created in the barn downstairs was a splendid music-room with a dais for the orchestra, looking three ways through mullioned windows to the gardens and the hills beyond. A kitchen wing was also added, kept low in construction in order not to compete with the original work. Large open fireplaces and chimney pieces, raftered roofs and beams, oak panelling, shutters and floors were all added to what both contemporaries and successors congratulated Prentice on, as " a very characteristic piece of Cotswold building". The Australians wrote of it in 1954, during the tour of Queen Elizabeth II and Prince Philip and because of the Queen Mother's long association with the house, as a "house of royal memories".

In the great room which Lady Maud Bowes-Lyon called her music room were held the elegant soirees of the early years of this century. Today this room dances seventy-five couples to the noise of a beat group, often the "Autocrats" appropriately named by their founder and leader the 2nd Lord Colwyn, son-in-law of Mr and Mrs Morgan of Morgan Cars at Malvern in my South Worcestershire constituency. This is a contemporary use for Lady Maud's great music room, beloved of my family for its warmth and comfort, huge log fire and the 23 inch colour television set on which my family watch me perform.

Those prominent in public life and politicians and publicists cannot evade the responsibilities and the duties which the television imposes. I have never tried to shirk this responsibility though neither have I ever solicited a television appearance or broadcast. I always wait to be asked. And, if one really can get used to a television camera and perform, unruffled and undisturbed by anything, however nasty or caustic, hurled by interviewers such as Robin Day, David Frost, Bernard Levin or their lesser satellites and imitators, then television becomes an ally. I regard it as mine and in recent years have appeared on hundreds of programmes, political and non-political, in colour and in black and white, BBC and Independent, in the United States, Canada, France, West Germany, Italy, Holland, Eire and Scandinavia. To show that I am a professional, I carry my fully paid-up membership card of AFTRA, the American Federation of Television and Radio Artistes. More publicity and propaganda may attend one television programme than a hundred utterances in the House of Commons and often as effectively. Televising the House of Commons would be no substitute and would probably destroy the informality and even intimacy of the Commons, which is at the very heart of Parliamentary debates. I love the variety and excitement of much television work and the spontaneity, which enables me to say much what I like, with a minimum of preparation and a maximum of effect. Moreover, I get paid for it. I need to be paid for it in view of the very high costs associated with being a Member of the House of Commons, my pittance of a Parliamentary salary and penal taxation. When I say variety, I do not mean it in the theatrical sense, but diversity ranging from "Panorama" to "What's my Line?", and in subject from defending Prime Ministers to defending Irene against Soames Forsyte. My fear is that I become more a television performer and less a Parliamentarian, which would be a pity but not a surprise. Today, politics and television are inseparable and you cannot have one without the other. Wilson knows it. Heath knows it. I know it. Also, I enjoy exposure. Nothing I like better than Robin Day or someone opposite me, hostile, waiting to pounce and savage me and grubbing around looking for chinks in my armour. I know that I will be able to clobber him given half a chance. Not so many of the journalists who write half truths, wallow in calumnies, vent party political spleen against particular politicians and public figures they happen to dislike, sure in the knowledge that their newspapers would never print any kind of reply from the assaulted. But not the Robin Days about the behaviour of whom many people complain to me. I spring to their defence. I like their militant style. It would be poor television without it. Anyway, I choose to expose myself in the interests of my political philosophy and party. I choose to, and that's my affair: but not my funeral.

After almost fifteen years in Parliament, I had to give up my seat because of illness and to my astonishment a newspaper which had rarely had a good word to say for me, or my works, up to that moment, wrote thus:

> Sir Gerald was one of a star-spangled trio who could pack the House of Commons with Tory and Labour MPs within seconds after their names appeared on the board—the other two: Winston Churchill and Aneurin Bevin.
>
> *Daily Mail*, 25th March, 1964.

And, as I worked my passage back to the House of Commons as Member for South Worcestershire, the *Daily Express* was very encouraging:

> It is good news for Parliament and the people that Sir Gerald Nabarro has now overcome his ill-health and is seeking a way back to the Commons. Sir Gerald's rumbustious spirit added down-to-earth qualities to proceedings. He is on the short list for the South Worcestershire seat. That, or some other Tory constituency has the opportunity to earn the public's gratitude by selecting him.
>
> *Daily Express*, 12th January, 1965.

All of which shows that newspapermen have hearts of gold and are dedicated to the truth.

Politics should be both grave and gay and one of the obvious consequences of politics and television is that my face becomes rather well-known; which prompted this delightful piece of levity in the *Sunday Times*, on 8th June, 1969, in the series "My Face and I":

> My moustache has always been my greatest attribute and the cause of my fortune. I have always had a moustache since hair grew on my face. I have never shaved my upper lip which accounts for the soft and silken texture of the hairs which have never been known to irritate, scratch or to blemish a lady's face when in close proximity to her. Had I no moustache I should have been indistinguishable from any other grey and faceless politician such as Mr Harold Wilson.
>
> No additive or cosmetic is employed on my moustache. I despise users of pomade d'Hongroise. My moustache is brushed vigorously four times per day and combed with a special small blunt-ended Kent comb, which avoids scratching my cheeks and keeps every hair in place.
>
> Finally, there is a recent case on record of a man in Cheshire who so admired my facial and hirsute idiosyncrasy on television that he spent two years growing a replica which has now been brought to resplendent fruition. He recently obtained from me a coloured and autographed photograph of myself as a memorial to his personal inspiration.

However, to return to more serious matters, the political pundits will tell you that if a Member of Parliament takes a knighthood, his career is finished. Thus in the autumn of 1962, I had to weigh the risks of being included in the Prime Minister's New Year Honours List in 1963. I reflected that I had always declined office in Conservative administrations, during the twelve years since 1951, believing that a determined and individualistic backbencher could influence the course of events much more effectively than by accepting Ministerial office, which dooms him to a single portfolio. However capacious that portfolio, be it the Treasury, the Board of Trade, Housing, or Social Welfare, the Minister is confined to speaking to a single brief. All rather inhibiting, I thought, and still think. I love the wide open spaces of politics, the television screen, the radio, the press, where I can speak on any and every topic of my choice in the national interest. Not for me the single brief, the one portfolio, the speech carefully read at the Despatch Box in the Commons, deviating not one comma from the typescript prepared by the bureaucratic underworld of a Department of State. I love my freedom to "blow off" on public platforms all over Britain, advancing the cause of my party and disseminating my Conservative philosophy. Thus my old friend Anthony Wedgwood Benn, MP, went to speak at Bristol University in May, 1969 and his audience was "NIL". In August 1968, at the height of the holiday season, I went to speak at a Conservative fete in the Vale of Alford, in the Liberal held constituency of West Aberdeenshire and more than 5,000 people paid for admission. And just to assure myself that Aberdeenshire was not in some way peculiar, I journeyed to Alnwick Castle (the seat of the Duke of Northumberland) three days later and spoke there for my friend, Viscount Lambton, MP, who has sat for Berwick-on-Tweed since 1951. Again the crowd listening was above 5,000 and the fete raised more than £3,000 for Conservative Party funds in a single day. These are the fruits of freedom. They do not ripen so lusciously for holders of ministerial office. Moreover, I have always regarded myself as a one man Tory propaganda machine, self-projecting, self-propelled and self-publicised, though Conservative Central Office does help me from time to time. So numerous are the invitations to speak that they outnumber my acceptances by twenty five to one. Enoch Powell may be more sought after than me: so may Ted Heath, but I doubt whether any other politican has been in 1968 and 1969, and I am appropriately gratified that I am helping my country and my Party. I believe in my Party and I believe that Labour are wreckers. I say so on every public platform, everywhere.

"... and it doesn't carry purchase tax, sir"

Daily Mail, 1st January, 1963.

In 1969, I spoke at a couple of hundred functions in South Worcestershire and scores of large gatherings besides in every part of Britain: at Penzance, at Inverness, Poole, Glasgow, Edinburgh, Newcastle-on-Tyne, Birmingham, Manchester, London, Dudley, Bradford, York, Henley-on-Thames, Coventry, Stourbridge, at Invergordon, Kettering, Worcester and so on. The places where I speak are as widely dispersed as the subjects I speak on. The speeches are made at every sort of function, including eve-of-poll meetings at Bye-elections in the toughest spots for my Party, such as Colne Valley, Rotherham and West Bromwich. The Tory May Day on 4th May, 1969, in Trafalgar Square, was an exercise in human exposure and an object lesson for the Prime Minister and his ticket-holders in the Royal Festival Hall. And to Prince Philip, Chancellor of Edinburgh University, who told an interruptor to "shut up and grow up", I say you have seen nothing and heard nothing until you contemplate the like of my "scream-ins" at the University of York, in May 1969 and the University of Aston in Birmingham, in February, 1969.

So, bearing all this in mind, after I received the following letter:

PERSONAL & CONFIDENTIAL

Admiralty House,
Whitehall, S.W.1.
December 3rd, 1962.

Dear Nabarro,

I have it in mind on the occasion of the forthcoming list of New Year Honours to submit your name to the Queen with a recommendation that Her Majesty may be graciously pleased to approve that the Honour of Knighthood be conferred upon you in recognition of your political and public services.

I should be glad to know if this would be agreeable to you, and I will take no steps until I have your reply.

Yours sincerely,

HAROLD MACMILLAN.

—I decided to reply, "Yes, I should be honoured, Sir, thank you very much." The Honours List was published on 1st January, 1963 and on that day, too, the Chancellor of the Exchequer reduced Purchase Tax right across the board, to three rates only, 25% (including motor cars), 15% and 10%. Today they are 55%, $36\frac{2}{3}$%, 22% and $13\frac{3}{4}$%, doubled to yield an exorbitant £1100m in 1969/70. The *Daily Mail* called me "Sir Purchase

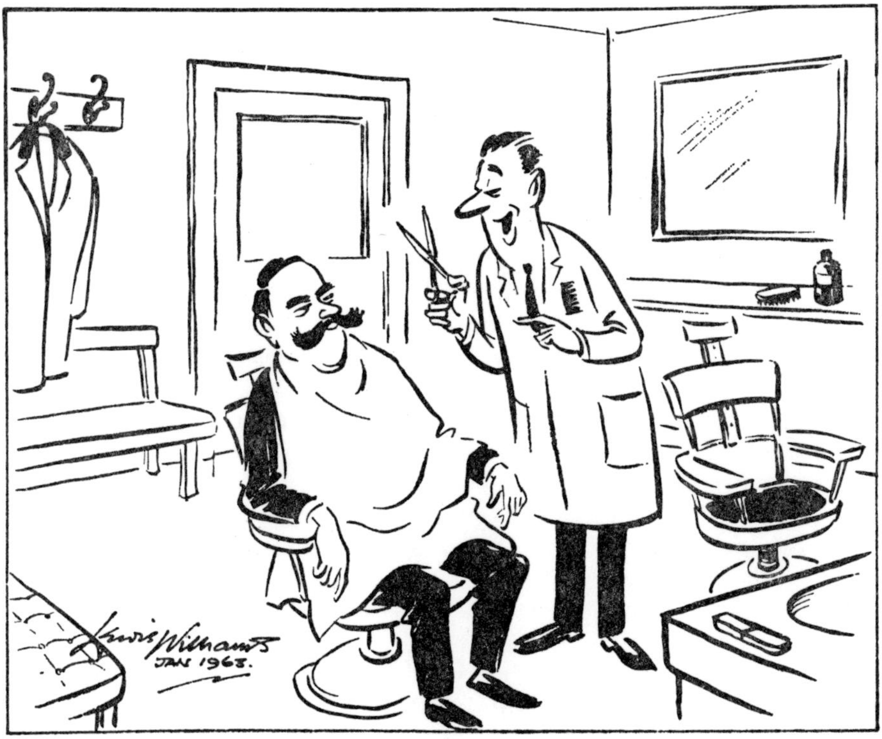

"PERHAPS JUST A LITTLE OFF WHERE THE SWORD COMES DOWN, SIR —!"

Birmingham Mail, 1st January, 1963.

Tax" and the *Daily Telegraph* observed that my television and radio fans would be pleased. "Cassandra" in the *Daily Mirror* said:

> Mr Gerald Nabarro, knighted in the New Year Honours list, said today: 'Eighteen years in the Army is rewarded by a long service and good conduct medal, or "rooty-gong" as the old soldier calls it—18 years of undetected crime.
>
> 'I entered political life in 1945: today, after 18 years, I have got my "rooty-gong". I am proud to have it. I hope I shall be worthy of it.
>
> 'I have not joined the Establishment.
>
> 'My New Year 1963 resolution is to intensify my efforts to guide Government policies into channels which will result in my party, the Tories, winning the next general election'.
>
> Of the cuts in Purchase Tax Mr Nabarro said: 'I am thrilled because that is what I have been campaigning for. It is a particularly happy New Year present to millions of our women who use cosmetics which have been so inflated in price in recent years by the iniquitous Purchase Tax.
>
> 'Incidentally, when I started this Purchase Tax campaign five years ago, the tax on cosmetics was 90% and now it is down to 25%.
>
> 'I shall continue to press the Chancellor to complete the reform of Purchase Tax in his next Budget in April', he said.
>
> 'I particularly want to see him bring all gambling into the Purchase Tax schedules, including fixed odds betting, betting shops, chemin-de-fer, bingo and the other games of chance which ought to be swelling the revenue and giving the Chancellor the financial sinews to reduce Purchase Tax still further and so help our export trade by which the British nation lives.'

When I went to the Palace to be dubbed on 5th February, 1963, watched by my wife and two sons, Rupert, 18, Captain of Rackets at Harrow, and Jeremy, 17, Worcestershire Junior Squash Rackets Champion and also at Harrow, Queen Elizabeth the Queen Mother officiated and deputised for Her Majesty, who was touring Australia. As I came up from kneeling, to attention, and looked straight into those gorgeous blue eyes and touched her outstretched hand with the tips of the fingers of my right hand, she said: "How very nice, Sir Gerald, to be meeting you today: you were so good last night on 'What's My Line?'." I could manage to stammer only: "Thank you, M'am, thank you most warmly for your kindness, M'am."

It was a good crop of knighthoods, including Sir William Carron (now Lord Carron) the Trade Union leader, Sir Denning Pearson, head of Rolls Royce, Sir Geoffrey Lawrence, QC, of Prices and Incomes repute, and a

Tory predecessor of Aubrey Jones; and Sir Leslie Thomas, MP for Canterbury, Parliamentary Private Secretary to the Rt Hon. Charles Hill, MP, for many years, and son of a former Socialist Cabinet Minister, the Rt Hon. Jimmy Thomas, MP.

I believe in the honours system: so does Harold Wilson. All civilised countries have them.

25. *Ten Canons of my Tory Faith for the Seventies*

THE leader in *The Times* on December 9th, 1968, began:

> "If one is British, one can only feel
> heartsick about the state of the country."

I am heartsick, for our affairs are in a worse state today than they were a year ago. Devaluation has not succeeded; inflation continues unchecked; the balance of payments is still heavily in deficit; our mountainous overseas debts remain; taxation, further increased, is scandalously onerous and abstruse; a swollen bureaucracy "cocks a snook" at Parliament and arrogates to itself supra-statutory powers; gambling and sport are the nation's major pre-occupations; and morals are on the slippery slope.

A large part of the urban population believes that the world owes us a living. The more intelligent section of the community suffers from a malaise deriving from over-government in recent years created by meddlesome matties, nosey-parkers and busy-bodies prying into every aspect of industrial and commercial life and the private affairs of every individual citizen. A "test census" will soon be asking for each person's income, though the lawful requirement is that only tax inspectors, in absolute confidence, may demand such information; the citizen will be too frightened to defy the bureaucratic interrogator for fear of committing a misdemeanour and being dragged before the magistrates. The bureaucracy is daily becoming more arrogant and intrusive.

Parliament churns out statutes comprising hundreds of pages of incomprehensible gibberish. The nation's financial statutes are in such a state of disarray that hordes of accountants disfigure every undertaking and only a tiny minority of citizens understand their own tax position; mechanically and drearily they meet the ever increasing fiscal imposts put upon them. Freedom is being eroded in every section of our national life. Sixty thousand additional central government civil servants and at least sixty thousand local government officials excluding teachers, police, firemen and other professional working personnel, have been recruited in five years to deal with such crack-pot paraphernalia as Selective Employment Tax, the Industrial Reorganisation Corporation, the proliferating "NEDDIES", big and small, which with many other quasi-governmental organisations take business and professional men away from their work and waste a mountain of public and private wealth. Small wonder that national and local taxes have increased so terrifyingly. Industrial discipline is beyond control. Men often strike with little pretext or none. Men out of work, with their earnings related benefits, their repayment of P.A.Y.E. formerly deducted from wages, their special social service allowances for needy wives and children and family allowances and welfare foods, can cause unemployed and strikers to take home more pound notes, untaxed, than their nett wages would have been at work. Thus we pay a premium on idleness and reward the work-shy. The man who builds a business and sells it will find his income from the invested proceeds subject to surtax as "unearned" income above £2,000 a year, whereas the company or state servant retiring on an occupational pension of more than £2,000 a year will have his income regarded as earned and will pay no surtax up to £5,000 a year. Thus, sturdy individualism and self-reliance are penalised.

So voracious is the demand of the tax-man at all levels of society that tax-fiddling is now the first national sport.

The British nation is much less moral, much less scrupulous, much less law-abiding, much less honest and much less industrious than it was twenty years ago, or even five years ago.

Moreover, we have:

(1) Fatuously taught the young that a benevolent welfare state will provide a comfortable subsistence from cradle to grave.

(2) Acted in our magnanimity and grandiloquence as if we were a world authority instead of a former Imperial power now bereft of Empire but still, like a great albatross around our neck, with many mendicants.

(3) Run down our armed forces and dissipated our reserves in a dangerously militant world.

(4) Allowed our finances in the five years since 1964 to become utterly deranged and our foreign debts to reach £5,000m, including those contracted in the immediate post-war years, 1945 to 1950. A second post-war devaluation of sterling has increased our foreign debts and demolished international confidence in sterling as a reserve currency.

(5) Slighted our friends and alienated our allies by refusing to sell jet aircraft to South Africa, frigates to Spain or Greece, or arms to Portugal, our oldest ally and friend for more than three hundred years. We moralise and pontificate and huff and puff and preach and sermonise, with the only result that our erstwhile customers buy from our major industrial competitors, from France and Western Germany.

(6) Indulged too much welfare, using foreign bankers' money to pay for it, and practised too little enterprise.

A quarter of a century after the end of the last war, the magnificent achievements of the then vanquished Germany are in pungent contrast to our own present poverty. M. Jacques Brossette made this point very effectively in a French newspaper on 29th April, 1969, under the title: "Post-War paradoxes—Beggared Britain and Bloated Germany":

> Britain and Germany have just taken stock, on the same day, the one of her desperate impecuniousness, the other of her flaunting wealth. This is the strange contrast which has shown itself over the past twenty years between the victors and the vanquished. But why, on the one hand is there austerity from which there seems to be no escape and on the other, uninhibited prosperity?
>
> The accounts which have just been published simultaneously present two strikingly constrasting pictures. In London, the Chancellor of the Exchequer, Mr Roy Jenkins, called on his compatriots to tighten their belts by yet a few more notches when he announced the latest £340m deflation in a budget (15.4.1969) scarcely influenced by the approach of elections. If the taxpayers are for once spared any increase in income tax, consumers suffer the usual

sting of price increases: petrol, wines and so on—not to mention games of chance so beloved of this nation of gamblers.

Meanwhile in Frankfurt, Mr Karl Blessing, Governor of the Bundesbank, has been studying in his annual report, means of stemming the flow of capital which threatens to swallow up Germany's currency reserves. The hoard on which the Deutsche Mark now rests exceeds nine milliard dollars, or broadly speaking, more than double the French and almost as much as the gold reserves of the United States.

In many ways this superabundance of wealth may end by being just as embarrassing for Germany, pressed as she is with requests for assistance from everybody and under pressure to revalue her currency, as the wretchedness which is driving Britain into a semi-permanent state of beggary and making her take periodic trips beneath the Caudine Forks of her international critics.

Yet, we maintain in our domestic sphere a standard of living higher than that of almost any other nation in the world, including a welfare system which is characterised by the inadequate relief of the truly needy and the large family dependent on a small income and obligingly beneficent to everybody capable of self-provision. It is notoriously non-selective and wasteful.

The best of our industries are world leaders. The worst are still operating in penny-farthing conditions and the era of the first Industrial Revolution. Our science-based industries—in electronics, in plastics, in radar, in nucleonics, in mechanical, electrical, chemical and civil engineering—are often way out ahead.

Nationalisation is a worn out Socialist shibboleth involving heavy losses to our national economy in the last twenty years and a continuous drain on our resources. There is no evidence to support any theory that further extension of the state sector—say one quarter of all industry today—would be efficient or rewarding. Moreover, the stigma of state corporation boss-manship, with the attendant political control, has made it exceedingly difficult to find competent men to relinquish posts in the higher echelons of private industry and incur the opprobrium often inseparable from the post of State board chairman. Resort to the Etonian Lord Melchett as chairman of the British Steel Corporation, at £25,000 a year, is a case in point.

Great Britain enters the seventies as the sick man of Europe.

The onset of the seventies should roughly coincide with the return of a Tory Government.

The probability is that the Tories will govern throughout the seventies.

Their task, as in 1951, when Sir Winston Churchill inherited a bankrupt economy from Mr Clement Attlee fleeing after only twenty months of his second post-war Government, will be to restore our national economic and financial sovereignty: above all, to restore our faith in ourselves as British people, and to cast out the demoralising inertia and malaise of recent years.

Against the background of these formidable and sombre conditions I set down the ten canons of my Tory faith for the seventies:

1. THE MANAGEMENT OF OUR NATIONAL ECONOMY

The creation of new wealth for the repayment of foreign debts is the precursor to all else. We will completely recast the taxation system to place every incentive on harder and longer work, thrift and investment. Taxation of earnings will be reduced and taxation of spending increased. Indirect taxation including notably Selective Employment Tax and Purchase Tax should give way to a Value Added Tax, totally rebated on exports. Capital Gains Tax and the Land Betterment Levy should be abolished. No individual should pay more than 13/4d in the pound, or £2 out of every £3 earned, even on the highest income, to the State. The highest paid should always be left with £1 out of every £3 earned. No corporation should pay more than 50% of profits to the state, irrespective of distributions. There should be no investment allowances, initial allowances, cash grants or other artificialities to attract private investment. The market forces should determine these and availability of nett profits should assure that, after tax, adequate funds are retained for new plant, machinery and equipment for development, expansion and modernisation. Attractive depreciation and obsolescence allowances geared to the principle of earliest replacement of plant, when better machinery is available, should be the tenet of all depreciation provisions, for tax purposes. Personal savings up to £1,000 per person, per annum should attract tax relief. State retirement pensions would not be taxed as unemployment relief goes untaxed. The earnings rule for widows and pensioners would be abolished.

2. THE WELFARE STATE

Social services would be selective and with much greater emphasis on the genuinely infirm, sick, needy, the socially underprivileged and the disabled. Above £1,500 per annum income before tax, the recipient may join a private scheme for medical care such as British United Provident Association or Private Patients Plan, and charge the nett annual cost against liability to direct taxation. Similar provision should be available for dentistry. The state monopoly sought by Socialists should be broken. It is seen to be costly and inefficient. The private sector of medicine including particularly specialist and hospital services, nursing homes and convalescence should be encouraged as a viable, and indeed indispensable adjunct to the state services. It is analogous that private drugs, provision and insurance should also be partners of the state service. And, rewards and terms of service in this country for British doctors and nurses should be sufficiently good to prevent them taking their professional skills and British training elsewhere. We should depend in this country on our own doctors and nurses, not on Commonwealth immigrants who are much more urgently needed in their own home-lands, in India and Pakistan, the West Indies and West Africa, than they are here.

Our social policies should rest most largely on selectivity: generosity to the truly needy and insured self-care for the millions of men and women who are anxious, willing and able to minimise their calls on state-provided services and suitably covered by private insurance schemes, sturdily supporting their own needs and those of their families. The alternative is the breakdown of the National Health Service.

3. EDUCATION

Educational advance should depend at all levels on qualitative selection. Universal comprehensives will retard educational progress, however good the "stream" system may be. We should raise the school leaving age to sixteen years as soon as economically practicable and desirable and retain in secondary education the independent and grant-aided grammar schools which provide such excellent facilities and ought not to be sacrificed to the nostrum of egalitarianism in education, which totally comprehensive secondary education is demanding. We would not change the present division as to 95% state and 5% private fee-paying education. A small minority of private pupils is generally advantageous in giving parents willing to pay, an alternative to the state school on religious, boarding, or other grounds. Moreover, the principle of parental choice is specially important in giving state schooling the spur of competition from a well organised and progressive private sector.

As to universities, they have grown too fast in the sixties and need to consolidate in the next decade. Out of three million youngsters of university age about 200,000, or 7% are undergraduates at Britain's thirty-six universities. A minority are undisciplined, unruly, unclean and unpleasant and become involved in disturbances of the Grosvenor Square type and clashes with the police. Once brought before the Courts and found guilty of civil disorder, or assault, or inflicting bodily harm, or striking and impeding the police in the execution of their duty, these scholars should be unfrocked, lose their grants and be sent down. There are tens of thousands of industrious, well-mannered boys and girls trying very hard to obtain a place at a University. Without prejudice to lawful assembly and peaceful protest—the prerogative of students since the beginning of time—we should encourage the law-abiding and the decent youngsters and put the unruly and law-breaking element to work in the cold hard world. The overwhelming majority of tax and rate-paying citizens endorse these views and urge sterner discipline for students to be imposed by Parliament and university alike.

4. FOREIGN TRADE

Britain needs big mass markets free of tariff walls to secure progressive increase in exports on a scale to produce an annual surplus of funds for foreign debt redemption. Our policy should be the widest area of liberalised trade, on the model of the European Free Trade Area—Britain, Sweden, Norway, Denmark, Austria, Switzerland and Portugal. This should join the European Economic Community, comprising West Germany, France, Italy and Benelux (Belgium, Holland and Luxembourg). We should prefer this initial west European trading bloc to start as a "Zollverein", a Customs Union. Later, we should seek to attract to it the countries of the British Commonwealth and the United States of America and Africa, south of the Zambezi, notably the Republic of South Africa and Rhodesia. Thus, the Western World, with much of Africa and Asia and all Australasia, could become one great trading entity untrammelled by tariff barriers, rich in resources, paramount in scientific and technical skills and able generously to help the under-developed world. It is the politician's aspiration for the seventies and then the eighties as a step towards world government in the twenty-first century and the only really effective means of achieving world peace.

Meantime, we have to live and balance our payments overseas and look after our international investments. Trade barriers are the enemies of all this and the liberalisation of international trade is our principal hope for effective competition with Japan, West Germany, France, Italy and the United States.

To avoid recurrent currency crises and threats of further devaluation of sterling we should end our adherence to Bretton Woods and fixed exchange rates, "float the pound", and derive maximum benefit from our role as major international traders.

Deliberately, I omit any reference to the Treaty of Rome, a grave impediment to the creation of a larger Free Trade Area, because of political bonds.

5. BRITISH FARMING

Agricultural output in the thirty years, 1940 to 1970, has almost doubled. It will have to double again in the next thirty years up to the end of the century, if we are to sustain a population of sixty-eight millions in these islands by the year AD 2000 and achieve balance in our overseas trade, plus the required sums for debt redemption. I calculate that our farms could replace the major part of our temperate food imports, given two essential conditions:

(i) Preventing foreign dumped food, generally subsidised by the government of the country of origin, undermining our markets for our British produce.

(ii) Switching to Import Levies which though implying rises in food prices, should certainly give a better return to the British farmer and end the present paradox: the more British farm produce now sold, the higher the amount of subsidies payable by Treasury support, deficiency payments, and farm subsidies generally, at the taxpayers expense.

Our farming, the most highly mechanised in the world, is the greatest potential contributor to national solvency. Horticulture needs special treatment within the farming framework to ensure its maximum contribution to imports substitution.

This is not a second agrarian revolution. It is the proposed application of science and technology to good, advanced, full and effective husbandry and land use, which is our greatest national asset.

6. NATIONALISATION

No more at any price. It has been a costly, wasteful political experiment, the handmaiden of Socialism and the antithesis of competitive efficiency. There may well be large ventures to be sold off to Private Enterprise Corporations, in steel, road transport, telecommunications and so on. The more the better, though nobody will buy back coal, gas, electricity and the railways which will remain State owned.

As elsewhere, enough is enough for nationalisation.

7. DEFENCE

Our defences have been dangerously weakened since 1964 and without any significant reduction in cost. Actually, the cheapest major form of defence today is nuclear and it is inconceivable that we should ever be called upon to use nuclear weapons independent of our allies. Until international control of nuclear weapons is established we should maintain the nuclear deterrent by Polaris submarine, by missiles, by aircraft with nuclear roles. After the present commitment of £50m per annum for American military aircraft is completed we ought to revert to building our own. As for civil airlines, it is preposterous that Britain, with the most highly developed aeronautical industry in Europe and Rolls Royce engines, should dabble in foreign aircraft, military or civil. This drain on our balance of payments is a major contributory cause of our present deficit. Why should British manufacturers burst their boilers to sell in the United States of America when the dollars won so hard are promptly dissipated by a dissolute British Government buying aircraft from America which could have been built here in the first place? All this should be reversed in the seventies, when the next generation of aircraft, missiles, naval vessels and defence equipment is embarked upon.

British forces should remain in Malaysia, at Singapore, Hong Kong and in the Persian Gulf, preferably as part of mutual defence arrangements with India, Pakistan, Australia, New Zealand and South Africa, including the continued use of the Simonstown base. The forces in bases east of Suez, notably in South East Asia should be a condominium of British, Australian, New Zealand and Gurkha regiments. We should negotiate in Nepal the raising of another six Gurkha battalions and reform our Territorial Army at home, based on the four hundred years' old tradition of volunteer service, since the Trained Bands of the First Elizabeth. Every Territorial regiment should have county affiliations and recruit and train most largely in that County.

We should specially apply ourselves to the defence and security of the South Atlantic trade routes and the re-establishment of the Simonstown base in view of the Suez closure; oil tankers of 250,000 tons are already too large to pass through Suez anyway, and no doubt there will be 1m ton tankers by 1980. The British Army of the Rhine should be wound up, and the 55,000 British troops brought home to our strategic reserve in Britain with garrisons at Gibraltar and elsewhere by treaty, in the Mediterranean. West Germany can well afford to pay for and maintain her own defence today, with more than half a million men in the Wehrmacht. I would save the Argylls and the other famous regiments: we will need them one day. I would assure maximum troop mobility all over the world by the use of even faster transport aircraft than the VC10, which would give way to the Concorde in the mid seventies.

That is a defence policy for Great Britain.

8. TRADE UNION REFORM AND INDUSTRIAL PEACE

Many people have elevated trade union reform into a panacea for all our economic and financial ills. Deal with unofficial and "wildcat" strikes, they say, restore discipline in the workshop, put the worker in his place, and, hey presto, our troubles will be over.

Like most demagogy this has some truth in it, but not much. Desirable reform of Trade Union law can only be achieved strictly without prejudice to the absolute and inalienable right of the worker constitutionally to withdraw his labour. "Wildcat" withdrawal is a menace; so would be written permission from a trade union official to withdraw labour, which is the exact opposite of the "wildcat" withdrawal.

Somewhere between the two is a practical and workable compromise which may involve endless disputation to achieve, if at all. Here, Mr Peregrine Worsthorne put it in the right perspective when deploring both parties' committal to fractricidal strife with the unions (who bitterly oppose the reform of trade union law). He then called for another look at the possibility of a Coalition, which I regard as nearly impossible in present circumstances:

> The trouble here is that the Tories have also made trade union reform the principal plank in their platform, given it number one priority in the list of

the policies which they are committed to introduce immediately after being returned to power. In other words, they too would find themselves in a head-on clash with the TUC which would make the present Government's troubles look like child's play. Industrial strife would be on an unprecedented scale. It is by no means certain that a Tory Government, facing such passionate obstruction, would be able to press ahead except at a cost to industrial relations which no Government in its senses would want to pay.

One can easily argue, of course, that both parties have been profoundly irresponsible to build up trade union reform into this cardinal pivot of their economic policies. But this is what they have done. Indeed, the Tories have taken the lead here, almost forcing the Government to follow in their wake. As a result, both parties are committed to this fractricidal struggle; committed so deeply that it is doubtful whether any authoritative Government can emerge in this country until a battle has been fought and won with the trade union movement.

My own view is that this constitutes a tragic failure of statesmanship by both front benches, a bi-partisan folly of major proportions. But it has been committed. There is no going back on it.

The great question which needs to be asked is whether a bi-partisan folly can be corrected by partisan methods; that is to say, whether a blunder which each party has made separately can be put right unless they both join together to do so. In short, does the blunder which the Labour Government and the Tory Opposition have made in courting a battle with the trade unions require them to form a coalition for the purpose of doing jointly what they cannot succeed in doing separately?

The very suggestion of a coalition always sparks off cries of dismissive contempt. Neither Mr Wilson nor Mr Heath is likely to take it too kindly. In normal times they would be right. But these are not normal times; the situation is desperately abnormal. It may even be unique.

It is difficult to recall an occasion when party government has set itself such an intractable task: to challenge and defeat a *deeply entrenched vested interest* which has the power to paralyse the productive forces of the nation. It has always been the aim of parliamentary statesmanship to avoid such collisions, because parliamentary Government is not designed to cope with them.[1]

What Peregrine Worsthorne calls a "deeply entrenched vested interest" I call the Fourth Estate of the realm. Either description is apt, and so is the call by Mr Harold Wilson that economic recovery could not be achieved without the reform of the trade unions.

[1] *Sunday Telegraph*, 11th May, 1969.

A large majority of the electorate, I am sure, would support strong, equitable and clearly stated reform proposals, thus:

(1) A Registry of Employers Associations and Trades Unions should be established and all agreements between Employers and Employees shall be registered and legally enforceable in the courts, including provisions as to wages structures and rates.
(2) There should be a secret ballot, conducted by officers of the Ministry and a clear majority of 2 to 1 or $66\frac{2}{3}\%$ affirmation, before strike action is permissible.
(3) Any such strike should not take place until a cooling-off period of ninety days has elapsed.
(4) Meantime, the dispute should go to arbitration before an industrial court, and the findings would be binding on employers and employees alike.

There should, too, be a precise legal re-definition of a dispute; restriction of sympathy strikes and much consequential legislation. As Mr Walter Terry, Political Editor of the *Daily Mail*, pointed out on 12th May, 1969:

> All this happened in the United States, West Germany and Sweden years ago: there was screaming at first, now replaced by harmony.

I believe a great majority of Trade Unionists of all political parties and a great majority of men and women of Labour, Tory and Liberal political persuasions support these sensible and practical proposals. Of course, the anarchists, the Communists, the Trotskyists and other disruptive and alien bodies do not. These people are not concerned with Britain and her recovery. What matters to me is that the great majority of sensible, patriotic Britons support the principles for reform which I have enunciated. Industrial peace is imperative if our national economy is to be restored. I am confident that good common sense will prevail and that, without a Coalition Government, we shall achieve this wide measure of Trade Union reform in the early seventies. So we should, too.

9. IMMIGRATION AND RACE

The United Kingdom of Great Britain and Northern Ireland accommodates 54 millions of population today, and by AD 2000, it will be 68 millions. This is normal growth, based on existing levels of live births per thousand heads of population, mortality rates progressively lowered by improved and improving medical skills and other factors. We are already greatly overcrowded and the influx of immigrants should be reduced to negligible proportions on grounds of population density alone. I am no racialist in saying this, just a realist and voicing my views on behalf of 80% or more of the population who take precisely my view. If we wish, we can review matters on New Year's Day, 1980, but I doubt whether we shall have reason to unless the majority of us change our opinions. Many other countries, including for example Australia, Canada, South Africa and the United States of America, have vastly more "Lebensraum" than we have in these British islands. Are they prepared to be more liberal in their immigration policies towards the teeming millions of Asia and Africa, who have plenty of space in their homelands but who want to leave, attracted by the prosperity of Western lands? Those former immigrants already here, whether of Indian, Pakistani, West African, West Indian or any other origin are British citizens. They should be treated on terms of absolute parity with indigenously born Britons, before the law, in employment, in housing, in schools and the remainder. There should be no discrimination of any kind on account of race, colour or creed. All are equal citizens, here in Britain.

We in Great Britain have neither the space nor the resources until the year AD 2000 while our population climbs from 54m to 68m to accept large-scale further immigration. That is firm and final.

10. MY COUNTRY RIGHT OR WRONG

Dr Johnson once said, "Patriotism is the last refuge of the scoundrel". I am no scoundrel but I want to see Britain recover her greatness built on the sure foundation of economic strength. Of course we should continue to aid those under-developed countries and former colonies, notably in Africa. Any money I give them would be spent in Britain, on British goods and services, not spent with our industrial competitors. It would be "tied aid" and rightly so. British taxpayers' money, spent in Britain for the benefit of British taxpayers and the development of less wealthy lands overseas. As Disraeli said in 1863, in the context of the former American colonies:

> The United States of America were colonies and we should not forget that such communities do not cease to be colonies because they are independent.

And, talking of America and Americans, let me quote a favourite of mine among American men of letters, Ralph Waldo Emerson, who said at Manchester in 1847:

> So . . . I feel in regard to this aged England, pressed upon by transitions of trade and competing populations, I see her not dispirited, not weak, but well remembering that she has seen dark days before; indeed, with a kind of instinct that she sees a little better in a cloudy day, and that, in storm of battle and calamity, she has a secret vigour and a pulse like a cannon.

Britain will recover, prosper and lead again. That is my conviction. I believe in patriotism: Great Britain is my country, right or wrong.

Index

Note: Entries marked * refer to Parliamentary constituencies.

ILLINGWORTH'S